Metropolitan Jews

Historical Studies of Urban America

EDITED BY TIMOTHY J. GILFOYLE, JAMES R. GROSSMAN, AND BECKY M. NICOLAIDES

Also in the series:

A CARNIVAL OF PLOTS: CHICAGO, CLAN NA GAEL, AND THE MURDER OF DR. CRONIN *by* Gillian O'Brien

A CITY FOR CHILDREN: WOMEN, ARCHITECTURE, AND THE CHARITABLE LANDSCAPES OF OAKLAND, 1850–1950 *by* Marta Gutman

A WORLD MORE CONCRETE: REAL ESTATE AND THE REMAKING OF JIM CROW SOUTH FLORIDA *by* N. D. B. Connolly

URBAN APPETITES: FOOD AND CULTURE IN NINETEENTH-CENTURY NEW YORK *by* Cindy R. Lobel

CRUCIBLES OF BLACK POWER: CHICAGO'S NEIGHBORHOOD POLITICS FROM THE NEW DEAL TO HAROLD WASHINGTON *by* Jeffrey Helgeson

THE STREETS OF SAN FRANCISCO: POLICING AND THE CREATION OF A COSMOPOLITAN LIBERAL POLITICS, 1950–1972 *by* Christopher Lowen Agee

HARLEM: THE UNMAKING OF A GHETTO *by* Camilo José Vergara

PLANNING THE HOME FRONT: BUILDING BOMBERS AND COMMUNITIES AT WILLOW RUN *by* Sarah Jo Peterson

PURGING THE POOREST: PUBLIC HOUSING AND THE DESIGN POLITICS OF TWICE-CLEARED COMMUNITIES *by* Lawrence J. Vale

BROWN IN THE WINDY CITY: MEXICANS AND PUERTO RICANS IN POSTWAR CHICAGO *by* Lilia Fernandez

BUILDING A MARKET: THE RISE OF THE HOME IMPROVEMENT INDUSTRY, 1914–1960 *by* Richard Harris

SEGREGATION: A GLOBAL HISTORY OF DIVIDED CITIES *by* Carl H. Nightingale

SUNDAYS AT SINAI: A JEWISH CONGREGATION IN CHICAGO *by* Tobias Brinkmann

IN THE WATCHES OF THE NIGHT: LIFE IN THE NOCTURNAL CITY, 1820–1930 *by* Peter C. Baldwin

MISS CUTLER AND THE CASE OF THE RESURRECTED HORSE: SOCIAL WORK AND THE STORY OF POVERTY IN AMERICA, AUSTRALIA, AND BRITAIN *by* Mark Peel

THE TRANSATLANTIC COLLAPSE OF URBAN RENEWAL: POSTWAR URBANISM FROM NEW YORK TO BERLIN *by* Christopher Klemek

I'VE GOT TO MAKE MY LIVIN': BLACK WOMEN'S SEX WORK IN TURN-OF-THE-CENTURY CHICAGO *by* Cynthia M. Blair

Additional series titles follow index

Metropolitan Jews

*Politics, Race, and Religion
in Postwar Detroit*

LILA CORWIN BERMAN

THE UNIVERSITY OF CHICAGO PRESS   CHICAGO AND LONDON

LILA CORWIN BERMAN is associate professor of history and the Murray Friedman Professor and Director of the Feinstein Center for American Jewish History at Temple University.

The University of Chicago Press, Chicago 60637
The University of Chicago Press, Ltd., London
© 2015 by The University of Chicago
All rights reserved. Published 2015.
Printed in the United States of America

24 23 22 21 20 19 18 17 16 15   1 2 3 4 5

ISBN-13: 978-0-226-24783-0 (cloth)
ISBN-13: 978-0-226-24797-7 (e-book)
DOI: 10.7208/chicago/9780226247977.001.0001

Library of Congress Cataloging-in-Publication Data

Berman, Lila Corwin, 1976– author.
    Metropolitan Jews: politics, race, and religion in postwar Detroit / Lila Corwin Berman.
        pages cm — (Historical studies of urban America)
    ISBN 978-0-226-24783-0 (cloth: alk. paper) — ISBN 978-0-226-24797-7 (e-book)   1. Jews—Michigan—Detroit—Social conditions. 2. Detroit (Mich.)—Ethnic relations.   I. Title. II. Series: Historical studies of urban America.
    F574.D49J515 2015
    305.8009774'34—dc23   2014047019

♾ This paper meets the requirements of ANSI/NISO Z39.48-1992 (Permanence of Paper).

Contents

Introduction: Jews and the American City   1

CHAPTER 1. Locating and Relocating the Jewish Neighborhoods of Detroit   18

CHAPTER 2. Keeping House in the City: The Local Politics of Urban Space   47

CHAPTER 3. Changing Jewish Neighborhoods   77

CHAPTER 4. From Neighborhood to City: The Formation of Jewish Metropolitan Urbanism   106

CHAPTER 5. The Sacred Suburban Sites of Jewish Metropolitan Urbanism   150

CHAPTER 6. Urban Crises and the Privatization of Jewish Urbanism   189

CHAPTER 7. Epilogue: Back-to-the-City Jews and the Legacies of Metropolitan Urbanism   217

Acknowledgments   245

Archival Collections, Interviews, and Abbreviations   251

Notes   255

Index   309

Introduction

Jews and the American City

This book is about the relationship between power and place in post-war American Jewish history. When I started to study modern Jewish history, I never imagined I would write about the role of place. Indeed, early on in my Jewish education, I had learned that Jews did not much care about physical places: the text, not the shrine, stood at the center of Judaism. A long history of movement from one place to another trained Jews to crave stability in ideas not places, to develop attachments to stories not spaces, and, on the broadest level, to transcend geography. Zionism served as the sole exception and, even so, through much of Jewish time, Zion was an idea as much as a place.

One could imagine that this formulation—synoptically Jews as the People of the Book and the Wandering People—would work quite well in explaining post–World War II American-Jewish life. Jews moved with alacrity to suburbs in the decades after the Second World War, participating in a large-scale migration away from urban centers. They left behind old sacred places and built new ones as they reconstituted Jewish life in yet another landscape. The places they left receded, remaining memories perhaps, but little else.[1]

Such an explanation might make sense were it not for the fact that the city—as a real and imagined place—continued to orient American Jews' political, economic, cultural, and spiritual lives, even as they journeyed away from urban centers after World War II. In these decades, Jews reinvented the geography and meaning of the city, as they responded to the broad range of forces that transformed twentieth-century urban life. The place of the city—ever changing and remade—remained nonetheless vital to Jews' sense of their power, possibilities, and identities. City space grounded Jewish political and cultural life in twentieth-century America. Yet the relationship between Jews and urbanism was anything but straightforward since the parameters and defining elements of city space shifted enormously over that century, much as the concerns of Jewish politics and identity changed over time.

To understand the political and cultural terrain of postwar American Jewish life, I had to overturn my long-held belief that Jews did not much care about physical places. I started by reading an emergent body of literature that advocated and identified a "spatial turn" in how we understand human experience. And I spoke to colleagues whose insights about space and its connection to identity and politics encouraged me to pay close attention to the ways in which Jews' attachment to place resonated throughout the postwar period and beyond.[2]

By no means did Jews engage with their physical settings in uniform ways. On the most basic level, the nature of one's surroundings—small town, large city, immigrant neighborhood, suburb, and so on—mattered, as did individual Jews' economic status, level of religious observance, national backgrounds, connection to Jewish institutions, and political proclivities. Yet, in this introduction, I use the term "Jews" in a broad and categorical way to set out the terms necessary for understanding my subject matter: Jewish urbanism. My intention is to bring new perspectives to the renderings of several important twentieth-century histories, including white flight, suburbanization, and the development of American-Jewish political and cultural identity. The bulk of this book is quite specific in its attention to how one Jewish population living in one city, Detroit, in the postwar years reinvented its urbanism. The implications of this study, however, suggest that a deeper attention to Jews' shifting relationship to urban space and the idea of the city in the twentieth century will reframe how we think about the American urban experiment and modern Jewish history.

Mapping the City in Jewish Time

Jews oriented themselves around city space in the modern era. Their historical experience in modern Europe and the United States predisposed them to invest their energies and passions in cities. In a relatively brief historical time period—from the 1800s to the 1930s—the global Jewish population became almost entirely urbanized, a feat impossible in earlier centuries when cities were much smaller and preindustrial economies could never have supported such a high concentration of people in such confined spaces. Many different kinds of people lived in cities, yet no group other than the Jews became so fully a metonym—a part standing in for the whole—for urban.[3]

The status of consummate urban dweller did not necessarily do Jews any favors. Just as the predominantly Christian characterization of Jews as a "wandering" people had communicated a pre-Enlightenment antisemitic belief that Jews were naturally—organically—rootless and, thus, unable to contribute to a land-based economy or nation, the Jewish-urban equation provoked and confirmed antisemitic renderings that correlated urban excesses with Jewishness. The city, a producer and product of modern economic, political, and cultural forces, reflected the anxieties that Europeans and Americans felt about modernity.[4] Much like modernity, the city threatened to corrupt morals, undermine authority, disrupt hierarchy, and thwart productivity, even as it positioned itself as the bastion of progress. Inhabitants of the city suffered most from these depravities, unless they were responsible for creating them, in which case they stood to profit from them. In nationalist European discourse and nativist American pronouncements, the Jew emerged as the ideal type for urban and modern exploiter.[5]

Sociologists have maintained that twentieth-century cities embodied the crucial binary tensions of modernity: between diversity and unity; between private and public; between anonymity and surveillance; between interaction and atomization; between power and powerlessness; and between men and women. As a field, modern urban planning concerned itself with protecting these distinctions and rationalizing them onto the map of the city. Yet the multiple and overlapping subcultures that defined urban life challenged the spatial boundaries of these divisions. In his 1938 article "Urbanism as a Way of Life," Jewish sociologist Louis Wirth set forth the possibility that American cities thrived on structural oppositions, but that the "way of life" in cities emerged from a constant process of shuttling between these binaries. Even as early sociologists may have overessentialized the city and overdrawn the tensions operating within it, they offered compelling explanations for the revolutions in social relations, social control, and the market that occurred in cities.[6]

Late to the privileges of national citizenship, Jews sought spaces that could support individual emancipation without trampling group loyalties and universal concerns. The modern Jewish question (or, as some termed it, problem) asked: How can one be part of a people, a nation, and humanity all at once? Nowhere did a resolution to that question seem more feasible than in modern cities, where the particular, private, parochial, and distinctive often coexisted with the universal, public, cosmopolitan, and civic.

In the United States, Jews were among the groups that depended on the slippage between the city's tensions, and by the early decades of the twentieth century, they worked to balance the private protections and public privileges offered in the interstitial spaces of city life. As urban planners, activists, artists, politicians, and critics, Jews tended to see cities at their best when they made room for individuals and groups to thrive in a productive tension. Ethnic neighborhoods adjacent to large public universities, or workplaces committed to equal pay for all employees, or theaters and art museums dedicated to public exhibitions all ushered individuals into a civic realm without demanding that they abandon the privacy of their group interests or their subculture. Even Jews who cared little about nurturing a separate Jewish group identity and for whom assimilation seemed the logical end point of American acceptance, such as Wirth, tended to judge cities only as successful as their ability to balance parochialism and cosmopolitanism.[7]

Without a doubt, American cities failed in myriad ways to serve their inhabitants. Particularly in periods of economic struggle and political turmoil, city policies and patterns tended to harden the lines of difference among urban dwellers and inscribe racial, religious, and cultural divisions and hierarchies into city space. In cities teeming with people, the assignation of group identity—whether defined religiously, nationally, linguistically, racially, economically, or sexually—to spatial divisions helped rationalize the overwhelming project of governance. Various urban groups participated in the effort to organize city space around lines of difference by claiming certain areas as particular or special to their group and, through various means, keeping others out. These divisions of urban space, however, also reflected hierarchies, many of which were generated and reinforced by the structures of urban policy and economics. Top-down policies, such as where to direct public monies or where to stimulate private development through public subsidies, designated certain urban zones as worthy of investment and others as acceptably neglected. Leaders tended to claim that these divisions reflected preexisting patterns. Thus, they rarely took responsibility for their role in engineering the distribution of power and making social divisions, especially those corresponding to race, ethnicity, nationality, and class, appear fixed in urban space.

The Formation of Jewish Metropolitan Urbanism

Jews played a critical role in redrawing urban maps during a series of decades when American city leaders feared that multiple forces threatened to disrupt the order of urban space. The entrance of millions of newcomers, including European immigrants and black Americans, into northern and midwestern cities in the early twentieth century had set cities on a course of rapid growth and also carved up urban space in new ways. As early as the 1920s, sociologists and urban planners sought to foist a coherent structure upon the changes and introduced models of social theory that correlated the degree of a group's assimilation into American life with its geographical mobility. Policy makers and speculators concerned with the valuation of urban space also fixated on urban maps, hoping to determine which areas were worthy of investment, which could give quick returns, and which were zones of racial and ethnic change.[8]

Over the postwar period, Jews increasingly entered positions of urban power, whether elected or not, that enabled them to make and, often, benefit from continually shifting urban policies.[9] For midcentury Jews, as urban activists, planners, elected officials, developers, and engaged citizens, to participate in redrawing urban maps promised emancipation from the ways in which dominant powers throughout history had employed space to confine and control Jewishness. Moreover, by gaining the power to define the cartography of Jewish and urban space, Jews developed a simultaneously quixotic and pragmatic approach to urban politics that shifted alongside their own geographical movement.

This book explains how the locus of Jews' political and cultural perspectives shifted in the decades after World War II from the sphere of neighborhood-based urbanism to citywide urbanism and, finally, to what I term "metropolitan urbanism." One could think of these three spheres as an inverted pyramid, with Jews' focus shifting from the smallest area, that of the neighborhood, to the largest, the metropolitan zone that encompassed city neighborhoods and suburbs. Yet through the lens of personal responsibility and obligation, the pyramid flips since the neighborhood generally demanded the broadest investment from individuals, while the city and then the metropolitan region, despite their geographical breadth, tended to depersonalize and narrow individuals' obligations to the city.

The changing spaces of Jewish urban concern corresponded with chronological shifts in urban policy, especially related to race and class, and Jewish self-definition. In the immediate postwar years, Jewish urban politics were organized around local and neighborhood-based concerns that focused on their immediate place of residence. Individual homeowners and renters could pitch in to improve the neighborhood, or, in the language of the day, "stabilize" it in the face of a changing urban landscape and the settlement of black people in once-presumed Jewish spaces. From their urban neighborhoods, Jews had expressed their firmest support for progressive politics by voting overwhelmingly for President Roosevelt four times over, by supporting New Deal legislation, and by advocating early civil rights reforms. In all cases, the vast majority of Jews developed a strong belief in a government responsible for and capable of creating a world where individuals could thrive, without having to renounce their group identities or their neighborhood ties.[10]

A marked shift in the terms and spaces of Jewish urbanism emerged in the 1950s as Jews saw their neighborhoods buffeted by changes beyond their sphere of local control. Amid the rapid growth of suburbs and an urban housing shortage that most profoundly affected black people, Jews witnessed and participated in changes in neighborhood space. Once-presumed Jewish residential spaces no longer felt Jewish when black people moved into the neighborhood, even though non-Jewish white people had long occupied many of the dwellings in so-called Jewish neighborhoods. As these changes occurred, Jews also were becoming vested in larger political processes that operated beyond the neighborhoods in which they lived. That more Jews than ever before entered city government, often in appointed though increasingly in elected roles and through civil service jobs, and that urban Jews had accumulated greater levels of wealth than ever gave them confidence to address the problems they perceived in their neighborhoods from a broader citywide perspective.[11]

Those same characteristics that historians suggest turned Jews into whites served as the foundation for a new Jewish urban identity. Jews' increasing urban power in economic, political, and cultural terms offered them privileges reserved for white Americans but did not align their interests neatly with the generalized whiteness that historians often describe as characterizing the postwar years.[12] As their urban power grew, Jews came to believe that they could play a broader role in the fate of the city, and, at the same time, they felt more empowered to assert that their own agenda should be central to the city's future.

Increasingly, Jews believed that the forces making their neighborhoods difficult for them to live in were city problems, not just Jewish problems. In the late 1950s and early 1960s, Jews turned toward citywide solutions to problems, such as the disruptive forces of black settlement and infrastructural neglect, that earlier Jewish leaders had believed were endemic to Jewish neighborhoods. In many ways, the neighborhood remained the impetus of Jewish involvement in urban affairs, but Jewish leaders and activists explained that neighborhoods were only as strong and stable as cities.

The critical turning point in Jews' urban identity occurred just as Jews contemplated leaving and left cities. This is because they believed that their decisions to move to the outer limits of a city or its suburbs did not preclude the centrality of the city to who they were and how their lives operated. When Jews left cities after World War II, they reinvented the boundaries of urbanism by continuing to tie themselves politically, economically, spiritually, and culturally to the city. In forging a place-based identity that did not directly correspond to the actual place in which they lived, Jews created a new kind of urbanism—a metropolitan urbanism—that broadened the range of possible spaces and behaviors that Jews nonetheless understood as urban oriented. Different from a neighborhood- or city-based consciousness, this new metropolitan consciousness enabled Jews to see themselves as still enmeshed with city life without feeling beholden to reside within it.

In the late 1960s and early 1970s, the tensions in Jewish metropolitan life ran high. Cities and the progressive democratic ideologies that had shaped them faltered in the face of federal disinvestment from urban life and growingly vociferous expressions of radical political ideologies from the left, the right, and black separatist groups. Jewish urbanism had grown in tandem with a particular strain of midcentury American liberalism that balanced a progressive social agenda (namely, to alleviate poverty, provide opportunities through social welfare programs, most importantly education, and to improve group relations) with a fundamental respect for a capitalist market structure and those policies that would most protect it from collapse. Jews tended to support progressive race-neutral laws that offered "fair" treatment to all groups and provided protections for those who were unfairly treated. Yet they also believed in protecting the capitalist market and believed, in turn, that the market would protect them.

Beginning in the mid-1960s, however, this hybrid of a progressive social agenda and classically liberal economic model, to which many Jews and almost all of the official voices of the Jewish community subscribed, faced serious challenges, most pronounced in urban environments, where fairness policies and free market protections seemed incapable of solving cities' problems.[13]

Throughout the first half of the twentieth century, Jewish urban liberalism had been predicated upon a progressive belief in the public sphere, that is, the government, as the broker and protector of fairness and the capitalist market. What some historians and critics have perceived as the crisis in Jewish liberalism in the 1960s and 1970s occurred less as a crisis of liberal ideology and more as a crisis of liberal democratic ideals, when the public sphere no longer had the funds nor the political support to act as an enforcer of fairness. Whereas many Jews by the late 1950s and early 1960s had put their faith in legislative and government-based changes to chart the course for successful urban life, by the end of the 1960s and early 1970s, more Jews than ever before supported private sources, including faith- and business-based ones, to improve and invest in cities. Jews' belief in the efficacy of private efforts to heal broken cities—to be the agents of their version of liberalism—grew during the Nixon administration, when urban programs suffered from massive funding cuts and shrinkages. Jews, by this time predominantly suburban dwellers, remained among the staunchest advocates of government intervention in cities, but they also became growingly disenchanted with urban governance, as they felt more and more distant from the channels of public urban power.[14]

Historical Frameworks

In examining how Jews reinvented the terms of their urbanism in the postwar era, I suggest a much deeper interpenetration between the geographical space of cities and suburbs than many historians have acknowledged. Through the lens of metropolitan urbanism, I explain the ways in which the city remained an essential and yet mutable touchstone for American-Jewish political, cultural, and spiritual identity. My point is that Jews reconstructed their relationship to the city at critical historical junctures and that the process of reinventing their relationship to urbanism hewed closely to the changing contours of Jewish political, cultural, and spiritual identity. Even during those moments when Jews expressed ambivalence toward, removal from, or loathing of the city, they tended to see the city as a reference point for what it meant to be Jewish in America; they remained "Metropolitan Jews."

In considering urbanism through a metropolitan lens, that includes the city and its surrounding suburbs, I draw attention to the ways in which these spaces were mutually constituted and not simply constructed in opposition to one another. Significantly, my reframing of the geographical dimensions of Jewish life offers a new way of thinking about Jewish political identity beyond the poles of liberalism and conservatism and takes into account the intersection of geographical space, modes of individual and collective power, and the structures of American law and policy.[15]

Metropolitan Jews argues that Jews who migrated away from American cities and to suburbs in the postwar years understood their movement through an urban framework because they felt connected to the idea of the city as a space of orientation in American and Jewish life. Jews believed in cities and persisted in reinventing their relationship to cities because they thought there was no better place to be a Jew than in a city or in a region defined by its proximity to a city. The difference, however, between being physically rooted in city space and feeling existentially (whether politically, culturally, historically, or spiritually) connected to the city was vast and consequential. This book tracks how and why Jews reinvented their urbanism over time and the ways in which the city remained a central element of Jewish identity, even as most Jews left city space.

Although many other American groups similarly engaged in the process of urban reinvention in the twentieth century, Jews had a particular stake in the matter. More than many other postwar whites who left cities after World War II, Jews saw their identities as tied to the modern city. This was in part due to their historically shaped belief that cities offered them unprecedented levels of freedom, protection, and access to power. Of course, this could change, and the fact that the majority of American Jews left cities in the decades after World War II indicates that Jews believed they could thrive outside of cities. Yet running parallel to the demographic reality of Jewish migration to suburbs were the myriad ways that Jews oriented their lives toward ideas, political movements, aesthetic trends, and spiritual modes that they set in the conceptual and physical space of urban America. Indeed, part of the way that Jews grounded themselves in the suburbs was through asserting their new relationship to the cities they had left. They defined in what ways their lives would now be very different from and in what ways their lives would remain consistent—or, at least, conjoined—with the urban spaces that had been so transformative of Jewish life. On both counts the city, as a space and as an ideal, remained a critical reference point for American Jewish identity.

Historians have long noted the gap between the rhetoric and behavior of white urban and suburban liberals, who espoused the belief in civil rights for all to work, live, and learn wherever they wanted but behaved otherwise by leaving neighborhoods, schools, and cities when whites no longer constituted the majority. Cheryl Greenberg, in her article about "liberal NIMBY-ism" (Not In My Back Yard-ism) and Jewish involvement in the civil rights movement, writes that American liberalism "emphasized public equality, to be legislated and enforced by government action. . . . It did not, however, require personal or private actions beyond this."[16] Greenberg, similar to other historians of postwar Jewish life, argues that Jewish self-interest fueled the overwhelming support that rank-and-file Jews gave to civil rights. Employing the logic of a slippery slope, Jewish leaders explained that bigotry sanctioned against one group would serve as an allowance for bigotry against other groups, including Jews. Greenberg concludes, "The chief reason for many Jews' civil rights support—Jewish security—was unrelated to their own behaviors."[17]

In the postwar years, small pockets of Jews castigated Jewish liberals for their hypocrisy. So-called neoconservative Jews, for example, suggested that Jews needed to reconsider the terms of their power, both by fighting for more power and openly embracing the power they had to create a political order that better served them. Jewish leftists similarly focused their attentions on power, arguing that liberal Jews had become too subservient to dominant power hierarchies and could only truly help those who stood on the lowest rungs of society by calling for a revolution that collapsed the structures of American power. In both cases, mainstream Jewish leaders and communities were called to task for not matching their rhetoric and their behavior; neoconservatives believed Jews needed to change their rhetoric to match the way that most Jews already acted, and leftists believed that Jews needed to change their behavior to match their rhetoric.[18]

Most Jews, however, did not fundamentally change their rhetoric or their behavior. Rather, mainstream Jewish political identity in the postwar era was premised upon the rhetorical defense of a liberal, rights-based mode of governance that allowed individuals to pursue their profits and pleasures, that included a defense of basic social welfare programs, and that fought against the kinds of categorical restraints that would edge out a Jew or a black person because he or she was Jewish or black. By no means did this rhetorical position obligate Jews to behave contrary to their interests of securing privilege or power in a capitalist system. Indeed, it did not even obligate them to live in integrated neighborhoods, send their children to integrated schools, or remain in integrated cities. And, in fact, Jewish leaders in the 1950s and 1960s were much more likely to focus their civil rights activism on freedom and opportunity for all and not on integration specifically. By recognizing a basic continuity between the rhetoric and behavior of postwar Jewish political life, we can better understand how it was possible for Jews to leave cities and still assert a deep, albeit complicated, connection to them. The ways that most Jews understood their behavior (of leaving cities) did not contradict their rhetorical support for rights-based liberal ideals and their sense that the fight for these ideals would need to be won in the most densely populated and diverse places in the United States, in cities.

In the 1960s, Jews expressed growing ambivalence about and animosity toward cities. These feelings stemmed from their deep dismay that the sources of urban power no longer appeared to cleave as closely to rights-based liberalism as Jews believed was necessary to create a fair social order. Whether in the form of black radical politics or white conservative politics, urban governance took a turn away from the path that most Jews believed in, and this made it more difficult for Jews to feel invested in urban public life than they had in the past. At the same time, Jews also expressed ambivalence about moving to and living in the suburbs. Jewish leaders, even while often leading their congregations and communities to the suburbs, challenged the Jewish public to stay true to values that they located in the temporal and geographic space of the Jewish urban past and worried mightily about whether Jewish life could survive in the suburbs.

To be certain, contradictions emerged in how Jews thought about the ideal of the city and how they built their lives and communities in spaces removed from the mounting pressures that demographics and federal and state funding policies exerted upon city space. Many of these contradictions corresponded to the structural realities of American life, realities that so tightly drew privilege and geography into a relationship that one could assume a natural order to the inequitable economic and racial cartography of American cities.

The body of historical scholarship on whites leaving cities and on suburbanization is rich with insight into the large structural forces that precipitated urban crises in the 1960s, that subsidized white movement to suburbs, and that eviscerated liberalism.[19] On the whole, however, the scholarship presents a linear spatial, political, and cultural narrative about urban disinvestment. Such a linear model may help explain the experiences of many white Americans who left cities after World War II. Yet it also tells a reductive narrative of postwar American life, leaving readers and students with the impression that in the second half of the twentieth century, urbanism and liberalism simply gave way to suburbanism and conservatism.[20]

Historians and social scientists have long understood the postwar period of American history as marked by the massive departure of white people from cities to suburbs. With near uniformity, these scholars correlate "white flight" with white, middle-class detachment and disinvestment from city politics, culture, and people. Historians have drawn attention specifically to the landscape of the suburbs as a fortification against urban problems and as the setting for a new form of anti-urban, white conservatism. Kevin Kruse, in a study of postwar Atlanta, asserts, "White flight, in the end, was more than a physical relocation. It was a political revolution."[21] In similar fashion, Thomas Sugrue and Robert Self explain, "The mass migration of tens of millions of Americans to suburban areas realigned American politics."[22] Correlating a geographical migration with political transformation, these scholars designate the suburbs as a product of and producer of conservatism. As David Freund illuminates in his examination of suburban Detroit, "New racial thinking was decisively shaped by the powerful new institutions and private practices that fueled postwar suburban growth while also successfully excluding most black people from its benefits."[23] White conservative politics, invested in shielding white middle-class life from problems perceived as urban and nonwhite, may have gestated in cities, but they thrived in suburban sites of urban removal.

Woven into accounts of the new suburban politics of ex-urbanites is an attention to the historical transformation of European immigrants into white ethnic Americans. Historians explain that admission into the suburbs served as a geographic marker for European immigrants' acceptance into a white power structure that defined itself by the distance it maintained from a black, urban underclass.[24] Indeed, historians often illustrate Jews' acceptance into the white power structure by pointing to the rapidity of their suburbanization, noting that roughly one-third of all American Jews relocated from cities to suburbs in the postwar decades. Scholars who directly address Jewish urban departure tend to interpret suburbanization as proof of Jewish assimilation, while, ironically, explaining that mobility is an age-old Jewish skill, the legacy of a "wandering" people who never had the chance to become attached to geographic space—cities, neighborhoods, streets. Only through studies of nostalgia have scholars of American Jews considered the ties between Jews and the cities they left.[25]

The last two decades of scholarship about suburbs and white flight have created a tight and totalizing correlation between spatial migration to the suburbs and the political and cultural transformation of white Americans away from urban liberalism. In recent years, some scholars have sought to disrupt the now reflexive assumption that suburbs were bastions of white conformity and conservatism by pointing to the political, racial, and class diversity that existed in many suburbs.[26] Slowly, we are learning that the line dividing cities and suburbs was not nearly as stark as government policy, popular culture, and social criticism characterized it. Indeed, groups and individuals participated in the ongoing process of urban reinvention often from areas outside of city limits and often in ways that disrupt a neat political division between liberalism and conservatism.

Over the last half of a century, scholars and social critics have casually observed the centrality of the city to postwar suburban American Jews. In 1967, when sociologist Herbert Gans wrote about Levittown, a consummate postwar suburb, he noted that Jews, among all of the inhabitants, expressed the most favorable attitudes toward the city.[27] Marshall Sklare, another sociologist, wrote in 1972 in the pages of the Jewish intellectual journal *Commentary*: "The fact of the matter is that when Jews opted for suburbia they did so reluctantly. . . . For many, the absence of these [urban] staples [e.g., hallways, lobbies, elevators, corner restaurants] of the Jewish urban scene was a real deprivation. . . . Thus, even when Jews seemingly embrace suburbia, they still look for the urban virtues—convenience, cultural and social opportunities."[28] These observations could be understood as texts of apology, written to communicate a level of shame that American Jewish intellectuals felt about the true Jewish embrace of the suburbs. Indeed, even if some Jews were reluctant to move to the suburbs, the demographics belie that reluctance and show a population that agreed with the lifestyle and the landscape that suburbs offered.

That Jews retained a deep sense of their urbanism in the suburbs does not, in other words, indicate that they rejected suburban life. In their own right, suburbs became critical places of Jewish political mobilization and many Jews rested their political sights on suburban matters.[29] Furthermore, not every Jew living in every American city participated in the process of urban reinvention or understood cities as a cardinal point around which to orient political, cultural, or spiritual life. To begin with, some

Jews never lived in cities and instead settled in rural parts of the United States, though these Jews were in the small minority among American Jews.[30] Moreover, for traditionally observant or Orthodox Jews, city living was incredibly important, but for reasons of observance more than political, economic, or cultural ones.[31] And finally some Jews left cities after World War II vowing never, ever to return in body or mind. But for many Jews and their institutions that mediated the public face of Jewish life, the city remained central to Jewish political, economic, and spiritual identities even as Jews left it. These Jews hoped to find compatibility between their decisions to move their homes and families to the suburbs and their investments in urban life and ideals. The power of the metropolitan ideal was precisely that it enabled Jews to foster this vision of harmonious synthesis and, often, to turn a blind eye to the contradictions embedded in it.[32]

Jews gained power in the United States in cities, and they learned how to exercise it in cities, whether in the pursuit of more power or a different distribution of power: these facts were the most immediate motivators of Jewish concern for cities. They also confirmed Jews' longer historical consciousness that cities more than other geographic spaces offered haven, privacy, and, sometimes, civil protection for Jews. For Jews who had come to America during an era of booming urbanization and lived through a massive expansion of the government, cities proved that unity (embodied in civic or cosmopolitan space) could be formed amid diversity, and that diversity (embodied in the particular and the private neighborhoods and spaces that groups formed) strengthened unity.[33]

Destination Detroit

This book is set in Detroit for a number of good reasons. Before I get to them, however, I should admit that I do not believe this story had to be set in Detroit. From historical scholarship and demographic and survey data about Jews in other American cities, I have discerned parallel spatial, political, and identity patterns to those I found in Detroit. Following a chronological arc similar to the one I observed in Detroit, Jews living in many American cities experienced attachments to neighborhood, city, and, finally, metropolitan region and evidenced like expressions of urban identification and orientation. Throughout the book, I note these comparisons.

More substantively, through my research I also learned about relationships that connected urban Jews across the country in their quest to reinvent Jewish urbanism. In many instances, national Jewish organizations, often with headquarters in New York City, held conferences, conducted studies, published reports, and issued directives about Jewish movement away from cities. These organizations mined the data and reports from local Jewish groups. Beyond this, local Jewish leaders and researchers corresponded frequently with one another to share strategies and ideas about the changing nature of Jewish urbanism. From Strawberry Mansion, Parkside, and Wynnefield (Philadelphia) to Weequahic (Newark) to Dorchester, Roxbury, and Mattapan (Boston) to Pikesville and Park Heights (Baltimore) to Shaker Heights (Cleveland) to Boyle Heights (Los Angeles) to Hyde Park and Lawndale (Chicago) to northeastern Queens to Brooklyn's Brownsville and Crown Heights, Jews in the postwar years exchanged ideas about city life and suburbanization and joined in the task of reinventing their urbanism from a neighborhood-based orientation toward a metropolitan one.[34] I acknowledge that this evidence of substantive similarities that cut across Jews' experiences in many Americans cities is almost exclusively based upon correspondence among Jewish leaders and some survey data, and only more site-specific research would illuminate a broader swath and more fine-grained portrait of the Jewish trends in various cities.

This book, however, is about Detroit. Quite simply, I decided that if I wanted to talk about the relationship between power and place, I ought to write about a specific place. My choice of Detroit was not haphazard. With striking frequency, historians have looked to Detroit for explanations of twentieth-century urban transformations. Its rise and fall as an urban industrial center and its demographic shift from a white city to a black city parallel similar shifts in many other urban locales. The unique texture of Detroit—the role that the automobile industry played in defining the city, its distance from either coast, and the eventual thoroughness of its segregation and deindustrialization—has also attracted historians interested in documenting urban tensions and politics. Yet historians of Jewish urban politics and culture have almost entirely neglected Detroit, apart from local histories of its Jewish population. The fact of the matter is that for a medium-size Jewish community, Detroit Jews played outsized roles on the national Jewish stage, serving as leaders of national Jewish organizations and emerging as trendsetting philanthropists. In the neighborhoods and suburbs of Detroit, one finds an unexplored slice of American-Jewish metropolitan life that is connected to postwar Jews' experiences throughout the United States and illuminates the broader relationship between cities and suburbs.[35]

Detroit Jews shared in local and nationwide conversations about urbanism, neighborhoods, and suburbs. From the 1940s through the 1970s, Jewish leaders worked in close collaboration with an ever-shifting array of non-Jewish groups in Detroit and beyond, including a variety of political movements and interfaith organizations. These alliances changed over time, sometimes causing deep rifts within the Jewish community and also causing dissension among Jews and other groups, particularly black political movements, in Detroit. Detroit Jews corresponded frequently with Jewish leaders across the country and shared strategies for responding to urban transformations. Furthermore, Detroit leaders, Jewish and non-Jewish, aligned with national civil rights organizations, including fair-housing and fair-employment advocacy groups.

With a narrative whittled down already by geography, this book also does not purport to represent every form of Jewish identity and affiliation in postwar Detroit. I am interested in Jews' collective and public acts to reinvent urbanism and create metropolitan urbanism. Because of this, I have focused on community leaders, religious and secular institutions, and political and cultural movements in Detroit. But I have also spent a great deal of time with Jews who grew up in Detroit and many of whom still live in the metropolitan region: talking on the phone, e-mailing, sharing meals, sitting in their living rooms, riding in their cars, paging through old family albums, and allowing them to correct and revise my understanding of the way place and power worked in the city. My hope is that these generous folks and others will feel no compunction about continuing to correct me. Because *Metropolitan Jews* is a narrative about a place and not a particular person, however, it cannot represent the breadth of Jewish experience in the city (or even the breadth of Jewish experience in a single family or within a single individual—these things are not simple).

The first chapter offers readers a historical and geographical orientation to Detroit through the eyes of a historian who did not grow up in the city and who came to understand it in relationship to broad Jewish and American urban patterns. This is the touchstone for the rest of the book, which considers in a chronological and geographical fashion how Jews moved through the spaces I describe in that first chapter. The book traces Jews' decisions about where to live from the immediate postwar period through the early 1970s when Detroit, much as other urban American places, had weathered a destructive urban uprising long in the making and instituted new policies and modes of governance in an effort toward recovery. In order to understand the relationship between place and power, I examine how Jewish political activism and identity changed over time and space in Detroit. I do not believe it is possible or historically accurate to sequester Jewish politics from Jewish spiritual and cultural transformations. Indeed, throughout the book, I show the interpenetration of these forces and examine, in depth, the sacred spaces that Jews constructed as they moved their families, communities, and congregations away from the city.

Throughout the 1970s and 1980s, Detroit Jews felt a dwindling sense of investment in the city, even as some remained committed to the terms of metropolitan urbanism and maintained that the entire region depended on the health of the city. Thus, one might have expected the steady dissolution of Jewish metropolitan urbanism in the face of regional and national trends that calcified the divide between cities and suburbs in those years. In an epilogue, however, I describe a new, yet historically shaped Jewish urbanism that emerged in Detroit in the new millennium and ran parallel to narratives about the insolvency, death, and rebirth of the city. A new set of historical circumstances found Jews reimagining the terms of their power, privilege, and identity in relationship to their imaginings of the city. Detroit emerged as an iconic—invented and constructed, to be certain—symbol of American and Jewish life that asserted something particular about what it meant to be Jewish in America, no matter where one might actually live.

Jewish urban reinvention, delimited in multiple and changing ways by structures of law and policy, runs throughout much of Jewish history. This is not because Jews were naturally more urban or city-like than others. Rather it is because cities over time addressed the historical, economic, spiritual, and cultural conditions of Jewish life. At their best, cities offered Jews hope for a place and a time of this-worldly redemption from insecurity or powerlessness or injustice. In the United States in the twentieth century, Jews found their greatest sense of success and security in cities and in metropolitan communities that retained strong and self-conscious ties to urban ideals and spaces. Over time, even as city spaces grew more and more into abstractions for Jews who were moving away from them, Jews continued to believe that cities mattered and that Jews mattered to cities.

CHAPTER ONE

Locating and Relocating the Jewish Neighborhoods of Detroit

Elaine (née Zeidman) and Eugene Driker's backyard in the summer of 2012 provided one point of entry into Jewish Detroit. In the far corner of the well-manicured yard, nestled between the boughs of a stand of pines, a street sign announced the intersection of Dexter Avenue and Davison Street. A ten-minute drive south of the Drikers' Palmer Woods house, the Dexter-Davison intersection in 2012 was home to two gas stations, a liquor store, an empty lot, and the Dexter Avenue Baptist Church. On a summer morning, a few cars might roll through the intersection and a handful of pedestrians might make their way across the street. The sign staked in the Drikers' backyard, however, pointed toward a different intersection of space and time.

The Drikers, born in Detroit in the late 1930s, grew up near the intersection of Dexter and Davison, an area that Jews, for a time, recognized as the Jewish neighborhood of Detroit. The corner of their youth was the central axis of Jewish life in Detroit, where Jews came to shop at the Dexter-Davison Market and to pause in their errands for conversation and a chance to catch up with one another.[1] Similar to many Detroit Jews in their generation, Eugene and Elaine attended Wayne State, the public university about five miles southeast of the Dexter-Davison intersection and closer to the heart of downtown. In 1959, immediately after Elaine graduated, they married. Eugene finished law school at Wayne State, and the newlyweds set up home in a flat, the second story of a two-story home, close to their childhood homes.

After a short sojourn in Washington, DC, where their daughter was born, the Drikers returned to Detroit. By this time, the early 1960s, the map of the city had changed. Instead of settling near the neighborhood

FIGURE 1.1 Owner Norman Cottler (*second from the left*) in front of the Dexter-Davison Market, a neighborhood meeting ground, 1939. Courtesy of the Leonard N. Simons Jewish Community Archives of the Jewish Federation of Metropolitan Detroit.

where they had grown up, they moved to another second-story flat on the edge of the Bagley neighborhood that had become a Jewish area after World War II. Bagley, about three miles northwest of the intersection of Dexter and Davison and less than two miles south of Detroit's city limits, was already losing its Jewish residents to the suburbs by the 1960s. After renting for a few years, the Drikers bought their first home in 1965 in Green Acres, a mile north of Bagley, just about as far north as one could go without leaving the city. They lived there for ten years. Many of their neighbors, such as Carl Levin (elected to the United States Senate in 1979), were Jewish, and their two children attended Pasteur Elementary School, the neighborhood public school. In 1975, Eugene and Elaine moved from Green Acres to Palmer Woods, an elegant neighborhood, with curved streets and grand homes, located close to Detroit's northern edge. They would never characterize their neighborhood as a Jewish one, though some Jews, particularly wealthy ones, had lived in it for many decades and some continued to do so.[2]

None of the neighborhoods in which the Drikers lived remained Jewish or white. By the 1980s, each of these neighborhoods, much like the city of Detroit itself, housed a majority of black residents. Most Jewish Detroiters, similar to other whites in the city, left Detroit sometime between World War II and the early 1970s, after having lived in at least one, but

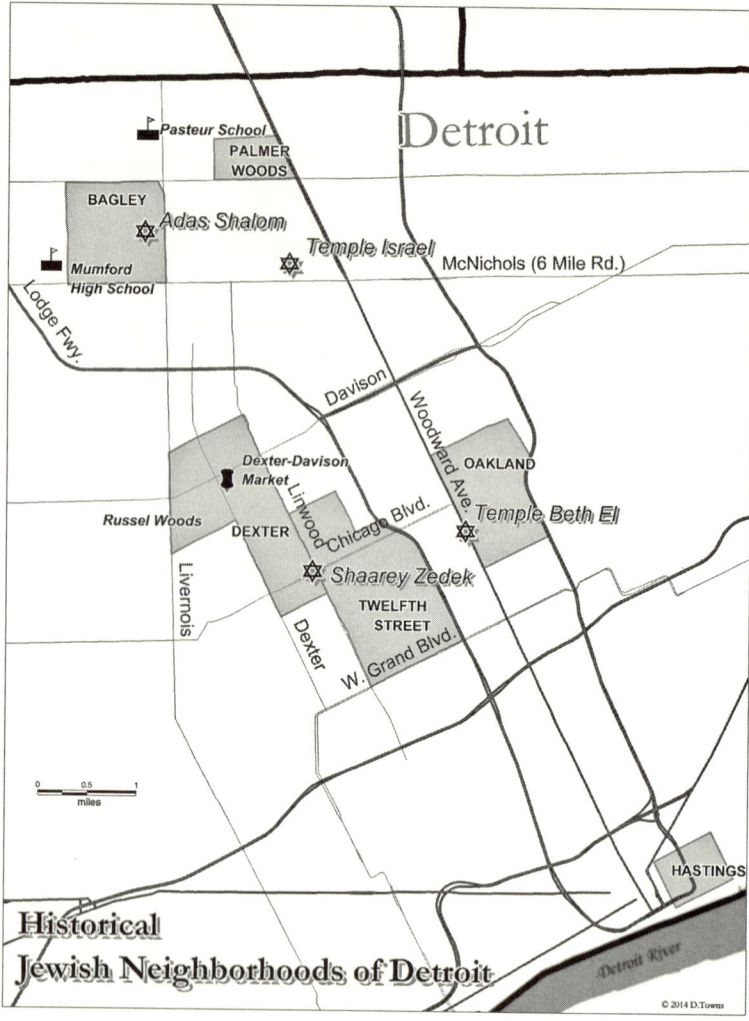

FIGURE 1.2 Overview of Jewish neighborhoods, synagogues, and landmarks in Detroit. Map by Patricia Becker and Douglas Towns.

often more than one, of these neighborhoods. This could be the end of the story of Jewish life in Detroit: Jews left it. The Drikers' decision to stay in the city was the exception.

Yet what was not exceptional—what was in fact quite typical—about the Drikers' story was the significance they credited to the city and its Jewish neighborhoods in orienting their political, cultural, and spiritual actions. Indeed, for the tens of thousands of Jews who journeyed away from Detroit after World War II, the city remained a place of engagement, and a space from which a new consciousness about what it meant to be a Jew in the United States emerged.

For the Jews of Detroit, the meaning of the city was interwoven with their experiences of living in, leaving, and imagining the Jewish neighborhood. A city street sign posted in the corner of a bucolic backyard made it difficult to know, indeed, where Detroit began and where it ended. One could read the sign as an epitaph, pointing to a time and place that no longer existed. But the sign itself offered a way to position oneself in time and place with respect to the city. Postwar Jews again and again sought to reorient themselves in the city, arriving at new markers to construct their relationship to the topographical and imagined space of Detroit and Jewish Detroit.

Even as Jews lived on the streets of Detroit, occupied its homes and apartments, and shopped in its stores, they understood their lives in the city through ideas about what it meant to be a Jew and an American, living in a city at a particular moment in time. The space of Detroit and the idea of Detroit were inseparable since both were formed in the nexus of the same historical, political, economic, and cultural forces.[3] Though my intention in this chapter is to orient the reader to Detroit, the urban policies that shaped it, and the Jewish neighborhoods that helped create its contours, my argument is that for Jews living in Detroit—and I believe other American cities—after World War II, the city's map shifted many times over in its representation of ideas about space. The map of postwar Detroit and its Jewish spaces reveals historical transformations, multiple understandings of single blocks, intersections, and buildings, divergences among memories, experiences, and desires set in space, and a variety of power relationships mediated by urban policies, economic structures, and collective and individual attitudes. Maps must be specific about time and place, even as they try to capture something general about space and its uses.

On the Idea of the Neighborhood and Detroit's First Jewish Neighborhood

Early twentieth-century sociologists understood the neighborhood as a crucial building block of urban identity. By studying the urban neighborhood, they believed they could better understand the forces of conflict, harmony, and progress that were forming American society. These sociologists, many of whom focused their fieldwork on the city of Chicago, believed that groups and individuals passed through neighborhoods as they rose in socioeconomic status. One could measure an immigrant or ethnic group's level of success by answering a basic geographical question: How far had the group moved from its earliest settlements?

In the sociological imagination of the early to mid-twentieth century, each urban neighborhood constituted its own reality. University of Chicago sociologist Robert Park explained in a 1925 essay, "In the course of time every section and quarter of the city takes on something of the character and qualities of its inhabitants.... The effect of this is to convert what was at first a mere geographical expression into a neighborhood, that is to say, a locality with sentiments, traditions, and a history of its own.... The life of every locality moves on with a certain momentum of its own, more or less independent of the larger circle of life and interests about it."[4] The neighborhoods of a city each represented an ecosystem, replete with its own set of social, cultural, and economic realities. Well into the mid-twentieth century, sociologists maintained that certain neighborhood characteristics endured even as different ethnic groups moved through them. The nature of a neighborhood—the rate of criminality that existed within it or the socioeconomic profile of its inhabitants—was organic to that neighborhood.[5]

Setting aside, for the moment, their neglect of the historical forces, including laws, economic policies, and hierarchical power structures, that shaped neighborhoods, early sociologists were onto something crucial when they drew focus to the unique geographical spaces that constituted cities. A neighborhood may have been a constructed artifice, but it also felt real and vital to its inhabitants who thought of their identities as shaped by the space in which they lived and the answer they gave to the question, where are you from? Indeed, popular discourse on urban neighborhoods, in part molded by the expert culture of sociology, tended to confirm the scholarly perspective that neighborhoods constituted their own realities. The shorthand of a neighborhood name (in Detroit, Twelfth Street or Dexter-Davison, for example) did not simply designate a topographical area; to the residents of a city, it also offered a rich indication of the kind of people who lived there. The linguistic partitioning of neighborhoods was often starker than their generally indistinct topographical boundaries.

The earliest geographic space in Detroit to bear the sobriquet of a Jewish neighborhood was hardly distinct in topographical form or human composition from other immigrant groups' neighborhood turf. Initially, a German settlement, the area became known as the Hastings Street neighborhood, referring to the business thoroughfare that cut through the neighborhood. Slightly to the east of the heart of downtown and close to the Detroit River, the Hastings Street area was part of the east side of the city, where working-class immigrants, predominantly German and Polish, had settled well before the twentieth century. German and Central European Jews found their footing in the neighborhood and by 1880 were in the kinds of professions—proprietors, managers, and white-collar workers—that propelled them into the middle class. The elite among these Jews integrated into the political life of Detroit, serving in elected positions at the city and state level in the late nineteenth and early twentieth centuries. Interestingly, after 1920, no Jew served on Detroit's elected Common Council until 1962. Clearly an indication of the trajectory of Jewish power in those decades, this fact reveals the outward political power that German Jews attained in the city, and, then, the retrenchment of outward Jewish political power as Eastern European Jews came to predominate and direct their energies toward internal political matters negotiated within neighborhood spaces and as antisemitism rose.[6]

With the settlement of Eastern European Jews in Detroit in the early decades of the twentieth century, German Jews left the Hastings Street neighborhood for areas to the north and west of it, especially several blocks east of Woodward Avenue near Warren and Oakland Avenues. Their reasons for moving were varied. Some viewed the Eastern European Jews as uncouth and not worthy neighbors, but the motivation for better housing stock trumped most other concerns. Documentary journalists from the first decade of the twentieth century reported on the "ghetto" conditions that existed in Hastings Street and identified a few blocks where most Eastern European Jews clustered. Not nearly as densely inhabited as New York City's Lower East Side, Jewish Hastings Street still struck reporters as overcrowded and teeming with foreignness and a "queer Yiddish dialect."[7] The local elementary school, the most populous in the state, had a predominantly Jewish student body, and synagogues and kosher markets lined the streets in this small quadrant of the city. The steady entrance of new Jewish immigrants into the city and the Jewish institutions that had been built over the last half of a century in the neighborhood continued to mark the Hastings Street area as the city's central Jewish neighborhood. Secular, socialist, and religious institutions stood side by side, asserting the internal diversity of the Jewish population, even as reporters saw a uniform mass swelling into the ghetto streets.[8]

FIGURE 1.3 A delicatessen on Hastings Street, 1911. Courtesy of the Leonard N. Simons Jewish Community Archives of the Jewish Federation of Metropolitan Detroit.

The Hastings Street neighborhood was home to a variety of ethnic, religious, and racial groups, and it also represented the densest concentration of Jews in the city. By 1920, roughly 60 percent of the Jews in Detroit lived there, and most lived on blocks with very little ethnic diversity.[9] In other words, Jews inhabited a neighborhood that was diverse, but they resided in relatively homogenous pockets. In their home lives, Jews may have been surrounded primarily by Jews, but in the larger neighborhood Jews were just one of many other populations.

Alongside the internal diversity of the neighborhood and its rather indistinct boundaries from other ethnic neighborhoods, a high level of residential mobility also characterized the Jewish sections of the neighborhood. Many of the non-Jewish groups in the neighborhood tied themselves to its space through their housing investments, purchasing real estate hungrily. The housing stock of Detroit tended toward freestanding homes, whether single family or divided, much more so than apartment buildings, and many immigrants understood real estate ownership as a path toward economic stability in their new country. Surveys from 1900, however, show that Russian Jews had a far lower rate of homeownership than other immigrant populations in Detroit, and they moved more often—generally to bigger homes or nicer streets—than many other immigrants.[10]

Jews' low rates of homeownership did not signify their lack of investment in the neighborhood. To the contrary, they invested in the area through the businesses and institutions they established. Because Jews did not receive a particularly warm welcome into the automobile industry, far more Jews than members of other immigrant groups became proprietors of their own stores and businesses, a fact that tied them to the economies and political struggles of the neighborhoods in which they lived. Of the roughly thirty-five thousand Jews who lived in Detroit in 1920, one-third were business owners or in retail, and proportionally far fewer Jews, when compared to the general population, were identified as laborers, a pattern that would continue into the 1950s and beyond.[11]

Jews maintained their stores in the Hastings Street area much longer than they kept their homes there. Even as they left the neighborhood for more middle-class housing, they remained involved in the neighborhood's economic and political life, through memberships in merchant organizations and involvement in neighborhood political counsels. Also, many Jewish political and social organizations maintained their headquarters in the neighborhood. For example, the United Jewish Charities, established in 1899 and committed to providing relief, education, and support to new Jewish immigrants and their children, kept its stronghold in the Hastings Street area, and, thus, tied Detroit Jews to the neighborhood, whether through philanthropy, voluntarism, or need.[12]

With consistency throughout the early decades of the twentieth century, Jews left the Hastings Street neighborhood to move north to the Warren and Oakland areas and then, increasingly, north and west toward the Twelfth Street neighborhood. Prior to the 1920s, there is no evidence that religious or community leaders castigated Jews for leaving the neighborhood. After all, it suffered from poor infrastructure, was plagued with water and sewer problems, and stood close to factories. The leaders who concerned themselves with planning and serving the Jewish community did not believe that individual Jews should remain there. Rather, most assumed that a steady flow of immigration would naturally ensure an enduring Jewish presence in the neighborhood and would support the Jewish institutions and businesses located there.[13]

Only with the passage of restrictive immigration legislation starting in 1917, did Jewish movement away from the Hastings Street area present a challenge to the Jewish nature of the neighborhood.[14] Without a steady supply of new immigrants to replace the Jews who left the neighborhood, leaders worried about the fate of the area. In 1923, the United Jewish Charities of Detroit charged a social researcher who had earlier served on its staff to study the contours of Detroit's Jewish community. The survey itself, as communal surveys often are, was premised upon a foregone conclusion: Jews were moving away from the Hastings Street neighborhood. The data not only named this trend as an empirical reality, but it also created the justification for reapportioning Jewish agencies' resources to plan for (and thus encourage) more movement. At the same time, the survey bemoaned the material losses that the Jewish community would face if the neighborhood, with its Jewish institutions and buildings, no longer remained a center of Jewish life. How could the community best prepare to avoid serious losses on these investments?

Whereas earlier discussions of Jewish movement from the neighborhood had simply indicated that mobility was an "inevitable" process, when the threat of the demise of the neighborhood became apparent, leaders turned their attention to unnatural forces that were hastening Jewish movement. The 1923 report attributed the most recent spate of Jewish movement away from the neighborhood to "the steady increase of the Negro population and their pressure upon the Jewish districts for housing facilities."[15]

An observer could have named countless forces other than the migration of blacks to Detroit that exerted pressure on Jews' downtown settlement. In the first two decades of the twentieth century, Detroit became a true industrial hub and a thriving modern city. In those twenty years, the city had climbed its way up from the thirteenth most populated city to the fourth, behind only New York, Chicago, and Philadelphia. New immigrants and migrants flooded into Detroit, enticed by plentiful jobs. While newcomers tended to settle in the downtown center of the city, close to jobs and near familiar ethnic or religious communities, people who had lived longer in the city moved away from the downtown. Indeed, Detroit quintupled its geographic size from 1900 to 1926, when, through the rapid annexation of land adjacent to the city, it reached its 139-square-mile size. The population explosion still led to crowding in the downtown area, but, until World War I, Detroiters had the luxury of space to ease that pressure.[16]

The number of blacks migrating from the South to join the ranks of laborers in Detroit increased during World War I, just as the number of immigrants from foreign countries slowed. This meant that fewer European immigrants, including Jews, were replenishing the population of downtown settlements. In their place, blacks were streaming into the city, and their numbers quickly rivaled that of white European immigrant groups.

Additionally, during the war, Detroit builders were forced to suspend housing construction so that all of the city's resources could be devoted toward war production. For the first time, despite Detroit's geographical expansiveness, the city's housing stock could not keep up with its population growth. Neighborhoods grew increasingly overcrowded and the possibilities for residential mobility, especially for nonwhites, were suddenly choked.[17]

Flattening the broader context that spurred Jewish mobility and depleted the Jewish population in the Hastings area, the author of the 1923 Jewish survey drew a causal link between "the pressure of the Negro population" and what it perceived as a growing instability of Jewish life in the city, exacerbated by the lack of a clear Jewish geographic center and faltering communal investments in the Hastings neighborhood. The report depicted Jews as playing a passive role in their own mobility, simply reacting to the pressure of black settlement. In the eyes of community builders, the problem was not that Jews did not want to live with blacks; the problem was that Jews had invested in the Hastings Street neighborhood and now their investments, primarily brick-and-mortar structures that housed synagogues and Jewish agencies, were becoming a "financial problem."[18]

With a nod to the nascent field of modern urban planning, the author concluded that unless Jews could predict their movement through space and create a rational map of their future, their community institutions would be unable to serve them. A coordinated, unified Jewish community must know where it was going so that it could plan its material investments accordingly and determine when to sell, and when and where to buy. And a good plan apparently had to give due consideration to where other groups, most importantly blacks but also white Christians who might bar Jewish settlement, were moving.

Planning for Jewish Neighborhoods

Just as Jews in Detroit confronted the travails of creating an urban infrastructure that could best serve their population, the urban planning movement grew into national prominence. Wed to concerns about urban corruption, delinquency, and hygiene, the burgeoning movement asserted that scientific inquiry and management could best order urban life. Cities, if properly managed, might be more than haphazard collections of people; they could be highly orchestrated organisms that improved the lot of their residents and, perhaps, humanity. Jewish social welfare organizations, such as the United Jewish Charities that sponsored the 1923 survey, were quick studies of urban scientific management. Jewish charitable and communal institutions, which proliferated in the 1920s, maintained that precise research into Jewish patterns—of residence, mobility, education, family organization, profession, and more—could illuminate the path toward a more coherent and ordered Jewish urban existence in the future. Three years after the release of the study, Detroit Jews formed the Jewish Welfare Federation to help manage Jewish life in the city. With sufficient research and coordination, precious community resources would be allocated judiciously and not invested poorly in synagogues or Hebrew school buildings only to be abandoned a few years later.[19]

Jews who lived in American cities in the early to mid-twentieth century experienced a residential geography reminiscent of European urban organization: certain areas of most American cities became known as Jewish areas and were defined as such by a balance of the choices Jews made about where to live, and the external pressures they experienced that confined them to restricted geographic areas. Jewish law and practice had long focused on how Jews might gain control of the space around them and might, in some fashion, colonize it as Jewish space, even when non-Jews often controlled the terms of that space. From ghettos or Jewish quarters, Jews created the basis of their political and communal organization. In the late eighteenth and early nineteenth centuries, Enlightenment ideals and the possibility of Jewish emancipation into the modern category of citizenship challenged long-standing Jewish forms of social and political organization. The possibility of Jewish citizenship in a modern nation-state pivoted upon redefining Jews as individuals and not primarily as members of a collective, as they had been treated for centuries. Thus, in yearning for the freedoms and privileges of individual-based citizenship, Jews also had to confront the communal costs of it.[20]

Despite American paeans to freedom of mobility, Jews, similar to other ethnic and racial groups, found that public policies and various forms of coercion delimited their residential possibilities in cities. By the 1920s, zoning laws wed private concerns about undesirable people (blacks, Jews, Catholics) and places (such as factories or boardinghouses) to public policy by stipulating land-use regulations. Stemming from urban planning theories, zoning ordinances ordered the use of space and, at the same time, rationalized racial and ethnic hierarchies by maintaining that certain kinds of property were not suitable for certain kinds of people. Restrictive covenants, a corollary of zoning laws, gave broader power to individual citizens and collectives to protect their property by, in effect, extending the reaches of private property to the house next door or the plot of land down the street.[21]

In the interwar period, the geographic sphere of Jewish concern focused almost entirely upon the Jewish neighborhood, in the case of Detroit, the Twelfth Street area and, by the mid-1930s, the more northwesterly Dexter-Davison neighborhood. This is not to say that Jews did not care about the broader city, nation, or world, but Jews concentrated their resources and investments—whether communal ones or private ones—on their neighborhoods, and defined the geographic spaces of their neighborhoods by the limits of their resources and the discrimination they experienced.[22]

The patterns of Jewish mobility in interwar Detroit reflected the city's intolerance toward the growing religious and racial diversity in its midst. Nativism ran high in interwar Detroit, compounded by periods of economic insecurity and, eventually, the Great Depression. Henry Ford's antisemitism, chronicled in his self-published newspaper the *Dearborn Independent*, the emergence of the Ku Klux Klan throughout the state, and growingly rigid lines of social segregation in Detroit's social club scene all constricted the spaces in which Jews felt comfortable. From populist rhetoric, meant to raise the ire of the working class, to elitist pronouncements, meant to show the upper class that Jews threatened their rarified existence, to zoning and restrictive policies, antisemitism etched itself upon the map of interwar Detroit.[23]

Ironically, during these same decades that witnessed the rise of public expressions of antisemitism and nativism in Detroit, Jews also solidified their socioeconomic success in the city and took advantage of the opportunities that the city provided for advancement among its white working and middle class. In the 1930s, while Jews, similar to everyone else, suffered deprivations during the Great Depression, Jews in Detroit had lower rates of unemployment than non-Jews. (This pattern was evident across urban America.) By 1934, Jews' median income was significantly higher than non-Jews' income, and their employment patterns continued to place them in more white-collar professions than their non-Jewish counterparts.[24]

The small number of truly wealthy Jews still found themselves excluded from the social institutions, such as the Detroit Athletic Club, that defined elite Detroit. In response, Jews formed their own downtown eating and social clubs. For example, in 1934, a group of wealthy, mainly German-descended Jews organized the Standard Club, an eating club that met in the Detroit-Leland Hotel. The men who signed the Articles of Incorporation (and chose to list their residential addresses, as opposed to their downtown business addresses) lived within blocks of one another in gracious homes in an area called Boston-Edison that stood in the northern regions of the Twelfth Street neighborhood. This was the space that by the 1930s had become the Jewish neighborhood—leaving the Hastings Street area the distinction of having become the "old" neighborhood.[25]

Temple Beth El, the city's largest Reform congregation, had led the way in designating the Twelfth Street neighborhood as Jewish. In 1922, its leaders, many of the same men who formed the Standard Club, insisted that the time was at hand to move the congregation from the Hastings Street neighborhood to a new location two and a half miles north, close to the Warren and Oakland areas where some Jews had settled and on the eastern edge of what would become the Twelfth Street neighborhood and the new core of Jewish life in the city. These men raised money, mainly through their own wealth, to erect a neoclassical building on Woodward and Gladstone and mark the neighborhood with the presence of institutional Jewish life in the form of a classically Reform and, thus, anti-Zionist American synagogue.

Twelfth Street quickly attracted Jewish families whose wealth, politics, and spiritual proclivities did not mirror those of the Temple Beth El leaders. In close proximity to the affluent Jewish families and institutions lived many middle-class and lower-middle-class Jews as well. Elaine Driker spent her early years living in a house in the center of the Twelfth Street neighborhood. Only a few blocks south of the gracious homes of the Standard Club founders, the house was a modest, redbrick, two-flat (or two-family) home. This was, in fact, the hallmark of the neighborhood, a place where the physical distance separating the very wealthy, the comfortably middle class, and the still struggling lower middle class was not so great. For most of Detroit, class lines translated into geography much more neatly. Olivier Zunz's study of the urban development of Detroit notes that by the 1920s "social class now served to define urban space in terms stronger than ever before and equal to those of ethnicity."[26] Not so for the Jews, whose emerging settlement patterns revealed occupational diversity unrivaled by any other white ethnic group. To be certain, class distinctions were as obvious as the size of the homes in the Twelfth Street neighborhood. Yet streets with varying socioeconomic profiles intersected and abutted one another. Jews in the interwar period were

FIGURE 1.4 Albert Kahn's Temple Beth El on Woodward and Gladstone, circa 1922. Courtesy of the Temple Beth El Buildings Collection XXXX.06, Rabbi Leo M. Franklin Archives, Temple Beth El, Bloomfield Hills, Michigan.

aware of class distinctions within the community, but they also inhabited shared class space, a reflection of the ongoing power of their ethnic ties to draw the map of Jewish Detroit.

Within the Twelfth Street neighborhood, political and religious diversity thrived alongside class diversity. By the 1920s, synagogues affiliated with the Reform movement and burgeoning Conservative and Orthodox movements lined the streets. Secular and socialist institutions, such as the Sholem Aleichem Institute and the Workmen's Circle, and secular (often socialist) Zionist groups joined the roster of neighborhood organizations. And children in the neighborhood had their pick from fifteen different Jewish supplementary schools, including one affiliated with the communist International Workers' Order.[27]

Although community leaders in the early 1920s had talked about using the tools of scientific management to plan for Jewish mobility, the residential patterns that emerged were less a function of planning and more a function of the vagaries of interwar Detroit. Increasingly, Jews had the resources to improve their housing situations, but they did not always have the freedom, sense of security, or desire to strike out on their own and live beyond the Jewish neighborhood.

The ability to define themselves geographically offered Detroit Jews a fairly undemanding mode through which to enact Jewishness. One simply had to live within a set of street boundaries to be Jewish. To be certain, non-Jews lived in the Jewish neighborhood, but the density of Jewish settlement, the number of Jews at the local public schools, and the businesses that catered to Jewish needs all gave Jews the sense that they inhabited Jewish space. None of this, however, enabled Jews to believe that their space was unchanging.

Changing Neighborhoods

By 1937, approximately seventy-one thousand Jews lived in Detroit, making it the sixth most populous Jewish city in the United States.[28] The frequency of studies into the demography of Jewish Detroit paralleled the rise in the city's Jewish population. The Jewish Welfare Federation of Detroit and the newly formed Jewish Community Council of Detroit both bankrolled a seemingly endless stream of surveys and interviews. Although they varied in their stated goals, each study revealed a desire to protect Jewish life from the internal and external forces that Jewish leaders perceived as threats to the strength of the community. Beginning with the 1923 report, the organized Jewish community devoted itself, in particular, to conducting population studies that documented where Jews lived and where they were moving.

A study from the mid-1930s, financed by the Jewish Welfare Federation, indicated the investment that Jewish leadership had in tracking Jewish movement. The author of the study, who completed his research while on fellowship at the University of Michigan, had used data from the 1935 Michigan census to create a sample of roughly 10 percent of the Jewish population. He found that just over 10 percent of Jews lived in the Hastings Street area, but that 80 percent of the Jewish population lived in two adjoining neighborhoods: the Twelfth Street area and the neighborhood that he termed Dexter. Twelfth Street, when compared to Dexter, was closer to the downtown; had older housing stock, predominantly from the early decades of the twentieth century; and a greater diversity of housing—from the very large homes on Chicago Boulevard and surrounding blocks where Standard Club members lived to the two flats on Clairmount where Elaine Driker spent her earlier years. The remaining Jewish population lived in a smattering of other areas that were north and west of Twelfth Street and Dexter and farther away from downtown.[29]

Although relative socioeconomic diversity had characterized Jewish residential settlements in Detroit, by the mid-1930s class distinctions could be mapped more clearly than ever before on Jewish space. Both core Jewish neighborhoods—Dexter and Twelfth Street—still possessed blocks with large homes that housed upper-middle-class residents. But as one moved north and west on the city map, Jewish income levels tended to rise, as did the cost of housing. The Twelfth Street neighborhood contained more lower-middle-class spaces—two-flats, smaller plots of land, narrower streets—than the Dexter neighborhood with its more solidly middle-class housing (single homes and more spacious two-flats) and landscape.

For the purposes of his report, the researcher for the Jewish Welfare Federation distinguished between the two neighborhoods, reflecting Jews' self-consciousness about the difference that a few blocks could make. The Hastings neighborhood had been separated from Twelfth Street by a couple of miles, so even though the borders of each neighborhood were fuzzy, a clear distance divided one from the other. Twelfth Street and Dexter, however, were contiguous with each other, with the latter neighborhood extending the former to the northwest. The researcher, however, understood that Jewish families in the 1930s endowed their moves from Twelfth Street to Dexter with significance not immediately visible in the neighborhoods' geographic proximity. A move to Dexter represented the arrival of Detroit Jews into a far more comfortable and secure American middle-class world than ever before. At the same time, Dexter also was the ground from which Detroit Jews invested unprecedented levels of resources in the idea and space of the Jewish neighborhood, anchored by Jewish institutions and Jewish homes.[30]

Eugene Driker's parents were Russian immigrants, who, by the time he was born in 1937, had moved into the Dexter neighborhood, eventually buying a single-family home right on the border of Russel Woods, an upscale area of the neighborhood. Never prosperous, his father was a proprietor. He owned a laundry and dry cleaners and then a candy store right on Dexter Avenue, only a few blocks from the family's home. Elaine's family moved to a nearby block when she was a young teenager, first renting a lower flat and then a single-family home.

By the mid-1930s, the federal government had determined that homeownership was the next frontier for creating a productive, loyal American citizenry. Not only were homeowners more invested than renters in the stability of their streets, neighborhoods, cities, and ultimately nation, but their home purchases could also pump dollars into a beleaguered

American economy. The newly established Federal Housing Administration (FHA) offered certain sectors of America's citizenry subsidized housing mortgages, operating according to the logic that healthy home-building and -buying sectors would redound benefit to the American economy and, ultimately, national strength and unity.[31]

Detroit was a city of homes, not apartment buildings. By 1940 housing units in apartment buildings constituted only about 14 percent of the city's total housing stock, and as the home-building industry took off, that percentage would only decline.[32] The archetypal Jewish neighborhoods most Americans imagine are New York City ones, abounding with low-rise tenement buildings and concrete stoops. Not so for Detroit. Though Detroit Jews had a lower rate of homeownership than the city's non-Jewish population, a full half of all Jews owned their homes by the mid-1950s, a marked increase since the 1920s when roughly one-quarter of Jews had been homeowners. Furthermore, among the younger generation of Jews, the number of homeowners was even higher.[33] Beginning in the interwar era, whatever area bore the tag of the Jewish neighborhood, whether Twelfth Street, Dexter, or later the Bagley area in northwest Detroit, that space reflected the highly subsidized nature of homeownership in the United States. Federal funds, funneling into home building and protecting low-rate home mortgages, were essential to the cartography of Detroit and the settlement patterns of Jewish Detroiters.

During World War II, Detroit, the so-called arsenal of democracy, suspended most nonmilitary-related industrial activities, and the tide of Jewish movement halted. For roughly a decade, very few Jews relocated to new neighborhoods, creating what in retrospect was a punctuated and ephemeral sense of stability for the middle-class Dexter neighborhood. That sense of stability, as fleeting as it was, also reflected shifts in national civic discourse away from publicly tolerated nativism toward a more consolidated hierarchical structure that defined access to privilege through skin color. By the end of World War II, the expressions of antisemitism that dogged Jews in the interwar year had become decidedly less acceptable. This did not mean that antisemitism evaporated, but it lost its traction in the public realm, where public relations experts trumpeted American civility, if not equality, as the foot soldier in the fight against totalitarianism. Expressions of interfaith solidarity, often crafted by Jewish communal relations agencies such as the American Jewish Committee, grew ubiquitous in print, radio, and television. Detroit's Father Coughlin, the vitriolic radio preacher who spewed antisemitism into the radio waves in the 1930s, had become entirely marginalized by the end of World War II, and the KKK was in decline.[34]

For the vast majority of American Jews in these years, urban neighborhoods became the setting for a feeling of "at homeness." These were places where Jews could participate in the culture of middle-class American life and still feel tied to perceptibly Jewish spaces. In writing about interwar New York City, historian Eli Lederhendler proposes that Jews inhabited two urban utopias in the city: a cosmopolitan democracy and an "ingathering" of Jewish people.[35] A Jew living in a Jewish neighborhood in any number of American cities might have imagined he had found an answer to the diasporic dilemmas that had plagued Jews for so many centuries: how to live as a Jew in a non-Jewish nation. What historians have termed "the cult of American-Jewish synthesis" gained its most self-conscious expression in midcentury urban neighborhoods, where political, economic, and cultural forces aligned to offer Jews some sense of resolution to the historical tension between particularism and universalism. A Jew was at home because he or she could live in the Jewish urban neighborhood and still venture often into the wider American city.[36]

Jews who came of age during the 1940s and early 1950s have created the iconography of the Jewish neighborhood: block after block of two-parent families familiar from one's synagogue, Hebrew school, or parents' social circle; elementary and secondary schools that were almost entirely Jewish; the sound of Yiddish phrases in the street; and the smells of Jewish bakeries and delis. Philip Roth's Newark, New Jersey, or Philadelphia's Strawberry Mansion, or the Bronx, or Cleveland Heights all share this lore of the World War II–era Jewish neighborhood.[37] Nostalgic as many portrayals of the postwar Jewish neighborhood may be, most of these urban neighborhoods shared certain geographical and demographic characteristics, including Jewish density and propinquity (generally over 60 percent of the residents on the central blocks in these neighborhoods were Jewish). Yet the neighborhoods were also in close proximity to non-Jewish spaces in the forms of shared business districts or downtowns.

In its rhetorical power, human composition, and reflection of urban economic and political policies, the Jewish neighborhood simultaneously asserted boundaries while creating unbound spaces of exchange and tension among Jews and with non-Jews. In the Dexter and Twelfth Street neighborhoods, nearly as many white ethnic Catholics (Greeks and Poles predominantly) as Jews inhabited the neighborhood space. The fact that most of the Catholic children attended parochial schools fueled Jews' perception that the neighborhood was Jewish. Yet two towering Catholic structures, the neo-Gothic Blessed Sacrament Cathedral and the Sacred Heart Seminary, loomed over the neighborhood. A combination of willed blindness and different institutional, educational, and recreational patterns prevented most Jews from identifying the neighborhood as shared, as opposed to Jewish, space.[38]

Jewish Life at the City Limits

After its final land annexation in the 1920s, Detroit grew to roughly four times the size of the island of Manhattan.[39] Thus, Detroiters could move far from the downtown area without leaving the city limits. The 1950 U.S. Census revealed that Detroit's population had increased by over 13 percent in the past ten years and that over 70 percent of that increase had occurred in the city's northwest neighborhoods.[40] Racial restrictive covenants, however, governed most of the property in the far reaches of the city to the west and east, making migration to all but a few swaths of land in the outer arc of the city impossible for black Detroiters.[41]

Already in the 1930s, small numbers of Jews had left the Twelfth Street and Dexter neighborhoods to settle in the northwestern extents of the city. In the broadest terms, the northwestern area extended across a quadrant of land west of Woodward Avenue and east of Greenfield Road (roughly four miles), and bound on the south by Six Mile Road (or McNichols Road) and on the north by Eight Mile Road. (The mile markers indicate the distance north from the intersection of Michigan Avenue and Woodward Avenue in downtown Detroit; Eight Mile Road is the city's northern border.) By the 1940s, Jews were forming a new area of Jewish density set around Bagley Elementary School, on the blocks between Livernois and Wyoming. But as was the case for most Jewish neighborhoods, the boundaries demarcating the beginning and the end of the Bagley neighborhood were indistinct.

In 1943, fifty-two Jewish men lingered in a Bagley-area storefront that had been transformed into a makeshift synagogue for Yom Kippur. These men were predominantly homeowners in the neighborhood, and they wanted to worship where they lived, even if they had to hold High Holiday services in a store. That evening, they gave themselves a name—Northwest Hebrew Congregation—and began to meet regularly for worship, first, in a building at the intersection of Livernois and Seven Mile Road and, then, in the more centrally located Bagley Elementary School. Two years later, they

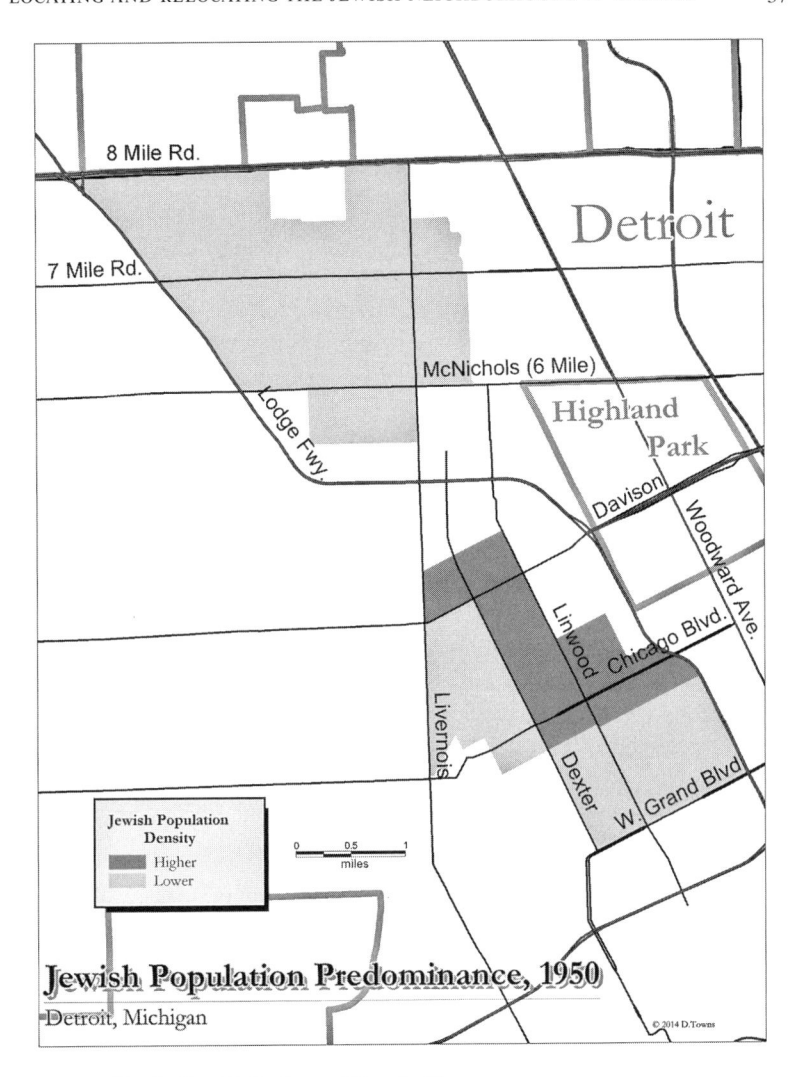

LOCATING AND RELOCATING THE JEWISH NEIGHBORHOODS OF DETROIT

FIGURE 1.5 Map by Patricia Becker and Douglas Towns.

planned a synagogue building and bought land down the street from the elementary school, next to the Mayflower Congregational Church. They formally affiliated with the Conservative movement, hired a rabbi and a cantor, and purchased twenty-five acres of land in the already established Northwest Memorial Park cemetery, west of the neighborhood and outside of the city limits. Finally in 1951, their synagogue building was complete. Searching for a more "spiritual" name that did not merely designate geography, the congregation renamed itself Adas Shalom (literally, Congregation of Peace). Yet synagogue leaders took pride in their congregation's geography, noting in a dedication volume for the new building that theirs was a truly American synagogue built "out of the distinct need of a geographical district for a place of worship, rather than out of the desire of a group of people to build a synagogue patterned on a national background."[42]

Jewish builders had helped orchestrate the geographical shift in the Jewish population. By the late 1940s, several Jewish-owned building companies invested in developing specific sections of northwest Detroit. Jewish builders encouraged a concentrated pattern of Jewish settlement in northwest Detroit by steering Jews toward the ethnic housing market. Similar to the "ethnically distinct housing market" that historian Deborah Dash Moore has written about in interwar New York City, Detroit's housing market developed a niche to serve the Jewish population in the postwar period.[43] In 1949, Kopman Building Company's advertisements in the *Detroit Jewish News*, the newspaper that served Detroit's Jewish community since 1942, described the northwestern area as the "Fastest Growing Jewish Section in the City." In concert with other building companies and real estate firms (predominantly Jewish-owned ones), Kopman encouraged Jewish families to come see for themselves the new setting of Jewish life in Detroit.[44]

A survey done in 1958 found that 62 percent of Detroit's Jewish families, compared to just over a third in 1949, lived in the Bagley area, mostly in the handful of blocks surrounding the elementary school and Adas Shalom. Proximate to this neighborhood was a larger swath of Jewish life, simply called "northwest" by Detroiters. While one might think of this area as liminal—only a mile or two south of the city limits and the expanding suburbs—for Jews in the late 1940s, 1950s, and early 1960s, the northwest was the site of a new set of Jewish neighborhoods, close to a business thoroughfare, with Jewish stores and offices, and anchored by public schools that served large Jewish student bodies. At the same time, the neighborhoods' geography and built topography seemed to announce mobility at every turn.[45]

The Lodge Freeway (eventually designated as M-10) cut across the northwestern edge of the neighborhood. Constructed throughout the 1950s and finally completed in 1959, the Lodge connected northwest Detroit to downtown, passing right through the Twelfth Street neighborhood. On the federally funded expressway, commuters could easily travel from homes in Bagley or northwest Detroit to jobs downtown. Yet the highway also linked to a northwestern extension that brought families to the western edge of

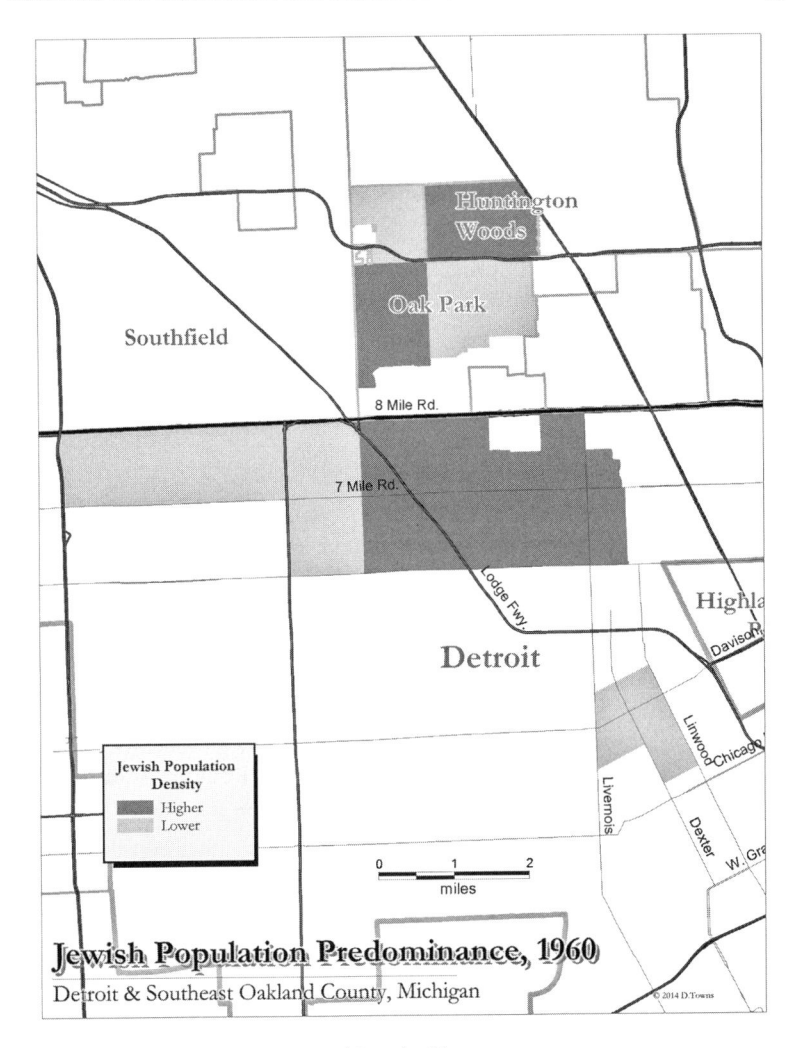

FIGURE 1.6 Map by Patricia Becker and Douglas Towns.

Oak Park and into the middle of Southfield, the suburban corridor that Detroit Jews started to populate in significant numbers by the late 1950s.[46]

When Elaine and Eugene Driker returned to Detroit in 1964 after a brief period of living in Washington, DC, they rented the second floor of a two-flat home around the corner from Adas Shalom. The Detroit they returned to had a sizably smaller Jewish population living in the city than the one they had left; in 1958, 79 percent of the Jewish population remained within the city limits, but by 1963 that number had dwindled to

55 percent.[47] Eugene had just started his private law practice, and the family lived on one of the more modest blocks in the Bagley neighborhood. As renters, not homeowners, the Drikers were in the minority among the Jews in the neighborhood. They witnessed few new Jewish families purchasing homes in the area, and they sensed that the neighborhood was fast losing its Jewish identification.

In those years, the Jews who lived in northwest Detroit were moving even farther northwest to the suburbs of Oak Park, Huntington Woods, and eventually, Southfield. Distance-wise, these suburbs were closer to Bagley than Dexter, Twelfth Street, or downtown were to Bagley. A move out of the city, in other words, took Jews only a few miles farther northwest from where they had already been living. The northwest neighborhoods within the city also had already felt suburban, with their single-family homes, front lawns, and backyards—and, in fact, builders and real estate agents often used the word "suburban" to describe them. Yet the true suburbs of Detroit stood outside of the city limits, a fact that became determinative of elections and referenda, tax structure, and school districting.

Jewish Neighborhoods in the Suburbs

Over the course of the 1950s, Jewish settlement patterns transformed the northwestern suburbs of Detroit into Jewish spaces. While a statistically insignificant number of Jews resided in the suburbs at the end of the 1940s, by 1958 a full fifth of all Detroit Jews lived in two contiguous suburban communities, Oak Park and Huntington Woods, that covered approximately 6.5 square miles of land.[48]

Some Jews and Jewish institutions left for the suburbs with a sense of defeat that they had been unable to make a satisfying life for themselves in the city. Most, however, expressed optimism that the suburbs would become a newer, better location for American and Jewish life than the city had been. Suburban planning commissions, driven by the building industry and federal incentives for home building in the suburbs, helped create that landscape of optimism. Land-use plans rezoned vast tracts of suburban land for residential building and determined precise codes that set standards for large lot sizes, and mandated the construction of single-family homes as opposed to multi-dwelling units (whether two-family homes or apartment buildings). In 1956, the Oak Park Planning Commission, flooded with zoning requests, approved nine new residential subdivisions. Planning commissions throughout Oakland County, which encompassed the northwestern suburbs of Detroit, made similar policy decisions to accommodate and spur on the 73.5 percent gain in population that occurred in the county in the single decade from 1950 to 1960.[49]

With new homes priced to sell to white middle-class families who could easily obtain federally insured mortgages, suburbs promised a life of order and stability. Responding to the shifting demographics, the Jewish Community Center of Detroit opened a branch in Oak Park in 1956. (Nonetheless, community leaders hedged their bets on the city and in 1959 opened the "main" branch of the Jewish Community Center in the thriving northwest area.)[50] White religious institutions sailed through zoning hearings; their presence in the suburban landscape would act as an anchor to the new towns constructed at a breathless pace.

Detroit Jews were fast becoming dispersed across a vaster geographic region than ever before, yet certain aspects of the Jewish neighborhood endured in the suburbs. For one, Jews still moved to areas of Jewish residential concentration. By 1960, Jews made up roughly 40 percent of the population of Oak Park and Huntington Woods, and they were on their way to creating similar density in neighboring Southfield.[51] Furthermore, Jewish institutions located themselves in the orbit of Jewish suburban life. By 1960, many Jewish institutions had fit themselves into the 1.5-square-mile area that constituted Oak Park. In the fall of 1959, the Jewish proprietors of the Dexter-Davison Market expanded its operations now to include a branch in Oak Park in addition to its store in the Bagley neighborhood. (Despite retaining the name, it had closed the doors of its Dexter neighborhood location in the early 1950s.) An article in the *Detroit Jewish News* praised the modern conveniences offered at the Oak Park branch, including parking for three hundred cars, eight checkout lines, and a "hi-fi system." Reassuring naysayers, the owners explained, "Our slogan 'Where Old Friends Meet to Shop' will truly apply in our new Oak Park store."[52]

With so many features resembling life in Detroit's urban neighborhoods, it is striking that when Jews moved to the suburbs, they no longer claimed their residential space as part of a Jewish neighborhood, even if most of these suburbs still had an observable Jewish core to them. Unlike New York City, where the difference between city and suburb was often as obvious as the difference between an apartment building and a house, Detroit's urban neighborhoods were full of houses. From the 1920s onward, Jews in Detroit lived in neighborhoods full of freestanding homes, though often divided into two or four flats, with small yards, and streets lined with trees. By the late 1940s, single-family homes had predominated in the Jewish neighborhoods in Detroit. Many American cities, such as Philadelphia, Pittsburgh, Cincinnati, and Baltimore, boasted of similar-feeling residential neighborhoods within their city limits.

The idea of a Jewish neighborhood, however, endured as an urban, not suburban, construct. Many of the urban Jewish neighborhoods in Detroit had been walkable, each one located in close proximity to a business thoroughfare. But even before the majority of Jews left Detroit, the ubiquity of cars and new highways reoriented urban neighborhood life around car-based movement and consumer habits.[53]

Although Jews clustered in certain sections of suburban Detroit, the idea of a suburban Jewish neighborhood never entered the common parlance to describe suburban topography. For some Jews, the suburbs represented freedom from the confinements—lack of privacy, a feeling of being stuck in an insular place—of the urban Jewish neighborhood. Who, then, would want to think of their new residential space as yet another Jewish neighborhood? Increasingly, Jews added the adjective "old" to their talk of Jewish neighborhoods (as in, the "old neighborhood") to indicate the distance, in time and space, between the city and the suburbs. Oak Park, Huntington Woods, and eventually, after the 1967 riots in Detroit accelerated patterns of Jewish movement already in place, Southfield, Farmington Hills, and West Bloomfield defined the new topography of Detroit Jewish life. The Jewish press, real estate advertisements, correspondence among Jewish leaders, and minutes from synagogues and other Jewish institutions rarely, if ever, employed the term "neighborhood" to define these new suburban centers of Jewish life. Nonetheless, the very names of these places, at particular moments in time, functioned as shorthand to announce Jewish space and to communicate features, especially the relative socioeconomic status, of the people who inhabited it.

The rhetorical absence of the term "neighborhood" convinced many social critics and historians that Jewish suburbs were lesser than urban Jewish neighborhoods. With the rising influence of new urbanism in the 1980s and its romanticization of tightly woven, densely populated neighborhoods, historians described suburbs as places of defeat, malaise, and bourgeois excess, places where diversity, creativity, intellectual intensity, and radicalism came to die. This is wrong. We know that reading groups, theatrical troupes, activist circles, political protestors, the working class, nonwhites, immigrants, and many others carved out spaces in suburbs to foster their various cultural and political forms. Yet the criticism of the

American suburb, couched almost always in comparison to the city, reflected the deeply interconnected geographical and historical formation of suburbs and cities. Critics of suburbs protested that connection while ironically reinscribing it in the persistent definition of suburbs and cities in relation to one another.[54]

Through building subsidies, loan-making programs, highway construction projects, and tax incentives, American policy makers hardened the divide between particular neighborhoods within cities, and between cities and suburbs, with the weight of material consequences. Whether one lived in one neighborhood or another, or in the city or the suburb, carried real economic and political significance. This was not because neighborhoods or suburbs and cities were intrinsically different (as early twentieth-century sociologists were wont to argue) but because state policies and the citizenry that benefited from those policies made life and the available privileges within them different. And this was a self-sustaining system. Once one landed in a space of privilege, whether a particular neighborhood or a suburb, one became materially invested in maintaining spatial divisions, since the existence of the divide actually had policy significance and protected the resources and infrastructure that made certain spaces better to live in than others.[55]

Jewish Urbanism beyond Nostalgia

When the Drikers bought their first home in 1965, they made an uncommon choice to remain in Detroit's city limits. They purchased a single-family home in a tree-lined neighborhood called Green Acres, slightly east and north of Bagley and still in northwest Detroit. Similar to Jews who moved to the suburbs, the Drikers benefited from federal subsidies to help them pay for their home. They paid the down payment on their $19,000 home using a small government pension fund Eugene had earned while working in the attorney general's office in D.C., and they qualified for a conventional mortgage (though many whites who moved to suburbs opted for federally backed mortgages).

Neither Eugene nor Elaine remembered any black families on their block, but some prominent and comfortably middle-class black families lived on adjacent blocks. For example, Arthur Johnson, who came to the city in 1950 to serve as executive secretary of the National Association for the Advancement of Colored People's Detroit branch, lived a block away and became a close friend. The Drikers' two children attended Pasteur Elementary School alongside many black students. Yet by the time their younger one was in second grade, the Drikers no longer believed the school was serving their children well, so they sent the children to private schools in the suburbs. "This was the grand compromise," explained Eugene. The family wanted to stay in the city—"city life had become part of our family's DNA"—but they did not believe their children would thrive in the city's schools.[56]

Ten years after they moved to Green Acres, the Drikers sold their home for $36,000, close to two times what they had paid for it. They bought a stunning home in Palmer Woods, less than a five-minute drive east and slightly south of their home in Green Acres and still within the city limits of Detroit. The Drikers knew that the $97,000 they paid for the home was a bargain. To purchase something comparable—over five thousand square feet, five-and-a-half bathrooms, and stunning craftsmanship—in the suburbs would have required a much larger investment and would have controverted their substantial investment in the city. They bought the home from a Jewish family, likely departing the city for the suburbs.

As children in Detroit's Dexter neighborhood, Elaine and Eugene had known of Palmer Woods and the neighborhoods bordering the exclusive Detroit Golf Club as the ritzy area of town with few Jews. Throughout the 1940s and 1950s, at a time when most Jews lived in the Dexter and Bagley areas, wealthier Jewish families gradually moved to the gracious homes with large yards near Palmer Park in the so-called University District of northwest Detroit, where half of the families were Jewish and the other half Catholic members of the Gesu Parish. The actual number of Jewish families in these areas never reached as high as it did in the more populous Jewish neighborhoods of Detroit—the Hastings Street area, Twelfth Street, Dexter, or Bagley—though certain blocks were home to almost exclusively Jewish families. Indeed, many leaders in the Jewish community whose financial success translated into communal power settled in the streets near Palmer Park.

Temple Israel broke ground for its first permanent home adjacent to Palmer Park in 1948. A Reform congregation, Temple Israel had split from Temple Beth El in 1941, primarily as a reaction against Temple Beth El's anti-Zionism, once an acceptable feature of classically Reform congregations but, with the spread of Nazism through Europe, an increasingly controversial position for Jewish institutions. The new congregation's leaders believed they had chosen a plot of land that would soon become the heart

FIGURE 1.7 Eugene and Elaine Driker in front of their home in Palmer Woods, 2014. Courtesy of the Drikers.

of upper-middle-class Jewish Detroit. A brochure printed to help raise funds for the building boasted of its location, "This is a neighborhood that will never deteriorate because of its proximity to Palmer Park."[57] A sanctuary, with the capacity to seat seventeen hundred worshippers, further revealed the confidence that Temple Israel's leadership felt in its choice of location. In 1980, the congregation relocated to West Bloomfield, a suburb considerably farther north and west than the inner-ring Jewish suburbs of Oak Park and Southfield. Well before Temple Israel left Palmer Park, most of the Jews the Drikers knew lived in the suburbs.

Back to the street sign in the Drikers' backyard in 2012, a sign that marked a place to which one could drive easily. By most measures, the intersection of Dexter and Davison one would find in Detroit in 2012 was not the intersection signified by the street sign in the Drikers' yard. To get to that place, one would have to speak to Elaine and Eugene, maybe sit in their backyard, where they would reminisce about the Dexter-Davison Market, down the street from a drugstore and a men's clothing store, near a thriving branch of the Jewish Community Center, in the heart of a neighborhood they would describe as Jewish. To be certain, the placement of the sign, a gift from a friend, in their backyard represented a form of nostalgia, a desire to return through memory to a home of one's past. Historians' inquiry into the shaping and consequences of Jewish nostalgia for places of the past has made for important scholarship.[58]

The yard sign, however, symbolized something beyond nostalgia because it represented a form of political, economic, and cultural orientation critical to the formation of Jewish life in the twentieth century. In material and conceptual ways, the city continued to shape how Jews understood and lived their lives, even as they journeyed away from it. As a psychological phenomenon, the rise of Jewish metropolitan urbanism is implicated in structures of nostalgia. But as a historical phenomenon, Jewish metropolitan urbanism materially affected the ways that Jews functioned in the world: the forms of political activism they practiced, the economic investments they made, the religious and communal ideas they embraced, and the cultural ideals they strove to attain.

The twentieth-century forces that shaped Jewish metropolitan urbanism can be traced to the streets that cut through putatively Jewish neighborhoods, where people struggled to define what it meant to live in an American city full of so many people unlike one's self. In the same decades that Jews made their way through urban space, a mix of structural forces (laws and policies) and individual attitudes hardened the line between white and black space and built the racial landscape of northern American cities. These two geographical narratives—Jewish urban migration and the segregation of urban space—must be plotted together, not because one created the other but because they were constituted together. In the late 1940s and early 1950s, Jewish leaders, businessmen, merchants, housewives, and political activists spent an endless amount of energy thinking about how the entrance of black residents affected their neighborhood spaces and what they might do to "stabilize" those spaces, even as they were packing their bags, figuring out how to be friends with and sometimes make a profit from the new residents in their midst, or organizing to keep Jews in the neighborhood. The map of Detroit itself changed as individuals, groups, policies, and laws reinvented urban life.

CHAPTER TWO

Keeping House in the City
The Local Politics of Urban Space

The men came back from work on a November evening in 1944, dirt on their clothes, tired, and ready to retreat into the modest comfort of their 1920s-built wood-frame homes. As they made their way down the street, one called out that he had heard a house on their block of Fullerton Street was being sold to "colored people." He instructed the group of men who had gathered around him to "grab" their hammers. His plan was to bash in the windows of the house. Whether out of fatigue, complacency, or decency, none of the men followed his orders, even as they all agreed that they did not want a black family moving onto the block. Theirs was a white block, with a mix of Catholic and Jewish families, north of the local high school and the business district that anchored Dexter-Davison and the Twelfth Street neighborhoods.

Standing among his neighbors, one man watched quietly until the group dispersed. Once in his own house, he wrote down everything he had observed and then mailed his report to Detroit's newly established Interracial Committee. As the air-raid warden of his block, he had come to know the neighborhood men well, and he suggested that his contact with them had made him come to expect their bigoted behavior. With the precision of an ethnographer, he explained that a white family had purchased the for-sale home only six months ago, yet upon discovering the number of Jewish families living on the block, the owner decided to sell the home because he "did not care to live among Jews." Immediately, a rumor circulated that the owner intended to sell to a black family. Nearby residents understood this as an insult to their block that would hit each homeowner where it hurt most, in their pocketbooks. The Jewish and non-Jewish residents were all middle-aged homeowners who worked at semiskilled or unskilled jobs and had families to support. Their homes were their biggest assets, and they could ill afford to watch their property values decline, as they correctly believed would happen if black families settled on their block.[1]

How many Jewish men stood among the group, eager to prove they were just as angry about the turn of events as their non-Jewish neighbors? Our informant did not include this detail nor have I been able to discern whether he was Jewish, though I suspect he either was Jewish or felt connected to the Jews on his block, given the nature of his report and his sensitivity to the anti-Jewish feelings that had fueled the neighborhood tension. One could assume that many Jews might have shied away from the group, nervous about the ire that could come their way, though some might have joined in the show of anger, hoping to prove their commitment to keeping the block white.

Throughout the 1940s, Jews in Detroit became increasingly involved in their neighborhoods' politics. They concerned themselves with the very local questions about neighborhood and block life: Who lived where, who was moving, and why? Whether acting as individuals, who owned or rented homes in a neighborhood, or members of a collective (a Jewish institution, a neighborhood association, or a block club), they understood their neighborhood concerns in clearly self-interested terms. For themselves, their families, and their community, they wanted their neighborhoods to be good places, a judgment connected to whether the area remained Jewish enough and, for the homeowners, whether their property retained its value. One would be hard-pressed to find instances of activism when self-interest does not play a role. The significant historical questions are what fueled Jewish self-interest in neighborhood and urban spaces at different moments in time: how did Jewish self-interest change over time, over space, and from individual to individual; and when and why were neighborhoods deemed to be no longer hospitable to Jewish life?

For Detroit Jews in the 1940s, theirs was primarily a local form of activism focused on making their blocks and their neighborhoods secure and comfortable places to live. By no means were Jews in agreement about how to do this. For example, leftist Jews believed that persistent class inequality fueled neighborhood tension, and they made common cause with other leftist groups, including black ones, over the class struggle. Yet over the course of the 1940s, mainstream Jewish institutions marginalized leftist Jews, concerned that their forms of activism were thin cover for communist plots to overturn democracy. To make alliances with the political left threatened to call into question Jews' loyalty to the United States, just at the moment when most Jews were starting to feel secure in the possibility of being Jewish and American.[2] Other sectors of the Jewish population—including secularists, laborers, merchants, Orthodox, and professionals—varied in their assessment of Jewish neighborhoods. Furthermore, non-Jews, including Catholics and blacks, shared neighborhood space with Jews and brought with them their own, often internally diverse, valuations of neighborhood life.

Values and perceptions about good neighborhoods were inextricably linked to a web of policies that defined the way Americans understood where they lived, especially in urban environments. A crucial reason the Fullerton Street residents worried about blacks moving onto their block was that federally backed mortgage-making agencies all but guaranteed their property values would diminish, in time, if the block lost white residents to black ones. As many historians have revealed, redlining practices designated areas where blacks lived as too risky to merit government-insured mortgages.[3] The policy may have emerged from a preexisting perception that black neighbors turned a block or a neighborhood into a risky zone, but it also transformed that perception into a reality with material ramifications for homeowners, homebuyers, landlords, and renters. Nonetheless, until the late 1950s, most liberal whites, Jews and Jewish leaders among them, did not approach their neighborhood struggles by advocating remedies to the city, state, or federal policies that put demographic and economic pressure on their neighborhoods.

Postwar liberal social scientists, urban planners, and community leaders instead tended to offer white urban dwellers a different prescription to their urban woes: to monitor their own actions and attitudes with an eye toward maintaining neighborhood stability. According to sociological and social policy wisdom of the time, the human composition of neighborhoods changed through a natural process of "succession." As groups passed through different neighborhoods, they gradually became incorporated (or assimilated) into the city organism.[4] These early sociological theories about urban space influenced social policy experts' thinking about how to manage cities—and, also, how to generate assets and wealth from the urban enterprise. Echoing urban sociologists, social policy experts explained that a group's movement away from one neighborhood to another was to be expected and a positive sign of progress as long as the speed of movement was not somehow unnatural, whether too fast or too slow. An unnatural pace could drive up or down the price of property and disrupt the ability of the free market to regulate property transactions, opportunity, and progress.

The belief in a "natural" and "free" market that governed neighborhoods, group life, and economic progress emerged as central to postwar liberal urban politics. Yet the market itself was regulated by policies that fostered unequal opportunity on the basis of race and favored precisely the kind of instability that plagued urban neighborhoods. A homeowner stood to gain more material assets by exploiting the instability—selling at a high price to house-hungry black families, or moving earlier than other white families on the street—than by trying to allay neighborhood volatility.

Operating within the forces of the housing and rental market and the policies that regulated it, an increasingly powerful liberal Jewish establishment, including community relations councils, and chapters of the American Jewish Committee, the American Jewish Congress, the Anti-Defamation League, and the Jewish Labor Committee, sought to manage urban transformations in Jewish neighborhood spaces.[5] Jewish leaders crafted a narrative that pivoted upon a natural pace of movement that would compromise neither Jews' access to property gains and the attendant benefits, including high-quality schools, good public infrastructure, and public safety services, nor their commitment to racial liberalism. Stability served as the language of choice for liberal Jewish leaders because it implied a natural balance between change and conservation that neighborhood residents could achieve by having a good attitude and behaving civilly. Residents were reassured that they could sell and buy property and move from one neighborhood to another so long as they did not interrupt natural market forces by acting rashly.

Liberal Jewish leaders maintained that individual actions and perceptions mattered to the fate of Jewish neighborhoods, and that the fate of Jewish neighborhoods foretold the future of Jews' place in the predominantly urban environments in which they found themselves in the 1940s. Very few Jewish leaders wished for Jewish neighborhoods to remain fixed in space, and very few pledged their commitment to residential racial integration. The spirit of progress, premised upon faith in the market economy, recommended against both. Instead, most liberal Jewish leaders attempted to frame a narrative that rendered Jews' decision to leave neighborhoods in the language of naturally paced upward mobility and urban transformation, not racial intolerance. The former narrative squared well with a liberal vision of individual and group rights, while the latter did not. A mob of angry homeowners might stop a black family from settling in a neighborhood, but it would also create the perception of instability and volatility. Better, it seemed, to focus on the merits of the neighborhood and convince homeowners that they should only sell their homes when it made sense in the due course of events, whenever that was.

Riots and Responsibility

In the fall of 1937, the rabbi of Temple Beth El, the city's largest Reform temple, chastised Jewish merchants in the Hastings Street area for behaving unethically toward black customers. In a sermon he delivered, he asked all Jewish merchants to deal fairly with blacks who entered their stores and called to mind the biblical injunction from the book of Deuteronomy: "Just weights and just measures shall thou have."[6] Over the last decade, as Jews in Detroit had gained socioeconomic power, they also confronted the sets of unequal relationships between whites and blacks upon which nodes of their own urban power rested. When Jews encountered blacks, they tended to do so through the realm of unequal economic exchange, reflecting Jews' positions as the merchants and landlords to black customers and tenants.

Jews who made their living through sharing economic space with blacks became the subject of liberal Jewish pronouncements about race and about how to avoid tension with blacks. Rarely did these statements question the economic structure that placed blacks in subordinate positions. Instead, as in the case of the rabbi's sermon, the pronouncements called for individuals who directly interacted with blacks (often Jews in a lower-class strata than the wealthier and German-born congregants of Temple Beth El) to be fair in their practices and encouraged Jews to help blacks gain their economic footing in the capitalist market-driven economy.

The Jewish Community Council, a centralized Jewish organization founded in 1936 that aimed to coordinate Jewish activity and relations with non-Jews throughout the city, also turned its attention to the tension brewing in the Hastings Street area in the late 1930s. As one of the city's first Jewish institutional bodies committed to reflecting the needs of Yiddish-speaking, leftist, and Eastern European Jews, the council's sphere of concern focused more squarely on the Hastings Street area, where recent immigrants settled, owned stores, and built livelihoods that depended on black dollars, than on Temple Beth El's sphere of interest.[7] The rabbi at Temple Beth El may have cared about what was going on in the Hastings Street neighborhood on a general level and, also, because some of his congregants were merchants there, but the Jewish Community Council still saw the neighborhood as central to its mission and the home of its constituents. In 1937, the council worked with Hastings Street area Jewish merchants to form the East Side Merchants Association. According to publicity, the group sought "to promote a better relationship between Jewish merchants and their Negro customers."[8] Displays of altruism formed a significant part of the association's efforts to build a "better relationship" with blacks. For example, the group collected funds to donate to the United Negro College Fund and a handful of black churches.

Much as Progressive-era middle-class reformers had employed the language of uplift in the early twentieth century to convince new immigrants to Americanize and adapt to middle-class norms, Jewish leaders in the 1930s addressed the problems that arose between Jews and blacks through the language of reforming individual attitudes and practices. Elite Jewish community figures, such as Fred Butzel, joined forces with middle-class black reformers in the Urban League to support programs in the black community that employed a similar rhetoric of individual improvement.[9]

Yet many Jews and blacks, especially those whose daily lives were shaped by interracial economic relationships, remained dubious of reformers' efforts. In the late 1930s, the *Detroit Tribune*, a black weekly newspaper, published a three-week exposé on "Jewish Exploitation of Race." A highly visible case in which a Jewish merchant fired a black female employee and dumped her belongings onto a busy street had precipitated the journalistic attention. A group of onlookers reported that when confronted and reminded that his customers were primarily black, the shopkeeper retorted, "I don't want any more nigger business."[10] Around the same time, a similar incident gained attention: a Jewish shop owner, upon discovering a black girl shoplifting, beat her.

The two cases highlighted Jewish merchants' abuse of their power over black people and specifically black women. These Jewish merchants, according to the exposé, took the exploitation of black people to a new level, not only price gouging for profit but also inflicting physical abuse on black women (even a girl) who were unable to defend themselves against men's physical aggression. A group of black residents in the neighborhood picketed Jewish stores and distributed leaflets that announced, "We are calling your attention to the circumstances in which our people are living, how they are exploited by the Jewish landlords and storekeepers."[11]

In internal correspondence, Jewish Community Council leaders lashed out harshly against what they perceived as exaggerated charges of Jewish exploitation, when only a few Jews were involved in the incidents. The leaders claimed that the exposé was a show of "Negro anti-Semitism."[12] The best public defense, in the eyes of the council, was a good study that would prove Jews' overwhelming goodwill toward blacks. The Detroit branch of the National Association for the Advancement of Colored People (NAACP), with a roster of Jewish supporters and hoping to quell rising black separatist movements that threatened black middle-class aspirations, joined the effort to conduct a study focused on the Hastings Street area. With a grant from Wayne State, sociologist Donald Marsh assembled a team to start its research in the early 1940s. Titled "Some Aspects of Negro-Jewish Relationships in Detroit," the results were not published until 1945.

Over the time it took Marsh to conduct the study, two racial incidents occurred that only heightened black and Jewish liberals' desire to find racial harmony in the shared spaces of black and Jewish life. First, under pressure of the wartime housing shortage, Detroit's Housing Commission had pledged in 1941 to build new housing for white and black workers. Not once considering building an integrated housing project, the commission struggled to determine where to locate the black project, since nearby neighbors would inevitably protest that the presence of a black housing development depreciated their housing values. After much deliberation, the commission determined to build the project for black war workers in a relatively sparsely populated area of northern Detroit. They named it after black abolitionist Sojourner Truth.

Even before the first black family moved into the project, Detroiters saw tensions mounting in the surrounding area that, while remote from dense white population centers, still housed whites. Anticipating the opening of the project, a small handful of Jews, including the leader of the East Side Merchants Association, helped create an interracial coalition called Sojourner Truth Citizens Committee to support the project.[13] In February 1942, as the first black family moved in, blacks and whites gathered on the streets and fighting broke out.[14]

Among the white activists who opposed the project, it became common wisdom that Jews and communists—and not government officials—had orchestrated the Sojourner Truth project to further their radical agenda and their own profit. One of the major opponents of the project, who helped foment the riots, explained to a researcher that Jewish builders such as "Nathan Strauss and his friends" reaped hefty financial gains from building projects for black families, and charged that these same Jewish builders would never tolerate black projects in their own neighborhoods. He further argued that Jewish builders underhandedly deflected criticism about their own exploitative practices against blacks by co-opting civil rights groups, such as the Civil Rights Federation, which he characterized as a "communist front."[15] Despite the tenuous logic, the white rioter did his best to connect Jews to capitalist-driven economic exploitation of both blacks and whites, as well as to anti-American, anti-capitalist radicalism.

Indeed, Jews did play a role in the efforts to secure the opening of the housing project for black workers, and some of these Jews were members of organizations with ties to the Communist Party. An important spokesperson for the Sojourner Truth Citizens Committee was a Jewish man named Jack Raskin, who also occupied a top leadership position in the Civil Rights Federation. Jews, such as attorney Ernest Goodman, alongside blacks, had helped establish the Civil Rights Federation in the 1930s, and Jews remained staunch supporters of the federation through the early 1940s as Raskin assumed leadership of it. Raskin had used his sway in the Jewish community to encourage several Jewish community leaders, including a prominent Reform rabbi, to join the fight for the Sojourner Truth project.

Throughout the 1940s, however, Raskin and his Civil Rights Federation fell out of favor with liberal black and Jewish leadership.[16] Black and Jewish liberals believed that the organization had veered toward the communist left and, thus, sought to disentangle themselves from it and the causes it supported. By the time of the Sojourner Truth riots in 1942, Jewish support for the housing project had dampened, in part because Jews were concerned that their support of the project would align them with communist elements. After the riots, Detroit city officials managed to settle black residents into the new homes peacefully, but they also determined in moving forward they would choose neighborhoods in which to erect public housing projects based upon a racial calculus that matched the racial composition of the neighborhood with that of the project.[17]

Another riot, this one erupting in the heart of the Hastings Street neighborhood in June 1943, a year and a half after the Sojourner Truth riots, only further raised the stakes on the findings of Marsh's report about blacks and Jews.[18] Marsh immediately instructed his researchers to collect survey data about the riot. Already, from data collected before the riots, Marsh and his team had concluded that "no wide-spread nor deep-rooted antagonism" existed among blacks toward Jews and that Jews manifested

FIGURE 2.1 Jack Raskin (*far right*) escorting Mary Paige (Mrs. Richard Davis) after she served time in prison for allegedly sympathizing with communists and helping to recruit soldiers for the Spanish Loyalist Army, February 16, 1940. Courtesy of Walter P. Reuther Library, Archives of Labor and Urban Affairs, Wayne State University.

"vastly more tolerance" toward blacks than other whites.[19] Furthermore, the study showed that Jewish shopkeepers tended to charge lower prices than black or other white shopkeepers, and that blacks felt no more animosity toward Jewish landlords than other white landlords. So reassuring were these conclusions about the absence of general tension between Jews and blacks, that the NAACP, the Jewish Community Council, and other liberal Jewish and black groups rushed to distribute copies of the study locally and nationally.

The data gathered after the riot, according to Marsh and his researchers, only confirmed the group's earlier findings: whatever tension erupted between Jews and blacks had nothing to do with a special problem between the two groups. Rather, trouble spots emerged from those pockets of abject poverty within the black community and not from deep-seated black antisemitism or ubiquitous Jewish exploitation.[20] Over time, the study's conclusions influenced other studies and helped shape the city's approach to Jewish-black tension. Just months after the 1943 riot, the city sponsored a study of religious and racial conflict. In a section devoted to Jews, the authors explained, "True, Jewish storekeepers had great property damage in the June riots. But these owners were mainly attacked as whites and not as Jews."[21] The study then appended a lengthy section of results from Marsh's survey on "Negro-Jewish Relationships."

In a city experiencing strife over race and religion, Marsh's study and the post-riot report depicted Jews as standing apart from that tension and, even, threw down the mantle of leadership to Jews to use their unique neutral position to mediate conflict. Jews emerged as marginal to the two central conflicts in the city: labor versus management (because few Jews worked in the auto industry, where unionism maintained a stronghold in the city), and blacks versus whites. Liberal city leaders and Jews among them endorsed the report's conclusion that Jews should continue to be in the "forefront in a wide range of social welfare activities" and help the city "cope" with its problems.[22] Jewish leaders hoped to sculpt the East Side Merchants Association, which had maintained a low profile for some time, into just that sort of mediator. In 1947, the Jewish Community Council tried to revitalize the mainly defunct organization to gather Jewish merchants together and to strategize about how to avoid another riot in the Hastings Street area. Yet by then, many Jewish merchants were closing shop in the neighborhood, frustrated with their inability to obtain property insurance since the 1943 riot and unwilling to tie their economic future to a black neighborhood.[23]

Although the Marsh report had suggested that stark class differences accounted for eruptions in tension between Jews and blacks, it made no gesture toward uncovering the forces behind those class differences. The post-riot study similarly discussed poverty and class tension as exacerbating the city's problems, but did not point to any systemic reforms that could redress class differences. Instead, both reports issued a call for those people who stood on the fortunate side of class divides—such as most Jews and other members of the middle class—to fulfill their "civic obligations" by participating in charitable activities and supporting programs intended to educate Detroiters about the ills of prejudice. These approaches to ameliorating city tension were typical of World War II–era liberalism and its eschewal of class reform or efforts that threatened to undermine capitalism or confront the systematic racism legislated into market forces. The post-riot report, in fact, blamed some of Detroit's problems on "rabble-rousers, labor agitators, and Axis agents," all code for radical forces, whether to the left or the right of what liberal Detroiters believed was the sensible center.[24]

Monitoring Neighborhood Change

Hastened by the rioting and studies that indicted the city for its lackadaisical attitude toward "intergroup tension," Detroit's mayor, Edward Jeffries, established the Mayor's Interracial Committee at the end of 1943. His charge to the committee revealed the imprecision that suffused community relations work in the 1940s: he instructed the committee to work "to cultivate better attitudes among the people of the community." In its attention to attitudes and not, for example, economic structures or policies that marginalized certain groups of people from power and wealth in the United States, the committee's charge fit well with the emerging liberal belief in individual remedies to prejudice.[25]

During the early years of its activity, the Interracial Committee suffered from a muddled agenda and inefficiency. Case files tracked incidents of discrimination in restaurants, schools, employment, police activity, and within city government. Community informants reported the bulk of these early cases and varied in their attention to detail. Most of the cases contained no indication of a resolution and, thus, simply appear as a record of bad things that happened in Detroit. The case file for the Fullerton Street incident, for example, which was reported in great detail and then filed with the Interracial Committee, listed no follow-up or outcome. The informant seemed to sense as much when he wrote that likely nothing could be done to improve the situation since his neighbors "don't understand anything except what concerns their own interest."[26] At best, his report portrayed resignation, faithfully recorded. Indeed, Mayor Jeffries had not granted the Interracial Committee any enforcement power. Thus, in its first few years, its work amounted to taking reports and filing them according to a color-coded system based upon the type of incident described.[27]

By the time Jeffries was up for reelection in 1945, his Interracial Committee faced criticism from liberals, including labor leaders, black leaders, and white leaders. Although Jeffries painted himself as no friend to these liberals in the 1945 election, appealing to racism and antisemitism to mobilize his white base against his opponent, he did commit himself to strengthen the Interracial Committee by hiring a new director, George

Schermer. Schermer, a native of Minnesota, had most recently worked for Chicago's Housing Authority.[28]

Under Schermer's sway, the Interracial Committee, although still involved in collecting cases about discrimination in a wide array of realms, focused the bulk of its attention on housing and race. In the early 1950s, Schermer reflected that from 1945 through 1948 "the pressure of housing need within the Negro community was so great, and white neighborhood resistance to change, supported by the general housing shortage, was so strong" that the committee devoted its energy to "softening resistance, improving police techniques in meeting threatened violence, and mobilizing community support behind the concept of open market practices."[29] Schermer worked quickly to endear himself and his agency to existing community groups and groom them to serve as informants to the Interracial Committee and, even more so, to help control potentially explosive situations that often came about when black families bought homes—or were suspected to have bought homes—in white areas.

Schermer cultivated particularly close relationships with the leading figures in the Jewish Community Council. Schermer was not Jewish, but he lived in the Boston-Edison area of the Twelfth Street neighborhood, on a block close to some of the finest Jewish-owned homes in the neighborhood and at a time when many Jews were leaving the area. He periodically attended Jewish Community Council meetings and had a clear conviction that Jews were among his crucial allies in creating a new approach to urban housing.[30] Furthermore, as he came to know the map of Detroit, he realized that one of the steady streams of black movement in the 1940s flowed into what was still known as a Jewish neighborhood, the southern part of his own Twelfth Street neighborhood.

Even before World War II, Jews in Detroit had begun to migrate away from the Twelfth Street area. In 1925, when Shaarey Zedek, the largest Conservative congregation in Detroit at the time, sought a new site for its building, congregational leaders purchased a plot of land on a block that was northwest of the neighborhood, gambling on the Dexter area, as opposed to the Twelfth Street area, becoming the center of Jewish life.[31] Shaarey Zedek's leaders understood that the housing stock in the Twelfth Street neighborhood likely would not accommodate the needs of an upwardly mobile Jewish population. Although its northern streets boasted of grand homes, most of the Twelfth Street blocks contained modest housing stock, built in the early part of the twentieth century to accommodate the swelling immigrant population of the city.[32]

Because the Twelfth Street neighborhood was contiguous with Dexter, Jewish survey data often conflated the two areas. In 1941, the Jewish Federation combined them for statistical purposes and reported that 80 percent of all Jews lived in the Twelfth Street and Dexter area.[33] Still when Jewish leaders turned their attention to the Twelfth Street neighborhood, many did so with a measure of personal remove. With only a few exceptions, the Jews who served on the Jewish Community Council board lived in Dexter or in the growing neighborhoods even farther north, such as Bagley or the Palmer Park area. Jewish Community Council leaders, after all, tended to be professionals—doctors, lawyers, and academics—and had the means to afford better housing. Yet the ongoing presence of Jews in the Twelfth Street neighborhood and the simultaneous migration of blacks into it meant that Jewish leaders remained concerned about it, a fact that tied the neighborhood and Jews closely to the city's Interracial Committee.

In the summer of 1946, Schermer learned that a Jewish man who lived in the Twelfth Street neighborhood had received a postcard written in Yiddish urging residents to protect their property from black intrusion. Schermer immediately contacted the Jewish Community Council. The council performed its own investigation and then assured him that the "propaganda is the work of one or two individuals and not related to any organized community effort." Despite the postcard's call to stop a "nigger family" from moving onto the street, to maintain the "white" character of the neighborhood, and to organize a meeting to determine "what can be done," Schermer trusted the council's assessment and did not order a police investigation.[34] His faith in the Jewish Community Council's ability to police its own constituents and his agreement with a general strategy to suppress publicity about anti-black incidents made the Interracial Committee and the Jewish Community Council good allies.

Together, the council and the Interracial Committee charted a series of steps that they came to believe effectively regulated what they, similar to other urban liberal groups, called "neighborhood change" and "panic." Focusing on remedy, not reform, the two groups maintained that local, neighborhood-based activism would best defuse the panic ignited by black families moving into the neighborhood. The real problem, they agreed, was the panic itself. If people could learn that their neighborhood was undergoing a gradual process of change, then they could react in more rational ways. Close monitoring of each block and each house would enable the agencies to counter invidious rumors about rapid black encroachment and reassure white residents that theirs was still a stable, good neighborhood. Their approach sought to empower residents to take an active role in safeguarding neighborhood standards and working toward a tolerant community. Yet, ironically, neither agency trusted that individuals could navigate the treacherous terrain of postwar politics. Fearful of co-optation from the right and the left, Schermer and Jewish Community Council leaders believed the outside forces of fascism and communism were threats to their work and necessitated careful monitoring. Thus, these liberal agencies took it upon themselves to supervise closely neighborhood activism and employ their bureaucratic channels and representatives in an effort to orchestrate the kind of organic activism they desired.

In the fall of 1946, the Jewish Community Council decided to perform a series of persuasive interviews with the Jewish residents of the Twelfth Street neighborhood whose homes were listed for sale in order to understand reigning attitudes about race and the neighborhood, improve them if necessary, and start a neighborhood movement against so-called panic selling. The guideline for interviewers set forth hypothetical questions that a homeowner might ask ("Can one sell a home to Negroes?" or "Won't real estate value drop?") and outlined answers all carefully balancing between homeowners' rights to sell their property and the Jewish Community Council's desire to stem panic selling. "Sell to anyone you wish," the guidelines explained. "But don't sell out of panic—because of prejudice." Elsewhere, the guide explained, "If there is to be a change in the character of Twelfth Street, it should be orderly, over a period of time."[35] Seeking to distinguish between natural neighborhood change and panic, the Jewish Community Council urged restraint. In other words, their goal was to modify people's behaviors—prejudice and panic—but not to modify the larger systems in which people behaved.

Quickly the Jewish Community Council learned that Twelfth Street neighborhood residents perceived their material surroundings deteriorating apace blacks' settlement in the neighborhood. Although Jewish institutions, such as a large Jewish Community Center building and Temple Beth El, remained rooted in the neighborhood, the center of Jewish religious, commercial, and communal life had shifted north and west into the Dexter-Davison area. Realizing that unless residents saw proof to the contrary, they would associate black entrance into the neighborhood with decay, the Jewish Community Council sought to put the responsibility for improving the material conditions of the neighborhood in the hands of each and every resident.

In January 1947, the council facilitated a meeting with a small group of neighbors who determined that the first priority was to clean up the public and visible spaces of the neighborhood and to educate new residents (primarily blacks) about the standards of orderliness expected in the neighborhood. Louis Fraiberg, an English professor and part of the council's leadership, led the charge to organize a cleanup drive in the neighborhood and suggested holding a spring event that focused on just a few blocks to serve as a catalyst for other similar efforts throughout the neighborhood.[36]

Despite thousands of posters, press coverage in Jewish and general newspapers, and, even, a radio spot, the cleanup drive neither abated tension nor changed white residents' concern about black settlement.[37] Throughout the summer of 1947, the Jewish Community Council and the Interracial Committee collected data showing more white residents leaving the neighborhood and documenting growing black and white dissatisfaction. Frequently, the reports cited material shifts in the neighborhood, such as overcrowding, lagging trash collection, and deteriorating housing stock. One report noted that in 1938, only 10 percent of the housing units had more than 1.5 people per room. It continued, "This has undoubtedly changed quite basically in the past nine years, with war marriages, movement in with parents or in-laws, the high birth rate in recent years and other similar factors." According to the same report, property surveys showed that a significant proportion of the housing was in need of repair, and monthly rental rates were far lower in the Twelfth Street neighborhood than in other Jewish areas (though they were by far not the lowest in the city).[38]

Jewish leaders and city officials understood rising rates of overcrowding or dilapidated housing as a function of a natural form of neighborhood succession. The Jews who remained in the Twelfth Street area were the ones who had not yet been able to leave. One report explained, "The lower status that [Jews in the Twelfth Street neighborhood] had no reason to be aware of or recognize in the past has rather suddenly been projected into their social horizon by virtue of the fact that Negro families as the representatives of a low status group in society, have been moving in around them."[39] The report continued that as a result of feeling demoralized and degraded, some Jews had stopped keeping up their homes. In interviews, some residents blamed the city for neglecting the area, not controlling a rat infestation, or not cleaning the streets frequently enough, yet reports suggested that Jews had once worked harder on neighborhood upkeep and now, as many Jews were moving away, the remaining ones did not care.

Intersecting with Jews' perception that black families' settlement in the neighborhood led to its degradation was the fact that black newcomers promised economic gain to homeowners ready to sell. A Jewish real estate agent reported that homes in the Twelfth Street neighborhood were selling for between $8,000 and $12,000, prices above his expectation of actual property valuation.[40] Another Jewish agent wrote a letter to the Jewish Community Council explaining that he and several other Jewish real estate agents had been "selling property in the 12th Street area to colored" simply because the profits were so high. Similarly, some landlords realized they could make greater profits renting their properties to house-hungry blacks instead of whites, even if this meant, as one person reported to the Jewish Community Council, evicting recently settled Displaced Persons in order to free up space for black renters.[41]

Historian Beryl Satter, in her study of a Jewish neighborhood in Chicago, has revealed that housing values in "changing neighborhoods" often became inflated because blacks had access only to a very narrow slice of the housing market in northern cities, had little chance of receiving government-backed credit, and, thus, found themselves at the whim of duplicitous and exploitative selling and renting schemes. Indeed, so uneven were the black and white housing markets that the Federal Housing Administration eagerly insured mortgages to finance the purchase of rental properties intended to serve black renters. The expectation that blacks would pay rents well above market value served as assurance to the federal agency that the owners of multi-unit buildings in black areas would earn high yields and repay banks with little trouble.[42]

A 1947 report found that residents believed that real estate agents, with their door-to-door solicitations and reports of black settlement, "precipitated much of the outward movement of the White families."[43] A Jewish real estate agent, who admitted to profiting from sales to black families, suggested that unless the council stepped in and exerted force to stop Jewish agents from selling to black families, then nothing would stop the neighborhood from becoming predominantly black. His fear, he explained, was that Jewish real estate agents' willingness to sell homes to blacks fueled "dislike for the Hebrew people." With such high profits to be made in selling to black families, only pressure from the Jewish community in the name of community stability and safety could prevail upon real estate agents to reform their practices.[44]

The predominantly liberal leadership of the Jewish community and the city's Interracial Committee assumed that over time the composition of a neighborhood would change, but they believed in a natural or gradual pace for that change. This was consonant with sociological assessments from the early part of the century that explained urban migration in ecological terms. Each immigrant or ethnic group, according to regnant sociological theory, naturally moved through city neighborhoods as its status improved.[45] Thus, one could expect a neighborhood to play host to different groups over time, as each group passed through the socioeconomic landscape provided by a particular neighborhood (working class, middle class, etc.). But when the pace of the change happened too quickly, the ecological system, deeply connected to economic forces, became fragile, and neighborhoods, instead of maintaining their character, fell prey to forces of decay.

Much of liberal work in the neighborhood in the late 1940s revolved around issues of perception: how clean were the streets, how neat were the yards, and how neighborly were the residents. By changing the perception of the neighborhood, Jewish and city liberal leaders did not believe they would forestall the natural process of change. They believed in that natural process and saw it as a function of a well-operating market economy. Instead, they set their sights on improving neighborhood appearance—streets, alleys, and playgrounds—to slow the pace of transformation to an assumed natural rhythm.

Liberal leaders also turned their attention to the sphere of individual interaction, believing that the more tolerant individuals were, the more natural the pace of transformation would be. Despite a rumor that some Jewish residents were agitating to create a restrictive covenant prohibiting black settlement in the neighborhood, most reports indicated that Twelfth Street Jews were fairly welcoming to black newcomers. Throughout the summer of 1947, the Interracial Committee interviewed several black residents who all concurred that their Jewish neighbors had been welcoming to them. One black woman, who had lived with her family in the neighborhood for nine months, noted that her Jewish neighbors had complained about a black family who had turned their home into a boardinghouse. She noted that she and "other Negro families agreed with the Jewish people in their objections."[46] The Interracial Committee and the Jewish Community Council credited the Jewishness of the neighborhood for "the orderly and peaceful manner" in which black settlement occurred. Whatever Jews' private attitudes may have been, reports explained, they did not react to black settlement with overt hostility.[47]

In its assessment, the Interracial Committee determined that the best course of action was to help to minimize tension as the neighborhood shifted from being "exclusively white" to predominantly black. In a memo to Schermer, a field investigator suggested that the focus of the committee's attention must be on "the normal problems of the community—such problems as play space, recreational facilities, school programs, community social activities, community appearances, etc." He emphasized, "The fact of recent Negro occupancy in the area should play little apparent or direct part in the stimulation of the programs."[48] The committee and the Jewish Community Council gave little thought to the possibility of a truly integrated neighborhood, since a potent combination of legal policy, market regulations, and individual attitudes mediated against that, but both groups believed they could help ease what they thought would be an eventual racial transition that would allow social and economic progress to continue at a stable clip.

Lingering in the shadows of efforts to stabilize neighborhoods were the threats of radicalism, threats that Jewish leaders felt with particular acuity. Jewish Community Council leaders were well aware that they walked a tightrope in their housing and neighborhood activism between leftist forces decrying capitalist ideals of private property and rightist forces that drew on fascist and racist ideals of white privilege. In 1947, the director of internal relations for the Jewish Community Council cautioned leaders that a "strong left wing element . . . is ready to step in and take control unless we are careful."[49] He realized that groups advocating integration and fair housing were under increased governmental scrutiny for sowing seeds of national discord and aligning with communist interests.[50] The Jewish Community Council often found itself on the defensive against accusations of communism. In 1949, when "radicals" protested in front of two stores in the Twelfth Street area that allegedly would not hire black employees, rumors swirled that the council was behind the pickets. The council immediately distanced itself from the protest. Its leaders reassured the store owners and neighbors that they would never force an employer to hire a black person and that their methods bore no similarities to those of radicals.[51]

Mainstream Jewish leaders and the Interracial Committee vigorously defended private property and denied any connection to radical activism. They rarely advocated integration. The endgame for the organizations was neither to engineer an integrated neighborhood nor to reform the policies and economic structures that stood in the way of integration. Rather, they hoped to foster tolerance and maintain neighborhood standards during a process of neighborhood transformation and racial transition that they believed was an inevitable part of progress.

A Neighborhood Association for Gradualism

In the fall of 1947, the Jewish Community Council joined forces with the Interracial Committee and the NAACP to create a neighborhood association, the Midtown Neighborhood Council, charged primarily with slowing the process of the neighborhood's transformation into a black neighborhood. For the Jews who continued to reside in the Twelfth Street area and the Jewish businesses and institutions located on its streets, the desire to stabilize the neighborhood emerged from their immediate circumstances. Their homes, their shops, and their synagogues were tied to the fabric of the neighborhood. Yet the Midtown Neighborhood Council led few Jews to believe that their future rested in the Twelfth Street neighborhood; rather, it was committed to regulating the pace of inevitable movement.

The Midtown Neighborhood Council resembled in form hundreds of other white neighborhood and homeowners' associations that emerged in postwar Detroit and across the United States. The formation of a neighborhood association was a common response to property owners' fears that their neighborhood was losing its status and stability, often because of the entrance of people of color into it. Community meetings at people's homes and school auditoriums, as well as neighborhood-based activities and leadership were typical of these sorts of associations. Neighborhood associations also generally thrived on social coercion and peer pressure. A publicity flyer for the Midtown Neighborhood Council explained, "The Council is composed of your friends and neighbors."[52]

If in form the Midtown Neighborhood Council resembled other white urban neighborhood associations, in its ideals it was rather distinctive from most. Unlike many surrounding neighborhood associations, it repudiated intimidation and violence against black families as strategies for preserving the character of the neighborhood. Instead, it focused on facilitating small, practical improvements in the neighborhood, building goodwill between Jews and blacks, and dispelling rumors of the neighborhood's rapid transformation into a black neighborhood.

At the end of 1947, the Jewish Community Council tried to drum up support for the nascent Midtown Neighborhood Council by circulating a statement entitled "Let's Think Clearly." Distributed in late 1947 and throughout 1948, the statement indicated well the group's investment in a rational and calm reaction to what it believed was an inevitable demographic and geographical shift. "We believe that Jews should and can live in harmonious relationships with their neighbors regardless of their race, color or creed. Such spirit would make for a better community and will make any transition which is occurring or may occur in the Twelfth Street area an orderly process over a relatively long period of time."[53] Already, in the early fall of 1947, the Jewish Community Council had met with Max Wohlgelernter, the rabbi of an Orthodox congregation located in the heart of the Twelfth Street neighborhood. With his support, the council wrote Detroit rabbis urging them to devote one of their High Holiday sermons to discussing the value of harmonious relationships between Jews and blacks and the "necessity for discounting rumors and not giving way to panic."[54] Later that fall, in the *Detroit Jewish News*, the Jewish Community Council urged "the Jewish Community who live in the Twelfth St. area" to practice "conduct . . . as to bring credit to all Detroit Jewry."[55]

Schermer, head of the Interracial Committee, focused his attention on lobbying the city to make visible improvements to the Twelfth Street area. In a letter to a member of Detroit's Common Council, he specifically distanced the neighborhood group's concerns from black settlement or racial tension: "I don't think the group has many questions about race relations, they've been through that. They want to know how to keep their alleys clean."[56] It seems unlikely that Schermer believed all of the residents of the neighborhood already understood the problems of prejudice and, thus, did not need that education. Instead, he determined that the city's limited resources would best be used making material improvements to the neighborhood. He encouraged leaders of the Midtown Neighborhood Council similarly to put their energy into concrete actions to make the neighborhood a good place to live: traffic control, trash collection, rat and roach extermination, park development, and street repaving.[57] These were the kinds of improvements that Schermer and the predominantly Jewish founders of the Midtown Neighborhood Council believed would stabilize the neighborhood, stem panic, and enable racial succession to happen at a gradual and assumedly natural pace. Schermer and other liberal leaders certainly did not disavow educational campaigns against prejudice—in fact, they were endlessly involved in them. Rather they also sought to control the perception that neighborhoods such as Twelfth Street were riven with racial unrest.

Adapting the strategy the Jewish Community Council had used in the neighborhood in 1946, Schermer enlisted his own field agents and the Jewish Community Council in 1947 and 1948 to perform frequent interviews with neighborhood residents and keep a record of homes that posted for-sale signs. In these ways, he hoped to head off incidents related to race and racism before they made their way into the media and fueled the perception that racial unrest plagued the neighborhood. Should a false rumor develop about a black family moving in or should a particular block exhibit the warning signs of hysteria and, even, violence, then these interviews could not only expose budding problems, but they could also act as interventions. Residents would see that the city and Jewish communal structure cared about what was happening. At the same time, the city and the Jewish community would avoid the unwanted publicity about racial tension.

In mid-November 1947, Jewish attorney Nathan Shur filed a report with the Jewish Community Council summarizing his interviews with residents on a block of Taylor Street near Max Wohlgelernter's Orthodox congregation and the heart of the Twelfth Street neighborhood. In each of his door-to-door visits, Jewish women greeted him with resignation about the inevitability of leaving the neighborhood. Women provided the on-the-ground information for the Jewish Community Council and, thus, gained substantial power to shape the narrative of what was occurring in the neighborhood. Sociologist David Riesman, famous for his 1950 book *The Lonely Crowd*, wryly observed that his door-to-door interviews almost always yielded interviews with housewives: "I have been struck by the eagerness of the housewives to talk to somebody (and not only to a man!) who is not a salesman (occasionally, they must be weaned away from the TV)."[58] Beyond whatever excitement they may have had about talking to a male researcher, postwar Jewish women played a crucial role in the valuation of neighborhoods and in determining when those spaces were no longer hospitable to Jewish life. Historians explain that women gained power in neighborhood politics because they were at home more often than men; inhabited the neighborhood in a different, more daily way than men; and had more exposure to their children's schooling experiences.[59]

An elderly woman, answering Shur's knock in November 1947, told him that she was about to be evicted from her home because her landlord had sold it to a black family. Wohlgelernter, the rabbi of the nearby synagogue, had unsuccessfully tried to intervene on her behalf to stop the owner, presumably a Jewish person, from selling to blacks. Shur did not bother explaining in his report why the change in ownership necessitated the tenant's displacement; likely it was obvious at the time that a new owner would enact a rent hike, in proportion to the inflated price at which the white landlord would have sold the property to a black person, and a new landlord would also realize that black tenants when compared to white ones paid higher rents on the same property.[60]

Two other women, both homeowners who were trying to sell, told Shur that they had little doubt that black families would purchase their properties. Both claimed it was impossible to sell to white families and neither felt comfortable living in the neighborhood anymore. The more garrulous one complained that the schools were "crowded with colored students," and she and her neighbors did not want their children to attend them. Other public spaces, a local theater, the supermarket, and street corners, according to the woman, had also become black spaces. Shur elaborated, "She was very peeved because Community Council had not attempted to stop the influx of Negroes in the neighborhood last year, when it would not have been too late." In her view, similar to the assessments of other women on the block, the neighborhood was no longer amenable to white or Jewish life. So quickly were blacks moving in, that some homeowners did not even have time to post for-sale signs. The worst part, according to this interviewee, was that Jews had themselves to blame for the neighborhood situation since a Jewish real estate agent had been the first to sell a home in the neighborhood to a black family. Many homeowners were boycotting him as a result, Shur reported, but this did not change the swift pace of movement.[61]

Even as the Jewish Community Council amassed evidence that the Jewish neighborhood of Twelfth Street was fast fading, it continued to invest money and staff hours in the Midtown Neighborhood Council. During the winter of 1948, the Midtown Neighborhood Council organized a large neighborhood meeting, attended by three hundred people, and endorsed the Jewish Community Council's housing statement entitled "Let's Think Clearly." It received favorable press attention for both actions.

Throughout 1948, the Jewish Community Council claimed success in the Twelfth Street neighborhood. The terms of its success had nothing to do with building a pathway toward successful integration; rather the council and the Interracial Committee believed it had tamped down the swells of panic by managing people's perceptions of the neighborhood, creating an apparatus to monitor individuals' behavior, and making some efforts to maintain the aesthetics of the neighborhood. As early as the spring of 1948, the Jewish Community Council announced its success: "The panic [has begun] to subside, the rate of exodus from this neighborhood lowered, and in general, the situation [has become] more stabilized."[62] Schermer, from the Interracial Committee, publicly shared the council's assessment.[63] A memo from the early 1950s, written to reflect on the history of the Midtown Neighborhood Council, recalled the feeling of triumph in 1948 and explained, "Apparently from what one can judge, this initial mass-participation approach was successful in allaying fears and panic, and as a result of house-to-house canvassing by volunteer workers, individuals who had listed their property for sale in many cases withdrew their listings, and, in other cases, although their property remained for sale, had removed the larger signs in front of their houses so that streets in the area did not give evidence to the passerby of visible preparation for flight."[64] The Jewish Community Council believed it had done something right and worthy of imitation. In the mid-1950s, its leaders would write up the case of the Midtown Neighborhood Council as a model of successful neighborhood stabilization for urban Jewish neighborhoods across the country.

As was their wont, the Jewish Community Council leaders worked fast to commission a study to prove just how stable and calm the neighborhood had become. With the proper results, they would show that Jews had not fled the neighborhood at an unnatural pace, and that when Jews left, the neighborhood remained in good shape for its next inhabitants. To complete the study, the council hired Bernard Rosenberg, a native Detroiter who had since moved to New York, first to earn his doctorate at the New School for Social Research and then to join the faculty at Hunter College.[65] Under Rosenberg's supervision, Wayne State graduate students interviewed neighborhood residents and turned ethnographic data over to him.

Unfortunately for the Jewish Community Council, Rosenberg's report did not tell the narrative they hoped it would. To the council's dismay, Rosenberg concluded that the Midtown Neighborhood Council played only a minor role in the temporary abatement of white movement away from the neighborhood and that Jews and other whites were continuing their rapid flight away from it. Furthermore, he revealed that the numbers of whites in the neighborhood had been artificially inflated by the arrival of Displaced Persons (DPs) from World War II, suggesting that Jewish agencies settled half of the one thousand DPs who arrived in the city over the last three years in the Twelfth Street neighborhood.[66] Rosenberg's report never saw the light of day, and he had to plead with the Jewish Community Council to receive his full compensation.[67]

In a lengthy letter, Joseph Fauman, who headed up the Jewish Community Council's research into group relations, chastised Rosenberg for downplaying the importance of the Midtown Neighborhood Council. "Actually," Fauman insisted, "the Midtown Council succeeded in its endeavors."[68] He admitted that the gains were not always great, but he believed

Rosenberg offered only criticism of the organization and provided no assessment of what it had done well and how it could continue to succeed. Rosenberg retorted that the neighborhood group had ceded any chance to play a meaningful role in the neighborhood when it decided to "deflect [its concerns] away from race."[69] Rosenberg understood, it seems, that the Jewish Community Council's efforts to create a natural pace of neighborhood transformation had sidelined the particular dynamics of black settlement in the neighborhood. In his estimation, "race" could not be made invisible by goodwill programs or efforts to keep the neighborhood tidy when policies thwarted black access to housing throughout the city through racial restrictions and exploitative home-financing arrangements.

To the extent that the Jewish Community Council was ready to admit the shortcomings of the Midtown Neighborhood Council, it placed blame at the feet of real estate agents. Fauman explained, "Now in all of our work in the area, informants have pointed out again and again the influence and activities of these dealers in causing the panic and tension. . . . Without exception our informants feel, and submitted evidence, that real estate dealers were responsible for the panic."[70]

More than anything else, the Jewish Community Council objected to losing control over the narrative being told about the neighborhood. Jewish leaders could not deny the fact of Jewish movement, but they had a vested interest in creating a record that showed Jews' commitment to the neighborhood's stability. Through crafting the proper narrative, they hoped to shield Jews from blame for the degradation of the neighborhood, especially for opening the floodgates to black settlement, and from accusations of unfairly engineering and profiteering from that settlement. In their efforts, they placed Jews squarely on the side of liberal, not communist and not fascist, urban politics.

Real Estate and Regulation

By the late 1940s, none of the seven census tracts with the highest concentration of Jews in Detroit could be found in the Twelfth Street neighborhood.[71] For the Jewish institutions in the neighborhood, this posed a problem. In 1948, the United Hebrew Schools, which had occupied its first building in 1919 in the Hastings Street area and then had established sites in the Twelfth Street area, created outposts in the Dexter and Bagley neighborhoods. Yet its leadership was self-conscious about the pace of

Jewish movement and averred, "It has always been the policy of the United Hebrew School leadership not to abandon an old neighborhood as long as there are some pupils of school age there, and at the same time to follow the movement of the Jewish people and to serve them wherever they settle in large numbers."[72] Similarly, by the end of 1948, the Jewish Community Center planned to erect a new building in the Dexter neighborhood, as it also promised to maintain services in the building that stood on Woodward Avenue, on the eastern edge of the Twelfth Street neighborhood.[73]

Neighborhood Jewish institutions, much as the Jewish Community Council and the Interracial Committee did, trained their eyes on neighborhood stability, not integration. Many of them promised to remain an ongoing presence in the neighborhood, although within the decade almost all of them closed their doors and moved away. Liberal leaders' pronouncements about stability and institutions' pledges to stay in the neighborhood could not occlude the stream of incidents that illustrated tension and unrest in the neighborhood. Throughout 1949, residents repeatedly brought conflicts over property and black settlement in the neighborhood to the Interracial Committee and the Jewish Community Council to adjudicate.

One incident involving an apartment building on West Philadelphia Street that had recently been bought by a black man revealed the way that racist economic policies structured tension between whites and black newcomers. According to the white and primarily Jewish tenants, the new owner had stated his intention of converting the building's rental units into owner-occupied ones and was targeting only black buyers by advertising the properties as "for colored occupancy only." The existing tenants reported that they were being forced out of the building upon threat that they would be the last whites left in the building and the neighborhood. According to Jewish Community Council reports, a group of the tenants, almost all Jewish, approached the council for help in the winter of 1949: "They left the impression that we were witnessing a recurrence on this block of the panic which so upset the whole Twelfth Street area two summers ago."[74] The Jewish Community Council referred the situation to the Interracial Committee.

The Interracial Committee started its investigation by contacting a man named David Hersh, the black owner's Jewish attorney. In a letter to Hersh, Schermer wrote, "The Interracial Committee holds that limitations placed on the availability of housing based on race or religion are contrary to fair practices and damaging to the community welfare." The letter offered several suggestions for remedying the situation and ended with the hope that the owner and Hersh would "give these recommendations serious consideration and will find it possible to act in conformance with them."

What amounted to a plea for community-spirited action, the letter packed no punch; after all, the Interracial Committee lacked the power of enforcement, and neither the black owner nor Hersh had violated any laws. Hersh diplomatically responded that the owner was not trying to stir up problems and was "purely interested in business aspects." This, of course, was the problem. From a business perspective, the owner—and his Jewish attorney—stood to make more money from sales to blacks than to whites, especially if the attorney helped draw up and arrange financing plans.[75]

The gains of selling property to black families were institutionalized into American home lending policies. These policies systematically and legally excluded the vast majority of black people from access to federally backed and bank credit on the grounds that black people and black neighborhoods were unsound investments for banks, lenders, or the Federal Housing Administration. Instead, black people who wished to invest in property or purchase a home almost always had to come up with their own cash or buy "on contract." Contract sellers, usually white real estate agents and lawyers and, sometimes, partnerships among many, abided by no specific regulations when it came to extending credit because they did not seek federal protections. Thus, they tended to write unforgiving terms into land contracts, for example, stipulating that even a single late or short payment could result in total repossession of the property by the contract seller. Just as significantly, contract sellers set their own interest rates, generally well above the rates available to buyers who qualified for bank mortgages, whether federally insured or not. Thus, land-contract sellers stood to gain profit from three sources: inflated prices, high interest rates, and repossessions and resales, often through new land contracts.[76]

The Jewish Community Council and the Interracial Committee made no gesture to suggest the regulation of land-contract practices and did not correlate these practices with the racial tensions they observed in the Twelfth Street area. They did, however, attempt to explore the legal remedies available to them to stop "serious incidents involving protest to non-white occupancy of homes" and other forms of racial tension that disrupted neighborhood stability.[77] In 1949, they met together with police officers and legal counsel, hoping, in vain, to persuade the city's police department to take broader measures to control racial intimidation. Prior to the meeting, Schermer and the Jewish Community Council president had consulted national Jewish organizations, the American Jewish Congress and the Anti-Defamation League (ADL) in New York City, seeking advice about what legal powers they could use to quell racial tension arising in urban neighborhoods. Both groups explained that violence and efforts to incite violence were already punishable under existing laws. The ADL suggested that although a new law was not necessary, one could function "as a statement that community sentiment strongly opposes the type of violence that has been developed in Detroit to intimidate Negroes who seek to move out of Negro ghettoes thereby enforcing continued segregation."[78] The Interracial Committee and the Jewish Community Council surely knew that violent activities and acts to compel violence were illegal; instead, they were searching for a legal mechanism to stop the kinds of incidents, while not necessarily violent, that often resulted in ends quite similar to violent housing protests.

Strikingly, the Interracial Committee and the Jewish Community Council representatives made no claims that they were working toward residential racial integration. Rather, they focused their efforts on finding ways to protect groups and individuals from those forces—such as public protests or panic selling—that destabilized property value. The police representatives and legal counsel suggested that civil, not criminal, action was likely the best path forward to deal with housing trouble. A representative from the police department at the 1949 meeting explained that unless violent action or clear disruptions of the peace occurred, the police had no jurisdiction over housing-related incidents. In an ensuing discussion about stopping peaceful protests aimed to prevent blacks from moving into a neighborhood, the county prosecutor demurred, saying he would have to study each incident and see if there was any leeway for police intervention.[79]

Schermer likely realized he and the Jewish Community Council would come up empty from their 1949 meeting with the police department. The year before, he had made enemies with Harry Toy, the police commissioner of Detroit, when Schermer suggested that the police department shirked its full responsibility to intervene in anti-black picketing occurring in a white neighborhood to the east of Twelfth Street. "If nothing else," Schermer had written to the commissioner, "I would like to be able to say most emphatically to community leadership that the police and the Prosecutor have done a most thorough-going job," yet, sadly, he did not feel that was the case.[80] In retaliation, Commissioner Toy accused Schermer of "sid[ing] with the Communists" by seeking "recrimination against the [police] Department" and using the Interracial Committee as a prop to incite racial tension.[81] Schermer characterized the charges against him and the committee as "ridiculous," and in a letter to a Catholic representative on the Interracial Committee, he wrote, "We have been instrumental in isolating the Communist elements so that a vital non-Communist leadership has emerged in the Negro community and in Detroit at large, which functions very well in keeping the Communists from confusing issues."[82] Still, Schermer's perceived radicalism and the Interracial Committee's efforts to reform the housing system would eventually lead to Schermer's removal and the committee's disbandment in the early 1950s.

The cases that the Jewish Community Council encountered in Jewish neighborhoods rarely drew police attention and likely would not have even if a more sympathetic police commissioner had held power. The incidents were not violent and generally did not involve angry mobs. Take the West Philadelphia Street case, described above, of the new black building owner who wanted to sell only to blacks and the Jewish tenants who felt threatened by this. No violence had occurred—the Twelfth Street neighborhood had no reports of physical violence related to black settlement throughout the 1940s—and no angry mob had amassed, yet liberal leaders felt certain that such actions were undermining the stability and natural transformations in the neighborhood.[83]

Jewish leaders, on national and local levels, tended to seek neighborhood remedies, much like the Midtown Neighborhood Council, to the kinds of racial tension they witnessed in their neighborhoods. But they were uncomfortable addressing the economic forces, policies, and thinly veiled racist perceptions that rested behind neighborhood tension. They did not wish to draw attention to the fact that some Jewish landlords, homeowners, lawyers, and merchants profited handsomely from black settlement in their neighborhoods and traded on stimulating white movement away from their neighborhoods. And, given the rising pitch of anticommunism, even those who perceived the flaws in the economic system governing private property transaction felt little confidence exposing them.

By the late 1940s, a few liberal Jewish leaders suggested that legislative actions could help ease the pressure of black settlement on Jewish space. If black families were able to move anywhere in the city without being scared of violent reprisal, then Jewish neighborhoods might not be such attractive targets for black settlement or for those who exploited the constraints of the black housing market for their own profit. The American Jewish Congress, with its Commission on Law and Social Action, and the

ADL committed themselves to lobbying for legal remedies to housing discrimination far earlier than most other Jewish agencies and only slowly did the Interracial Committee and the Jewish Community Council turn toward citywide legislation about housing.

Instead, real estate agents throughout American cities became the subjects of increased scrutiny by the late 1940s for the role they played in perpetuating housing discrimination. Especially those agents working in marginal neighborhoods, where the boundaries between black and white spaces had become fuzzy, found themselves blamed for panic, hysteria, plummeting housing values, and interracial tension.[84] In the spring of 1949, the Detroit Interracial Committee and the Jewish Community Council reached out to the real estate community, hoping to convince it, not with the force of law but only with the power of persuasion, to join the effort to stabilize neighborhoods and slow the pace of black settlement. In a letter to a group of real estate agents, Schermer explained, "Persons operating in the real estate business are in a particularly good position to serve as a constructive educational influence in those situations where the neighbors become concerned about the neighborhood changes."[85]

Lacking any leverage to demand compliance with his vision, Schermer turned to Jewish communal leaders, whom he believed could control the behavior of Jewish real estate agents and would want to protect their own investments in the real estate world. In a report documenting white ethnic groups' role in housing discrimination, Schermer contended that although Jews were rarely openly hostile to black settlement, they nonetheless bore a special burden and responsibility to quell racial tension around housing issues. In the first place, he found that antisemitism pervaded both white and black responses to housing problems, so Jews were consistently perceived as central actors. He also believed that Jews' real estate dealings often caused racial tension, convincing whites that Jews brought blacks into the neighborhood and convincing blacks that Jews took advantage of their powerlessness in the housing market. In private conversations with Jewish leaders in 1950, Schermer encouraged them to confront Jews who were involved in the real estate industry.[86] Understanding that Jewish real estate men were often deeply dependent upon the Jewish community and relied upon a close ethnic network to help fuel their businesses, Schermer believed that Jewish leaders could hold sway over their business practices.

Already in the spring of 1948, a researcher at the Jewish Community Council had monitored one month's worth of newspaper advertisements for homes for sale in the central blocks of the Twelfth Street neighborhood. He found that Jewish and black agents persistently characterized the properties they were selling as suited for "colored" people. In a letter to the NAACP, the researcher suggested that Jewish and black leaders intervene to stop members of their communities from steering black buyers into the neighborhood. He wrote, "If these practices which are recommended can be implemented, it should serve to remove the stimulus to panicky movement from the area and hence prevent the inevitable repercussions which follow panic."[87]

In a retrospective report from 1950, the Jewish Community Council went as far as to lay total blame for the panic in the Twelfth Street area on real estate agents: "Real estate dealer activity precipitated a near hysteria by early 1947."[88] Yet liberal Jewish leaders waded into murky waters when they tried to tell real estate agents to stop engaging in real estate practices that caused "panic." The heart of their concern was that these agents were selling to black families at an unnatural speed, but they could not quantify what would be a "natural" speed. They also realized how hypocritical they, promoters of civil rights, would sound if they told real estate agents to stop selling homes to blacks—a policy that would abrogate their commitment to group rights and protections. Furthermore, Jewish real estate agents often invested in community institutions through charitable giving and pro bono work, and many Jewish leaders relied upon these acts of largesse. Over the course of the 1950s, liberal Jewish leaders scrutinized real estate agents' behavior, characterizing it as annoying, aggravating, and destabilizing, yet always stopping short of delivering a truly damaging assessment of the real estate industry, the market economy it fueled, its profit-making structure, and its reliance on a system of race-based hierarchy.

CHAPTER THREE

Changing Jewish Neighborhoods

In 1955, Harry and William Gross, a father-son real estate team, acquired Hurd Realty in northwest Detroit. The Gross men explained that they would still maintain their original office on Linwood at the crossroads of the Twelfth Street and Dexter neighborhood, where they had made millions of dollars in sales from "people who are selling their homes in changing neighborhoods." But now, with an expanded office close to the Bagley neighborhood and more listings than ever in northwest Detroit, they could move right alongside their sellers who "immediately become buyers, and approximately 80 percent of them buy homes in the northwest section."[1] By the mid-1950s, "changing neighborhoods" rested at the heart of the urban real estate market and Jews' relationships to cities. And, to be certain, there was money to be made in neighborhood change.

In the late 1930s, roughly 10 percent of Jewish men in Detroit worked in the real estate and insurance industries.[2] A similar study of Jewish occupational life in Detroit from the late 1950s found that a slightly higher percentage (about 13 percent) of Jewish men in the city worked in finance and real estate. More than half of those men made over $20,000 a year, putting them in the city's top earning bracket and giving them a median income well above other professional men.[3]

For Jews, a people who historically engaged in trade because they were excluded from owning and working the land, land trade—buying, selling, and developing property—became one of the pillars of personal and communal wealth in twentieth-century America.[4] In many ways, real estate was a perfect profession for the mid-twentieth-century Jew. It demanded little start-up capital and almost no overhead, so it was a profession well suited for an immigrant population and their children who rarely had access to family capital. It was also the kind of work that relied on strong networks of trust, such as ethnic networks, that gave people the confidence to invest in one another and take risks without worrying that they would be cheated. Finally, it was a good profession for people with connections to groups that tended to move often. The more that Jews moved, the more work real estate agents and financiers had, and the more extensive—and lucrative—their work became. Urban Jews relied on Jewish real estate agents to enable them to leave their old neighborhoods and move to new ones. Of course, not all Jews used Jewish real estate agents, but many did as evidenced by the brisk business that Jewish real estate firms did in Jewish neighborhoods.[5]

By the middle of the twentieth century, Jews and Jewish institutions profited, as individuals and as a community, from real estate activity. Jews, like other Americans, bought and sold homes and amassed investment gains and equity in doing so. The *Detroit Jewish News* happily reported in 1951 that the Real Estate and Building Division of the Allied Jewish Campaign, a massive fund-raising campaign from which almost every Jewish agency in the city benefited, was "doing well and still plugging."[6] Jewish real estate men gave back to the community, often in very public ways, in hopes of gaining exposure for their community-mindedness and their businesses.

Yet as much as the Jewish community relied upon real estate agents to help them invest in property and yield gains from their investments, Jewish communal leaders also demonized real estate agents for undermining the goal of community stability. Real estate men were on the front lines of Jewish migration within and away from cities, and by midcentury they were the focus of community tension and ambivalence about those moves. In 1951, leaders of Detroit's Jewish Community Council wrote to their Cincinnati counterparts, "We feel that what would ordinarily be a gradual migration is being made more than just that because of the activities of six or seven 'sharp operators' who call themselves real estate brokers, many of them Jewish."[7] Jewish real estate agents disproportionately served Jewish clients and, thus, worked in Jewish neighborhoods in the midst of racial transformation, often entering into buyer and seller agreements with black newcomers. Urban leaders repetitively used the word "unscrupulous" to describe real estate agents. Jewish leaders worried in particular about the ways in which real estate agents' tactics were damaging to Jewish life, thwarted neighborhood-based activism, and compromised a liberal civil rights agenda. When the real estate agents happened to be Jewish, as they often were, then leaders also worried that the perceived misdeeds of a handful of Jews would reflect poorly on all Jews and fuel Americans' perceptions of collective Jewish wrongdoing and avarice.

Over the course of the 1950s, liberals tried to figure out how to protect private property rights without compromising civil rights. Ever vigilant about distancing themselves from communism, they exercised great caution when it came to criticizing private property and market forces. Liberal leaders maintained that people should be able to sell their private property to whomever they wished and to make a profit from doing so. These were the "natural" forces that enabled a market economy to work by creating value from demand. Yet those who lived in urban Jewish neighborhoods—who perhaps had left these neighborhoods or had watched as their friends and relatives left them—witnessed how private property transactions legitimated discrimination and perpetuated societal divisions by drawing profit from legalized race-based exploitation. Racial hierarchies guided the logic of economic policy, including financing structures, which regulated the market. Thus, insofar as Americans understood the market economy as operating according to natural forces, hierarchies of race became naturalized, too.

Urban Jews in the 1950s believed that in order for their neighborhoods to remain viable places for Jewish life to thrive, they would need to redress abuses in the real estate market that interrupted fair property transactions, but they tended to focus their attention narrowly on real estate agents' practices. Beyond convincing Jewish families that the neighborhood was still a good place to live, as they had done in the 1940s, urban Jewish leaders sought to persuade real estate agents to reform practices that they believed challenged the natural workings of the market system. Extending their belief that a certain level of movement away from Jewish neighborhoods was natural and a sign of progress, they did not seek to revolutionize the market system when it came to property transaction; instead, these leaders aimed to rid the real estate market of those forces that they saw as impeding its natural protective mechanisms.

Specifically, leaders called for agents to stop pressuring Jewish residents to sell property well before natural proclivities would dictate. Jewish leaders had faith that without real estate agents' fueling neighborhood panic, the real estate market would be able to operate in a pure state, enabling people to buy and sell property when they could afford to do so. They characterized real estate agents who traded in unnatural or artificial means to induce sales as threats to the mechanisms of capitalism and democracy. For liberal Jewish leaders, who believed in this distinction between the natural market forces and artificial ones, the difficulty remained in identifying what distinguished these broad categories and, then, persuading real estate agents and residents to accept those categories, especially at a time when mobility implied success in the minds of American Jews and other white Americans.

Where Are You Running?

By the early 1950s, the Jewish population of the Twelfth Street area had become so depleted that Albert Mayer, a Wayne State sociologist who year after year churned out demographic reports commissioned by the Jewish Federation of Detroit, observed that the neighborhood was on the brink of becoming "a place where 'Jews used to live.'"[8] The largest concentration of Jewish residential life could be found now in the Dexter neighborhood, though Mayer suggested that if Jews' migratory trends continued, this would not be the case for long. He did not mention, though it was clear from the detailed census tables he appended to his report, that the Dexter neighborhood, while still home to 40 percent of Detroit's Jews, now hosted a growing number of black families. In the census tract with the largest number of Jews, located in the heart of the Dexter area, the black population had grown to 115 families in just a few years. This was still a small number when compared to the over twenty-five hundred Jewish families who lived there, but to residents and Jewish leaders the change mattered.[9]

Even so, in the early 1950s, many Jews and their businesses and institutions were not ready to give up on Dexter, though their commitment to the neighborhood tended to be framed as a bold act. In January 1950, Ben Pupko, proprietor of a fine linens and home goods store, took out an advertisement in the *Detroit Jewish News* that announced, "WE ARE NOT MOVING FROM DEXTER." The advertisement explained, "We want to stay out of the high rent district . . . so we can continue giving you the best value in Detroit."[10] Less than two months later, Ben Pupko's brother Abe opened a branch of the family store, now called A. Pupko's (as opposed to B. Pupko's) on Livernois Avenue on the eastern side of the Bagley neighborhood, ostensibly the "high rent district" Ben Pupko mentioned. A brief article in the *Detroit Jewish News*, more an advertisement than a news report, commented that this move "marked another step forward

CHANGING JEWISH NEIGHBORHOODS

FIGURE 3.1 Celebrating the start of construction on the Temple Israel building near Palmer Park. Architect William Knapp (*left*) shaking Rabbi Leon Fram's hand, with Louis Schostak (*inside left*) and Harry LeVine (president of the congregation), 1949. Courtesy of the Archives of Temple Israel, West Bloomfield, Michigan.

in the history of this 40-year-old firm," and then heaped praise on the expanded quarters and air-conditioned interior. The article noted that Schostak Bros. and Co. handled the property acquisition.[11]

While Louis Schostak, of Schostak Bros. and Co., helped Jewish-owned businesses acquire retail property in northwest Detroit, he also served on the building committee for Temple Israel, the Reform congregation that had broken off from Temple Beth El in the early 1940s. Under Schostak's guidance, the synagogue bought land in northwest Detroit, close to Palmer Park and about a mile east of the new Pupko store, and erected a synagogue building there.[12] Neither the real estate market nor Schostak was blind. By guiding a synagogue to move to a particular area of the city (or eventually the suburbs), helping a high-end store acquire land in near proximity to it, and acquiring nearby property for more retail and residential development, a real estate developer could hedge his bets on a profitable future.

Yet many liberal Jewish leaders worried that the same real estate men who helped Jews and Jewish businesses and institutions relocate and amass new assets were corrosive to the Jewish community. In the summer of 1950, Louis Rosenzweig, an attorney and the chair of the Jewish Community Council's internal relations committee, invited Jewish real estate

FIGURE 3.2 Temple Israel, 1951. Courtesy of Walter P. Reuther Library, Archives of Labor and Urban Affairs, Wayne State University.

agents with interests in the Twelfth Street and Dexter neighborhoods to discuss the "procedural, ethical and advertising nature" of real estate sales.[13] Representatives from four of the major Jewish firms attended, though some, such as Benjamin Rich (whose advertisements read "Get Rich Quick!"), declined the invitation.

At the meeting, four representatives from the Jewish Community Council as well as a leader of the local chapter of the ADL took the real estate agents to task for the "immoral aspects of creating artificial panic for financial gains."[14] Indeed, the only time anyone mentioned residential integration as a possible solution to the community's woes came when a real estate broker mildly suggested that the group's time might be better spent teaching "Jewish people . . . to live with Negroes" than scolding real estate agents for selling homes to black people. Instead, the meeting focused almost exclusively on how to keep Jews and other whites from leaving neighborhoods at an unnaturally rapid speed, while allowing demographic change to occur in a "slow and orderly fashion." Rosenzweig and other council leaders emphasized that "millions of dollars of communal property [was] at stake if the area change[d] rapidly in character." The representative from the ADL went so far as to suggest that one possible remedy would be to mandate "sales be made only to Jewish persons."[15]

So full of anxiety about black settlement in Jewish neighborhoods was the meeting that one of the leaders felt compelled to assure the attendees that the tone of the conversation should not "be interpreted as an anti-Negro one."[16] These Jewish leaders did not know how to explain what distinguished selling a property to a black family from destroying a Jewish neighborhood. So in their rhetoric, they tended to conflate the two, even as they also pronounced themselves champions of civil rights, opponents of racial restrictive covenants, and bearers of goodwill toward blacks. They rested their attention on the behavior that characterized real estate transactions and not the transactions themselves; whether a Jewish person sold a property or a black person bought a property mattered less than the extent to which a real estate agent had preyed upon panic-inducing factors. How to characterize and stop panic selling came to occupy the minds of midcentury urban Jewish leaders.

Just as Jewish leaders were meeting with real estate agents behind closed doors, the Jewish Community Council initiated a publicity campaign against panic selling. A flyer, distributed door-to-door and reprinted in local newspapers, asked readers a series of aggressive questions, starting with the flyer's title: "Neighbor, Where Are You Running To?" The text continued, "Why not wait until you meet your neighbor before you judge him? . . . Are you being panicked by some unscrupulous real estate dealers . . . ? Are you going to sacrifice your life savings because of a lot of unfounded rumors by men who will profit by it?" The "it" of the last question made little grammatical sense, and it left vague what exactly real estate brokers were profiting from: white prejudice, rumors, or, perhaps, the ability to exploit blacks who had little economic protection in the postwar housing market? Turning to the language of intimidation, the flyer warned that any neighborhood where whites moved "will also eventually be for all Americans, of all nationalities and colors." One could not escape, "So, don't do anything foolish!"[17]

The *Michigan Chronicle*, a black newspaper on the political left, reprinted the flyer and praised it in an accompanying editorial. Noting, as the flyer did, that the Supreme Court, as of its 1948 decision in *Shelley v. Kraemer*, had declared restrictive covenants unconstitutional, the editorial explained, "In Detroit in particular this means that for the first time in many years, large groups of people are going to be given an opportunity to demonstrate in their every day [sic] living whether they really believe in Democracy or not."[18] One can imagine that the same editorial page would have had a different assessment of the Jewish Community Council's

> **NEIGHBOR, WHERE ARE YOU RUNNING TO?**
>
> Why not wait until you meet your neighbor before you judge him? . . . are you being panicked by some unscrupulous real estate dealers into leaving a good home neighborhood near the downtown area for another of very doubtful value and probably overpriced?
>
> Are you going to sacrifice your life savings because of a lot of unfounded rumors by men who will profit by it?
>
> **Think Hard First!** Then, if you must, sell, remember: nobody wants to be forced into a ghetto. The street you might be moving to will also eventually be for all Americans, of all nationalities and colors.
>
> If your heart won't admit that all men are entitled to decent homes, then remember:
>
> 1. The United States Supreme Court has ruled that there is only one class of citizens.
> 2. The United States Supreme Court has ruled that there are no exempt and excluded neighborhoods.
>
> **So, don't do anything foolish!**
>
> THE OLD NEIGHBORHOOD WHERE YOU RAISED YOUR CHILDREN AND MADE YOUR FRIENDS IS STILL THE BEST LOCATED IN OUR CITY.
>
> **So why run, neighbor?**
>
> JEWISH COMMUNITY COUNCIL OF DETROIT
> 803 Washington Blvd. Bldg.
> Detroit 26, Michigan, WOodward 3-1657
>
> Dr. Shmarya Kleinman, President   Louis Rosenzweig, Chairman
> Jewish Community Council   Internal Relations Committee
> Sub-Committee: Robert Nathans, Irving Schlussel, and Mrs. Oscar Schwartz

FIGURE 3.3 "Neighbor, Where Are You Running To?" 1950. Courtesy of Walter P. Reuther Library, Archives of Labor and Urban Affairs, Wayne State University.

meeting with real estate agents. Whereas the flyer could be interpreted as demanding that white people adjust to the reality of residential integration, the meeting had focused entirely on ways that the pace of white movement away from the neighborhood could be slowed to its "natural" rhythm so that Jews could adjust their communal and private investments accordingly.

A column published in the *Jewish Daily Forward*, a Yiddish national newspaper, similarly praised the flyer for singling out "people who have a financial interest in creating" panic and warning Jews against playing into their moneymaking schemes. The columnist agreed that getting to know one's neighbors, as the flyer instructed, was the building block of creating a stable Jewish neighborhood. He wrote, "Experience has shown that those Negroes who move into the Jewish section have been excellent in their behavior and quite pleasant as neighbors." Of course, once enough of one's neighbors were black, then few would think to call the neighborhood Jewish any longer. Stuck in this contradiction, the columnist floundered to find clarity: "Naturally, we do not say that no one should sell his home to Negroes. This would be discrimination. A normal exchange of homes should take place, and no discrimination of any kind should be practiced. We only wish to caution and warn against panic."[19] Concluding with an insipid plea for normalcy, the columnist, similar to the Jewish Community Council, advocated a normal pace of Jewish movement and did little to suggest that residential integration constituted normal.

Some Jews at the time were unimpressed with the campaign against real estate panic and pointed out the deep contradictions embedded in it. Most articulate was Bernard Edelman, a Jewish real estate agent who had sent a representative from his firm to the Jewish Community Council's real estate meeting. In a series of letters to the council, he methodically set out the flaws in its attack against real estate agents. To one of his missives, he appended a for-sale advertisement from a local newspaper. Below its listing of the property's location (on the northern edge of the Twelfth Street neighborhood), the ad specified "unrestricted." "Gentlemen," he wrote, "I've discovered that you people object to the word restricted in real estate advertisements. I think then that the enclosed ad will make you very happy." With sarcasm dripping from his prose, Edelman continued, "Thanks to the encouragement one gets from your office many realty brokers are introducing colored families into complete [sic] white sections causing considerable ill feeling toward Jewish people." He explained that if real estate agents sold homes to whoever wanted them—black or white—"leading synagogues will be forced to move." With a rhetorical flourish, he ended his letter by questioning just who was creating panic: real estate agents or liberal Jews, such as the members of the Jewish Community Council, who sang the praises of nondiscriminatory real estate practices and then protested the results when too many blacks moved too quickly into Jewish neighborhoods. Edelman characterized liberal Jews as endorsing slow movement for purely self-interested reasons so that Jews and Jewish institutions would not take a hit on their property investments.[20]

Edelman, who eventually left the real estate business in disgust, would have seen that printed on the flip side of the thousands of "Neighbor, Where Are You Running To?" leaflets distributed throughout the

Twelfth Street and Dexter neighborhoods was a not-for-sale sign. The Jewish Community Council encouraged Jews to display it in their front yard to ward off panic-inducing real estate agents. The council intended the sign as a pithy value statement: this house is not for sale, and nor are its occupants' values and beliefs. Yet, much like the discussion with real estate agents about panic selling, the matter was not so straightforward. Indeed, the sign (which appeared in other U.S. cities at the same time) could also be read as a populist attack against integration, a de facto restrictive covenant meant to assure neighbors that this home would never be sold to blacks.

Valuing Property

According to liberal leaders, real estate agents could stir up panic in an entire neighborhood simply by suggesting that a black family had looked at a home. This was because homeowners believed there was an intrinsic relationship between property values and race, such that the more attractive a neighborhood became to black people, the less a piece of property would be worth. At the same time, real estate agents convinced homeowners that if they acted ahead of the curve—before most white homeowners thought to get out—their property would yield returns higher than market value. Real estate agent Benjamin Rich (of "Get Rich Quick") frequently mailed postcards to nearby homeowners after he sold a home. "You have a new neighbor," the card read. "If you want to sell your house see us for quick action and top price."[21] By coupling pace and price, the postcard expressed the urgency of the situation without once mentioning race.

By the late 1940s, the Jewish Community Council had cultivated informants in the main Jewish neighborhoods and requested them to report when black families bought homes or, even, when rumors circulated that blacks were considering buying property. In the summer of 1950, real estate agent Bernard Schatten, who had recently attended the Jewish Community Council's real estate meeting, purchased a single-family home on a pleasant block in the southern reaches of the Dexter neighborhood. The council learned that he intended to sell it to a black family, and a staff person talked to nearby neighbors who confirmed the reports. The council assigned one of its informants, a Jewish woman who lived in the neighborhood, the task of reporting on and minimizing the panic that Jewish leaders were certain would ensue from this sale. Council staff members encouraged her to organize block meetings and help improve neighborhood communication to stop rumors. These were the kinds of techniques they believed had worked successfully for the Midtown Neighborhood Council and would help now in preventing real estate panics.[22]

At the same time, city officials tried to disprove the correlation between black settlement in a neighborhood and declining home values, hoping that empirical research could also thwart panic sales. Detroit's Interracial Committee assigned its research assistant to study the question. Unsurprisingly, the researcher chose a Jewish neighborhood with an influx of black families (he did not name the neighborhood, but it was almost certainly the Twelfth Street area) as his experimental group and an all-white neighborhood as his control group. By tracking home prices over the past few years, he found that values in the Jewish/black neighborhood actually increased more steadily than they did in the all-white neighborhood. "Thus," he concluded, "we find that the belief that 'Negroes devalue property' to be completely unsubstantiated by the data of this study."[23] A decade later in 1960, a five-year study commissioned by the National Committee Against Discrimination in Housing would similarly conclude, "The odds are about four to one that house prices in a neighborhood entered by nonwhites will keep up with or exceed prices in a comparable all-white area."[24] Yet it was a mistake to read the data as indicating a race-blind housing market. That housing values increased in the short term would not surprise historians who have come to understand that blacks, at the mercy of racist housing policy and housing shortages, were often charged severely inflated prices for homes. In the long term, prices in the Twelfth Street neighborhood would spiral downward, as the city neglected the neighborhood's infrastructure, as black families strapped with high interest and expensive monthly housing payments could not maintain the homes they purchased, and as employment practices continued to make it difficult for many black families to earn a living wage.[25]

Still, when George Schermer spoke at neighborhood meetings in the 1950s, he claimed that the only force that truly caused housing values to decline was panic. And the Jewish Community Council worked quickly to propagate this belief, creating pamphlets and educational materials to show people that if they remained calm and maintained a natural pace of movement, then the market would function smoothly.[26] The primary purpose of proving to homeowners that their property levels would not decrease after blacks moved in was to convince them that even if they did not move immediately, they could move eventually without taking a loss on their home investment. The returns would endure a slower pace of movement.

For midcentury liberals, the belief that the real estate market could naturally regulate itself as long as individuals did not panic validated their approach to private property rights and urban policy. A free market, they maintained, could not possibly be racist since it only responded to economic forces. Ironically, in this very same era, the real estate market operated under heavy federal regulations to stimulate home building and subsidize home buying. At least since the 1930s, with the passage of the National Housing Act, the private real estate market had never been left to develop according to a natural rhythm, whatever that would have been. Economic forces did not operate free from race and class hierarchies.

For many residents of the Jewish neighborhoods in Detroit, the decision to move or to stay blurred the line between economics and emotion, which is why panic-selling tactics worked and, also, why so many Jews felt exploited by them. In September 1950, some of the wealthiest homeowners in the Twelfth Street area met together. These were the homeowners from the Boston-Edison district, the high-end northern section of the neighborhood. Likely, many Boston-Edison residents would not have described themselves as living in the Twelfth Street neighborhood, especially once the neighborhood started to lose its Jewish character in the mid-1940s. Yet the Midtown Council had included these streets in its reports on the neighborhood and clearly the fate of these upper-middle-class streets could not be separated from the fate of the rest of the neighborhood.

Led by George Schermer and convened at his home, an elegant three story with a columned porch and dormer windows, the Boston-Edison group considered itself more enlightened than most, recording in its meetings the following self-assessment: "There are probably few areas in the city where there is a higher proportion of people endowed with a liberalism of attitude with respect to racial, religious and cultural differences than the general area including and surrounding the Boston-Edison section. If there is any place in town where a stable, cosmopolitan community can be maintained this should be it."[27] As liberal cosmopolitans, they would not worry about living alongside people who were different—as long as those people shared their values about liberalism and cosmopolitanism and as long as they could afford the real estate on their blocks. The wrong class of people would hurt their section of the neighborhood, but they assured themselves that the upscale nature of their blocks would act as a natural impediment to keep those people from moving in.

Other neighborhood residents, who did not have the protection of large expensive homes to reassure them that their blocks would remain stable, continued to worry about their property values and the less empirical but equally important feel of their neighborhood. Annoyed by the aggressive language of the "Neighbor, Where Are You Running To?" campaign, some Twelfth Street residents accused the council of expecting them to make sacrifices to guard an abstract ideal about liberalism and community good. A Jewish woman who lived in one of the apartment buildings in the Twelfth Street neighborhood contacted the Jewish Community Council after receiving its flyer in 1950. She wrote, "This particular campaign is being waged by the Council in an aura of hypocrisy, in view of the fact that the majority [of the leaders] have long since moved away themselves, but exhort those still remaining to 'hold fast' so that the Jewish community may enjoy a reputation for interracial goodwill."[28] Another Jewish resident of the neighborhood found the campaign equally hypocritical and simply signed his letter "disgusted." Not only did he complain that the same Jewish leaders demanding a gradual pace of Jewish movement had for the most part already left the neighborhood, he also argued that none of these liberal Jews were honest enough to acknowledge the problems that really did arise when blacks moved in.[29]

The Jewish Community Council could not deny these charges: most of its leaders did not live in the heart of the neighborhood where black families were settling, and the council made few efforts to publicize the kinds of problems plaguing the neighborhood on the heels of black families' arrival. Instead, they set their sights on slowing the pace of Jewish movement by denying rumors that more blacks were moving to the neighborhood than truly were, providing empirical testimony to the ongoing strength of housing values, and going after real estate agents for trying to "break" blocks and systematically sell homes to black families.

Liberal Housing Politics in the Era of Jewish Communist Fears

Liberal Jewish leaders in the early 1950s rarely endorsed residential racial integration as a solution to their urban neighborhood woes, even if occasionally in their pronouncements they mentioned integration as an ideal. To be certain, they encouraged Jews to reach out to black neighbors and not to judge them according to prejudiced preconceptions. But their explicit goals were stability and the protection of Jewish investments in the city, and not specific remedies for housing discrimination. In matters of employment discrimination, on the other hand, Jewish liberals tended to be outspoken supporters of legal remedies. For example, the Michigan Committee on Civil Rights, which had been established in 1948 to lobby for the passage of the state's Fair Employment law, included many Jews (and many Jewish Community Council leaders) who expressed support to end segregation in employment and extend legal protections to minorities who faced discrimination in hiring and firing decisions.[30] Housing integration, however, was a separate matter. Many of the same Detroit Jews who eagerly supported fair employment policies balked when it came to offering support for the Detroit Council for Better Housing, a housing reform group committed to integration and critical of the city's housing policy. The Jewish Community Council offered tepid endorsement of the group in 1950, deferring the decision to affiliate formally with it.[31]

The political climate in the city recommended liberal Jews' cautious approach toward housing desegregation. In 1950, Albert Cobo, a Republican with a solid base of support from white conservatives in the city, was sworn into the office of mayor. Under his leadership, racist homeowners associations and pro-segregationist groups gained legitimacy and power. Liberals in the city felt more besieged than ever, as they lost their footing in city politics and felt pressed to erect a stark boundary between themselves and leftists who were targets of governmental suspicion, investigation, and imprisonment.[32]

The year Cobo entered office, controversy over an integrated housing cooperative erupted that tested liberal and Jewish commitments to housing activism. A private group of primarily union-affiliated individuals had been moving forward for some time with plans to construct an integrated housing cooperative, the Schoolcraft Gardens Cooperative, in northwest Detroit. The conservative shift in city politics in 1950 emboldened nearby homeowners associations to organize mass resistance to the plan. By March of that year, these associations proposed a rezoning ordinance to the city's Common Council that would make it impossible for the cooperative to be built. Schermer, certain that the rezoning ordinance was a racist ploy, urged Cobo to block the ordinance and warned him that racial tension could erupt if the white conservative forces prevailed.

Calling upon liberal groups to protest the effort to disband the cooperative, Schermer went quickly to his friends at the Jewish Community

Council. Dutifully, the Jewish Community Council distributed Schermer's statement against the ordinance to its constituents and urged the Common Council not to approve the rezoning ordinance. Yet aside from one rabbi, B. Benedict Glazer of Detroit's large and important Temple Beth El, Jewish leaders remained relatively quiet on the issue. As nervous as Schermer may have been about stirring up racial tension, Jews were just as nervous about being targeted by white conservatives as rabble-rousers and, worse, communists.[33]

Under the cover of an interfaith coalition, Jewish leaders were much more willing to challenge white conservative elements in the city. By the end of March, with a split Common Council and the matter of rezoning on Mayor Cobo's desk, Jewish leaders met with other religious leaders in Detroit to create a list of recommendations for how the mayor could deal with racial tension. Among their demands was that greater enforcement power be given to Schermer and the Interracial Committee. Notably, the group did not specifically demand the mayor's support for the housing cooperative. Perhaps to leverage the situation for his own political gain, Cobo responded that the Interracial Committee's future and Schermer's retention had not yet been decided. Hinting at a quid pro quo, he also tried to pressure the interfaith group into backing his new slum clearance plan, a plan that the Detroit Council for Better Housing and the Jewish Community Council had opposed on the grounds that it did not provide adequate housing for the black residents who would be displaced.[34] In the end, Cobo approved of the rezoning ordinance and denied the private group the right to build an integrated housing cooperative.

Without a doubt, most Jewish liberal leaders disagreed with the mayor's decision, but none had issued a persuasive case as to why the racist desires of nearby homeowners should not trump the integrationist desires of other private citizens. Likely, at least one of the reasons that Jewish leaders supported the project was because it promised more housing for blacks—a promise, they hoped, that would alleviate pressure on their own neighborhoods. For the same reason, they opposed Cobo's slum clearance plan to displace black people without providing sufficient new housing for black families.

National Jewish organizations in the early 1950s issued statements supporting racially integrated public housing as a necessary answer to the severe housing shortages throughout urban America.[35] These same organizations, however, did not make any similar statements about integrated private housing and neighborhoods. They were unwilling to challenge the sacred ground of private property rights. In the first place, Jews benefited from laws and policies that protected white homeowners in the name of private property rights. Furthermore, liberals and, especially, liberal Jews realized that local, state, and federal authorities viewed outspokenly reformist positions on private housing and support for integration as warning signs of communist proclivities. Too much activism on this front might very well draw unwanted attention.[36]

A housing case in December 1951 confirmed liberal Jews' fears that becoming overly active in housing and integrationist politics could come back and haunt them. In December 1951, Detroit's Interracial Committee received a complaint from Morris Davidson, a Jewish man who lived on Elmhurst Street in the heart of the Dexter neighborhood. Davidson explained that he had recently sold his home. Throughout 1951, the *Detroit Jewish News* filled page after page announcing synagogues and stores moving out of the Twelfth Street and Dexter areas, and reporting synagogues, a new Hebrew school branch, and stores moving northwest into the Bagley neighborhood.[37] Davidson's decision to move, therefore, was not at all unusual. The problem, however, was that Davidson had sold his home to the Graham family, a black family, and had since been receiving retaliatory threats from his neighbors. Davidson even claimed that a small fire had been set in his garage.

Immediately, the Interracial Committee contacted the Jewish Community Council. This had become common practice—whenever a Jewish person was involved in a dispute that made its way to the Interracial Committee, the Jewish Community Council was notified and asked to participate. The council representative and the Interracial Committee urged Davidson to act with "restraint" and not to try to "counter-organize" his neighbors. They assured him that the police would protect him and his family and that likely the matter would blow over quickly. Davidson's wife openly flouted this advice. She felt that they were being asked to suppress information about the sale and the intimidation they had received for it. She wanted everything to be public and said she intended to gather her neighbors and introduce them to the Graham family.[38]

Over the coming weeks, the Interracial Committee and Jewish Community Council representatives grew suspicious of the Davidsons: Why would the family want to put on display the fact they had sold their home to a black family? When asked, Graham, the black buyer, said he and his family did not want the attention and were happy to move quietly into their new home. And the police never corroborated that a fire had been set in the Davidson's garage. On December 29, 1951, and January 1, 1952, articles in the *Pittsburgh Courier*, a black newspaper, and the Communist

Party's *Daily Worker* confirmed both groups' misgivings about the Davidsons. The articles reported that the Davidsons had brought their complaints to the Civil Rights Congress, a left-leaning organization that had once attracted considerable Jewish support but had fallen out of favor with Jewish liberals in the postwar period because of its alleged ties to the Communist Party.[39] Suddenly, the Interracial Committee and the Jewish Community Council appeared to be sharing a platform with an organization connected to the Communist Party. When confronted, the Davidsons said they would tell the Civil Rights Congress to back away from the case as long as they believed that the liberal organizations were taking the necessary steps to address the situation. Under pressure, the Interracial Committee agreed to facilitate a meeting with neighbors and, also, try to organize a neighborhood group similar to the Midtown Neighborhood Council to stop the panic in the area.

Yet in the coming weeks, the Davidsons continued to complain of threatening phone calls and, even, claimed to smell gasoline around their home one afternoon. The Grahams, yet to move into the home, reported no intimidation. Whether the Davidsons reneged on their promise and felt that it was now in their interest to bypass the Interracial Committee is unclear. But shortly after the gasoline incident, the Civil Rights Congress papered the neighborhood with a plea for activism. Addressed to the "residents of the Dexter Boulevard area," the letter described a "reign of terror and violence" that had ensued in the neighborhood since the Davidsons sold their home to a black family. Contrary to the restraint that the liberal leaders had recommended, the Civil Rights Congress warned, "Jewish people in particular cannot let themselves be trapped into participating in pogroms." The letter compared the Davidsons' travails and liberals' complacency to the circumstances that had precipitated "the degradation and destruction of minorities" in Nazi Germany.[40] The *Daily Worker* even more bluntly accused the Interracial Committee and its supporters (in this case, clearly liberal Jews) of engaging in a "coverup" operation, and "spending time redbaiting the Michigan Civil Rights Committee" instead of protecting the Davidsons and their two children.[41]

The Jewish Community Council reacted to the accusations swiftly and coordinated a meeting with Schermer, the detectives, and police officers who had been involved with the case. The Davidsons were not invited. The Jewish Community Council and the Interracial Committee felt pushed into a corner, as each tried to rebut allegations of racism, while maintaining sufficient distance from communist and fellow traveler forces. The police and detectives justified their inaction by explaining that they doubted any of the intimidation represented coordinated neighborhood activity. Furthermore, most of the incidents the Davidsons reported rested on flimsy evidence. That the Davidsons' support of the Civil Rights Congress was now common knowledge did not help their credibility. According to the discussion at the meeting, the Civil Rights Congress "had attempted to exploit several other similar incidents." The minutes of the meeting also recorded the suggestion that perhaps "the Davidsons are tending to exaggerate this incident in their own minds, partly out of understandable concern for their family's welfare and partly out of a tendency of persons in left-wing groups to think in terms of extremes." The police were ordered to guard the property and soon the Davidsons moved out of the neighborhood. In a similar case in 1950, the Jewish Community Council discovered early in its investigation that the Jewish and black individuals involved were affiliated with the Communist Party. The council avoided becoming a public presence on the issue, but managed to keep the matter quiet, and aside from one minor incident, the neighbors left the families alone.[42]

Moving forward, the Jewish Community Council and the Interracial Committee were determined to better contain the narratives about race and neighborhood incidents. When a group such as the Civil Rights Congress gained control of the story and leafleted the neighborhood with its version, the Jewish Community Council and the Interracial Committee lost their footing. They could not possibly make common cause with the Civil Rights Congress—to do so would have only confirmed what Mayor Cobo and other conservative forces in the city already believed about white and Jewish liberalism: that it was just a front for communism. But they also had to reckon with the moral clarity of the Civil Rights Congress's pro-integrationist and anti-capitalist position when it came to ending racial discrimination, and they worried that Jewish residents might look to the communist group and not the liberals for the answer to their neighborhood woes.

By the time the House Un-American Activities Committee (HUAC) announced it would hold hearings in Detroit in early 1952, Schermer likely knew his days working for the city of Detroit were numbered. In public talks, his rhetoric grew bolder as he suggested that only large-scale changes would eradicate the racism embedded in the housing market, though he also believed that a fair housing system could coexist with capitalism. To a group of women civic activists, he explained, "Basically, most of us want to maintain an economic system that is as free, as private, as competitive and flexible as possible and practicable, with due modifications to secure the common welfare."[43] And underscoring his level-headed approach, he assured a group of home appraisers, "I am not speaking as a starry-eyed social dreamer who thinks it would be just wonderful for Negro and white people to live side by side.... I am not speaking for integration, I am speaking against restrictive market practices."[44] His prescription, he explained, was simple: "Remove race, color, or ancestry as a factor in doing business. Open up the market." This became the basis for an open occupancy movement that flourished by the late 1950s and early 1960s among housing activists. As Schermer averred, open occupancy was hardly a radical proposal; rather, it represented an effort to free the market economy from its reliance on emotions and disallow the actions of those who would manipulate race into a market force. Open occupancy supporters believed that a truly free market would pay no heed to race, neglecting in their logic the fact that economic purchasing power and racial hierarchy were already knotted together in the United States.

Convinced of the commonsense pragmatism of his plan, Schermer expressed frustration that anticommunist campaigns had depicted anyone in favor of reforming housing as a communist sympathizer. In a letter to Congressman Charles Potter, sent in advance of the HUAC hearings in Detroit, Schermer wrote, "In order to assure confidence in the findings of your committee among minority groups it is imperative that non-Communist minority group and civil rights leadership be asked to tell their experience in combating Communist influences."[45] Neither HUAC nor Cobo's administration was interested in supporting moderate liberal reform; Schermer knew this. After writing a scathing report that exposed the depths of racism in Detroit's private and public housing system and gained attention from housing activists nationwide, Schermer resigned under pressure in 1952. Almost immediately, Cobo dissolved the Interracial Committee and convened the Commission on Community Relations, charged with a very similar mandate but now clearly owing its existence—and its allegiance—to the conservative mayor.[46]

In losing Schermer, liberal Jews in Detroit lost an ally. Schermer had lived in a Jewish neighborhood and had made it a point to talk to Jewish leaders and approach them first when Jews were involved in a housing situation or any other incident that fell within his purview. In 1955, when the Jewish Community Council reviewed its work over the past ten years, it credited Schermer with helping to stop the panic that had swept the Twelfth Street area in 1947. However, the review continued, since 1952 things had "seriously deteriorated," in no small measure due to Schermer's departure and because the new Commission for Community Relations "no longer does the job it was set up to do."[47] Even under Schermer, the Interracial Committee had been hard-pressed to do much beyond generate reports documenting racial tension and seed neighborhood meetings and grassroots organizations to ease tensions. Without the power of enforcement, liberal agencies and civic groups could make statements eschewing prejudice and discrimination, but little else.

Changing Neighborhoods: A Local and National Issue

In 1952, member organizations of the National Community Relations Advisory Council (NCRAC) sponsored the first nationwide study of housing from a Jewish perspective called "Equal Opportunity in Housing: A Handbook of Facts." From that point forward, NCRAC, founded in 1944 as a Jewish defense organization and a coordinating body for other Jewish community relations groups (primarily Jewish community councils) in cities across the country, committed itself to solving the problems of housing discrimination and neighborhood change. The 1952 handbook, distributed to urban community relations organizations, made the case for Jews' investment in housing problems: "The Jewish organizations sponsoring this pamphlet are peculiarly alert to the dangers to democracy arising from racial or religious residential segregation. Jewish experience under European despotism gave rise to the word 'ghetto.' The revival of that institution in American cities demands action."[48]

In truth, housing problems had more pressing relevance to Jewish life than Jews' generic concern for the protection of democracy. A memo from NCRAC to Jewish leaders explained that its deep concern with "neighborhood change" emerged from "the movement of Negroes into predominantly Jewish neighborhoods" and the sense that Jewish neighborhoods were disproportionately targets of black settlement when compared to other white urban neighborhoods.[49] NCRAC resolved in 1953 to create a permanent committee on Discrimination in Housing and charged the committee with studying neighborhood change and making recommendations to urban Jewish communities struggling with the problem.[50]

By the early 1950s, the terms "neighborhood change" and "changing neighborhood" appeared with higher frequency than ever in the Jewish and non-Jewish press, Jewish institutional records, and rabbis' sermons throughout American cities. The word "change" represented a careful choice; it was value neutral and communicated a measure of inevitability since change is always happening. In creating a common vocabulary, the discourse of neighborhood change also provided the comfort of shared experience. Even as neighborhood change seemed to point to a very local phenomenon, it also gestured toward something more general and ubiquitous than any single place. As discussions about neighborhood change universalized the problem, Jewish leaders still fixated their attention on short-term efforts to stabilize specific neighborhoods, but they also thought about the connections between their own neighborhood problems and broader forces. Real estate practices remained foremost on their minds and pushed them to think about how the practices in one neighborhood affected other places. Gradually, Jewish leaders also confronted city policies, such as slum clearance and urban renewal, which made it difficult to find solutions to the problems of changing Jewish neighborhoods solely within the Jewish neighborhood.

When NCRAC decided in 1953 to conduct a study of neighborhood change, it invited urban Jewish leaders from across the country to join the enterprise. Boris Joffe and William Cohen, leaders of Detroit's Jewish Community Council, were among the eleven representatives chosen to join a group of men that included high-profile national leaders from organizations such as the American Jewish Congress and the Jewish Labor Committee. They gathered in New York City in January 1953 to create an agenda for a national effort to help Jews encounter "tension resulting from changing neighborhoods, usually involving the movement of Negroes into predominantly Jewish communities."[51]

The men on the committee all agreed that the issue could not be met with a simple mandate that Jews desist from all forms of housing discrimination. Decisions about where to buy a home and when to move always rested on personal preferences and affected one's most precious assets—family and wealth. The members of the housing committee acknowledged, "Discrimination in housing is perhaps the most important and the most difficult of all fields of discrimination, particularly in the area of private housing."[52] The group believed that housing represented a personal decision and that people had the right to surround themselves with the material circumstances they desired and could afford. But it also deemed certain forces artificial and harmful in influencing housing decisions. The group did not seek to change the structure of private property in the United States; rather, the committee of Jewish leaders sought to purify the housing market. The leaders hoped that by ridding the market of discriminatory forces disrupting its assumedly natural mechanisms of self-regulation, the right to private property would be equitably protected.

NCRAC members acknowledged that for all the positive action that Jews had achieved to combat other forms of discrimination, such as employment and educational, "one area in which progress has been less rapid is that of discrimination in housing."[53] Jewish leaders were concerned that unless they made a case for the immediate relevance of housing discrimination to Jews, most Jews would not embrace it as an important cause. For community leaders, who were involved in thinking about Jewish institutions and their futures, the case was as evident as the synagogues that were saddled with buildings in once-Jewish neighborhoods and the Jewish institutions trying to figure out the next place to move, hoping that their brick-and-mortar investments would last beyond a decade. For many other Jews, however, the case was not nearly as clear. To be certain, many mourned what they saw as the demise of old Jewish neighborhoods. But new homes and attractive mortgages were available to them.

By the mid-1950s, NCRAC leaders pursued a dual-pronged agenda to help direct Jewish attention to housing problems in American cities. First, they attempted to convince Jews that housing discrimination was akin to any other form of discrimination and, if tolerated, it would eventually hurt all minority groups: "Believing as we do that all forms of racial and religious discrimination are inconsistent with Jewish religious and ethical values and the American ideal, we pledge our efforts toward the application of the principle of equality to every citizen's great necessity, a home for his family."[54] Second, they sought to persuade Jews that it was in their self-interest to stop discrimination in public and private housing. Otherwise, Jewish leaders warned, Jews would make easy prey for unscrupulous real estate agents looking to make a handsome profit by steering black families into the few neighborhoods, including many Jewish ones, that eschewed violence, and by blockbusting—using one or two strategic sales to black families as a means to get an entire block's worth of white families to move. According to a 1953 statement released by the NCRAC: "Such practices prevent the natural and gradual movement of families, whatever their origin, in all parts of the city in accordance with their means and desires. Thus, in the long run, solution of the problems caused by neighborhood changes must be sought in the elimination of discrimination."[55] The problem with housing discrimination was not that Jews suffered directly from it; only a few neighborhoods still excluded Jews from settling in them. The problem with housing discrimination, in the eyes of Jewish leaders, was that it unnaturally deteriorated the bulwark of Jewish life and investment: the urban Jewish neighborhood.

Joffe and Cohen, the two Detroit representatives to the 1953 NCRAC meeting, rather bullishly reported that the Jewish Community Council in Detroit had succeeded in "slowing down the movement of Jews out of the [Twelfth Street] area and . . . allaying panic." Their triumphant boast earned them the task of gathering data and cataloguing the effective ways that urban Jewish neighborhoods had dealt with neighborhood change.[56] An initial report on their findings, based upon surveys sent to twelve major cities with large Jewish populations, did not offer conclusive evidence that neighborhood change disproportionately affected Jewish neighborhoods more than other white urban neighborhoods. Nonetheless, Joffe and Cohen suggested that Detroit's set of responses to neighborhood change, which increasingly focused on monitoring real estate agents' behaviors, could serve as a guide for other American cities, and they plainly asserted, "Jews are more often involved in changing neighborhood problems [than other groups]."[57] The insight that Jews were special victims of neighborhood change because of the demographic trends of black settlement became common wisdom in urban areas throughout the country by the mid-1950s.

Detroit leaders, in offering their actions as a national model, believed they could help other Jewish leaders slow the pace of Jewish movement and work toward ridding the housing market and real estate industry of artificial discriminatory mechanisms. Yet the means of doing so by the mid-1950s still rested almost entirely on the strategy of persuasion: Jews could learn to see their neighborhoods as good places to live even after blacks moved in; real estate agents could be dissuaded from steering and blockbusting; and neighborhood associations could keep their hands on the pulse of neighborhood life, defusing conflict before it occurred.

In 1954, Will Maslow, who had recently joined the national leadership of the American Jewish Congress as its general counsel, wrote, "We must recognize that for some problems, such as racial and religious discrimination by private landlords, it is visionary at this time to talk of comprehensive legislation. No legislature in the country is ready to compel lily white neighborhoods to admit Negro householders."[58] Although Maslow believed that social attitudes could change as a result of legislative reform, he also maintained that prematurely enacted legislative changes were bound to fail. Even though that same year a new Federal Housing

Act passed providing broad-based incentives for urban renewal projects and slum clearance, Maslow did not believe that necessary popular support existed to regulate discrimination in the private housing industry. With a measure of resignation, he concluded, "For years we will have to rely on the slow forces of persuasion and example to induce home owners in 'good' neighborhoods that their world, financial and social, will not tumble down if a Negro moves on that block."[59]

"It's Good to Live in the City." So said the Detroit City Plan Commission in a mid-1950s pamphlet about neighborhood conservation geared to persuade Detroiters to stay committed to living in their urban neighborhoods. Acknowledging that some urban neighborhoods had suffered blight and neglect over the past decade as federal money had been channeled away from cities, the authors of the pamphlet assured readers that the new Housing Act of 1954 promised to help cities improve their infrastructure. But individual action was still the building block of good city life and could return real value to neighborhoods on the brink of depreciation. The pamphlet instructed, "So the place to start is to talk to your neighbors. Get your neighbors to agree that you are living in a good neighborhood and want to keep it a good place to live."[60]

The Jewish Community Council continued to charge individuals with organizing block meetings, seeking out the truth instead of believing rumors about house sales, and resisting real estate pressure all in the name of slowing the pace of neighborhood change and creating a positive neighborhood environment. It even offered ongoing support for the East Side Merchants Association, a dwindling group of Jewish merchants who owned businesses in the Hastings Street area, explaining, "Its purposes are not only to eliminate unethical selling practices but also to develop a sense of responsibility to the community which the merchants serve, which might be translated in the Association's support of various civic and neighborhood endeavours."[61] Even as liberals started to think about the forces—whether unscrupulous real estate agents or discriminatory financing practices—beyond local neighborhood ones that caused urban neighborhood deterioration, they maintained their focus on individuals and neighborhoods.

In 1955, *Redbook* published an article entitled "We Refused to Give Up Our Homes" about a neighborhood in New Jersey. The subheading explained, "When Negroes moved in, the whites of Teaneck, New Jersey had three choices: drive them out, sell their own houses at a loss—or find a fair, peaceful solution." According to the article, the whites (many of whom were Jewish) chose the last option, the right option. They were able to succeed in finding a "peaceful solution" because of their own efforts to talk to each other and the new black homeowners who moved in and their ability to resist the emotions of panic. As a newcomer to the neighborhood, a white man, summed up, "I just happen to believe in democracy and want to live it."[62] Detroit Jews passed around reprints of the article. They had followed the situation closely since the past summer when the *New York Times* reported on the efforts of a group of neighbors to stop whites from fleeing Teaneck, and an editorial in the *Detroit Jewish News* had admonished, "Detroit especially should watch the results in the New Jersey city. Our community was among the first to suffer from rumors and from wholesale flights that have caused the Exodus of old to pale into insignificance compared with the exoduses that have changed neighborhoods in our city."[63]

Despite outward bravado that Detroit Jews would beat the odds and remain committed to their urban neighborhoods, many Jewish leaders by the mid-1950s quietly believed that city officials were willing to sacrifice Jewish neighborhoods if it meant insulating other white areas from black settlement. One internal document blamed the Commission on Community Relations for being far less effective than the Interracial Commission under Schermer had been in supporting blacks "in their right to buy and live where they choose." The report continued, "The result of the Commission's failure . . . has meant that the fear of violence has kept Negroes out of many white non-Jewish areas and channeled them into areas of Jewish residence."[64] Most immediately, these actions "greatly increase[d] the capital costs to the Jewish community."[65] Housing discrimination, even when it was not practiced against Jews, directly hurt them and their neighborhoods.

Special Victims and Model Solutions

Although the hypothesis that Jewish neighborhoods were targets of black settlement was never proved with any sound empirical data, local and national Jewish leaders convinced themselves that this was the case and would continue to be the case unless something changed. Only if the housing market and real estate practices were reformed to ease the pressure on Jewish neighborhoods to absorb such high numbers of black newcomers, then, Jewish leaders suggested, Jewish urban neighborhoods might endure into the future. Formalizing a new approach, the Jewish Community Council created a Changing Neighborhoods Committee in October 1955. In its first meeting, Joseph Fauman, a Detroit-born sociologist who had been hired in the late 1940s as a staff researcher at the Jewish Community Council, explained that the council's approach to stabilize neighborhoods and slow the rate of change no longer worked in the face of new housing shortages confronted by black residents in Detroit.[66] Recent city policies drew on federal funds to displace black families in the name of "slum clearance, expressway development, and urban renewal or redevelopment programs" without planning for the resettlement of these families. Fauman explained, "The lack of violence as Negroes move into areas in which Jews reside has meant that disproportionate numbers of Negro families have moved and wish to move into these areas."[67]

As it became commonly accepted among Jewish leaders that Jewish neighborhoods were special victims of the city's racial and housing policies, they looked for solutions to their neighborhood woes outside of the confines of their own neighborhood space. Noting that blacks were barred from purchasing almost all of the new homes built in the last decade, the council's resident sociologist, Fauman, explained to the Changing Neighborhoods Committee just how far-reaching this discriminatory policy was. Blacks were forced to narrow their housing search to older housing stock and, thus, could not apply for the same attractive financing terms that whites buying new homes throughout the city had available to them and, instead, often purchased homes on land contracts with punishing terms. Fauman, lecturing the assembled group, concluded that a mix of economics and social policy channeled blacks able to afford homes into those few neighborhoods with older housing stock and with residents who did not threaten to respond with violence—in other words, into Jewish neighborhoods. By understanding black settlement as a response to forces beyond Jews' making, the Jewish Community Council fueled a rhetoric of Jewish victimization at the same time that it started to consider large-scale reform as the only answer to the changing-neighborhood problem.[68]

As pressure mounted on Jewish neighborhoods, Jewish leaders worried that Jews, especially those who were unable or did not wish to leave the neighborhood, needed strategies to feel in control of their surroundings without being blamed by or falling prey to the mentality of an angry mob. In the fall of 1955, Fauman and the council had watched a handful of blocks in northwest Detroit anxiously, concerned that Jews were being enticed to join a vigilante mob to patrol the neighborhood from black incursions. Fauman, acting as an undercover informant to the Jewish Community Council, attended a meeting among homeowners in the neighborhood and watched in disgust as the 350 attendees, three-quarters of whom he was certain were Jewish, agreed to try to raise the funds to buy a home rumored to be on the brink of being sold to a black family. Fauman wrote of the Jews in attendance, "The majority of them were young home owners under the age of forty. Quite a number of them were members of B'nai B'rith lodges who had come to the meeting on their way to bowling, and from the conversations I overheard were entirely in agreement with what was being done."[69] Only one person, a Jewish woman, spoke out against the tenor of the meeting. She compared the tactics being considered to those used in Nazi Germany and the American South. The crowd surged against her and accused her of being a communist.

Referring to this meeting in his first report to the Changing Neighborhoods Committee, Fauman explained, "In one area a large number of Jewish residents have been panicked by the threat of the sale of one home and have joined civic associations and lent their support to precisely the type of activities which have exacerbated Negro-white relations in the past and have been used against Jews as well." Fauman recommended that the council act on its commitment to "extending equality of opportunity in the sale and rental of all housing to all Americans," and that it direct its efforts to the "maintenance of areas of Jewish residence and communal facilities."[70]

In 1956, when NCRAC published its "Guide to Changing Neighborhoods," authored by none other than Fauman (along with a leader at the American Jewish Congress), the manual made clear that unless the Jewish community clearly addressed neighborhood change, it would lose whatever power it possessed to shape its own political and ideological narrative about Jewish attitudes toward race and racism. According to NCRAC, without a coherent statement about the Jewish approach to neighborhood change, Jews who left urban neighborhoods would appear to be fleeing from blacks; Jews who stayed in these neighborhoods would appear to be thwarting their own and the community's socioeconomic ambitions; and Jews who stayed in the neighborhoods and fought against the "changes" would appear to be making common cause with white racists or radical leftists. Of course, each of these scenarios could be true, and not just a matter of perception, but NCRAC hoped to craft a unified Jewish approach to neighborhood change that could sway Jews' behavior and, also, Jewish and non-Jewish perceptions of that behavior.

An introduction to the NCRAC manual stated clearly that "only programs that accord with our convictions as Jews and Americans that every man has a right to full equality" were included in the manual. The authors implied that these tests—the Jewishness and Americanness of any particular response to neighborhood change—were one in the same. Yet from its assertion that Jewish neighborhoods were disproportionately targets of black settlement to the difficulty the authors had defining why neighborhood change had to be managed, the manual revealed that Jewish convictions did not simply mirror or amplify American ones. The heart of the issue for the Jewish leaders who wrote and distributed the guide widely was not housing discrimination; rather, it was more specifically ending the kinds of discrimination that they believed caused aftershocks in Jewish neighborhoods and made racism or radicalism appear the only possible responses. The solution, according to the manual, was to rid the housing market of racial discrimination by monitoring the actions of buyers, sellers, and their agents.

The manual represented the first time that Jewish leaders used the term "open occupancy" as a programmatic solution to Jewish urban woes. In endorsing open occupancy, these leaders hoped to find a way out of the corner into which they believed they had been backed. They sought to create an activist housing market that could disperse black families throughout the urban landscape and, thus, break up the tight connection between race and geography that had long characterized American cities. In turning toward open occupancy, Jewish leaders stepped in time with broader housing reform efforts. NCRAC had initiated conversations with Charles Abrams, a housing activist who was Jewish, and asked him to read drafts of its housing statements. In response, Abrams suggested the group would suffer from myopia if it only examined its own neighborhoods without thinking about the implications of state and national housing policy. The Federal Housing Administration, he wrote, could be "the most important factor in encouraging and can be the most important factor in discouraging discrimination," particularly in private housing.[71] When it came time to draft the 1956 manual on changing neighborhoods, the authors quoted Abrams at length to explain the evolution of housing discrimination and why it plagued Jewish neighborhoods. As such, the manual asserted that individuals or even specific neighborhoods were not alone responsible for the situation that existed in cities.

One of the clearest pieces of advice offered in the "Guide to Changing Neighborhoods" was to involve "spiritual leaders" in the effort to end housing discrimination. The authors explained, "The moral values of religion and the prestige of community leadership can weigh the scales in favor of democracy in housing."[72] Furthermore, with religion on their side, Jewish housing activists could "make clear their total dissociation from the Communists" and leftist elements that NCRAC and other liberal Jews continued to fear would taint their liberal housing efforts.[73]

Importantly, the manual did not equate open occupancy with integration. Open occupancy aimed to remove discriminatory barriers in housing sales, but Jewish leaders understood its results in terms of fairness and rights (basic liberal ideals) and not necessarily racial integration. They understood racial integration as a much more radical social, political, and economic program that demanded the sharing of space, resources, and power with black families. In fact, the authors explained, "Minority groups in America have always shown some tendency to live together and there are many who believe, as to religious groups at least, that this tendency is desirable and necessary."[74] The idea of the ethnic neighborhood, so ingrained into American urban space, appeared to chafe against programs of integration; support for open occupancy, on the other hand, did not demand a disruption to that ideal.

Although it demanded activist governmental enforcement, open occupancy had a libertarian ethos to it. People should be able to move to wherever they wanted as long as they had the means to do so. Thus, the capitalist workings of the housing market could remain intact. Indeed, devotees of open occupancy believed that theirs was an effort to return the housing market to its pure capitalist workings by ridding it of discrimination that could artificially inflate or deflate market prices.

Midcentury liberal Jewish leaders expected that most Jews would want to live near other Jews and live in relatively urban areas—and they had demographics on their side to support these expectations. If through efforts to reform real estate agents' practices and legislative reform they could help make open occupancy a reality, then they believed they would have found a way to balance the ideal of a Jewish neighborhood with the ideals of capitalist democracy.

CHAPTER FOUR

From Neighborhood to City
The Formation of Jewish Metropolitan Urbanism

"For young moderns," the advertisement announced, drawing readers' eyes to a sketch of a chic woman and photograph of a tidy ranch home. She and the newly built home shared sharp lines—sculpted eyebrows and a flipped collar in her case, and a long low roof in the home's case. Readers of the *Detroit Jewish News* who would have seen this advertisement in the fall of 1959 learned that the house, like the woman, struck a balance between sophistication and middle-class comfort: "The carefree ease of suburban living, rarely found within city limits, awaits young moderns seeking every urban convenience in one of northwest Detroit's last and most fashionable residential areas."[1] Close to several already established white neighborhoods and an easy drive to the Lodge Freeway that connected the northwest of the city and its suburbs to downtown, Jewish builder Harry Slatkin's new development promised the best of urban and suburban living. His homes were priced at $17,000, affordable to white middle-class families with access to bank financing.

Still, these same newspaper readers might have perceived a eulogy cloaked beneath the sales pitch: What did the "last" residential area mean? The admen likely intended to imply that all other available land in the city had been developed. But the word "last" also suggested that Jewish residential life in northwest Detroit or the city more generally was entering a final phase. Only a few years earlier, in 1953, Slatkin had proposed extending an existing concrete wall in northwest Detroit to divide the "last fashionable residential area," his development, from other parts of the city's northwest reaches. Built in the early 1940s, the wall had offered proof to the Federal Housing Administration and its home loan assessors that a sharp line, in the form of a six-foot-tall concrete barrier, separated whites and blacks in northwest Detroit. Slatkin had hoped he might snake the wall around the property he owned to protect his investment from black settlement.[2] The city rejected his 1953 effort to elongate the wall, but Slatkin's housing developments, similar to many other residential developments in that area of the city, were bound by other walls—in the forms of individuals' attitudes, homeowners' associations, real estate practices, and federal policies—intended to keep blacks out.

By now, you might think, I get it; as went the Twelfth Street and Dexter neighborhoods, so went northwest Detroit. If one is interested only in the physical movement of people, then yes, this is not a new story line. Yet in the northwest areas of Detroit in the late 1950s and early 1960s, Jews' connection to the city underwent a transformation. In this space and this time, Jews came to see themselves through a geographic and ideological lens that broadened the sphere of their interests and investments beyond their neighborhoods and toward the city and, eventually, the metropolitan region as a whole.

Three key transformations occurred between the late 1950s and the mid-1960s that characterized the development of what I call Jewish metropolitan urbanism. First, Jews increasingly linked their neighborhood struggles with larger city, state, and national issues. They came to see their neighborhood problems as tied to broader city trends, and, thus, believed that solutions could not emerge solely from block activism and neighborhood associations. National Jewish organizations supported the new belief that Jews had to think and work beyond their neighborhoods and helped foster conversations among Jews living in different cities but also facing similar struggles.

Second, and connected to Jews' growing perception of their neighborhoods as part of a larger urban fabric, was the conviction that neighborhood struggles would not be solved through neighborhood activism alone; rather, legislation and the courts had to be harnessed to create lasting solutions. The fact that Jews at the time were gaining political power, through appointed and elected positions, enabled them to feel more confident that the political process could and should remedy the urban problems they experienced. Nonetheless, Jews also understood that their power was limited, and in these years, they became more skilled than ever before at working through coalitions, especially liberal ones, which stood on the eroding ground between the city's white conservatives and black separatist, nationalist, and radical groups.

Faith-based coalitions were among the most powerful ones in which Jews participated. The third characteristic of Jews' metropolitan urbanism was its reliance on the language and organization of faith and spirituality. Jews engaged with like-minded spiritual leaders to approach city problems from a moral high ground, often calling upon Judeo-Christian values to validate their efforts. They simultaneously invoked Jewish values, a supple yet forceful concept, to draw an intrinsic connection between being Jewish and working toward ideals of urban justice. Yet in asserting that Jews, by the very fact of their Jewishness, cared about injustices in the city, they also fostered a level of complacency, where the fact of one's Jewishness could stand in, at times, for concrete action.

From the northwestern city limits of Detroit, Jews developed a metropolitan identity that they eventually carried with them as they left the city. In the late 1950s, Jews in cities throughout the United States started to use the word "metropolitan" to describe themselves, even as a majority of Jews still resided within city limits. For example, in 1958, at a time when only 21 percent of the Jewish population had moved to the suburbs, the Jewish Community Council of Detroit changed its name to the Jewish Community Council of Metropolitan Detroit.[3] The term was appealingly flexible, denoting an urban zone without quibbling over municipal boundaries, township lines, or other kinds of political jurisdictions. It covered a broad terrain but still offered geographical specificity by rhetorically tying suburbs and newly built communities to the familiarity of the city. As residents of a metropolitan region, Jews could profess that they were still politically, culturally, and spiritually of the city, wherever they happened to live.

In this chapter and the next one, I chart the shifts that made Jewish metropolitan urbanism possible and historically significant, even if deeply marked by contradictions and ambivalence. This chapter focuses on the ways in which Jews from the late 1950s through early 1960s developed an identification with the city as a whole for a sense of orientation and as the locus of concern. The next chapter turns its attention to Jewish efforts, especially related to plans from the mid-1950s to the 1970s to relocate synagogues to the suburbs, to understand themselves as stitching together urban and suburban life through their political, economic, and spiritual lives.

The Politics of Home in the Northwest

By 1959, nearly half of all Jews in Detroit lived in the northwest zone of Detroit.[4] Although the area was relatively large, extending roughly five miles west from Woodward Avenue and two miles south of Eight Mile Road, Jews tended to settle in small pockets. The densest concentration of Jews lived in the one-square-mile Bagley neighborhood. By the early 1960s, the neighborhood's population was over two-thirds Jewish.[5] Bordering Bagley, especially to the north and west, were several other white neighborhoods. Though none had nearly as high of a concentration of Jews as Bagley, Jews lived in all of them. So when in the 1950s, black families started to move into these neighborhoods, Jews paid attention, especially to the homeowners' associations that formed quickly.

The Jewish Community Council, following its typical protocol, sought Jewish informants to attend homeowner association meetings and file reports. In the spring of 1956, Joseph Fauman, who had joined the council as a staff member in the late 1940s to research Jewish group relations, became a member of the Blenheim Forest District Improvement Association, an organization that served homeowners just north of Bagley. He recalled, "It was felt at this time that, as part of the Council's policy to help develop community organizations of neighborhood residents devoted to the maintenance of sound neighborhoods and open to all without regard to race, creed, color or national origin, it was most desirable for me to participate."[6] In time, he became the association's recording secretary, a position that gave him access to neighborhood rumors and activities. Often, he used his position to defuse the board's anxiety about black families buying homes in the neighborhood and enrolling their children in neighborhood schools. Despite his efforts, the board continued to worry that the settlement of black families would harm the neighborhood, and it was poised to do whatever it needed to do, including purchase homes on the market, to prevent blacks from moving in. Fauman wondered to his superiors at the Jewish Community Council whether he should remain a participant-informant on the board or whether doing so would compromise the credibility of the Jewish Community Council in the eyes of black Detroiters and others who believed in fair housing. Nonetheless, throughout the late 1950s, the council continued to send informants to neighborhood meetings in northwest Detroit, no matter how racist and vitriolic their tenor.[7]

By the beginning of 1958, the Changing Neighborhoods Committee (which had been created in 1955) authorized work to dispel rumors and organize neighborhood groups in northwest Detroit, a sign, if history was any guide, that it did not expect Jewish life to endure there for very long.[8] That year, at the Jewish Community Council's annual assembly, Fauman and Albert Mayer presented a panel called "Neighborhoods in Transition." Mayer, on the faculty at Wayne State University, had a regular contract with the Jewish Federation of Detroit to perform demographic studies. Far from detached scholarship, his demographic studies weighed in on pressing community questions. Just one year prior, in 1957, he had used his data to project the future distribution of the Jewish population and written that these projections could be "used as a guide in making a judgment in locating the site for the [Jewish Community] Center Main Building."[9] Leaders heeded his recommendation to build in northwest Detroit, though he warned that the life span of the building would be no more than twenty-five years, at which time the main center would surely move to the suburbs. Mayer translated his descriptive demography into prescription.

In their panel on "Neighborhoods in Transition," Fauman and Mayer explained that a number of factors contributed to high rates of Jewish mobility. Chief among these was the "ready made" housing market that black homebuyers offered to Jews. "Negro purchasers," they explained, "have encountered no embarrassment or resistance when seeking to buy homes in predominantly Jewish neighborhoods."[10] Fauman must have realized this was an overstatement since the Jewish Community Council had very recently shifted its attention to the northwest area precisely because it was concerned that Jews were participating in ugly housing incidents. In the fall of that year, a rumor started in the Bagley neighborhood that a home recently put on the market was going to be sold to a black family. As soon as the council's Changing Neighborhoods Committee learned of plans for a meeting, it contacted "friends who live in this neighborhood" and urged them to attend and report back. From its informants, the council learned that one hundred people showed up for the meeting, and a plan to pool resources and buy the home failed only because the group could not raise the necessary funds. A member of the Changing Neighborhoods Committee reported on the pivotal role that it had played in mollifying the situation: "Several persons we alerted made strong appeals to judge neighbors as individuals. As a result, no action was taken to buy up the house and no further meetings of this nature have been called."[11]

In the neighborhoods surrounding Bagley, however, the Changing

Neighborhoods Committee found that it could not quell rumors and racist responses quite as handily. These neighborhoods all had Jews living in them, though in none of them were Jews nearly as dominant a group as they were in Bagley. Members of the Changing Neighborhoods Committee were concerned that even if Jews did not directly participate in racist neighborhood activities, they would be brought into them as victims, since they would be blamed for bringing blacks into the neighborhood. In early 1959, the Ruritan Park Civic Association that served several blocks just south of Bagley met to drum up support for an "option agreement." In its literature, the association explained that the agreement was a nonviolent means to maintain the value of the neighborhood and "protect our homes." People who signed it agreed to act in a community-minded way and seek the neighborhood association's approval before selling their home to anyone.[12] The Changing Neighborhoods Committee planted "friends" at the meeting "so that persons there could be advised against panic selling or affiliation with an organization having a racist background." Nonetheless, a number of Jews (and non-Jews) signed the informal restrictive covenant, described by a member of the Changing Neighborhoods Committee as an "unenforceable restrictive covenant which might tie up in red tape the sale of property to 'undesirables' (Negroes)."[13]

The Ruritan Park Civic Association threatened to erase the thin line separating liberal neighborhood activism from racist neighborhood activism. Using liberal language, the leaders of the association explained, "We believe in equal opportunity for all in employment, housing and all phases of life." They simply did not believe that black families had to pursue their equality in white neighborhoods. The group also requested that neighbors watch out for one another and let the association know immediately if they saw a home being shown to "undesirables."[14] Indeed, the Jewish Community Council similarly instructed its members and friends to notify the council with any rumors about homes being shown or sold to black families. For example, in the spring of 1959, a Jewish woman, Betty Stearns, informed the council about a rumor concerning the sale of a home on the border of Bagley and Ruritan Park. The staff person asked her to keep an eye on the situation and to "continue to assure her neighbors of the necessity for not spreading unfounded rumors or engaging in loose talk which would only result to the detriment of all the residents."[15] The Jewish Community Council generally believed a matter was resolved successfully when rumors were proved wrong and the home was either taken off the market or not sold to a black family.

The similarities between tactics used by liberal Jewish leaders and overtly racist homeowners associations did not end here. In the fall of 1959, the Ruritan Park Civic Association called a neighborhood meeting to talk about three homes being sold through black real estate agents. The leaders assured residents that the sellers had all signed option agreements, but that the problem was finding enough white buyers. Liberal leaders, including Jewish ones, concerned about neighborhood change and real estate practices shared the worry and, in fact, shared one of the Ruritan Park Civic Association's strategies: limiting the number of for-sale signs as a way to convince white buyers of a neighborhood's stability. Association leaders instructed residents not to post more than two for-sale signs on any block for fear that too many signs would "prove alarming to prospective purchasers."[16] The Jewish Community Council would soon endorse a city ordinance to put similar restrictions on posting for-sale signs.

Liberals and the racist homeowners' association were furthermore joined by their burgeoning efforts to commandeer the legislative process in their favor. Just as the Jewish Community Council started to lobby for fair-housing laws and city ordinances, the Ruritan Park Civic Association urged its residents to broaden their political horizons as well and pressure legislators against fair-housing policies. The leaders instructed, "Vote against legislators who support so-called 'Civil Rights' legislation that in reality has the effect of taking away your right to live in a neighborhood of your own people."[17] Mrs. Shapiro, who attended a Ruritan Park Civic Association meeting in January 1959 at the behest of the Changing Neighborhoods Committee, reported that the bulk of discussion had focused on defeating fair-housing legislation.

By the early 1960s, the predominantly Jewish and liberal population in northwest Detroit created its own neighborhood association. The Bagley Community Council, incorporated in October 1961, served the four thousand families who occupied a one-square-mile area. Over two-thirds of the residents in this area were Jewish. Adas Shalom, a Conservative synagogue, anchored Jewish life in the neighborhood. A Congregationalist church and the local elementary school (Bagley Elementary School) also grounded liberal activism in the neighborhood.[18]

From its inception, the Bagley Community Council set about the task of distinguishing itself from neighboring homeowners' associations through its Jewishness and liberalism. Jews constituted over half of its board members and an even greater percentage of its membership, and the Jewish Community Council funded a part-time secretary for the group.[19] Jacob

Segal, the rabbi at Adas Shalom, played an active role in the group and mobilized his congregants' support. In an article published shortly after the Bagley group was founded, the *Detroit News* explained, "There are homeowners' groups and homeowners' groups. They can be a force of sane, humane preservation of what makes a neighborhood good to live in, or a force—unwittingly or otherwise—for disorder and hate." Bagley was the former. The article continued, "Its members have taken the only stand compatible with our American ideal: That a man be judged by what his individual works show him to be, not prejudged by what his race, creed or national origin lead narrow minds to assume he is."[20]

In its composition and political proclivities, the Bagley Community Council appeared an offspring of the Midtown Neighborhood Council, the Twelfth Street group that had vowed to stabilize the changing neighborhood. As the Bagley group formed, initially through a meeting of the Bagley Elementary School Parent Teacher Association, neighbors talked together about the local changes that concerned them: ripped screen doors; unkempt lawns; multiple families living in single homes.[21] And much as it had over a decade earlier for the Twelfth Street group, the Jewish Community Council took the lead in organizing a plan of action that involved cleanup efforts and frequent neighborhood meetings.

Yet whereas the Twelfth Street group had set its sights clearly on the neighborhood, the Bagley group tied its work to a much larger urban frame that intersected with city, state, and federal housing policies. Irving Rubin, the Jewish man who was elected the first president of the group, worked for the Michigan State Highway Department and guided the Bagley Community Council to think of its activism in broad political terms. Doubtful that a moral case would convince white families to stay in the neighborhood, Rubin suggested that only a serious legislative effort throughout the city could change the demographic trends that had long hurt Jewish neighborhoods in the city.

Similar to other liberal Jewish leaders, Rubin set an agenda for the Bagley Community Council to endorse open occupancy and self-consciously disentangled open occupancy from integration. In a presentation to the Jewish Community Council, Rubin explained, "We are not for integration and we are not against integration. We are for an open housing market all through the city."[22] A fair-housing market, he suggested, would prevent certain neighborhoods from believing they were "safe" from black settlement and would convince homeowners that "fleeing is futile."[23] In distancing open occupancy from racial integration, Rubin suggested that one could sign onto the goal of ridding the housing market of unfair discriminatory measures without endorsing social or political programs aimed to redistribute space, power, or resources equitably among black and white people.

Whereas the Midtown Neighborhood Council had thought of its work on the neighborhood level—as an effort to solve a neighborhood problem—the Bagley Community Council envisioned itself as operating on a citywide stage in a way that, it hoped, would benefit the neighborhood. Neither the problem nor the solution could be found solely in the neighborhood. Indeed, the more Jews set out to influence city politics and the more they thought of themselves in broader urban terms, the less they felt tied to the particular space of their city neighborhoods.

The Jewish Neighborhood Reimagined

Demographer Albert Mayer noted in 1958 that Jews had become more geographically dispersed than ever and this fact made it much more difficult to think about Jewish life in terms of one—or even a handful—of neighborhoods.[24] Yet the idea of the neighborhood endured as a communal value; that is, Jewish leaders believed that Jewish life was best lived in close proximity to other Jews and Jewish institutions. At a Changing Neighborhoods Committee meeting in the fall of 1959, one member discussed the "values emerging from the deep integration of institutions into community life, of psychological rootedness in place and peoplehood." He continued, "Communities constantly moving and running live on the surface of Jewish life, and experience only a superficial sense of Jewish identity and belongingness."[25]

Jewish leaders and ordinary Jews romanticized the Jewish neighborhood in the late 1950s in response to fears that American-Jewish life was becoming inauthentic or untrue to itself in its middle-class incarnations. In the eyes of social critics, the growing middle class clawed its way into conformity without realizing how ruinous—for self, community, and nation—this conformity truly was. Some of the most notable figures voicing this criticism were Jews themselves, who lamented the cultural, political, and spiritual losses connected to socioeconomic and geographic mobility. And whether or not they were Jewish themselves, many critics highlighted Jews as consummate middle-class Americans, through whom one could observe the cancerous conformity of middle-class suburban living. William Whyte, in his 1956 book *The Organization Man*, observed, "Not only does suburbia tend to attract Jews who are less 'different'; it speeds up the process in which anyone—Jewish or non-Jewish—becomes even less 'different.'"[26] Without a doubt, popular social criticism of the 1950s weighed heavily on Jews' concerns about leaving urban neighborhoods.

The homeowners in Russel Woods, a small enclave of upper-middle-class housing in the Dexter area, had believed briefly that the combination of their liberalism and their economic status could protect their half a square mile from the forces that were eroding Jewish urban neighborhood life. In its early days, a civic association, founded just as the area was being developed in the 1920s, had guarded the racial and economic profile of the neighborhood, using zoning ordinances to maintain the single-family and white Christian uniformity of the area. With little fanfare, Jews started to move into Russel Woods after the Great Depression. By 1952 about 60 percent of the homeowners were Jewish, primarily intellectuals and professionals with liberal political views.[27] In 1955, the first black person bought a home in the neighborhood, but almost immediately sold it to the all-white neighborhood association. The new owner had purchased the home on a land contract with undesirable terms and claimed to be reluctant, in any case, to settle in a white neighborhood. Yet a few weeks later, a black lawyer bought a different home and settled in Russel Woods. Over the next year, black families purchased forty neighborhood homes, many of them bought through land contracts, which required small down payments from buyers but charged punishingly high interest rates and enabled sellers to hold the deeds to the homes until the final payment was made.[28]

In the late 1950s, a group of predominantly Jewish residents of Russel Woods decided to form a new neighborhood association that allowed black residents to join and embraced a liberal vision of the neighborhood as a cosmopolitan and stable urban space. Edward Pintzuk, president of the newly formed association, praised Russel Woods in a neighborhood newsletter from 1959 for balancing the "fine qualities of suburban living—our beautiful homes with spacious lawns, and majestic trees—... with the advantages of city living."[29] Pintzuk, a Jewish podiatrist with clear leftist leanings, also wrote deep analyses of the housing market for the neighborhood newsletter. The integrated neighborhood association understood Russel Woods' precarious position as the one remaining island of Jewish settlement in the Dexter neighborhood and worked tirelessly

FIGURE 4.1 Russel Woods, c. 1960s–1970s. Courtesy of Walter P. Reuther Library, Archives of Labor and Urban Affairs, Wayne State University.

to protect its class character, describing it self-consciously as a "prestige community."[30] Similar to Boston-Edison homeowners, the association leaders believed that the true threat to the neighborhood had everything to do with class and little to do with race, and that if the upper-middle-class character of the neighborhood could be maintained, then the neighborhood itself would continue to thrive. The Russel Woods association improved traffic patterns, maintained vacant lots, stopped illegal parking, and prevented a bar from opening in the neighborhood, thanks to a group of Jewish attorneys who proved that the establishment violated a zoning ordinance prohibiting bars from being built too close to religious spaces (in this case, a synagogue).[31]

When by the end of the decade, over half of the residents in Russel Woods were black, the neighborhood association leaders came to understand that race and class would not be separated as neatly as they had hoped.[32] Some of the leaders entertained the idea of creating a campaign to target "Caucasian" homebuyers as a way to "conserve" the neighborhood and mount a defense against real estate agents. The plan received reprobation from the Jewish Community Council for potentially stirring up "serious community relations problems."[33] Local Jewish sociologists who studied the Russel Woods neighborhood believed that as individuals, the Jews who lived in it possessed "little prejudice themselves" against new black neighbors. But these same experts contended that individual attitudes were no match to persistent real estate solicitations. A full 60 percent of the residents, after all, reported being contacted on a weekly basis by real estate agents hungry to help them sell their homes. Furthermore, sociologists noted that city policies had created a housing shortage for black residents and put disproportionate pressure on Jewish neighborhoods.[34]

In the late 1950s and early 1960s, Jewish activists continued to assert that the Jewish neighborhood, wherever it was located, was worth saving but the only way to do so was to move ideologically, if not physically, beyond it. Activists in the Jewish Community Council's Changing Neighborhoods Committee suggested renaming their group the Neighborhoods and Housing Committee in order to indicate a newly broadened sphere of concern. One committee member explained, "The basic thesis of [this new] approach would be: to the extent that Negroes can and do obtain housing all over Detroit and in all sections of the tri-county area, to that extent abnormal pressure of Negro buying into the Jewish community might be reduced."[35]

Shmarya Kleinman, former president of the Jewish Community Council and a doctor who lived close to the upscale Palmer Park area of northwest Detroit, became the spokesperson for shifting the name and the purpose of liberal Jewish urban activism away from the neighborhood and toward the city as a whole.[36] Kleinman's involvement in Russian socialist politics before he came to the United States and his ongoing ties to progressive Jewish organizations such as the Jewish Labor Committee and the Workmen's Circle primed him to see Jewish neighborhoods through the frame of a larger political system.[37] In early 1960, as chair of the Changing Neighborhoods Committee, he explained, "It has now been universally recognized that work in neighborhoods, in blocks, even in areas of the city, will not alone be effective in normalizing housing patterns and in stabilizing neighborhoods on an integrated basis. The main emphasis has to be placed on achieving an open housing market all over the city. . . . Times have changed."[38] Even as he gestured toward integration as an ideal, Kleinman believed the more immediate and efficacious goal was citywide open occupancy. In a letter to Jacob Segal, the rabbi at Adas Shalom in the Bagley neighborhood, Kleinman wrote, "According to a re-evaluation of the challenge before us we dropped our emphasis upon 'change' and adopted an emphasis upon equal access to housing opportunity as the key to our problem."[39]

In confronting housing discrimination and not simply "neighborhood change," Jews navigated the difficult terrain of determining how an issue might be a Jewish one even when Jews were not always directly involved in it. A 1960 investigation revealing that Jews, among other minorities, had been systematically handicapped in their ability to purchase homes in the Grosse Pointe suburbs of Detroit stood out for Jewish leaders as the exception that proved the rule: in only very few cases did Jews face housing discrimination.[40] A NCRAC report from 1960 explained, "All of us are cognizant . . . that discrimination against Jews in housing is trivial in comparison with discrimination against Negroes; that it is an irritant and an affront to Jews, whereas it is a deprivation as well as a deep indignity to Negroes." Jewish leaders, the report admonished, should not concern themselves with the "occasional *Judenrein* [Jew-free, a term used by the Nazi regime] apartment houses or neighborhoods, but with those festering and unresolved problems created by the persistence of racial housing segregation in the cities and suburbs."[41] A few years later, NCRAC "took some gratification in the fact that Jewish organizations and individuals are prominently represented in citizens' fair housing bodies."[42] To liberal Jewish leaders, fair housing was a Jewish issue.

The realignment of Jewish urbanism with citywide and not uniquely Jewish interests occurred throughout the United States in the late 1950s and early 1960s. In part, national Jewish organizations, such as NCRAC, orchestrated the shift. By the late 1950s, NCRAC advised its constituent community agencies to lobby for nationwide open housing legislation. Starting in 1959, it requested those same agencies to mail the national office copies of their "statements of principle on housing discrimination."[43] Jewish organizations that lacked such statements heard this as a call to write one. Leaders of Detroit's Jewish Community Council communicated directly with NCRAC to ask for advice about how to craft a new statement about Jews' investment in open housing that balanced "our democratic and equalitarian American tradition" with "something . . . from the fact and practice of our Jewishness."[44]

In 1958 and 1959, Detroit Jewish leaders also collected open housing literature from Cleveland, Philadelphia, Queens, and several other urban communities in an effort to educate themselves.[45] After reading an article about Chicago's Hyde Park neighborhood, the president of the Jewish Community Council, Abraham Citron, wrote the author, a University of Chicago sociologist and a Jewish man, to discuss parallels between liberal activism in Hyde Park and in Detroit: "We here must deal with this problem on a city-wide, perhaps even tri-county-wide basis. I doubt if one neighborhood can be stable on an integrated basis unless many neighborhoods move together toward this goal."[46] Similar to Kleinman, Citron positioned residential integration as an abstract goal, but not a policy guide. He closed his letter with a request for twenty-five copies of the article to distribute to Jewish leaders in Detroit.

In the fall of 1961, reviewing the accomplishments of the recently renamed Neighborhoods and Housing Committee (which had replaced the Changing Neighborhoods Committee) over the past two years, Kleinman declared that a "major shift in orientation and practical aims" had occurred. He explained, "We are no longer in the patch-up or remedial business to stop panic, but are working to destroy all the props of discrimination in housing." Kleinman continued, "We consider that this is not only a Jewish issue, nor just a neighborhood issue, but a city, state and national issue."[47] Of course, the Jewish neighborhood had been central to the evolution of Jews' investment in the broader issue of open housing. Yet by the late 1950s and early 1960s, liberal Jews steadily moved away from their concern with changing neighborhoods and embraced citywide open housing.

Over the next several years, paralleling a shift toward a more progressive spirit in the city's and nation's governance, liberal groups increasingly turned to legislative answers to housing discrimination as a means to enforce the rhetoric of goodwill. Jewish leaders worked to guide the Jewish public to use its vote to redress housing discrimination, and, thus, to understand the changes occurring in Jewish neighborhoods as demanding a broader, citywide response than neighborhood activism could offer.

The Spiritual Politics of Jewish Urban Activism

When Jews left cities, leaders worried that the spiritual life of the community would wither. Many believed that an essential element of Jewish collectivity sprung forth from the experience of living together in a city. The theories of midcentury rabbi Mordecai Kaplan held great sway over the postwar generation of rabbis and their ideas about community. Hundreds of American rabbis trained under Kaplan, who taught at the Conservative Jewish Theological Seminary from 1910 to 1963, and generations of twentieth-century rabbis read his writings. First in an article he wrote in 1920 and then in his 1934 tome *Judaism as a Civilization*,

Kaplan advanced a "social" definition of Judaism: "That viewpoint," he explained, "will enable us to shift the center of spiritual interest from the realm of abstract dogmas and traditional codes of law to the pulsating life of Israel [i.e., the Jewish people]. We will then realize that our problem is not how to maintain belief or uphold laws, but how to enable the Jewish people to function as a highly-developed social organism and to fulfill the spiritual powers that are latent in it."[48]

Kaplan's formulation of spiritual life as coterminous with collective life, an adaptation of French Jewish sociologist Émile Durkheim's theory of religion, was so appealing because it unbound spirituality from theology by defining spirituality in distinctly human terms. What people ate, the music they listened to, the books they read, and the conversations they had, all of these things in Kaplan's definition could become acts connected to the spiritual life of Jews, defined by their collective survival. Perhaps more than anything else, where people lived, the streets on which they walked, the stores they patronized, the buildings they frequented, and the people who lived in their midst pulsated with spiritual meaning.[49]

Morris Adler, the rabbi of Shaarey Zedek, Detroit's largest Conservative congregation, considered Kaplan one of his teachers and felt a firm conviction that Jews enacted their Judaism through community and through the way they inhabited the places in which they lived. In 1956, Adler wrote a column in his synagogue's newsletter about neighborhood change on his own block in the Dexter neighborhood. A black family, he explained, had moved into the home next door to his. "What should my approach to them be?" he asked and then answered that he and his wife would accept them "openly and without prejudice" because the couple knew what it meant to enact democracy and to live according to true Jewish values.[50] The Jewish Community Council reproduced the column and sent it to all of its members. Yet many members of the council were also congregants at Shaarey Zedek, and they would have known that their synagogue owned land in the suburbs and had imminent plans to leave the city, joining the trend of several other Dexter-area synagogues.

In the same year that Adler wrote his column, Temple Beth El, the city's largest Reform congregation, hosted housing activist Charles Abrams to deliver a lecture entitled "Changing Neighborhoods." Temple Beth El's rabbi, Richard Hertz, and his board devoted substantial time and resources to coordinating the event, cosponsored by the Jewish Community Council, the local chapter of the American Jewish Committee, and Detroit's Commission on Human Relations. The organizers hoped Abrams would help Jews improve their relations with black newcomers to their neighborhoods. Yet reflecting the emergence of a broader Jewish perspective on urban housing, they also looked toward Abrams, well known for advocating judicial and legislative action against housing discrimination, to offer advice beyond the neighborhood sphere. In the wake of the lecture, Hertz wrote in a letter to Abrams that the housing activist had given "our people an enthusiastic lift."[51] Yet even more so than Adler, who expressed reservations about moving Shaarey Zedek to the suburbs, Hertz in those very same years passionately sought to move Temple Beth El out of the city.

At the precise moment when legions of Jews and synagogues left American cities, Jewish leaders cited urban-oriented activism as a constitutive element of Jewishness. In powerful terms, they connected urban activism to the spiritual core of Jewishness; a Jew was a Jew, in part, because he cared about the places—almost always imagined as urban places—where people struggled with poverty and discrimination. At a 1960 meeting of rabbis gathered to discuss changes occurring in northwest Detroit, the Jewish Community Council instructed the group, "We have a tremendous spiritual investment in the rootedness of this community, in its feeling of wholeness, future, and security."[52]

Even if Jews no longer inhabited the urban neighborhoods that Kaplan and other thinkers had imagined as forming the setting of Jewish collectivity, urban-oriented Jewish activism could become a new grounding of Jewish community. In the early 1960s, the Reform, Conservative, and Orthodox movements issued national statements compelling Jews to participate in the struggle to grant blacks full civil rights. The United Synagogue of America, the Conservative movement's denominational body, wrote, "We affirm that the Jew, as Jew, is inherently and personally committed to participate, to whatever degree he can, but participate he must in the struggle of the Negroes."[53] The statement passed by the Union of Orthodox Jewish Congregations similarly mandated "Jews to set an example in their personal lives of conduct of brotherly love extended equally to all good men."[54] When Jewish religious leaders demanded specific actions of their Jewish communities, they tended to focus on ways that Jews could act, often in interfaith coalitions, to improve race relations across cities and harness so-called inherent Jewish values to pressing social problems. But they almost never tried to make the case that Jewish values obligated Jews to remain in urban neighborhoods.

In 1960, for example, Jewish Community Council leaders joined a Catholic priest and a Protestant minister to initiate a "Covenant Card Campaign" in Detroit. Drawing on models from Cleveland, Minneapolis, and Ann Arbor, the group collected signatures from householders who promised to "welcome as neighbors any responsible person regardless of race, religion, or national origin" and then planned to publish the list of signees to show "there is no 'safe' place for a bigot, that in all sections of our city people of good-will are prepared to eliminate discrimination in housing."[55] In several ways, this campaign marked a crucial stage in the development of metropolitan Jewish urbanism. First, it was executed by an interfaith group, the kind of group that would gather many times over in the coming years to promulgate statements against housing discrimination. Second, it relied on "good-will," but appropriated language from case law and new legal statutes. A sample covenant card elided the boundary between moral behavior and law: "I believe that every person has the moral and legal right to rent, buy, or build a home anywhere.... I believe it is imperative for our metropolitan Detroit area that all persons of good will unite with others of like conviction to take an active role in helping to achieve this freedom of opportunity in housing."[56]

The Jewish Community Council's "Statement on Open Occupancy," released in 1961, similarly blurred the language of goodwill and legal compulsion: "If men of good will speak out they will find each other in every neighborhood.... [They will create] the fully open communities worthy of the stature of American democracy."[57] Yet neither the council statement nor the covenant card addressed the means of legal enforcement to ensure nondiscriminatory behavior. Rather, individuals were expected to feel inwardly compelled by religion or democracy to act. An interfaith statement written around the same time depicted open occupancy in similar terms as a religious or moral good and a democratic principle. For its force, it relied on moral persuasion, not legal enforcement: "We earnestly urge all who are members of churches and synagogues to wield their influence on the neighborhoods and neighborhood associations."[58]

Beyond the Neighborhood

The transformation in Jewish consciousness away from local neighborhood activism toward a citywide and, eventually, metropolitan perspective gained sanction in spiritual language and from spiritual leaders, but was made possible by Jews' growing economic and political power in the postwar years. A survey from the late 1950s found that almost three-quarters of Detroit's Jewish household heads (all men) held white-collar jobs.

Furthermore, Jews in the city had attained levels of education commensurate with the white Protestant population. Finally, a greater number of Jews than ever before held political posts, due, in part, to gubernatorial appointments made in the late 1950s.[59] As Jews entered new positions of power, they also gained the skills to navigate modes of power, such as the law, to achieve their desired ends.

In the mid-1950s, a Jewish man named Mel Ravitz emerged as an activist for housing reform in Detroit and, in his efforts, he helped solidify a new alignment of Jewish and urban interests. Ravitz, born in New York City in 1924 but a resident of Detroit from a young age, earned his doctorate in sociology from the University of Michigan and then joined the faculty of Wayne State. In 1953, Detroit's City Plan Commission hired him to work on neighborhood conservation projects mandated by the Federal Housing Act for all cities receiving federal urban renewal funding. In 1957, at a city banquet, Ravitz described block-by-block community organization as a "fundamental element not only of a successful neighborhood conservation program, but the very corner stone [sic] of democratic community life."[60] A frequent guest at Jewish community meetings and a participant in Jewish Community Council meetings, Ravitz had advocated the kind of neighborhood activism so central to Jewish urban identity throughout the 1950s.

Much like other liberal Jews, however, Ravitz grew disenchanted with neighborhood activism in the face of large-scale forces—such as discriminatory housing policies—that compromised the power of local organization. By the late 1950s, he entered the world of fair-housing activism, through parallel Jewish communal and city government routes. Indeed, those two paths merged many times over, first, as he tested out ideas about city planning in front of Jewish audiences and, later, as he sought a Jewish base for his Common Council (the name of Detroit's city council) campaign in the early 1960s.

In 1959, Ravitz spoke to Jewish Community Council members about Detroit's housing problems. After reviewing the basic facts about the housing shortage and urban renewal projects that tore down old developments in the central city without providing new homes affordable to the predominantly black residents in those inner city areas, Ravitz turned to consider the specific role that Jews could—and should—play in the housing market. In his words, "moral and practical" reasons dictated Jewish involvement in housing reform. Drawing on the force of spiritual and moral language, Ravitz explained that Jews were the inheritors of a "tradition which is especially sensitive to social inequality and social evil."

Still, whether or not Jewish values held any claims on a particular Jew, no Jew could evade the problem of housing discrimination because it had a direct consequence on Jewish space; this was Ravitz's "practical" reason that compelled Jewish involvement in housing reform. Acknowledging that blacks moved into many neighborhoods, Ravitz, similar to other Jewish leaders, also asserted that they moved without fail into Jewish ones. He explained, "So long as there are <u>limited</u> outlets for Negro population needs, the Jewish community will feel strong pressures. One answer is to open the entire community as a housing market to all groups."[61] Indeed, this was the answer that he dedicated the next several years of his life to legislating into practice. Ravitz threw down the gauntlet of leadership to the Jewish community: "Only in a liberal community can there be real freedom and security for Jews. . . . We should not offer less but more leadership; we should give more time and care to this basic community problem [that should be] one of our primary concerns."[62] Many Jewish leaders agreed with Ravitz's charge and over the next years, they joined civic organizations, such as the Greater Detroit Committee for Fair Housing Practices, devoted to fair housing.[63]

Detroit Jews may have found housing reform work compelling on a voluntary and morality-enacting basis, but in the late 1950s, they were not in agreement about the wisdom of legislating against discrimination in the private housing market. They considered public and private housing two separate matters and, thus, agreed that discrimination should be legally banned from public housing, but hesitated to endorse the same when it came to private housing. Although national Jewish organizations had already recommended that Jews lobby for nationwide legislation barring discrimination in all housing transactions, many Jewish leaders still worried about subjecting private housing sales to public scrutiny. A member of the Jewish Community Council's community relations committee explained that when "a liberty was involved"—the right to buy and sell private property—laws must protect, not compromise, it.[64] Similar to other white Americans, Jews benefited from the freedoms that the so-called private housing market offered them in the form of mortgage subsidies, tax breaks, and quick and relatively unregulated property transactions. They tended to ignore or simply not see the ways that public and governmental monies subsidized the private housing market and, thus, challenged a true division between public and private housing.[65]

For at least a decade, the Jewish Community Council had sought to deal with Jewish real estate agents quietly and privately, organizing meetings with them or encouraging council supporters to speak to agents who were sowing the seeds of housing panic. Under Schermer, the Interracial Committee (renamed by Mayor Cobo the Commission on Community Relations) had always referred cases involving Jews to the Jewish Community Council. Starting in the early 1960s, however, as real estate agents drew more scrutiny for using discriminatory tactics in their business practices and as the housing reform movement gained power, the Jewish community was less able to deal internally with Jewish real estate practices. In the spring of 1960, a black woman reported to the Commission on Community Relations that an agent working for Benjamin Rich's real estate firm (recall: "Get Rich Quick!") had knocked on her door to find out if she had black friends willing to buy homes from white homeowners in the neighborhood.[66] Perhaps because the incident did not take place in a Jewish neighborhood, the Jewish Community Council was not notified, even though Rich was Jewish. Later that year, the council determined to reach out to all Jewish real estate agents and "urge them to use all effective means at their disposal to minimize or eliminate practices . . . which indulge in scare tactics, panic tactics, block busting, or improper pressure depending on fear and prejudices." But they also resolved to rely more heavily on the Commission on Community Relations to intervene when "tension" arose.[67]

Benjamin Rich continued to be the subject of complaints, and by the spring of 1961, the Commission on Community Relations had received multiple affidavits from Detroit residents complaining about the methods that he and his sales associates used. Staff members at the commission met with Rich and urged him to stop intimidating homeowners, canvassing door-to-door, and sending postcards such as one they had on file that read: "We've just handed one of your neighbors a handsome check! You can have one too if you sell." Yet with no means of legal enforcement and acknowledging that none of his tactics were so blatantly discriminatory as to merit a formal investigation by the Corporation and Securities Commission, the Commission on Community Relations could merely plead with him. Rich denied the charges and glibly remarked that his salesmen "were especially successful in getting the listings of those who 'shouted the loudest' about not moving."[68] Under the thumb of conservative Mayor Louis Miriani, who replaced Cobo after his death in 1957, the director of the Commission on Community Relations squelched early stirrings for legislative reform of

FIGURE 4.2 Mel Ravitz celebrating his election to the Common Council with his wife, Eleanore Ravitz, November 7, 1961. Courtesy of Walter P. Reuther Library, Archives of Labor and Urban Affairs, Wayne State University.

real estate practices and argued that real estate agents policed themselves and, when problems arose, were responsive to the commission. Liberals, however, had begun to see the shortcomings of this approach.[69]

In the fall of 1961, Mel Ravitz, a committed member of the Jewish Community Council's Neighborhoods and Housing Committee, a resident of the Russel Woods section of the Dexter neighborhood in Detroit, a trained sociologist, and an avowed liberal, kicked off his campaign for a seat on Detroit's Common Council. His political aspirations had been buoyed by the 1959 election, when five Jews won judgeships and other elected positions in the city.[70] Furthermore, Ravitz knew he had the endorsement of liberal civic officials. In 1959, the president of Detroit's Housing Commission had praised him for his "fundamental grasp of the city's problems of housing and of urban renewal . . . the clarity of his thought, the penetration of his analysis and the soundness and practicality of his approach and suggestions."[71]

Ravitz leaned heavily on the Jewish community, especially those Jews who had entered private positions of power through their legal practices and real estate development ventures, for support. In 1960, he had informed the leaders of the Jewish Community Council of his intention to run for city office but asked that they keep the news under wraps until he was ready for their help waging an "all-out" campaign.[72] In the early fall of 1961, his campaign slogan, "For a Better Detroit," greeted readers of the *Detroit Jewish News* as did his platform to increase "cooperation between cities and suburbs to solve common problems," to help senior citizens, and to create jobs. The Women's Committee for Mel Ravitz, a group of thirty-five Jewish women, had raised the funds for the advertisement.[73] And the *Detroit Jewish News* celebrated his victory in November, announcing that he was "the first Jew to be elected to the Council since 1920."[74]

Legislating Goodwill

In 1962, as Ravitz took office, a spirit of progressive optimism pervaded Detroit. Jerome Cavanagh, a young white Democrat, had won the mayoral election, defeating the incumbent conservative Louis Miriani. White and black liberals believed, albeit briefly, that Detroit could be a model of the "New Frontier" social and economic policies on which John F. Kennedy had campaigned.[75] When Lyndon B. Johnson assumed office in the fall of 1963, his War on Poverty poured federal dollars into programs to alleviate poverty and discrimination across the nation. In the face of these trends, Detroit liberals grew more supportive of legislative interventionism to regulate city life and, especially, property than they had been in the past.[76]

In the spring of 1962, Ravitz wrote directly to Cavanagh, "I am still convinced that the problem of deteriorating neighborhoods is one of Detroit's major problems. I am further convinced that it will require bold and dramatic public action to mount the kind of campaign necessary to do anything effective about this problem."[77] Other members of the Common

Council shared Ravitz's concerns, and that year the city body deliberated over the passage of a Fair Neighborhoods Practices Ordinance (FNPO). At its heart, the FNPO attempted to define what constituted a discriminatory practice in the act of selling real estate. Aware that real estate agents often relied on innuendo and tacit assumptions about property value to make their sales, the framers of the FNPO tried to sharpen the distinction between acceptable and unacceptable behavior. Each of the acts prohibited in the ordinance targeted fairly common real estate practices, from alerting neighbors to recent sales as a way to suggest that the neighborhood was changing, to implying that the "presence or anticipated presence" of blacks would harm the neighborhood and posting advertisements targeted to particular racial, ethnic, or national groups. A full four out of the ten specified acts dealt with the mechanics of placing for-sale signs.[78]

Introduced by William Patrick, the first and, at the time, only black member of the Common Council, early versions of the FNPO mandated strict enforcement through fines against any racial discrimination practiced by real estate agents and sellers. James Brickley, a white Republican representative to the Common Council, amended the proposed FNPO and softened its terms of enforcement. In November 1962, the Common Council passed the amended version, now called the Brickley Ordinance.

Just prior to the vote, the Jewish Community Council, writing on behalf of 340 Jewish organizations in the city, issued a statement supporting the passage of the Brickley Ordinance. (They had also supported the earlier version, but by the fall of 1962, only the Brickley Ordinance appeared in front of the Common Council.) Agreeing that real estate agents bore responsibility for legitimating discrimination in the city's housing market, the Jewish Community Council explained, "The attempt to impose a legislative control on such unscrupulous approaches is viewed by us as a positive step."[79] Jewish leaders also likely hoped that Jewish or not Jewish, real estate agents would be forced to comply with a uniform standard, and, thus, the Jewish community would not have to endure the shame that Jewish real estate agents might bring to it for exploiting buyers and sellers or for facilitating black settlement in white neighborhoods.

Although in the past the Jewish Community Council had criticized the Commission on Community Relations for its ineffectuality, now Jewish leaders found it "gratifying" that the commission was named as the enforcement body in the Brickley Ordinance and were relieved that the commission and not the city police were given this power. Not only would it be more invested than the police department in supporting antidiscrimination measures, the commission also had a history of cooperation with the Jewish Community Council. Protestant leaders expressed similar enthusiasm for the Brickley Ordinance, as did presidents of various community associations throughout the city.[80]

As the Brickley Ordinance made its way into law in the fall of 1962, residents living in an apartment building that shared the block with Conservative synagogue Shaarey Zedek in the Dexter neighborhood faced the kind of intimidation that supporters of the ordinance hoped would soon be barred. Paul Silverstein, a Jewish representative at a mortgage company, sent a letter to the tenants informing them that the Jewish owner of the building "has sold this property and in the very near future the new owner is planning to integrate this building." In the context of the letter, the word "integrate" was an indication to white renters that the building would become a black one, and the new owner's plan likely involved charging higher rents to new black tenants, a practice fully sanctioned and backed by Federal Housing Administration codes.[81] Indeed, Silverstein offered to show the white (and predominantly Jewish) tenants other properties owned by his company located nearby or in different parts of the city "which we have no intention of integrating."[82] The building's manager filed a complaint with the Commission on Community Relations. Soon investigators spoke with Silverstein and the two other Jewish partners at the mortgage company. The mortgage men insisted they had done no wrong and denied trying to exploit "racial fears." Yet upon hearing that under a new law, the Brickley Ordinance, "such a letter would be a misdemeanor," the men apologized.[83]

Mention of a legal apparatus barring actions that played upon racial fears had intimidated the mortgage men into offering an apology, yet the case hardly proved the efficacy of the new law. To those involved in the real estate industry, the law felt capriciously regulatory. Real estate professionals worried that the stipulated prohibitions would interfere with their ability to make sales and do their business since in order to serve their customers, they had to accept that some people did not want to live in integrated buildings or neighborhoods. Those involved in the real estate industry also protested that the ordinance unfairly targeted them and not the sellers, buyers, and renters who actually acted upon racist beliefs. Both of these concerns would surface even more vociferously as Ravitz and other Common Council members attempted to strengthen the FNPO.

Some fair-housing activists also found reason to criticize the Brickley Ordinance, which even if it convinced a mortgage company to apologize for its thinly veiled campaign to intimidate white people into moving away from an integrated building, offered no larger framework for dismantling residential segregation. William Patrick, the initial sponsor of a far more regulatory FNPO, and Mel Ravitz voted for the Brickley Ordinance, while also expressing clear reservations about it. To their fellow Common Council members, they wrote that the ordinance "does not . . . focus attention on the basic problems inherent in the segregated housing pattern of Detroit and the fears and prejudices of many of the people the real estate man approaches."[84] Black liberal groups, such as the NAACP and the Cotillion Club (a group of black businessmen and professionals), voiced similar concerns about the Brickley Ordinance's shortcomings.[85]

The Brickley Ordinance aimed to tamp down the most overt discriminatory practices in private property transactions, while leaving untouched lending codes and economic policies that functionally segregated many urban neighborhoods far more effectively than real estate practices. In a market economy that used race as a factor for determining the availability of financing, a white dollar would always have more purchasing power than a black one. Indeed, an editorial in the *Detroit News* summed up the matter correctly, when it offered its support for the Brickley Ordinance on the basis of its apparent neutrality on the matter of residential integration: "The ordinance does not encourage or discourage integration."[86] Jewish leaders, similar to most white liberal leaders, occasionally invoked the word "integration," especially as an abstract ideal. Yet few focused their efforts on advocating legislative measures aimed to dismantle the economic policies that hampered broad residential integration.

The 1962 FNPO was most notable for its lack of enforcement. The month after it passed, Irving Rubin, president of the Bagley Community Council, reported eight violations of the new ordinance to the Commission on Community Relations. Instead of acting swiftly and to the extent of his enforcement capacities, the director of the commission balked. The *Detroit News* reported, "It was not the intention of his commission to embark on any punitive expedition to 'write tickets as fast as we can.' "[87] Instead, he planned to meet with real estate agents and educate them about the law.

Yet in the meantime, the temperament of Detroit's white electorate showed signs of backlash against liberal reforms. Shortly after the FNPO passed, the city introduced two millage (or property tax) proposals to increase funding for public schools. In both cases, the majority of white voters, expressing fear their tax dollars would be taken to subsidize schools in poor black areas, voted down the measures and communicated general resentment about the costs and sacrifices the mayor's progressive policies demanded of them.[88] First the Brickley Ordinance and now these millage proposals convinced the white majority that the city no longer had its interests in mind. Unlike other whites in the city, the majority of Jewish voters aligned with the Jewish Community Council, which urged voters to support the millage proposals. Through press releases, communication with its over three hundred member organizations, and collaboration with other liberal and religious groups in the city, the council created a lobbying campaign central to the white liberal agenda in the city.[89] The Jewish Community Council's lobbying prowess, however, would be no match to the forces that concatenated in 1963 and 1964 to eviscerate open occupancy, but for a fleeting moment, liberals in the city coalesced to support a citywide attempt to disentangle race from the housing market.

"Why Not Try God?": Interfaith Housing Politics

In March 1962, as Mel Ravitz and Mayor Jerome Cavanagh settled into their new city offices, a group of Presbyterian ministers had met with leaders of the Jewish Community Council. Struck by how quickly their congregants were leaving the northwest areas of the city and abandoning their churches, the Presbyterian ministers "wanted to know what the experience of the Jewish community had been with this problem."[90] The ministers hoped Jewish leaders would share their strategies for managing neighborhood change and convincing members of the community to welcome all neighbors "irrespective of 'race' or religion."[91]

Testifying to the power of the Jewish Community Council and the prestige it held in the eyes of non-Jews, the Presbyterians met with lay leaders of the council, not rabbis. Indeed, this unevenness marked the path of Jewish interfaith activism in the 1960s: lay Jews, with no particular spiritual training, often stood shoulder to shoulder with Christian clergy. Rabbis usually joined the conversation, but more often than not lay Jews involved in communal relations agencies orchestrated interfaith activism.[92] On panels with other faith leaders, Jews moved beyond their own neighborhoods and considered the problems affecting the city as a whole. Yet just as legislative advocacy enabled Jews to lobby for urban policies without the sense of individual urgency that neighborhood activism had impelled, the interfaith rhetoric of urban activism could provide a release from immediate personal action.

By the end of the first meeting, the group of Jews and Presbyterians decided to invite other clergy into its conversation and work together to organize a metropolitan-wide conference on housing. A few months later, 120 white religious leaders, including clergy and lay leaders, gathered at the Jewish Community Center adjacent to the Bagley neighborhood to talk about "neighborhood stability and open occupancy." Central to the all-white group's concerns was the steady migration of white people away from the city. A priest from the Archbishop's Committee, Jewish demographer Albert Mayer, the director of the Commission on Community Relations, the chair of the Jewish Community Council's Committee on Neighborhoods and Housing, the president of the Bagley Community Council, the rabbi of Adas Shalom, and Lutheran and Congregational ministers all spoke of their investment in ridding the housing market of discriminatory practices. Almost every participant expressed his conviction that no one neighborhood and no single group could solve the problems harming urban neighborhoods and precipitating white migration away from the city. Jacob Segal, the rabbi at Adas Shalom, explained, "I therefore feel that it is necessary for us to envisage a general metropolitan housing conference in the fall. We must try to solve the problem in the entire Detroit area—in order to make the solution feasible and enduring in any one segment of the city."[93]

Following on the logic that a single neighborhood or group could not solve the problems afflicting city dwellers, the group also maintained that reforming the mechanics of the housing market would far better stabilize urban life than focusing on individuals' attitudes toward black people. "The most fundamental factors have nothing to do with race relations," the white leaders concurred; instead, "the key to this question is the organization of those forces that desire the only solution that will work—open occupancy."[94] Attenuating race relations from open occupancy enabled the white leaders to skirt the controversial issue of integration or systemic changes to the housing market itself. Open occupancy promised to remove barriers from the housing market directly related to matters of race, without questioning the extent to which the nexus of race and economics structured the functioning of the market. A true dedication to racially integrated neighborhood space may not have demanded a full-scale remaking of the housing market. Liberal leaders, however, worried that a call for integration could issue a challenge to the terms of the market by prioritizing the goals of sharing space and power with black Americans over the protection of a free housing market and the financial gains that it offered white Americans.

Without an open housing market, the group maintained, white middle-class Detroiters—specifically those who eschewed intimidation as a method to keep blacks from settling in their neighborhoods—would inexorably leave the city. By defeating the practices that channeled black Detroiters to move to only certain areas of the city, the whole city would more equally bear what these white leaders still unmistakably thought of as the burden of black settlement. Furthermore, in removing race as a factor in the geography of the housing market, class would become the primary variable determining where a person could live. Yet because race and class were so tightly bound together due to years of economic, employment, and educational discrimination against black people, an entirely class-based housing market would mean that middle- and upper-middle-class white neighborhoods, where most liberal Detroiters lived, would only host the small minority of blacks who could afford to pay high housing costs.

Jewish leaders played a crucial role in the interfaith group's effort to organize a "metropolitan conference on open occupancy." Serving as the clearinghouse of communication among the group—as minute takers and organizers of meetings—the leaders of the Jewish Community Council encouraged rapid planning for a conference to take place in January 1963. Furthermore, they helped sculpt the public face of this interfaith alliance to mirror the council's own commitment to open occupancy and, as a council leader noted, "to move open occupancy toward the accepted norm of the community."[95]

Explaining the impetus for the conference, the leaders wrote, "Privately and independently, we were often shocked to realize that we felt more in common with those of other faiths who were dedicated and working on this problem [of housing] than we did with members of our own faith who were apathetic or negative." Theological differences may have paled in comparison to the moral claims of open occupancy, yet religious leaders also leaned on their spiritual authority to demand obeisance to the agenda of open occupancy. In the group's recommendations, it pronounced, "No man can have the right to call himself a good Christian or Jew and not work actively and diligently to solve this problem [of housing discrimination]."[96] With similar insouciance toward theological differences, Richard Hertz, the rabbi at Temple Beth El, explained, "We have tried legislation. We have tried court decisions. We have tried executive orders . . . and the messianic day of equality for all people has not come. Why not try God? Why not harness together the combined moral power of the greatest force for good on earth—religion!"[97]

Rendered as a generic force of good, religion could connect faiths—or, at least, those liberal faiths that did not get hung up on theological disputations or claims of exclusive truth—in common purpose. Jewish, Protestant, and Catholic participants had shared the hope that through coalition politics, they could prove to their own devotees that open occupancy and the disavowal of housing discrimination had become woven into an American religious creed or civil religion.[98]

Throughout the fall of 1962, the Jewish Community Council invited Catholic and Protestant clergy to attend its Neighborhoods and Housing Committee meetings. At one meeting in November, on the eve of the passage of the FNPO, a priest and an Episcopalian minister talked about their work in northwest Detroit, each offering an honest portrayal of the strengths and weaknesses of their approach. The priest explained that the archdiocese had recently embraced an "interfaith" approach to working in neighborhoods as it realized that some priests and parishioners were detractors from the cause of open occupancy. He hoped that in concert with other religious groups, the Catholic Church could standardize its commitment to ending housing discrimination. The minister agreed that interfaith activism could exert pressure on a single faith and set a new level of expectation. He admitted that Protestants "in the past have been the captive of cultural practices of segregation," but now due to interfaith efforts, clergy from various denominations were supporting open occupancy and moving toward a greater embrace of fair housing."[99]

When asked, both the priest and minister revealed that very few Protestant or Catholic churches were integrated, though this issue was put aside quickly since integration was hardly the point. Jewish leaders skirted the issue of religious integration for the most part since the black Jews in Detroit attended their own congregations, though when they did seek acceptance at a mainstream synagogue, they clearly felt a great deal of trepidation and uncertainty.[100] In 1960, for example, a man who had just moved with his family from New York to Detroit and described his family as "of the Negro race—and of the Jewish faith" wrote to Adas Shalom seeking membership in the congregation. Using wry humor that hardly cloaked his expectation for rejection, he offered a hyperbolic description of the "problems" his family might cause for the congregation. In closing he wrote, "Actually, the countless questions and embarrassing explanations which would be brought up involving my entire family could be enough alone to refuse us acceptance. As you can probably see, the risks you take in both loss of prestige and members, are very great. Even so, I have to be selfish enough to ask acceptance for one simple reason: We are Jewish."[101] Records do not indicate whether the man's family joined the synagogue.

Indication of the extent to which interfaith leaders willfully sought to exclude racial integration from their purview was the fact that throughout the early stages of planning the Metropolitan Conference on Open Occupancy, black leaders were simply not consulted. By the time of the conference, in January 1963, the white planners had rectified what they characterized as their "omission," and several middle-class black institutions, including the Cotillion Club, the Booker T. Washington Business Association, the Urban League, and the NAACP, were represented on the advisory committee.[102]

Public officials joined faith leaders at the 1963 conference, helping to create the semblance of a unified front against housing discrimination buoyed by the recent passage of the FNPO. Richard Marks, the director of the Commission on Community Relations, and Mel Ravitz and William Patrick, from the city's Common Council, all spoke at the conference, offering their support for an agenda set by the faith leaders. While religious leaders became fluent in policy language and legislative matters, public officials drew on the language of faith. In a public statement in favor of open occupancy released after the conference, Mayor Cavanagh explained, "It is an opportunity for all of us to put into practice the Judeo-Christian ideal that we are all children of one father."[103] By characterizing open occupancy as fulfilling "the Judeo-Christian ideal," he hoped to elevate the policy above reproach and above the specific circumstances of any one neighborhood or group into an issue with citywide and interfaith significance.

When Temple Beth El's Rabbi Hertz addressed the audience gathered together at the 1963 conference, he carefully distinguished between urban-oriented activism, which he deemed a spiritual necessity, and rootedness to actual urban space, which he did not see as essential to such activism. Jews, he argued, could maintain a commitment to racial justice without remaining in cities. The rabbi explained, "My people have had a long history in the battle for open occupancy. We have lived in some of the foulest ghettos of the world. We know what it means to be harried and haunted and harassed, the last to benefit and the first to be denied. . . .

The freedom to live where one wants is a precious privilege of first class citizenship devoutly cherished by Jews of this country."[104] Now that Jews finally had gained the right to live where they wished, they were obligated to work to ensure others possessed it, but they were not obligated to curtail their own freedom of movement in the name of fulfilling a vision of urban integration.

"My people," Hertz continued, set the mold for what it meant to experience injustice "because they were there." Yet they also possessed "special sensitivity" to fight injustice anywhere: "We never [have] forgotten the prophetic accent of the Bible's charge to my people: 'Justice, justice shalt thou pursue.'"[105] The rabbi rendered the obligation to fight injustice as a basic facet of the Jewish character, wherever the Jew may live. According to him, Jews' abhorrence of injustice was not tied to a specific place or behavior, but rather was an innate part of Jewishness. The rabbi's usage of prophetic language and his pussyfooting around the terms of Jewish obligation helped the liberal rabbi create an enduring link between Jews and social justice that would not dissolve even when they left urban spaces where poverty and injustice were far more visible than they were in the suburbs.

In its attention to open occupancy and not integration, and to urban activism and not the creation of enduring urban communities, the 1963 conference represented accurately the moderate agenda that characterized white liberalism in the city. A set of recommendations presented at the end of the conference charged Detroiters with "emancipat[ing] the housing market of our community from the unconscionable evils of discrimination for reasons of color, religion, or national origin." With fealty to capitalism, the group of liberal leaders advocated reforms that would free the housing market of what the mayor characterized as the "artificial barriers" of race, ethnicity, and religion.[106] The belief that an open housing market, allowed to operate naturally, would alleviate pressure on their neighborhoods had initially fueled Jewish support of the interfaith movement for open occupancy. Yet as the conversation shifted away from neighborhood solutions toward citywide and legislative ways to reform the housing market, Jews in Detroit invested in a broader political struggle removed from actual urban neighborhoods. Indeed, in the months after the Metropolitan Conference on Open Occupancy, a group of interfaith leaders, half of whom were Jewish, reconstituted themselves as the Metropolitan Detroit Conference on Religion and Race, broadening their purpose beyond housing issues. They worked to organize another conference on religion and race with the explicit aim of engaging suburban dwellers and lobbying for local and state open occupancy laws.[107]

The Retreat of Progressive Urban Politics and the Suburbanization of the Liberal Electorate

In the summer of 1963, governing a city that was now composed of almost 30 percent black residents, Mayor Cavanagh welcomed the Reverend Martin Luther King Jr. to Detroit and joined him and 125,000 others to walk down Woodward Avenue in the Walk to Freedom.[108] That same summer, a time when interracial and interfaith liberal coalition politics appeared to offer a path forward for the city, Mel Ravitz and William Patrick introduced the Patrick-Ravitz Ordinance to the city's Common Council. Their intention was to leverage the spirit of the times and strengthen the FNPO legislation by bringing more stringent enforcement and more precise definitions to the ban on racial discrimination in housing sales than expressed in the Brickley Ordinance.[109]

While liberals, including many vocal Jews, rallied around the Patrick-Ravitz Ordinance, white conservatives and the majority of members on the Common Council saw little wisdom in it and felt threatened by the rising forces of anti-discriminatory politics, the headline-grabbing Walk to Freedom, and the empowerment of black residents in the city. Fueling white conservatism was the rise of black leaders who rejected King's nonviolence in favor of more assertive means to defeat white racism. The Reverend Albert Cleage led the effort to create a new black political agenda of self-determination and separatism that helped unify black protest politics into a more militant and organized political structure and that drew on the burgeoning strength of the Nation of Islam and the Socialist Workers Party.[110]

Perceiving a moment ripe for unseating the city's liberal power brokers, a group of white leaders introduced a counterproposal called the Homeowner's Rights Ordinance (HRO) intended to invalidate the measures already passed into law by the Brickley Ordinance, not to mention those proposed by Ravitz and Patrick. Though the HRO attempted to justify racial discrimination through the language of individual rights and private property, it resembled the Patrick-Ravitz Ordinance (and Brickley) in its focus on the individual behavior of buyers, sellers, and their agents, and its understanding of private property as a right. Despite the fact that the Common Council voted down the HRO, it appeared as a city referendum in the fall of 1964.

Almost immediately, a liberal coalition of business, labor, religious, and civic leaders formed to oppose the HRO. Known as Citizens for a United Detroit, the group issued a major public relations campaign against the ordinance, characterizing it as "dangerous," "evil," and "immoral." In its effort to tread the line between white conservatism and the growing radicalism of the city's black leadership, this group of white and black leaders attempted to maintain a viable liberal space in the city. In August 1964, Irving Rubin, the president of the Bagley Community Council, organized a rally to protest the HRO. Appropriating the language from the ordinance, the rally was billed as a meeting "to protect your home."[111] Indeed, supporters and opponents of the HRO both had a stake in protecting private property rights, but disagreed on how to do so; supporters believed that sellers should have the right to rent or sell to whomever they pleased, while opponents believed that homeowners were exploited—as was their property—by profiteering and race-baiting real estate agents.

Jewish leaders felt a particular tug to defend a moderate liberal agenda in the city, believing that white conservatism and black radicalism undermined the protections and power that Jews had gained in the city. Officers from the Jewish Community Council and the Bagley Community Council, the rabbi of Temple Beth El, and Stanley Winkelman, owner of Winkelman's department stores, were key activists in and served as some of the leaders of Citizens for a United Detroit.[112] Unsurprisingly, the Jewish Community Council threw itself into the defeat of the HRO, mailing out over eleven thousand flyers against it, conducting home visits, organizing telephone canvassing, and spending significant sums on the campaign. For them, the ordinance presented a harsh rebuke to their brand of liberalism and their evolving belief that the protection of people's rights issued due cause for regulatory legislation against discriminatory behaviors and transactions. The HRO also threatened to serve as a spark for even more white reactionary behavior that could undermine the gains in acceptance that Jews had made over the past decades in the city. Black liberal groups, such as the NAACP and the Urban League, similarly worked tirelessly to defeat the HRO.

Nonetheless, on September 1, 1964, Detroiters passed the HRO by a margin of twenty-three thousand votes. Voter turnout was poor—only slightly over half of all Detroiters went to the polls that day, and of those, only 62 percent cast a vote either way on the ordinance. Additionally, black voters, whom the council believed would oppose the ordinance, had a low rate of participation and thus did not counteract the white conservative vote.[113]

At the time of the HRO's passage, the Jewish Community Council carefully emphasized in a press release that "areas containing substantial numbers of Jewish residents voted heavily against the ordinance."[114] Yet internal analyses presented a more complicated picture. While true that precincts in substantially Jewish neighborhoods voted sometimes as much as ten to one against the ordinance, the Jewish vote was rarely large enough to sway a precinct. With the exception of the Bagley area, which uniformly defeated the ordinance, most other assumedly Jewish precincts contained no more than 50 percent Jews. The ideals embraced by the city's Jewish liberal leadership were undermined by demographic realities that seriously compromised the Jewish public's electoral clout. For all of the outrage that liberal Jews expressed about the passage of the HRO, none of the leaders remarked upon the waning Jewish electoral presence in Detroit. The internal Jewish Community Council report denied any "white backlash" and maintained that liberal forces were alive and well in Detroit.[115]

In a 1963 discussion on Jews and cities held in New York City, William Avrunin, the executive director of the Jewish Federation of Detroit, had maintained that Jews made a "special contribution" to cities, wherever they resided in the "metropolitan community—including those of us who may live in the suburbs." Avrunin continued, "It is my conviction that Jews and the organized Jewish community have a stake in the core city, even if it does not include a single Jewish resident."[116]

A Test Case: Urban Schools

In the same 1964 referendum that found the majority of Detroit voters on the side of the HRO, voters also defeated a bond to build a new high school in the city. An editorial in the *Detroit Jewish News* described the two votes as linked by race: "the homeowners' scheme to prevent Negroes from living where they wish . . . and the school bond plan which would have enabled the city to construct new high schools from which Negro students would benefit. What a devilish result stemming from prejudices that are immoral, inhuman and unrealistic!"[117] Two years and a court judgment later, the HRO was overturned as unconstitutional, and a long list of individual Jews, most with ties to the Jewish Community Council, were among the plaintiffs in the case.[118] Eventually, in 1968, the state of Michigan passed its Fair Housing Act barring "an owner, a real estate broker or real estate salesman" from discriminating in a property transaction on the basis of "race, color, religion or national origin."[119] Still, the link between real estate discrimination and the weakening of the city's public schools would not be erased by a court judgment.

In surveys, far more Jews identified the quality of schools as opposed to the tactics used by real estate agents as the single most important factor causing them to leave urban neighborhoods. Yet Jews did not devote nearly the same amount of energy to urban school reform as they did to real estate reform. The personal sacrifices of deciding to send one's child to an urban school and working toward local, neighborhood-based school reform struck many Jews as high. And Jewish leaders and activists did not find a citywide school reform agenda that could be as politically flexible and ideal affirming as open occupancy served in the realm of housing reform. Open occupancy could be expressed as an effort to free the market that most Jews had faith in from the hindrances of discrimination. As a method of housing reform, it also had the advantage of demanding very little in the way of personal behavioral change. But Jewish leaders and Jews who still lived in urban neighborhoods in the 1960s were hard-pressed to figure out a way to promote the ideal of fairness and the protection of rights, which most believed in, without endorsing the ideal of active racial integration of the school system, a goal that struck most Jews as simply unrealistic given the range of obstacles.

In the summer of 1964, the parents of forty white children who attended Pasteur Elementary School, a school that served a comfortable middle-class neighborhood slightly northeast of Bagley, petitioned for a transfer out of Pasteur to an all-white elementary school three and a half miles west. The group expressed concern that Pasteur's quality was diminishing as classrooms were becoming overcrowded due to the growing number of black children in the school. A smaller group of Pasteur residents, including Jewish circuit court judge Victor Baum, successfully filed an injunction against the mass transfer.

The parents who had hoped to stay in the neighborhood but flee the slowly integrating school now had to decide whether to move. In a three-part series about neighborhood life in northwest Detroit published in the *Detroit Free Press*, one of the parents, a Jewish woman who had initially endorsed transferring her children out of Pasteur, reflected on her motivation for deciding to remain at Pasteur and work toward improving the school: "I love living in the city and I want my children to live in the city."[120] A pro-Pasteur group formed, and black and white residents, many of whom were highly educated and held powerful positions in the city, joined it. Jews, including Judge Baum, constituted a majority of the advocates for the school.

Informed by their conversations with the leaders of the nearby Bagley Community Council, Pasteur activists understood that unless its elementary school remained strong, families who had a choice in the matter would neither remain in nor move into the neighborhood. Even the Bagley neighborhood, viewed by the Pasteur group as a model of success, had to confront its residents' perceptions that the slow influx of black homeowners would, by and by, weaken the neighborhood schools. A 1964 study of the Bagley area found that homeowners expressed concern that as more black children attended neighborhood schools, the schools would reach a "tipping point" and precipitously decline, in terms of student conduct, classroom size, and school resources, no matter what action they tried to take.[121]

The Pasteur group determined to address the Detroit Board of Education directly and make a plea for two parallel measures: increased funding and resources for the Pasteur school; and a commitment, in the words of a Jewish attorney involved in the group, to making, "public education one of the stabilizing forces in an urban community undergoing change."[122] The plea suggested that the board of education would improve the entire school district by giving special attention to one of the remaining predominantly white and middle-class schools. The board of education agreed with the parents' reasoning and pledged to invest extra resources in the elementary school for gifted programming, remedial classes, a functioning borrowing library, and a system to track students according to their academic ability. A new principal, a white woman known as a top-rate educator, moved to the school, as did a full-time police officer. Undaunted by the situation, the principal told the *Free Press*, "The people in this area are generally liberal in racial matters, but they were realistic. They knew the facts. And the fact is when a school becomes all-Negro it does not get as much attention as the all-white school."[123] She hoped to right the balance, both by lobbying the board of education for more resources and by keeping a stable number of white students in the school. Aware of the demographics of her most powerful charges, the principal enthused, "I couldn't have fallen into a better situation, having a community this knowledgeable, this enthusiastic, and this powerful. Jews are education oriented and the combination of Jews and Negroes is dynamic."[124]

For the apparent success that the Pasteur parents had in funneling public money and resources into the school, they also understood that without a quality public high school, parents, who perhaps stayed in the city during their children's younger years, would inevitably leave. Mumford High School, located in the Bagley neighborhood, had long served as a beacon for the Jewish community in Detroit. Opened in 1949, just as the Jewish community was establishing a strong presence in northwest Detroit, Mumford quickly gained a reputation for its large Jewish student body and academic excellence. By 1965, however, Jewish parents and community leaders feared that the school's reputation was declining and observed that Jewish parents were pulling their children out of it and moving to the suburbs.

In April 1965, a group of civic activists formed the Mumford Action Program (MAP) under the premise that "good schools . . . [are] essential to the existence and maintenance of a stable integrated community."[125] Jewish institutions (such as the Jewish Community Council, the American Jewish Committee, and the Jewish Labor Council) represented the mainstays of support for the group, and Jewish individuals constituted well over half of the active participants. The finance committee, for example, was entirely Jewish, and five out of eight members of the education committee were Jewish.[126] Yet Jewish leaders' persistent avoidance of fully endorsing integration undermined the committee's ideological strength.

Through publicity campaigns, MAP worked to prove that the school was safe and maintained a strong white and Jewish presence. "In reality," a press release in 1965 explained, "discipline at Mumford High School is not now, and has never been a significant problem."[127] MAP, similar to Jewish neighborhood groups, relied on empirical evidence to disprove rumors and to persuade constituents that panic was unwarranted. In advance of the 1966–1967 school year, MAP intended to gather the names of all of the students planning to attend Mumford the following fall and use the list "to solicit others."[128] Yet much as the task of rumor denial in neighborhood work had the effect of drawing more attention to black settlement and Jewish concerns about it (why deny a rumor if it does not matter one way or the other?), MAP's efforts to prove that nothing was amiss with Mumford were compromised by the group's very existence and its clear focus on discipline and the school's declining Jewish population.

Shortly after its formation in the spring of 1965, MAP made the *De-*

troit News for endorsing the expansion of school officials' police powers to give them the right to search for weapons on school property and make arrests. Robert Alpern, a Jewish member of MAP's executive committee, explained to the reporter, "Many parents have already indicated their fears and concerns have resulted in a decision to move out of the neighborhood." He believed that the expanded police powers would quell parents' anxieties.[129]

To the contrary, the *Detroit News* article set off a storm of criticism against MAP. The Jewish left and many black leaders accused the group of equating growth in the black student body with an explosion of violent troublemaking. The director of the progressive and left-of-center Jewish Labor Committee, who had once heartily endorsed MAP, now explained, "MAP is creating the illusion of [disciplinary] problems that do not exist in fact."[130] Later, another leader of the Jewish Labor Committee accused MAP of believing that "physical danger" directly followed black entrance into the school. "I would like to suggest," he wrote, "that the posture of MAP is not congruent with good community relations. . . . If we are in favor of integrated schools then we must open our arms and welcome the newcomers without first searching them for knives and other weapons."[131] The fact of the matter was that aside from some progressive and leftist voices, few liberal Jewish leaders actively supported the economic policies that would dismantle the discriminatory measures encoded in the housing market and allow for true racial residential or school integration. By the end of the spring of 1965, the Jewish Labor Committee had retracted its support of MAP.[132]

Even progressive Jewish political leaders, such as Ravitz, who theoretically supported school and residential integration, and progressive Jewish organizations, such as the Jewish Labor Committee, refrained from putting forward the broad critique of the housing market and legal protections of private property that would have opened up the possibility for true residential integration. Reformatory measures, such as open occupancy, operated within the structure of preexisting economic policies and market protections. These continued to empower white homeowners and renters and give them the resources, in credit and in profits from past investments, to leave schools or neighborhoods that were tipping away from the perks of white privilege and tilting toward the detriments of black disadvantages.

Jewish activists found educational activism far more taxing than housing activism. In part, they may have believed that the problem of school segregation was a symptom of residential segregation, thus in their efforts to end residential segregation, they may have thought they would also, by and by, solve the problem of school segregation. Yet whereas with housing activism, they could focus their efforts on reforming the bad behavior of real estate agents—so much so that one complained that agents had become the "whipping boys" of liberals' efforts—in school reform, they did not identify a third-party enemy.[133] Some tried to foist blame on real estate agents, suggesting that they were spreading the rumor about school decline to get whites to sell their homes. But this line of blame was not particularly effective and did not address the problems that parents and children witnessed in schools that had become overcrowded and strapped for cash. Most white and Jewish parents correlated the new problems in the schools, which included more violence and less control over the student body, with the entrance of black students into the schools. The author of a study of the Bagley neighborhood concluded that although some neighborhood activists attempted to organize to improve the public schools, "work along these lines plunged [residents] into a thicket of intractable urban problems and involved [them] in issues of the utmost complexity."[134]

When white parents, such as the predominantly Jewish groups at Pasteur or Mumford, mobilized to improve their schools, they often received only tepid support from black parents. Although the NAACP and the Congress on Racial Equality had endorsed MAP, very few black individuals stepped into positions of leadership. So acute was the white and primarily Jewish bent of MAP, that in the late summer of 1965, school board officials provided MAP leaders with lists of black individuals whom they believed should be approached in order to gain some black members for the group.[135] A black woman who lived in the Pasteur catchment area explained that her black friends "covertly resent the leadership [of parent groups] being largely white, and often patronizing." She observed that the white women who formed the foot soldiers of the movement were affluent and had much more leisure time than black women to devote to organizational involvement. In response, a group of black parents formed a separate community group to improve the school and neighborhood. One noted, however, "Negroes want whites to stay because when a neighborhood is all-Negro the residents see themselves that the city doesn't do as good a job picking up the garbage, fixing the streets or giving police protection. And the school system too just doesn't seem to care as much."[136]

Although Jewish neighborhood residents in the late 1940s expressed the same sentiment that the city often neglected neighborhoods once blacks arrived, by the mid-1960s, many liberals saw this critique as the fighting words of black radicals. Jews, who participated in the city's power structures through political positions and private wealth and, also, continued to interact in the economic space of black life as merchants and landlords, feared the double edge of black communities' rising activism. If blacks blamed white power brokers for rigging the economic and political system against them, then Jews were implicated in that power structure. And if blacks blamed the local political and economic circumstances for making them beholden to white proprietors, then Jews, too, were implicated. When it came to school reform, Jewish leaders generally advocated giving blacks a voice in the process and supplying textbooks about black history, but they feared the nationalist and separatist rhetoric that growingly appealed to black communities in the city.[137]

In the belief that their neighborhoods, their schools, and the city operated as part of a metropolitan structure, Jews understood schools as just one piece of the urban experiment in need of reform. While the organized Jewish community devoted more of its energy to housing reform than school reform, very few Jewish leaders were willing to demand that Jews remain in urban schools or neighborhoods. These were private choices, and in the scheme of Jews' new consciousness about their role in city life, what I have called their metropolitan urbanism, these private choices mattered much less than Jews' ongoing public support for legislative reform and civil rights. Thus, Jewish leaders invested significant resources in convincing Jews to stand steadfast in their support of open occupancy and antidiscrimination measures, whether or not they voiced their views from within the city or beyond it.

The Decline of the Middle-Class Urban Housing Market

In February 1966, as the Homeowner's Rights Ordinance remained tied up in court, the Commission on Community Relations organized public hearings about housing in Detroit.[138] A number of Jewish real estate agents spoke in favor of open occupancy, even as they demanded reform to the FNPO. They believed that uniform compliance with nondiscriminatory regulations would help them do their jobs and would be good for the city's real estate market, which they feared was losing its middle-class center. In 1965, three Jewish real estate men, Allan Grossman, William Gross, and Irving Katcher, formed a group called the Independent Real Estate Brokers Association that lobbied for open occupancy and tried to rehabilitate the reputation of real estate agents. In a press conference,

Gross, the first president of the group, insisted, "The real estate profession is not engaged in any attempt to ghettoize . . . neighborhood[s], or any other area of this city. . . . We do not determine where buyers seek to secure houses and we cannot decide for homeowners when they want to sell. . . . Attacks on real estate brokers are not going to provide the solution."[139]

Katcher, who had become president of the Independent Real Estate Brokers Association by the time of the 1966 public hearings, protested that the language of the FNPO had left real estate agents vulnerable to prosecution for almost any selling practice in which they might engage. He specifically objected to restrictions on posting for-sale and sold signs, and argued that these kinds of measures fueled the specious belief that real estate agents were out to hurt neighborhoods for profit. Once laws provided "de-segregation in every . . . area of the City of Detroit and metropolitan area," Katcher argued, only then would open occupancy measures prove themselves effective and not simply slaps on real estate agents' wrists.[140]

When Grossman, a fellow member of the Independent Real Estate Brokers Association, testified, he concurred with Katcher that brokers could only change their practices if a statewide mandate went into effect. When confronted with a case that accused him of standing in the way of a sale to a black family, he denied the allegation (and the Civil Rights Commission eventually dismissed the case, as it did almost every housing discrimination case brought in front of it in 1966). Until statewide legislation passed, he argued, the responsibility was on the seller, not the broker, when discrimination occurred in housing sales.[141]

Albert Letvin, a Jewish real estate agent in the business since 1946, agreed with his colleagues that real estate brokers had become the victims of laws that did not work. He explained to the panel that he had been "blacklisted" by the Bagley Community Council for his long-standing practice of sending out "sold" cards to nearby neighbors after selling a home. Although he claimed to have desisted from this practice after the FNPO ruled against it, he reported the Bagley group continued to target him and coerced residents to sign a petition against him. One of the panel members, a Jewish woman, voiced skepticism that he had curtailed these practices and pressed him to explain the current solicitation tactics he used. In exasperation, she accused him of "call[ing] up the whole neighborhood" after he had sold a home to a black family. Letvin protested, and returned with a powerful indictment of the very people complaining about him: "I'm just saying that people make a move because they want to make a move. They would very much like to blame it on the real estate broker. It's a very easy out for them. They don't want to live in an integrated area. The basis they use is we're just badgered to death by these real estate people so we're just going to sell and move into another area. That's not the real answer. The real answer is examining their own hearts, their own conscience."[142]

Pushing back against Letvin's interpretation, a member of the panel contended that real estate agents presented themselves as experts and, thus, could intimidate, even dupe, people into feeling scared about black people moving into their neighborhood. Letvin retorted, "Let's take Bagley . . . these are people who are normally professionals, semi-professionals, or business people. These are not people that are intimidated by a phone call, or intimidated by a post card." Still, they may be annoyed, another panelist remarked, to which Letvin replied, "Unfortunately, we live in a world of many annoyances." The questioner retreated, and Letvin explained that he supported statewide legislation against "unscrupulous" real estate practices, but that unless these practices were banned in the entire state, then he could not, as a businessman, abide by them in the city.[143] Citywide reform was inadequate in an era when more and more of the city's middle class could simply decide to move to the suburbs and leave the city's ordinances behind.

Real estate agents saw as clearly as demographers that the city's white middle class was fast shrinking. Increasingly, to be a member of the white middle class meant to invest in real estate in suburbs. In the 1960s, responding to the real estate boom outside of the city, urban planners in Detroit searched for ways to keep the white middle class in the city by offering new kinds of housing options that tied together the privileges of white suburbia with the cosmopolitanism of the city. Attempting to compete with the new and modern lure of the suburbs, city planners in Detroit used urban renewal funds to build new housing stock in the city, literally on top of the old neighborhoods that carried the burdens of white neglect and exploitation. Unsurprisingly, given the ideals of metropolitan urbanism and the preexisting investments that Jews had in the city, Jewish developers, planners, and leaders offered support for these experiments, even as many also invested in suburban development.

The city's clearest effort to sustain middle-class residential life in the city came in the shape of a Mies van der Rohe–designed housing cooperative complex located just east of the old Hastings Street neighborhood. The site, cleared of 1,550 dwelling units that had been home to predominantly black families, languished in the 1950s until Walter Reuther, president of the United Auto Workers, agitated for action. The city formed a committee to establish "an integrated residential community . . . that can attract back to the city people who are finding housing in the outlying sections of the city and its suburbs."[144] The committee assembled a team of prominent modernist architects, including Victor Gruen, a Viennese-born Jew known for his suburban shopping complexes; Minoru Yamasaki, who would design New York's World Trade Center and, also, a new suburban synagogue building for Temple Beth El in the early 1970s; and Oscar Stonorov, a designer of public housing in Philadelphia. Eager for a coordinated process of development, the committee also hired Herbert Greenwald and Samuel Katzin, Jewish real estate developers from Chicago, to oversee the project. Through Greenwald's long-standing relationship with him, Mies van der Rohe joined the project as the chief architect.[145]

Built in the International Style in the early 1960s, with steel frames, large unadorned windows, and sleek lines, the complex, called Lafayette Park, offered high-rise rental units and a series of townhouse buildings for cooperative ownership. Despite early plans to create a mixed-income development, Lafayette Park was priced for middle-class renters and cooperative owners. And, much like suburban developments, this urban middle-class area benefited from federal subsidies, first through funds to dislocate poor and mainly black residents from their homes in the name of clearing bad neighborhoods, and then through financing that helped middle-class and mainly white people obtain better housing for their dollar than poor people for their dollar. Very quickly, the rental units filled and within just a few years, the cooperative townhouses had total occupancy and a long waiting list.

The developers' explicit commitment to racial integration differentiated the cooperative movement from the open occupancy movement, but in their unwillingness to foster true economic diversity, the developers resembled open occupancy liberals who had little interest in upsetting the capitalist structure of the housing market. On the whole, the residents of Lafayette Park were upper-middle-class professionals, highly educated, and with positions at Wayne State University or nearby medical complexes.[146] Within the first few years, only about 15 percent of Lafayette Park dwellers were nonwhite, yet residents prided themselves on having chosen and helped create a "stable integrated area in Detroit."[147] Although no comparable statistics reveal the number of Jews who lived in the complex, from lists of residents and their recollections, it is clear that Jews maintained a significant presence in Lafayette Park.[148]

The modest success creating a middle-class enclave in Lafayette Park did not prove to most whites that Detroit was a livable city. It did not spawn similar communities, and it did not channel enough new funds to the city's tax base to change the finances of the education system. Indeed, as much as Gruen may have felt committed to attracting people who were moving to suburbs to reconsider living in the city, he had also worked, as his biographer explained, to "express urbanity in the suburbs" and develop a model of "urban decentralization."[149] If the suburb could not come to the city, then perhaps the city could come to the suburb.

As Jews moved out of the city—by 1965, half of all Detroit Jews lived in the suburbs—fewer felt the local connection to urban woes that they had felt in the past, but many felt a dual-pronged ambivalence about, on one hand, fully committing to Jewish life in the suburbs and, on the other hand, continuing to invest in the political and economic life of the city.[150] In observing the formation of metropolitan urbanism, it is possible to understand why Jews believed that they might leave the city and remain engaged with it without falling prey to the hypocrisy of their own ambivalence. The characteristics of metropolitan urbanism—a sensibility that the city and Jews' investments in it could and should extend beyond Jewish space—enabled Jews to think of themselves as politically, spiritually, and culturally urban oriented without feeling beholden to the terrain of the city.

Ironically, Jewish liberals had turned toward a citywide view out of concern with their specific neighborhoods and the belief that if more urban neighborhoods adopted liberal values and nondiscriminatory attitudes, then Jewish neighborhoods would not feel such acute pressure from the entrance of black newcomers. Yet, as time passed, the citywide view and the sense that urban problems were bigger than the Jewish neighborhood and unsolvable by the actions of one group allowed Jews to see their decisions about whether to stay in the city as separate from their participation in metropolitan and urban-oriented political, spiritual, and cultural life.

CHAPTER FIVE

The Sacred Suburban Sites of Jewish Metropolitan Urbanism

A Jewish man wrote candidly to his rabbi in 1963, "We, being a sympathetic and kind people, and having felt the lash and the whip are probably less belligerent and somewhat more tolerant than others, but what we do in essence and stark reality, is just as evil and sinister as maybe some of the more quarrelsome and belligerent people do. In other words, we do not create any riots, or scenes, nor do we break windows or set fires, but we just quietly and politely without any fuss, pack up and move, which I must reiterate is just as dastardly and mean as some of the others."[1] The man's rabbi, Jacob Segal of Adas Shalom, the Conservative synagogue in the Bagley neighborhood, likely nodded in agreement as he read the heartfelt words. Segal was an active member of the Bagley Community Council and the Jewish Community Council, and a staunch supporter of open occupancy. In the early 1960s, unlike many of his colleagues at other large synagogues, Segal had so far prevailed upon his congregation to stay rooted and not purchase land for a new building in the suburbs. But he likely knew it was only a matter of time before his synagogue would move.

Demographics confirmed the ubiquity of Jews' strategy of packing up and moving from the city and its problems. By 1963, 38 percent of Detroit Jews lived in the suburbs. While a majority (slightly over half) of the Jewish population remained in the northwest neighborhoods clustered around Bagley, demographer Albert Mayer predicted that by the next decade, very few Jews would live within the city limits. He suggested, however, that political activism could change that fate: "If open occupancy on a Metropolitan basis including the suburbs is achieved before 1970, there is a greater possibility that the Northwest area might retain more of its present Jewish population."[2] In his formulation, Mayer proposed that the city and the suburbs become a single metropolitan organism, fused together by policies that undermined a stark division between the two areas. Whereas a metropolitan vision had first shifted the sights of Jewish leaders from their neighborhoods to the city more broadly, the metropolitan frame expanded even wider from the mid-1960s through the early 1970s as Jewish leaders sought to stitch together the city and its suburbs in specific and, often, limited ways. Central to their efforts was the desire to craft and control a public narrative about Jewish suburbanization. By placing it into a metropolitan framework, Jewish leaders hoped to smooth out the ambivalences that threatened the terms of Jewish political, spiritual, and cultural self-definition once Jews no longer made their homes in cities.

Over the course of the 1960s, Jews communicated double-sided—and, often, contradictory—ambivalence about the city and the suburbs. Progressive and liberal Jewish leaders, including Conservative and Reform rabbis, worried that something at the core of Jewish values would atrophy if Jews left cities for suburbs. Entangled with their ambivalence about Jews leaving cities was their anxiety about Jews' arrival into the American middle class.[3] Few could argue with the material benefits of reaching this destination, and as the last chapter explained, liberal and progressive Jewish leaders, for the most part, did not challenge the market system and structure of private property that had enabled Jews to gain the privileges of white citizenship. Still, many of these same Jewish leaders, echoing the concerns of other social critics, expressed angst about the spiritual, communal, and ethical depravity that they feared would accompany Jewish socioeconomic privilege.

At the same time, a growing number of Jewish leaders—and sometimes the very same ones who deprecated suburban life and worked to reform cities—also issued sharp rebukes of city life. Most tangibly, the rebuke took the shape of Jewish leaders' decisions to move their communal and religious institutions to suburbs. In their rationales for making these moves, Jewish leaders sometimes rested their decisions on simple demographics and the desire to follow their people, but many also explained the necessity of defining Jewish life apart from the city and its problems.

Thus emerged a metropolitan urban narrative that portrayed the city as simultaneously more minor and more significant than it had ever been; on one hand, the city was simply one node of a metropolitan region, yet, on the other, it served as the defining center of an expansive metropolitan area. The protean quality of the city, able to be perceived as a narrow marker and also as the anchor of an entire region, shaped Jews' consciousness of their role in new urban dramas set many miles away from their homes but experienced as close as their doorsteps.[4]

Writing in *Phylon* in 1963, Jewish social critic and Yiddishist Joshua Fishman characterized Jews, in this new metropolitan landscape, as "absentee landlords" from American cities. Playing on the term, he explained that not only did many Jews who left the city maintain real estate holdings in it, but even those Jews who did not own urban property still fashioned themselves as caretakers, albeit remote ones, of the city.[5] Aside from commuting to their downtown offices, one of the primary reasons that suburban Jews continued to return to the city was to attend synagogue. As absentee landlords of grand urban synagogues, many Jews only looked in on these properties—maintained by their membership dues and contributions—once a week, once a month, or perhaps just once or twice a year. The decision about whether to move a congregation out of the city, especially once the majority of its members no longer lived in proximity to the urban building, strained the terms of Jewish metropolitan urbanism. In almost every negotiation about whether and when to move, synagogue communities confronted the disjuncture between their avowed support for city life and what appeared to be an inexorable process of Jewish disinvestment from urban spaces.

Enmeshed in urban congregations' decisions to rebuild their sacred sites in suburbs was a set of complicated tensions that Jews expressed about the terms of their privilege and their connections to cities. Indisputably, the monumental synagogue buildings that postwar Jews funded and built in the suburbs paid visible homage to Jewish socioeconomic privilege—this has been the reigning interpretation of the postwar boom in suburban synagogue building.[6] But the buildings also participated in the process through which Jews reinvented their relationships to cities. In the deliberations that went into constructing these new buildings, Jews continued to reposition themselves within the framework of metropolitan urbanism, asserting a gulf between city space and their new suburban landscape while still connecting themselves to a host of spiritual, cultural, aesthetic, and political ideals framed by their self-perception as an urban people.

Jewish Reinvention through the Suburban Synagogue

Starting in the 1950s, when the bulk of the Jewish population still resided in the city, the *Detroit Jewish News* published frequent articles celebrating congregations' efforts to fund, design, and erect new synagogue buildings outside of the city. A 1950 article, surveying the landscape of suburban synagogue buildings, reported with pride, "Although the many new buildings which have been completed or are now in the process of construction vary widely in size, they have in common the beauty and utility characteristic of modern institutional architecture."[7] The reporter went on to observe, "A modern building in itself cannot bring renewed life to Judaism in America, but it can serve as a healthy shot in the arm. There can be no question but that the beautiful new synagogues which dot the Detroit community are going a long way in achieving that end."[8] That "shot in the arm," it seemed, was the opportunity to reinvent Jewish life in new, modern spaces that stood apart, in some fashion, from the pressures of the city. The task of either moving a synagogue from the city to the suburbs or establishing a new congregation in the suburbs contained multiple narratives about who Jews were and should be, and what the old space of Jewish life had to do with the new space.

Centralized denominational authorities, rabbis, and building committees understood that synagogue movement offered as much of an opportunity to recraft a narrative of Jewish meaning as it did to erect a new synagogue, and that these two goals would be best achieved if woven together. More so than the other Jewish denominations, the Reform movement involved itself deeply in the process of transplanting old synagogues and building new ones in the suburbs. On one level, Reform Judaism's institutional involvement in the suburbanization of Jewish life is ironic. Reform Jews tended to be among the most progressive and outspoken supporters of urban reform and civil rights protections. Furthermore, by the 1950s, the denominational body of the Reform movement devoted itself to a social justice agenda tied closely to urban life.[9] Yet it also makes good sense that the Reform movement worked tirelessly to orchestrate the process of synagogue suburbanization. A well-managed campaign would tread carefully and avoid the potential hypocrisies of an urban committed people deciding to move their congregations away from the city.

In 1953, almost immediately after he assumed the pulpit at Temple Beth El, Richard Hertz steered his congregation on a course to leave the city while still maintaining a sense of urban purpose. Housed at the time in a 1922 Albert Kahn–designed building on a corner of Woodward that had once stood between two large clusters of Jewish life, Temple Beth El, gradually became an almost solitary Jewish space in a growingly black area of the city. In 1953, Hertz wrote to the synagogue's leaders, "We must develop a long-range master plan that will embody our total physical needs and congregation program at the time when our present quarters must be completely evacuated and disposed of."[10] With little fanfare, the congregation purchased acreage in Southfield, a suburb just beyond the city limits and about seven miles northwest of the Bagley neighborhood.[11]

In the decade prior to World War II and during the war, economic depression and then wartime exigencies had sidelined synagogue building. Depleted resources and ration requirements forced Jewish congregations to forgo building and improvement projects. The new prosperity that Americans experienced after World War II fed a synagogue and church building boom that, according to one historian's estimation, amounted to the expenditure of $3 billion from 1945 to 1955 to erect new religious buildings.[12]

In the winter of 1954, Hertz traveled to New York City to meet with several architects.[13] His trip, far from his own brainchild, had been arranged under the careful supervision of the Reform movement's central denominational body, the Union of American Hebrew Congregations (UAHC). Embedded in the Reform movement's efforts to guide the process of postwar synagogue building were two prescriptions about Jewish life. First, postwar congregations should establish themselves in the suburbs outside of cities, whether this entailed moving a preexisting congregation or establishing a new one. In an official guidebook to synagogue building published by the Reform movement in 1954, one of the contributors maintained, "New urban sites should be selected only where there is evidence of a fairly permanent urban membership. In the design of an urban structure care must be taken that the building will not become an excessive burden if its particular membership begins to decentralize."[14] The other central plank of the Reform movement's postwar synagogue building plan involved aesthetics: postwar congregations should invest in a modernist style of design and architecture that would clearly differentiate between old urban synagogue buildings and new suburban ones.

Since the end of the Second World War, the aesthetics of synagogue design had gained renewed attention among Jewish leaders and critics. In a 1947 article, after reviewing the past trends in synagogue architecture, art historian and former curator of the Jewish Museum in Berlin Rachel Wischnitzer-Bernstein charged, "The present and future demand something new, expressive of the aspirations of a more self-conscious Jewishness."[15] Although she was not certain what the new synagogue would look like, she speculated that "after the bitter lessons of the war," it would recoil from historical forms such as neoclassical and Moorish designs.[16]

A forum published in 1947 in *Commentary*, a Jewish intellectual journal, invited three prominent Jewish architects and an art critic to speculate on the "Modern Synagogue Style." With uniformity, the group averred that modernism—as an aesthetic and an ideology—could best inform synagogue design. Eric Mendelsohn, who had practiced architecture in Germany and designed some of the most well-regarded modernist buildings before fleeing from the Nazis, explained that modernism made people "aware of their human limitations." Clearly reacting against fascism and Hitler's animus toward modernist art and architecture, Mendelsohn suggested the postwar world could be reconstructed as a more humane place by erecting modernist structures "built to human scale" that served as "social centers" where people would interact equally in a "democratic community."[17]

That same year, in 1947, the Reform movement organized two conferences on synagogue building, during which it made clear its institutional commitment to modernism as the guiding design principle for suburban synagogues. In a subsequent volume based upon the conferences, the president of the UAHC explained, "It is hoped that . . . the tendency of mimicry and simulation in the synagogue will become speedily an unhappy remembrance of things past, and that a stirringly creative period of synagogue architecture expressed in an esthetic modern idiom may be stimulated."[18]

In the wake of the two conferences, the Reform movement situated itself as a controlling force in the aesthetics of Jewish synagogue building by creating a body called the Synagogue Architects Panel. Leaders of the movement assembled a group of architects and then subsidized their usual fees in order to offer no-cost consultants for synagogue boards exploring the possibility of erecting new buildings. By the early 1950s, the panel consisted of roughly forty architects, among them many of the most prominent in the United States. The majority of those on the panel were Jewish.[19] Membership on the panel was a professional boon to those chosen to serve who, as a result, became familiar names to rabbis and building committees and well positioned to receive commissions to design new synagogues. At the same time, these architects also felt a measure of loyalty to the Reform movement for acting as their agent and patron and, thus, would likely advance its ideals. In 1952, a UAHC official commented, "The response to our consultation service on both synagogue art and architecture continues to be almost frighteningly large."[20]

What was striking (if not frightening) was the number of congregations that felt driven to seek official guidance on moving their synagogues to the suburbs and that were compliant when it came to accepting advice on the physical form of those synagogues. Although only Reform congregations had access to the services of the Synagogue Architects Panel, the UAHC also answered frequent queries from Conservative congregations and provided lists of architects and guidebooks to them. By the mid-1940s, the Conservative movement had established a Department of Synagogal Architecture to assist new and emerging congregations in their building efforts, but its work and connections with architects were far less extensive and well funded than the UAHC's.[21]

Not Your Neighborhood Synagogue: The Rise of the Metropolitan Synagogue

At the end of 1955, the *Detroit Jewish News* reported that Temple Beth El's board of trustees had determined, after a thorough study, not to build on the land it had purchased in Southfield. According to the synagogue's president, congregational membership was continuing to grow, as was religious school enrollment and worship service attendance in the Woodward building. Furthermore, the newly built Lodge Freeway now allowed for congregants living in northwest Detroit and the suburbs to drive to the synagogue in "a matter of minutes." Convinced that the Woodward property held historical value as a "landmark" and that the expense of building a new synagogue, estimated at $5 million, was prohibitive, the board, despite the rabbi's wishes, declared Temple Beth El's intentions to stay rooted in Detroit.[22] Yet its commitment to Detroit hardly indicated a commitment to the neighborhood space surrounding the synagogue building; rather, it reflected the growingly metropolitan nature of Jewish life. Throughout the 1950s and 1960s, Temple Beth El's metropolitan vision enabled the congregation to remain grounded in Detroit, though eventually its commitment to a metropolitan ideal of synagogue life would provide justification for its move to the suburbs.

Much earlier than most other synagogues, Temple Beth El envisioned itself as a metropolitan—and not a neighborhood—synagogue. By the mid-1940s, its congregants were already geographically dispersed. A 1945 survey showed that one-third of Temple Beth El's members lived either in the Dexter area or the upscale Boston-Edison section of the Twelfth Street neighborhood, and one-quarter of its members lived in northwest

Detroit. By the next decade only about 15 percent of Temple Beth El's members remained in the vicinity of the Twelfth Street or Dexter neighborhoods, with the majority living in the northwest area.[23] That Temple Beth El already thought of itself as operating beyond its building's neighborhood location as early as the mid-1950s explains, in part, why it did not move to the suburbs until the early 1970s. With the exception of the Isaac Agree Downtown Synagogue, a synagogue established in downtown Detroit in 1921 to serve Jewish businessmen who needed to chant kaddish (a mourner's prayer), almost every other synagogue in the city tied itself to the residential neighborhood spaces that surrounded it.[24]

It makes sense that a postwar Reform congregation, much more so than a Conservative or Orthodox one, would imagine itself through a decentralized geography. Reform Jews, in the first place, made no pretense of following Jewish law prohibiting car travel on the Sabbath. By the early 1950s, the Conservative movement revised its understanding of the Jewish law that had been interpreted to ban car travel, and it permitted Jews to use their cars to drive to and from religious services. Even so, Reform congregations continued to think of themselves as much less place bound than Conservative ones, which sometimes had the consequence of enabling them to remain tied to urban neighborhoods longer than their Conservative or Orthodox counterparts. This was not only the case in Detroit. For example, when most congregations in North Philadelphia moved to the suburbs in the 1950s, the city's large Reform synagogue, Rodeph Shalom, alone decided to stay put, despite the fact that the vast majority of its congregants lived far from its North Broad Street location. Philadelphia's Rodeph Shalom, similar to Detroit's Temple Beth El, had a robust membership and full coffers. Money and members enabled both congregations a measure of freedom not felt by smaller and less affluent synagogues. Furthermore, as an ideology, Reform Judaism, when compared to American Conservative and Orthodox Judaism, focused far more on formal statements of belief than it did on modes of Jewish practice, many of which depended upon a centralized residential Jewish community for enactment.[25]

For Philadelphia's Rodeph Shalom and Detroit's Temple Beth El, remaining in urban neighborhoods with few Jewish residents was made possible by the religious ideology of the Reform movement. It also wove into the spiritual and progressive mission that many postwar urban Reform congregations espoused. A grand urban synagogue on North Broad Street in Philadelphia or Woodward Avenue in Detroit stood as a symbol of Jews' rootedness to the city and their commitment to urban-inflected social justice agendas. More often than not, however, the buildings were empty symbols, quite literally, since they stood unoccupied, as daily activities occurred in satellite buildings removed from the inner-city neighborhoods and bankrolled by affluent congregants.[26]

Unlike Temple Beth El, Shaarey Zedek, Detroit's largest Conservative congregation, defined itself through its location in a Jewish neighborhood well into the 1950s. In the 1930s, it moved from its building in the Hastings area to a new home in the Dexter neighborhood. Its location, still convenient for Twelfth Street residents to attend services, yet easily accessible to the growing Jewish population moving northwest into Dexter, revealed its attachment to Jewish space and its self-definition as a neighborhood synagogue. When Jews in the Bagley neighborhood established Adas Shalom, also a Conservative congregation, Shaarey Zedek leaders expressed few concerns since Adas Shalom had clearly been built to serve a different neighborhood. Yet as the Dexter neighborhood's Jewish population waned, and northwest Detroit appeared to be the new center of Jewish life, Shaarey Zedek worried about its ability to sustain itself as a neighborhood synagogue. Had Adas Shalom not already built a Conservative synagogue in Bagley, it is likely that Shaarey Zedek would have moved there. In fact, in 1952, the board acquired a small plot of land slightly north and west of Adas Shalom and built a modest structure to house a branch campus of its religious school. Yet Shaarey Zedek's leaders realized that the neighborhood could not support two Conservative congregations.[27]

As Jews left the neighborhood surrounding Shaarey Zedek, synagogue leaders felt pressed to act quickly: What would a neighborhood synagogue be without a neighborhood? For a brief moment, synagogue leaders contemplated following Temple Beth El's urban-based metropolitan path and, even, approved the expenditure of $2,500 to complete a parking lot adjacent to the Dexter building and appointed a committee to explore renovating and expanding the synagogue building.[28] Maybe congregants would return to Shaarey Zedek, pointing their cars south on the new highways dominating the city's landscape. Yet for the Conservative congregation, less affluent than its Reform counterpart and more tied to a geographically centered form of Jewish life, the metropolitan model felt unattainable and foreign. Whereas Temple Beth El's Woodward building was grand and monumental, itself expressing a sweeping vision of its importance, Shaarey Zedek's was more modest. Albert Kahn had designed both buildings in a very similar neoclassical style, but built during the

FIGURE 5.1 Shaarey Zedek, in the Dexter neighborhood on Chicago Boulevard, 1932. Courtesy of Walter P. Reuther Library, Archives of Labor and Urban Affairs, Wayne State University.

Great Depression, Shaarey Zedek showed signs of frugality not visible in Temple Beth El's building; for example, in place of the massive portico columns that guarded the entrance to Temple Beth El, eight miniature columns were inset just below Shaarey Zedek's pediment.[29] Temple Beth El's physical form announced gravitas and self-importance fitting for a metropolitan synagogue and simply lacking in Shaarey Zedek's building.

In the winter of 1954, Shaarey Zedek's board approved the purchase of land in Southfield. While the decision mirrored that of Temple Beth El's board in its timing and the location of the land, Shaarey Zedek moved much faster in its plans to relocate. From 1955 onward, pleas to repair the Chicago Boulevard building and hire a full-time maintenance person fell on deaf ears, though the board agreed to install a timed light in the building in 1957 so that it would not appear unoccupied.[30]

Morris Adler, Shaarey Zedek's rabbi hired in 1938, remained noticeably aloof from the decision to relocate. His silence on the matter reflected his discomfort with the decision and his unwillingness to tie himself closely to it. Similar to Temple Beth El's Hertz, Adler was active in city affairs and spoke openly about his liberal politics. His 1956 synagogue newsletter column detailing his openness and acceptance toward a black family who moved next door to him and his wife had circulated widely among Detroit Jews.[31] Adler defined himself through his civic involvement in Detroit's liberal-leaning organizations, including the United Auto Workers and Michigan's Fair Election Practices Commission. So passionate was his commitment to the city that a fellow rabbi called him the "Bishop of Detroit."[32]

Unlike Hertz, however, who offered only encouragement and energy for the project of moving Temple Beth El and often seemed frustrated with the slow pace of his board's decision to leave the city, Adler offered caution about moving to the suburbs. In 1960, as his board feverishly raised money for its new building in Southfield, Adler worried that the new structure "would face the challenge of a native born population which had no memories or scars; of a Jewish community that had emerged

FIGURE 5.2 Albert Kahn, famed Detroit architect and designer of Shaarey Zedek on Chicago Boulevard and Temple Beth El on Woodward and Gladstone and its earlier building on Woodward and Eliot (now the Bonstelle Theatre at Wayne State University), 1931. Courtesy of Walter P. Reuther Library, Archives of Labor and Urban Affairs, Wayne State University.

FIGURE 5.3 Rabbi Morris Adler (*third from the right*) with the United Auto Workers Public Review Board, including Walter Reuther (*far right*), March 1957. Courtesy of Walter P. Reuther Library, Archives of Labor and Urban Affairs, Wayne State University.

from the proletariat to that of a large middle class wherein ideas of social justice seemed to be waning."[33] Evoking the activism of the proletariat Jewish past, Adler encouraged his congregants to see their new suburban home as looking toward—and not fleeing from—that past, the city. Yet suburban synagogue buildings also clearly stood as monuments to the privileges that Jews had gained in the cities, privileges predicated upon their acceptance into a white power structure and their skill in navigating the economic terrain of white middle-class life.

The Privileges of Synagogue Suburbanization

Even as denominational bodies such as the UAHC helped steer the course of Jewish synagogue design in the suburbs, the more powerful force behind synagogue suburbanization was real estate agents and developers who stood to gain significant benefit from the moves. Some already had holdings in the suburbs, although many also maintained urban properties and generated revenue from tight and predominantly nonwhite real estate markets that they then used as investment equity in the suburbs.

Synagogue building committees served as platforms from which real estate professionals could shape the suburban housing and retail real estate market, so it is no accident that they flooded the leadership and ranks of synagogue building committees. To be certain, these men (in Detroit, the prominent Jewish real estate professionals were all men) were logical choices to sit on building committees because they knew the industry, the regulations, and the challenges and brought with them invaluable experience and networks. Yet as sincere as they may have been in their belief that the suburbs would offer a better environment for Jewish life to thrive, they also gained significant financial advantages from their synagogues' relocations. To calculate their actual gains, one would have to consider not only the role that a new synagogue building played in increasing property values and demand in areas surrounding it but also the favors that real estate men were able to cash in when they hired their own companies or friends' companies to lay foundations, raise roofs, wire, dig pipes, paint walls, pave parking lots, and landscape for new synagogue buildings.

Real estate magnate Mandell (Bill) Berman claimed the credit, almost fifty years after the fact, for having "made all the decisions" and "built" Shaarey Zedek's new building.[34] Born in Detroit in 1917 and elected to the congregation's board in 1952 at the comparatively youthful age of thirty-five, Berman indeed shepherded almost every facet of the relocation and building process. In 1946, Berman had become a partner in Bert L. Smokler and Company, a real estate development and home-building enterprise with most of its holdings in the suburbs of Detroit.[35] In an interview from 1990, he recollected a "knock-down, drag-out battle" about purchasing the land in Southfield in the mid-1950s. "There was a lot of feeling we ought to stay [in Detroit]," he remembered, but he and the board prevailed and convinced the congregation to buy the acreage.[36] With land in hand, Berman was confident the congregation would accede to plans to move. And he was certain, given his deep familiarity with the building trades and real estate market, he was the one to make that move happen.

Berman, of course, did not act alone. A wealthy hotel developer and a number of other builders and architects served on the building committee with him. The hotel developer, a man named Louis Berry, who in 1962 was among the investors who bought the Fisher Building in Detroit,

FIGURE 5.4 Bill Berman (*second from the right*), with members of the Junior Division of the Jewish Federation of Detroit, 1949. Courtesy of the Leonard N. Simons Jewish Community Archives of the Jewish Federation of Metropolitan Detroit.

recommended the group hire an architect consultant immediately.[37] Three local architects, all congregants and part of a newly formed Architect Selection Committee, compiled a list of well-known synagogue architects, almost all members of the UAHC's Synagogue Architects Panel. Berry immediately recognized the name Percival Goodman on the list and in the summer of 1956 persuaded the board to spend $5,000 to retain him as a consultant. (Because Shaarey Zedek was not a Reform congregation, it did not benefit from the free consulting services provided by the UAHC.) Berry and Berman well understood not only that Goodman could offer them sound advice, but also that he brought enough celebrity to the project to impress congregants and drum up their support for the new building.[38]

Among Goodman's first pieces of advice to Shaarey Zedek's building committee was to buy a new plot of land. He feared the fifteen-acre plot purchased in Southfield in 1954 was too small to accommodate a truly monumental synagogue building and also noted that the landscape was

FIGURE 5.5 Percival Goodman addressing the Union of American Hebrew Congregations, 1957. Courtesy of the Avery Architectural and Fine Arts Library, Columbia University, New York.

rather flat and unattractive and plagued with water-drainage problems. Ever the businessman, Berman, who had brokered the first land deal, now saw the opportunity for gain in selling the fifteen-acre plot and investing in a new one. Already, in the last three years, the fifteen acres had appreciated more than 100 percent; land that the congregation had purchased for $75,000 sold in the summer of 1957 for $185,000.[39] From its profits and with just a little more fund-raising, the congregation put down $125,000 in 1957 on a forty-acre parcel of land that sold for just over half a million dollars. Still located in the suburb of Southfield, the new plot of land met with Goodman's approval and, as Berman noted, was also surrounded by land suitable for a housing development.[40] A few years later, Berman would work through township channels to rezone a portion of the land for a housing development that he oversaw. His home-building company helped settle Shaarey Zedek congregants, including Rabbi Adler, in new homes that abutted the synagogue land.[41]

Despite the fact that Shaarey Zedek was a Conservative synagogue, its leaders communicated with the Reform movement's UAHC for guidance about the synagogue building process.[42] Berman flew to New York City, where he met with a handful of synagogue architects, all of whom served on the UAHC Synagogue Architects Panel.[43] During this trip, he quietly brokered a deal to hire their consultant Percival Goodman as chief architect on the project, though publicly the Architect Selection Committee made the selection. In 1958, the group traveled to the suburbs of Cleveland to view the recently built Fairmount Temple, a true Goodman package; the architect had designed it, furnished it, and selected the artists whose works adorned it. Sufficiently impressed, the building committee voted to retain Goodman, thus confirming the deal Berman had already made.

The Architect Selection Committee, at Berman's behest, also decided to hire Sol King, a congregant-architect and a member of the firm that Albert Kahn (since deceased) had founded at the end of the nineteenth century, to work with Goodman.[44] Berman announced this arrangement as a cost-saving measure, though for the local architects it was also profit making. And for Berman, his behind-the-scenes maneuvering with Goodman and the local architects assured him a position of power in future negotiations.

Several other synagogue members also angled to profit from the move. For example, when it came to selling the old building on Chicago Boulevard, inside channels ruled the day. In 1962, Shaarey Zedek was in the midst of final sale negotiations with Ebenezer African Methodist Episcopal Church. At the eleventh hour, a member of Shaarey Zedek, who served as the attorney for Clinton Street Greater Bethlehem Temple of the Apostolic Faith, also a black congregation, brought a new offer to the table. The offer came in at $600,000, a figure $150,000 higher than the Methodist's offer and almost too good to be true. A quick phone call to the attorney gave the board all the information it needed to understand the offer and its urgency: Clinton Street was in dire need of new space since it was being forced out of an area condemned by urban renewal plans. The funds the Christian group would reap from the government would more than cover the $100,000 deposit on the Shaarey Zedek property. Whether they would be able to pay the rest of the cost was unclear, but the board was able to extract a promise

FIGURE 5.6 The men of Congregation Shaarey Zedek preparing to transport the Torah scrolls from Chicago Boulevard to the new building in Southfield, December 20, 1962. Courtesy of the Archives of Congregation Shaarey Zedek, Southfield, Michigan.

from the attorney that Shaarey Zedek could keep the deposit whether or not the purchase went through.

The attorney took fees, the synagogue benefited from insider knowledge, and the Clinton Street group handed over the federally subsidized payoff it had been given for evacuating its old building to Shaarey Zedek, all in return for a building that Shaarey Zedek had deemed undesirably located.[45] In this case, urban renewal dollars helped finance the synagogue's move to Southfield while lining the pockets of synagogue members who helped facilitate that move.

Even as it moved with a slower pace, Temple Beth El similarly empowered a few real estate men to make the decisions and profits from its eventual relocation. By the mid-1960s, Temple Beth El had sold its land in Southfield on the advice of Aubrey Ettenheimer, a synagogue board member and also the owner of a local building company. Ettenheimer explained, "At present values, it is much too valuable a piece of land to consider putting a Temple on."[46] The board had already received offers from hungry industrial bidders who were seeking suburban sites for their headquarters.[47] Sell the land for a handy profit, Ettenheimer suggested, and use the earnings to invest in a larger parcel of land.

Throughout all of this, Temple Beth El's leaders discussed the land transactions as investments that would help strengthen the metropolitan congregation, rooted, for the time being, to its corner on Woodward Avenue. In a letter sent to the entire congregation, outlining plans to sell the old land and purchase new acreage, the president emphasized, "As you know, and I state this to avoid any misunderstanding, there are no present plans to build a new Temple. Some of our members believe that our present edifice should always be the home of Congregation Beth El. Others favor an immediate northward move. Only time and other developments can determine what our ultimate decision may be. The proposal made is merely to protect our membership, in the event such a move becomes a necessity."[48]

At Ettenheimer's prodding, the congregation agreed to purchase land in Bloomfield Hills, a suburb even farther north from Detroit than Southfield. Ettenheimer pointed out that "experts" predicted Bloomfield Hills and the surrounding West Bloomfield area would become "the center of our present and future membership's population."[49] The new building site, abutted by land restricted for residential zoning and several "high-class residential homes with an average cost of $30,000 to $60,000," promised a suburban haven for the congregation and profitable development opportunities for Ettenheimer and others of his ilk.[50]

Similarly, at Adas Shalom a real estate agent and congregant named Max Sheldon worked indefatigably starting in the mid-1960s to convince synagogue leaders to acquire land in the suburbs through his realty company. "Being a member of Adas Shalom," he wrote to a member of the board, "I hereby pledge to reimburse ½ of my earned six percent in real estate commission to the Adas Shalom Building Fund at any time a parcel is acquired through Max Sheldon Realty Company."[51] Using tactics similar to the kinds that Jewish leaders, including Adas Shalom's rabbi Jacob Segal, protested in Jewish urban neighborhoods, Sheldon admonished the board that "time is of the essence." He offered his professional opinion that the congregation "should have acted two years ago, but it is still not too late."[52]

Similar to Sheldon, who was eager to help the congregation purchase land in the suburbs, many members of Adas Shalom's building committee also were enthusiastic about bringing more Jews into the suburbs, where they would buy homes and shop. After all, among the members of the building committee were Nathan Goldin and Samuel Hechtman, founding partners of a suburban residential development group called Practical Home Builders, and Sam Frankel, the scion of a suburban mall-development firm.[53]

In the summer of 1966 Adas Shalom entered negotiations to purchase a plot of land in Southfield owned by WXYZ, an ABC affiliate. For the deal to go through, however, the synagogue learned it would have to buy the full sixty-six acres of land, priced at roughly $10,000 an acre. So desirable was the land that several members of the building committee decided to enter into a private agreement with WXYZ and purchase the land, explaining "the Synagogue was apprised through their attorney that it would be quite expensive for the Synagogue to have 66 acres in their name and then sell the balance." Instead, the group, as private individuals, agreed to "advance the funds" to acquire the land and then develop the excess "for residential purposes." They informally pledged to return much of the profits to support "the building of our new edifice."[54] By the fall of 1966, the negotiations for the land fell through when WXYZ decided to require a full cash purchase. The men who had agreed to front the money for the down payment walked away from the sale.[55]

Using their real estate networks, the building committee quickly found a seventeen-acre site in Farmington Hills, a suburb to the west and slightly north of Southfield. Working with the various owners of the land, almost all of whom were Jewish and some of whom were members of the synagogue, the building committee, as individuals, bought up contiguous parcels of land and sold sections of them back to Adas Shalom once the synagogue generated the capital to afford them. The building-committee members, for the most part, did not directly profit from selling the land back to the synagogue (though in at least one case, when tempers flared, one charged interest), but they all gained residual benefits, whether in the form of having become the owners of land adjacent to the synagogue, suddenly valuable and ripe for residential development because of the synagogue's presence, or through establishing relationships with other land developers from whom they purchased the plots.[56] In the final assessment, the men did well for themselves by doing what they believed was good for their congregation.

The Price of Leaving the City

Without a doubt, then, there was profit to be made in moving urban synagogues to the suburbs. Yet this fact did not overshadow the high costs, tangible and intangible, that Jews paid to make such a move, nor did it resolve the ambivalence that many Jews and their leaders expressed about leaving cities and moving to suburbs. Urban synagogues, such as Temple Beth El, stood as a visible connection between Jews and the city and had enabled their members to believe that one's personal decision to leave the city need not indicate his or her total disinvestment from the city. That is, a Jew might still pray in and for the city, even if he or she did not live in the city.

Indeed, so important was this narrative of urban investment, that Temple Beth El's leadership actively concealed elements of its ongoing relocation plans from the congregation so as to avoid the community upheaval that it believed would meet such an announcement. Despite the fact that the synagogue entered into an initial contract with architect Minoru Yamasaki in December 1965, one month later, the president of the congregation wrote in response to a handful of congregants' criticisms, "Let me reassure you at the outset that at the present time there is no proposal for the erection of a Temple on our new site." He continued, quoting directly from the letter of censure he had received, "I share your views in reference to the necessity for 'rapid integration of Negroes into the community.' If all people felt as you and I do about it, there would be no 'fleeing' from neighborhoods. Unfortunately, however, you and I cannot control this."[57] Even in positioning himself as a supporter of "rapid integration," the synagogue's president backpedaled from asserting any control over the larger forces that undermined the goal and made it unrealistic.

In early 1967, in the midst of a campaign to raise funds for the building, the president of the congregation recommended confronting criticism about the move with a "complete program of indoctrination" to persuade obstinate congregants of the benefits of relocation.[58] Nonetheless, in the summer of 1967, mere weeks after the Detroit riots spread through the blocks around the synagogue, the rabbi and synagogue president issued a statement describing their congregants as "ambassadors of reconciliation" and depicting the synagogue's physical location as a "source of strength and stability . . . to our city."[59] Confused by what he perceived as dissimulation, one board member complained that the rabbi and a few others "appear to be proceeding full steam" with the move, but only behind closed doors.[60]

In 1969, Temple Beth El's leaders reassured members that should it build "a new edifice in the suburbs," the synagogue would remain "commit[ted] to the problems of the inner-city" and would work to preserve the spiritual intimacy and meaning that many believed resided in their urban synagogue.[61] That year, the president of the congregation, a lawyer named Archie Katcher, received an inquiry about the Woodward building from a member, who happened to be a real estate agent. (The record does not reflect that the agent was his brother, Irving Katcher, also a member at Temple Beth El and active in the Independent Real Estate Brokers Association.) The agent implied that he had a client interested in the property. Although the president deflected the inquiry, explaining that the board was not in the position to give "any serious consideration to make a sale," his excitement about the potential offer was palpable. In a note to his board, Katcher enthused that the real estate agent had informally offered a $500,000 down payment with a land contract guaranteeing the remainder.[62] It almost went without saying that the prospective buyer was a black church.

As appealing as the terms of the proposed sale may have sounded, the synagogue leadership also understood the practical and symbolic implications of selling the Woodward building. In some cases, synagogues sold their urban buildings before their new suburban buildings were fully finished. Often, these congregations would rent space in their old building while awaiting the completion of a new synagogue building. When black churches purchased Jewish urban synagogues, which happened with notable frequency in the postwar years, church groups generally preserved the Jewish symbols and Hebrew verses found on stained glass windows or carved into the stone face of the building. Still, some Jewish congregants would have found it painful to watch the slow dismantling of their sacred space, as they moved from owners to tenants. Neither Temple Beth El nor Shaarey Zedek chose to sell their urban buildings before their congregation moved to new suburban ones, even though in both cases the revenue generated from the sales would have been helpful.[63]

Despite expressions of protestation, the majority of congregants at Temple Beth El and Shaarey Zedek understood their synagogues' moves as mirroring the same migrations they were making from city to suburb. Indeed, campaigns to raise the significant funds necessary to erect new synagogues in the suburbs played upon the familiarity that Jews had with weighing the decision about whether and when to move their own homes. A fund-raising brochure put together by Shaarey Zedek's building committee in the late 1950s explained, "Just as the growth of a family overcrowds what once was an adequate comfortable home, so the steady growth of our Congregation has brought about uncomfortable crowding in our Synagogue, our spiritual home."[64] It was natural, a simple process of growth, the brochure asserted, to want to make a better home for oneself with more amenities and space. Yet the text did not stop there: "And not only has our Congregation grown, but our city's residential areas have changed. As we would desire for our immediate family, so too it is fitting that our spiritual home should be situated in a neighborhood in which we ourselves would be proud to live."[65]

By drawing an analogy between funding the new synagogue and buying a new home in a better neighborhood, the framers of the text had hoped to tap into an experience with which many of its congregants would have been familiar. Another Shaarey Zedek fund-raising brochure suggested that congregants consider the payments they were willing to make for their new homes, and the ways in which they sacrificed in order to afford new homes in the suburbs. "If the amount you are considering [giving to the synagogue fund-raising drive] does not represent a real sacrifice," the brochure instructed, "it is *not* your fair share."[66]

Indeed, the problem obliquely addressed in the brochure was that the tangible costs of building the sort of synagogue that the building committee hoped to erect were extraordinarily high. Individuals' moves to the suburbs and recent home purchases, so soundly supported by federal lending programs and inexpensive home-building practices, did not prepare them for the high cost of building a monumental synagogue. Although initial estimates put the total costs for Shaarey Zedek's new building at $3.8 million, midway into the project, Berman realized that the estimate was about half a million dollars short.[67] Berman blustered that he was not worried about raising enough money, yet naysayers clearly abounded. A flyer distributed to congregants in 1957 outlining the plans for the new building proclaimed, "No one in Shaarey Zedek should doubt our members' financial ability to make possible a new Synagogue if they really want one. If sister congregations in Detroit can do it, starting with far less membership, leadership or physical resources, then so can we!"[68]

In 1962, when the building was finished and dedicated, Shaarey Zedek's congregants still had been unable to raise enough money to pay for it and went into debt. The congregation relied on revenue raised from the sale of its old religious school building in northwest Detroit, a donation of an acre of land abutting the forty-acre plot, and compensation from the Michigan State Highway Department for repossessing a swath of front acreage to break even again.[69]

Temple Beth El's suburban building, dedicated a decade later than Shaarey Zedek's, cost its congregants over $7 million. Temple Beth El's leaders could rely on its wealthier congregants to pay the high premium, almost twice as expensive as Shaarey Zedek's building, for a new suburban building.[70] However, the synagogue's leaders realized that unless congregants were convinced of the wisdom of the move, they would not open their pocketbooks. Of course, one could build a much less expensive synagogue, but Shaarey Zedek's and Temple Beth El's suburban buildings were as costly as they were because their leadership invested in the aesthetics of the building, just as the Reform movement in the late 1940s had recommended. Both congregations hired star architects and artists to render a new kind of Jewish space that communicated cosmopolitanism while drawing a sharp line of division between urban and suburban space.

The Look of Suburban Cosmopolitanism

When Shaarey Zedek's building committee hired Percival Goodman in the 1950s, it well understood that his work reflected the modernist tendencies of synagogue architecture. He designed strikingly modern synagogues but offered congregations leeway to interpret modernism in a way that felt comfortable and familiar. No other architect consulted with as many building committees or designed as many synagogues, over fifty, in the United States as Goodman. Thousands of rabbis, synagogue board members, and congregants, whether they had any background in architecture or design, became Goodman's disciples, imbibing his love for functional modernist art and architecture. His ideals, about the primacy of community, the importance of creating flexible and functional spaces, and the value of modern aesthetics became central to the look of suburban Judaism. In later years, he reflected, "It became perfectly obvious that the least important part was, in fact, this prayer function."[71] But Goodman also knew that Jewish leaders would not entirely abandon the sanctuary idea, so he suggested melding it with the social hall, often through moveable partitions, and thinking about "the whole space as a single, holy kind of space."[72]

A triangular façade, which two congregants would later describe as the synagogue's "massive prow-like form," practically screamed out the difference between Shaarey Zedek's old building on Chicago Boulevard and Goodman's design for the Southfield building.[73] Goodman explained that the triangle symbolized Mount Sinai. Whether the front of a ship or the sharp ascent of a mountain, the front exterior communicated height

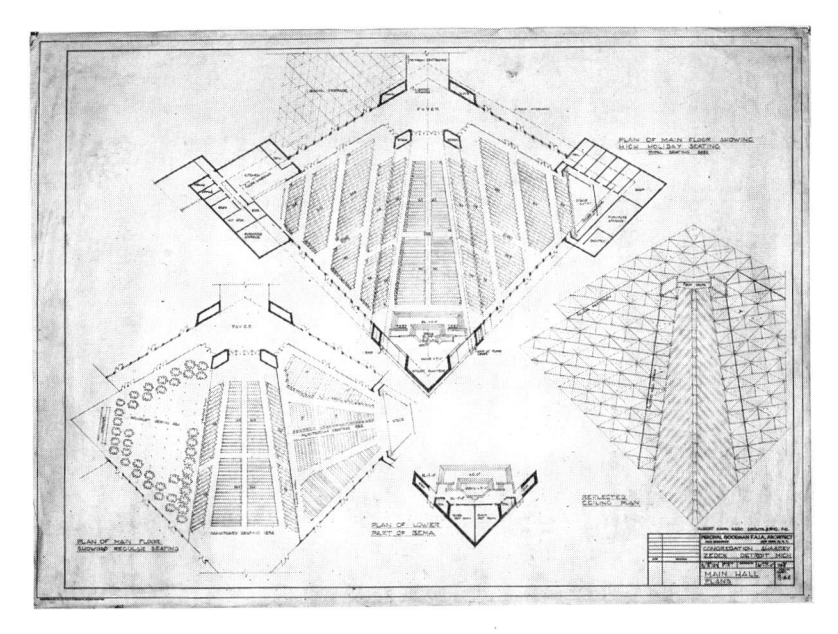

FIGURE 5.7 Percival Goodman's architectural plans for Shaarey Zedek's sanctuary and two flanking social halls, 1959. Courtesy of the Avery Architectural and Fine Arts Library, Columbia University, New York.

and verticality, echoed in the internal lines of the sanctuary. At its highest point, in the very front of the sanctuary, the ceiling soared to ninety-two feet. An ark, fashioned from white Israeli marble and framed in dark wood with stained glass panels radiating beyond the dark frame, extended toward the peak of the ceiling. Worshippers (up to eleven hundred of them and three thousand more if the adjoining social halls were combined with the sanctuary), who sat under a ceiling that sloped down to a more modest height of forty feet, gazed toward the inner shell of the triangular façade. As Goodman explained, "The Main Sanctuary is the dominant element because of its location and its height. The social halls flank it and form part of the same structure both functionally and aesthetically, for these halls, though typically used for celebrations are also extensions of the Sanctuary itself."[74]

While such a large sanctuary space was anything but functional for a congregation that rarely filled it, the sanctuary and the ark were the focal points of Goodman's design. He convinced the building committee to pay more than twice as much as he had allocated to the artists who fashioned

FIGURE 5.8 Exterior of Shaarey Zedek's new building in Southfield, circa 1962. Courtesy of the Avery Architectural and Fine Arts Library, Columbia University, New York.

the ark and the eternal light sculpture suspended in front of it.[75] Despite having decried stained glass (for blocking natural light needed to read prayers) and electric eternal lights (for feeling chintzy) in a 1947 polemic about the importance of functional design in modern synagogue architecture, Goodman was pragmatic enough to allow for both in his Shaarey Zedek design—and he handpicked the sculptor and glass artist.[76]

The verticality of the front of the sanctuary also did not cleave closely to the general principles of modernist architecture. Modernist architects tended to emphasize horizontal lines over vertical ones, believing in space that served human needs and rested close to the ground of human experience. Yet Goodman, similar to other modern architects who designed sacred spaces, seemed unable to free himself or his clients from the expectation that divinity should be communicated through height. How small a worshipper should feel in the presence of that sanctuary, that God!

Unlike its urban synagogue building, where visitors entered from the sidewalk up a set of front steps and almost immediately into the sanctuary,

Shaarey Zedek's new front entryway stood adjacent to an immense parking lot. A mammoth slab of freestanding concrete jutted out over the front entrance, creating a close and dark portico. Here, in the entryway, which led to a marble-floored expansive lobby, congregants might feel intimacy with their fellow congregants, under the cover of a canopy of concrete. They would also appreciate just how far they had come from their Chicago Boulevard synagogue, where a small parking lot had been tacked onto the back of the building's plot of land only as an afterthought and the dying gasp to keep the synagogue in the city.[77]

Although in the mid-1950s Temple Beth El's Rabbi Hertz had pronounced Goodman "the number one architect of the synagogue today," when it finally came time for Temple Beth El to choose its architect in

FIGURE 5.9 The main sanctuary in Shaarey Zedek's Southfield building, circa 1962. Courtesy of the Avery Architectural and Fine Arts Library, Columbia University, New York.

the 1960s, Goodman was no longer as new or exciting as he had once been.[78] Perhaps the fact that he had designed Shaarey Zedek made him seem hackneyed and not bold enough for Temple Beth El. Instead, the congregation retained Seattle-born Minoru Yamasaki, who had only designed one other synagogue (just outside of Chicago) but was fast gaining recognition for his innovative skyscraper designs. Yamasaki also had the added advantage of being local. In 1945, he started a firm in Detroit, and in 1962, he designed his first skyscraper for Michigan Consolidated Gas. Situated at the southernmost point of Woodward Avenue, the twenty-six-story precast concrete and white marble tower served as a model for the buildings he would design in the future, including New York City's World Trade Center. The next year, Yamasaki appeared on the cover of *Time* magazine, his face superimposed on one of his skyscraper designs.[79]

Mimicking design principles that were forming urban skylines would not make a suburban synagogue a city one—few suburban Jews wanted this to be the case since they had consciously chosen to move their synagogues away from the city and many felt ambivalent about the city they had left. But these principles could help connect suburban sacred space to an urban-oriented cultural ideal, where the city mattered as a sensibility, a place of culture, and the setting for spiritual ideas about justice. Temple Beth El clearly valued Yamasaki—and paid his steep fees—for his ability to shuttle between urban aesthetics and suburban space.

Indeed, as Jews moved out of the city, they increased their participation in urban arts and cultural life and joined the ranks of philanthropists supporting the arts in Detroit. In 1964, Alvin Toffler, a Jewish cultural critic, noted in his book *The Culture Consumers* that Detroit over the last decade had "witnessed a very perceptible change in the degree of Jewish involvement in community cultural life since the war."[80] Large cultural institutions, from the Detroit Symphony Orchestra to the Detroit Institute of Arts, changed their funding models from relying on a few high-level donors to embracing members of the "comfort class," such as Jews, who could be trained to give reliably.

In the late 1950s, for example, a Jewish lawyer named Alan E. Schwartz joined the board of directors of the Detroit Symphony Orchestra. Under his influence, the orchestra reached out to members of the Jewish community who had never funded the orchestra before but who had giving potential and an abiding interest in the arts. That same year, Jewish Detroit native Lawrence Fleischman joined the prestigious board of the Detroit Institute of Arts. Fleischman, the son of a Detroit carpet company owner, had

FIGURE 5.10 Architect Minoru Yamasaki showing synagogue leaders a model of the new Temple Beth El building, with Rabbi Richard Hertz on Yamasaki's right, circa 1970. Courtesy of the Temple Beth El Buildings Collection XXXX.06, Rabbi Leo M. Franklin Archives, Temple Beth El, Bloomfield Hills, Michigan.

a long-standing interest in visual arts. By the early 1960s, under Fleischman's leadership, the DIA expanded its funding base to embrace more public and private sources and tapped individuals, among them many Jews, who had never given before.[81]

As Jews raised synagogue buildings, some had already entered the world of cultural patronage, reflecting and augmenting their economic and political power in the city. For many Jews, however, their synagogue building campaigns served as a crucial source of instruction about how to support the arts and appreciate aesthetics that did not immediately feel comfortable, let alone recognizable.

Yamasaki imprinted the theme of movement onto the new Temple Beth El building, drawing on the biblical imagery of the tents that the Israelites pitched while they traveled through the desert during the exodus out of Egypt as the inspiration for his design.[82] Congregants may have been familiar with the story, but the design it fueled would have been far

FIGURE 5.11 Temple Beth El in Bloomfield Hills, 1974. Courtesy of Walter P. Reuther Library, Archives of Labor and Urban Affairs, Wayne State University.

less familiar. The main sanctuary paired vertical spaces with horizontal ones. A steeply ascending roofline resolved into a narrow plateau, like a spine that brought a level feel to the sanctuary despite the building's impressive height. An oblong oval served as the base for the sanctuary structure, where eighteen hundred worshippers could sit shoulder to shoulder. Large windows swept along the perimeter of the base. A worshipper inside could gaze onto the carefully landscaped campus, each window framing one segment of it as if naturalistic paintings hung side by side.

In March 1973, during the final phases of construction, the president of the synagogue wrote the congregation to announce that "the renowned sculptor" Bernard Rosenthal of New York City had been commissioned to create the main sanctuary's new sacred objects—the ark, a menorah, and the eternal light.[83] A graduate of the University of Michigan, Rosenthal had made his mark on the New York City art world with a commission to create a sculpture for Astor Place in 1967. The acclaim he received from this sculpture, *Alamo*, a cube that pivots on a single point, was likely just as instrumental in positioning Rosenthal to receive the Temple Beth El commission as his friendship with Percival Goodman and the fact that a twin of his Astor Place cube stood on the University of Michigan's campus in Ann Arbor.[84] Still $2 million short and hoping to convince congregants to increase their pledges, the president described the unprecedented opportunity the congregation had to bring truly contemporary and important art into its sanctuary. New checks came in.

When the new Temple Beth El building opened in 1973, congregants flocked to see the modernist sanctuary that their dollars had built. The year prior, Rabbi Hertz had acknowledged that the "move from the Inner City to the outer suburbs is hard," particularly because it involved accepting "what served well in [the Woodward] building for the last fifty years will not necessarily serve well in the new Temple."[85] Undoubtedly, some congregants were more attached to the actual building—its place in their own memory and family history—than they were to the location of the building in the city. Trying to rise above the hue and cry that plans to move had caused, one congregant reflected, "What concerns me more is what will be inside the building, and also what treasures will be left out."[86] His letter drew attention to the material objects adorning the Woodward Avenue building that might be left behind in the move.

An ornately carved monolith of dark wood, the Woodward ark was almost seventy years old and held sentimental value in the letter writer's estimation. Although the stained glass in the Woodward synagogue had not been with the congregation for quite as long, the writer also believed it evinced special attachment: "There is a certain deep feeling that I have each time I see the morning sun come through those windows. I feel 'at home' in Temple Beth El when I look out those windows, and I know that most of the members of the congregation share my feelings."[87]

Prescient, the letter writer understood how important these objects of memory were, and as congregants settled into the new building, they found themselves assembling often in its auxiliary chapel, adorned to Yamasaki's chagrin with the carved wooden ark and a handful of other ritual objects transported from the Woodward building. To get to the chapel, one passed through a glass-paned corridor, where colorful light streamed through the stained glass pieces, also brought over from the Woodward building. In this smaller chapel, with capacity for two hundred people, and a similar ancillary chapel space at Shaarey Zedek, congregants could feel closer to one another and the task of worship than they might in the massive modern sanctuary.

The new Shaarey Zedek and Temple Beth El buildings, dozens of others constructed in the Detroit suburbs, and hundreds built throughout American suburbs in the postwar years represented Jews' desire to implant themselves through foundations, steel beams, and paved parking lots in suburban soil. But they also carried with them references to an urban past: in the self-conscious opposition of the design schemes to the urban buildings; in the few objects transported from the city synagogues to the suburban ones; and in the continued calls that the rabbis and social justice committees made for Jews to engage with the people and problems of the city, who, in the main, were not Jews. The synagogues were important nodes in the landscape of metropolitan urbanism because they illustrated its core tension: Could one be fully engaged with the city without living within the city?

Spiritual Urbanism and Experimentation in the Suburbs

Critics and historians have not been kind to postwar synagogues. They have viewed the modernist forms these synagogues took as indicative of the soullessness and vacuity of postwar Jewish life: cavernous and cold sanctuaries, expansive social halls, massive parking lots, and costly upkeep with few returns.[88] Jews invested in these colossal synagogues, we are told, at the expense of meaningful Jewish life. For example, in 1972, a vocal student activist wrote, "We know that the plastic synagogues our parents go to are no more than haunted echo chambers of a once vibrant past."[89] While scholars categorize the efflorescence of new Jewish spiritual and political forms in the sixties and seventies as a reaction against middle-class suburban life, they rarely trace the lines connecting suburbs to new forms of Jewish spirituality and politics. Indeed, even as large monumental synagogues defined the Jewish topography of the suburbs, spiritual experimentation also found its home in suburban spaces. In suburban Jews' efforts to experiment with Judaism and bring new meaning to Jewish life, the city and urban ideals often remained crucial referents.

One example of this can be found in the suburbs of Detroit, where, in the 1960s, a new Jewish movement emerged self-conscious in its embrace of an urban and cosmopolitan Jewish identity even as its birthplace anchored it to the circumstances of suburbanization. Eventually termed Humanistic Judaism, the movement grew from one rabbi's charismatic leadership and his appeal to a small, liberal group of suburban Jews, mostly born in Detroit and starting their own families in the suburbs. The founder of the movement, Sherwin Wine, was born in Detroit in 1928. His parents were observant Jews and members of Shaarey Zedek. Wine studied at the University of Michigan and then moved to Cincinnati, where he attended Hebrew Union College and received his rabbinical ordination from the Reform movement. In 1958, he returned home to Detroit, after serving as a chaplain in Korea, and became the assistant rabbi under Richard Hertz at Temple Beth El. Although as early as his undergraduate days Wine had questioned theism and felt himself attracted to humanism, he kept his doubts about God quiet—quiet enough to gain him admission to and ordination from rabbinical school. But in the late 1950s, as he settled into the rabbinate at Temple Beth El, the captivating young man started to share with some of his congregants his disenchantment with a God-centered Judaism. In 1959, he left his pulpit at Temple Beth El to lead a congregation in Windsor, Ontario, just across the Detroit River. Yet he kept strong bonds with some of his former congregants, who in 1963 reached out to him to form a new Jewish congregation in the suburbs of Detroit.[90]

The men and women who sought Wine's rabbinic leadership felt dissatisfied with Temple Beth El. These were mainly professionals, married with a few children, and living in the suburbs of Detroit. The 1920s-era neoclassical building on Woodward, the rabbi who could be self-righteous in his pronouncements about what Judaism was and what Jews did, and the drive back into the city for religious services and holidays frustrated them.[91] Reform rabbis in northwest Detroit hoped to convince the dissatisfied suburbanites to join their congregations, which were much closer to the suburbs than the intersection of Woodward and Gladstone where Temple Beth El stood. Leon Fram, the rabbi at Temple Israel, the Reform congregation that had split off from Temple Beth El in the early 1940s and erected an architecturally striking building near Palmer Woods in 1950, quickly contacted the acting secretary of the schismatic suburbanites. He encouraged the group to reconsider the decision to form its own synagogue. "Once a family is in a car," he wrote, "it makes little difference whether they drive for five minutes or for twenty minutes. We have plenty of room . . . for all the residents in your area."[92]

Yet by the time Wine conducted his first service for the group on a Sunday in September, a spirit of experimentation and radicalism prevailed that would not fit with the norms of Temple Israel or the postwar Reform movement. The Sunday service—neither Friday night nor Saturday morning—was only the first clue that Wine intended to infuse the new congregation with his iconoclasm. Word spread about the charismatic rabbi who encouraged Jews to stop thinking about God and instead to focus their spiritual energy on human life. In November 1963, thirty-five families joined together to incorporate a new synagogue called the Birmingham Temple (a bit of a geographical misnomer since the congregation only met in Birmingham, a suburb of Detroit due north of Oak Park, very briefly).[93]

By 1964, interest in the new suburban synagogue swelled. That fall, one hundred families attended Friday evening services at the Birmingham Masonic Temple, where the congregation rented space. Wine, alongside lay leaders, had crafted a service that expunged God from prayers and focused on the immanent and human elements of Jewish ritual. The congregation established a religious school for its children and even held its first bar mitzvah.[94] As the congregation built its institutional apparatus, its aims became well known, not just as a source of curiosity, but also as reason for alarm.

By the mid-1960s, Wine was widely known by the epithet, "the Atheist Rabbi." Charged with not believing in God, Wine responded in 1964, "If by atheist you mean a person who denies the existence of a Supreme Being existing in time and space and having the attributes of a human being, then I am an atheist."[95] From articles published in the *Detroit Free Press*, regional Jewish newspapers, and, even, *Time* magazine and the *New York Times*, he gained recognition and, in many quarters, infamy for his conviction that Judaism should shed its dependence on the God idea.[96] Religion as "a matter of public relations," Wine wrote to his congregants, dictated that "one must belong to a religion. . . . My religion does not exist for me; it exists to inform my neighbor that I am respectable."[97] He saw little meaning in this form of exhibitionist religion that he believed had become the norm in most suburban and large metropolitan synagogues.

With increasing frequency, he was charged with the task of defending himself as a true rabbi and his congregation as a true synagogue. In 1964, Leon Fram, the rabbi at Temple Israel who also served as president of the Michigan Association of Reform Rabbis, convened a tribunal of area Reform rabbis who "confronted [Wine] with the rumors and accusations they had heard." Wine's responses, including his defense of atheism and his assertion that his congregation did not belong to the Reform movement and thus could not be censured by it, left Fram reeling. With clear exasperation, he told a reporter, "This Birmingham group . . . has a program aimed at losing all Jewish identity and of becoming a sort of cult. . . . It has violated a fundamental rule of Judaism."[98]

Solomon Freehof, the former president of the Reform movement's rabbinical association and a prominent national Jewish leader, agreed with Fram's assessment and suggested in the *National Jewish Post and Opinion* that by using the terms "rabbi," "synagogue," and "temple," Wine was "luring in new members by false and heartless pretenses."[99] Elsewhere, Freehof implied that Wine was a cult leader who dragged "innocent children and unsuspecting elders into a group dedicated to the propaganda of atheism."[100] Even Reconstructionist leaders, who themselves had to fight an uphill battle to gain acceptance for some of their radical ideas about the diversity of Jewish belief and practice, described Wine's philosophy as "untenable for a rabbi."[101]

Jewish leaders were not alone in condemning Wine for his iconoclastic ideas. In late 1964, the Birmingham Masonic Temple refused to continue renting its space to Wine's group, which had swelled to nearly four hundred members, explaining that Wine's atheism had prompted their decision.[102] Bishop Richard Emrich, a prominent Catholic leader in the city, added his voice to the rising condemnation of Wine. Writing in the *Detroit News* in the winter of 1965, Emrich analogized, "It is as if a General Motors official announced that he was opposed to cars."[103] Acting with a spirit of interfaith solidarity, Emrich defended Jewish leaders for speaking out against Wine, yet he also may have exerted subtle intimidation, suggesting that should Jews accept Wine's brand of Jewishness, then they would have moved beyond the pale of true American religion.

Wine was certainly not the first Jewish leader to propose jettisoning the idea of God from Judaism, yet his moment in time and setting in space electrified his ideology for supporters and opponents. On one hand, he spoke from a place of new Jewish security and self-confidence. By the 1960s, Jews felt more accepted in the United States than ever before evidenced by educational, employment, and social opportunities newly opened to them. From the setting of the suburbs, Jews perceived few impediments to their American success and comfort.

Yet Wine also tapped into the anxiety that limned Jewish life in the 1960s suburbs—and had, in fact, characterized Jews' encounter with modernity writ large: Could Jewishness survive in a new world that offered Jews more opportunities, rights, and freedoms to interact with civil society than in the past? A study of the Birmingham Temple, written in the late 1960s, explained that Jewish leaders "feared that the combination of location, ideology and a magnetic rabbi might prove so attractive to young college-educated Jews in a new suburban area, that the Birmingham Temple would grow at the expense of older temples, trapped with large buildings in neighborhoods of tensions and promulgating an unromantic ideology which quite possibly does not ring true to third and fourth generation American Jews."[104]

To be certain, Jewish leaders rejected the Birmingham Temple for its godlessness and countercultural tendencies, but they also saw it through their own anxiety about how to remake Judaism as relevant and meaningful outside of the city. Wine perceived the suburbs as a creative source for Jewish reinvention. As he was building his congregation from the ground up, many of the city's rabbis and synagogue boards were preoccupied with how to move a synagogue established decades or, even, a century ago, out of the city. Wine's congregants, some of whom experienced alienation from their families for joining the Birmingham Temple and most of whom lived in suburban subdivisions, often described the synagogue as their new "neighborhood" that served as a replacement for the closeness they had felt in their old urban neighborhoods.[105] The fact that Wine was a gay man, who only gradually came out to his congregants after many years of simply being assumed a bachelor, may have sensitized him to appreciate invented forms of community that could provide support even in the absence of traditional family structures. Homegrown in the suburbs, the Birmingham Temple recognized its community purpose immediately.[106]

When the members of the Birmingham Temple amassed the funds to erect their own building in Farmington Hills (a suburb west and slightly north of Southfield), they held to the modernist ideals of horizontal, human-scale spaces with far more orthodoxy than Shaarey Zedek or Temple Beth El had. Indeed, modernism's focus on the human realm perfectly complemented the Birmingham Temple's ideology. At the building dedication in 1971, Al Tobocman, a synagogue member and the architect, explained that the goal of "humanizing" space drove his design principles.[107] The function of the building—to house a group of Jews who had broken with the Reform movement—guided its form. These Jews, under Wine's instruction, had come to care exclusively about human, not divine, interaction and to use ritual to sanctify community, not God.

A simple brick-and-wood façade set off three conjoined rectangles: the central foyer, the sanctuary, and the administrative wing, which also housed a library. Inside, the space was low and open and lacked the grandeur of Shaarey Zedek or Temple Beth El. Large plate windows lined the front and back of the foyer, allowing natural light to illuminate the sheen of the dark brick floor and the wood panel walls. To the right, a set of doors opened into the sanctuary, designed, according to the architect, to

FIGURE 5.12 Birmingham Temple in Farmington Hills, designed by Al Tobocman, 1971. Courtesy of Walter P. Reuther Library, Archives of Labor and Urban Affairs, Wayne State University.

create a "more personal atmosphere."[108] Movable seats lined three sides of the room, and a dropped carpeted floor, with more space for seating, abutted a slightly raised platform or bimah. Echoing the materials from the exterior of the building, brick and wood served as the backdrop for the art on the bimah. Neither an ark nor a *shulchan*, or large table from which the Torah scrolls are read, imposed upon the bimah. This synagogue placed a single Torah scroll in a small niche in the library, where people could consult it but where it would never preside over the people.

The congregation, now rooted through its brick and mortar to suburban soil, never imagined itself an urban synagogue. Yet Wine guided his congregants to engage with the city as a sphere of this-worldly concern and identity. From the start, the suburban congregation dedicated itself to urban-oriented social activism. Congregants formed a Community Relations Committee in early 1964 and pledged themselves to participate in civil rights activities.[109] A Social Action Committee set its agenda to fight job discrimination, improve public education, and "aid inner-city youngsters" in Detroit.[110] Later, the congregation "adopted" an "inner-city" school and provided tutoring and other forms of assistance to the school.[111]

Echoing the turn toward legislative politics among Detroit's larger Jewish community, the Birmingham Temple likewise expressed its investment in the city by lobbying the state legislature to "take cognizance of the need for massive support for schools," to pass laws in favor of fair housing, and to bar employment discrimination in the city.[112] The progressive approach to Jewish spiritual life that marked the Birmingham Temple also informed the congregation's political proclivities and oriented the congregation toward the city and its struggles. At the same time, the congregation emerged as a product of the postwar Jewish suburbs, a new American terrain where Jews could experiment and reinvent, though rarely without ambivalence about what was being left behind and what was being made anew.

Death in the Suburban Synagogue

Twenty-three-year-old Richard Wishnetsky had purchased a sawed-off .32 caliber Colt revolver from a pawnshop in Toledo. The gun rested heavily in his suit pocket as he sat in the winter of 1966 in Shaarey Zedek's main sanctuary. The Southfield synagogue was crowded that day, with almost one thousand worshippers, including Wishnetsky's own parents, all there to attend a bar mitzvah.

Rabbi Morris Adler had just finished a sermon on Abraham Lincoln, whose birthday was celebrated that week. According to witnesses, Wishnetsky walked calmly down the aisle as the cantor started chanting the kaddish, the prayer of Jewish mourning. A tape recorder was running that morning and captured a gunshot, screams, and Wishnetsky's directive for everyone to leave the bimah except the rabbi.

Adler knew Wishnetsky; he had offered the troubled young man, a recent graduate of the University of Michigan, counseling a few times over the last couple of years. "You had better do what he says," the rabbi admonished the congregation, "this boy is sick." Then there was silence. Wishnetsky set his gun on the pulpit and took out a piece of paper. He read aloud: "This congregation is a travesty and an abomination. It has made a mockery by its phoniness and hypocrisy of the beauty and spirit of Judaism."[113] He stopped, warning an approaching person to back away while he finished.

"With this act," Wishnetsky concluded, "I protest a humanly horrifying and hence unacceptable situation."[114] Whispering the word "rabbi," Wishnetsky shot Adler in the arm. Screams. As the rabbi rose, the young man moved toward him and shot Adler point-blank in the head. Wishnetsky turned the gun toward his own head, fired, stumbled, and fell. His parents and sister watched from the pews. Five days later, Wishnetsky died. After spending a month in a coma, Rabbi Adler died as well.[115]

The *New York Times*, in its report of the tragedy, noted, "The shooting occurred in the modern new synagogue of Congregation Shaarey

Zedek."[116] Drawing attention to the building's newness and modernist aesthetic, the newspaper captured the dramatic tension between the yearnings of those who had worked so hard to design, fund, and erect the building and the act of madness that occurred in it.

Here in the fields surrounding Detroit, on a plot of land with rolling hills and an ample parking lot, abutted by a solidly middle-class new housing development, Jews who thought they had made it were unmade, at least temporarily. Wishnetsky intoned a prophecy of suburban ruin, not so different from social critics' vilification of the suburbs as breeding grounds of materialism, conformism, and vacuity. Unlike social critics, however, he used firepower to enact the prophecy and to stain the multimillion-dollar monumental synagogue with the blood of its rabbi and its disenchanted youth.

Two weeks before the murder-suicide, Adler had written a short essay about youth alienation from mainstream society. He argued, "The failure of society may be a root cause no less or perhaps more than the instability of the juvenile rebels."[117] Jews who moved to the suburbs believed they would find greater security and comfort for themselves, their families, and their communities away from the city. Such a public moment of suburban bloodshed interrupted that narrative and drew attention to one individual who felt himself so terribly failed by society and by Judaism.

That the murder happened in the gleaming new Shaarey Zedek sanctuary and that the sanctuary would now bear traces of the blood of the rabbi and the young man issued a pause, and one that Adler himself likely would have recommended, in a decade marked by Jews' growing prosperity and their migration to suburbs. An editorial published in the *Detroit Jewish News* while Adler still lay in a coma explained, "He is the chief spokesman for our people in Detroit. But he has gained the distinction also of being the interpreter of the acts of justice that are so vitally needed in our time so that there should be an end to racial and religious discrimination.... We pray that the powerful voice that had been interrupted may once again speak out."[118]

Indeed, without Jewish leaders such as Adler, Jews' ability to balance their narrative of upward mobility, as represented by the space of the suburbs, with their equally powerful narrative of Jews as the protectors of liberal urban social ideals of fairness and antidiscrimination policies was compromised. Adler's voice, similar to other progressive Jewish rabbis, had smoothed the contradictions in the postwar Jewish narrative of metropolitan urbanism and enabled Jews to believe it was possible to move away from the city and still remain engaged in it. When a year and a half later, Detroit Jews witnessed an uprising in their city, some Jewish leaders still sought to tie Jewish concerns intimately to the fate of the city, but many, albeit more gradually and less horrifically than Adler, simply silenced their efforts.

CHAPTER SIX

Urban Crises and the Privatization of Jewish Urbanism

The first night of the riots, July 23, 1967, fifty-nine-year-old Max Fisher, a prominent member of the Jewish community who made his fortune in the oil industry and, later, in real estate investments in Detroit, heard the report that the city was on fire. Ignoring authorities' efforts to seal the city, he called for a car to take him from his suburban home to his downtown office. He stood atop the thirty-story art deco Fisher Building, a building he along with two other principal investors, both also Jewish, had purchased just five years earlier, and surveyed the city. His biographer wrote, "For Fisher . . . the riots of Detroit touched a chord of sadness in him in a way he cannot describe. Ask him about it and he shakes his head. . . . Nothing in his past had prepared him to watch people, in the city he so willfully claimed as his home, burning their houses."[1]

Another prominent Jewish man, a mall and real estate developer in his sixties in the summer of 2008, told me that he, too, had been in the thick of the riots. "I was right in it," he insisted. And then he explained: he had been a member of the United States Army special reserve unit called up to restore order. "We were in a war zone, in the middle of a war zone. In the center of an urban area, totally unprepared." During the second week of his service, after the fires that reduced twenty-five hundred buildings to ash heaps had been extinguished and the military presence brought controlled stillness to the city blocks, this man took a short drive in his jeep.[2] "I went to see the house where my father had grown up because I was close by." He paused. "So what was it like?" I prodded. He stumbled at first, "I said, this is, what's going on?" Then his voice grew louder, "This is my city! What's going on here?"[3]

FIGURE 6.1 Max Fisher and the Fisher Building, which he purchased with a few others in 1962 and where he maintained a twenty-second-floor office, 1970s. Courtesy of the Max M. and Marjorie S. Fisher Foundation.

Whose city? He had not returned to the blocks of his own childhood home. Rather he had driven to the blocks surrounding his father's home, a home his father had left in 1941 before he was even born. While he attended college in Ann Arbor in 1964, his parents had moved out of Detroit, and when he returned to the Detroit area, he moved to Birmingham, an affluent suburb about twenty miles to the northwest of the city center. And Max Fisher, who had moved to Detroit in his early twenties, left the city for Franklin, another affluent suburb of Detroit, ten years before the riots. That both men, nonetheless, claimed Detroit as their city revealed the ongoing connections, financial, political, and psychological, they maintained to a city they had left. As the many chapters preceding this one have shown, the terms of Jews' connection to Detroit were neither straightforward nor consistent.

It is tempting to see the 1967 riots as a turning point in Jews' relationship with Detroit—the time, to put it crassly, when Jews broke up with the city. The riots serve as a convenient narrative device for encapsulating a complicated set of political, economic, cultural, spiritual, and personal changes that Jews experienced but did not foment. In this narrative, the riots acted upon Jews, and Jews reacted to them.

Yet as historians have shown, the urban uprisings in American cities throughout the 1960s did not function as much as turning points in the political economy of city life as they represented a coalescence of deep-rooted political and economic structures that had diverted funds and resources away from cities and limited nonwhites' access to opportunity.[4] Indeed, what is most striking about the role that the riots played in Jewish life in Detroit is how many patterns set well before them endured well after them.

In the form of what I have termed metropolitan urbanism, Jews had already started to redefine their role as stewards, if not inhabitants, of the city. In the decades before the riots, Jews set in motion a demographic pattern of suburbanization. Even as they broadened the urban field to include their lives in the suburbs, they also contracted their own urban activism, putting their faith increasingly in government programs to help improve the struggling city from which many had fled. From afar, Jews could lobby for legislative change and seek to redress the large legal systems that made inequality endemic to Detroit. They could also harness a spiritual vocabulary to urban activism, whether in their own synagogue spaces or in interfaith coalitions, and work to repair the city through non-state means—through good works and spiritual rightness.

Over the course of the postwar years, Jews had reinvented their relationship with the city, reflecting changing political and economic circumstances that affected Jewish and urban life. Jews' urban activism in the immediate postwar years had been characterized by local, individual, and communal efforts. Neighborhood associations, the Jewish Community Council's committees, parlor meetings with concerned residents, cleanup drives, door-to-door canvassing, all of these efforts relied on the power of the individual and the community to effect immediate and nearby change.

In the 1950s, as Jews increasingly questioned the efficacy of grassroots forms of organizing through the private individual or local neighborhood, they also gained more civic power. Furthermore, state interventionism, particularly in terms of civil rights and public works, expanded in the postwar years and promised a new vision of urban reform through public government action. Yet even as Jews expressed their faith in government action to reform urban life in the 1960s, the possibilities for state involvement in urban life became constricted. During the early to mid-1960s, many Detroit Jews had shared Mayor Cavanagh's optimism that Detroit could build itself into a model city, using federal government resources. Far fewer of these resources materialized than Detroiters hoped, especially as the war in Vietnam diminished federal funds. At the same time, the city's tax base persistently shrunk, a trend in which Jews played a role. By 1965, almost half of all Jews lived in the suburbs of the city.[5]

Although the federal government deployed U.S. armed forces to quell the riots in the summer of 1967 and gave its dollars to rebuild the city after the destruction, Jews, similar to other whites and blacks in Detroit, emerged from the riots less certain than before that the government could heal what commentators dubbed the "urban crisis." An examination of Jews' responses to the riots reveals two trajectories stemming from earlier sources: first, Jews' continued ambivalence and frustration with the city and, especially, the black leaders who articulated a vision of radical justice very different from mainstream Jewish leaders' liberal vision of fairness and remedial efforts to stop discrimination; and, second, Jews' growing investment in private, whether entrepreneurial or faith-based, efforts to determine the course of urban reinvention and stitch it to suburban Jewish concerns. Without a significant electoral voice in the city and under the sway of a federal government less and less willing to devote funds to urban improvement and social welfare programs, Jews came to understand their relationship to the city in terms of the private acts they chose to support.

Private Urban Activism after the Riot

When the *Detroit Jewish News* went to print on Friday, July 28, 1967, four days after the start of the riots, its editors declared, "Detroit is back to normal." In its eagerness to proclaim an end to the riots, the Jewish newspaper credited two sets of forces: President Johnson's order to send federal troops to Detroit, and community efforts to help the victims of the outbreak. The newspaper reported that Jewish Community Center buildings, the central offices of the United Hebrew Schools, and Temple Beth El were all declared "drop-off stations for non-perishables to be distributed among the victims of the rioting." Jewish Family and Children's Services had volunteered to help homeless victims find shelter, and Jewish attorneys were well represented among the lawyers defending individuals who had been wrongly arrested during the riots.[6] Such a premature attempt to put the riots behind the city, written while fires still smoldered and soldiers still patrolled the streets, revealed opposing visions for Detroit's recovery. In one, the president swooped in on the chariot of government intervention, commanding military forces to act at the will of a beneficent and mammoth government toiling for the good of its people. In the other, community leaders orchestrated private efforts of goodwill to help the city move forward.

What had been quiet and occasional doubt about whether government policy could really reengineer society into a place of racial and economic justice grew far louder than ever in Jewish responses to the riots. Prominent Jewish leaders voiced criticism of black leadership, arguing that it had not taken the proper responsibility for its community and that neither the government nor any other agency could restore justice unless black leaders stepped up their efforts. In its Friday edition, the *Detroit Jewish News* editorialized, "The people who must take the lead in assuring a return to sanity are the Negroes themselves. Negro leadership must assert itself. It must do its utmost to wipe out crime in its midst. And the white community must stand ready to help in every form."[7] In this formulation, the "white community" emerged as a handmaiden, awaiting black directives for how it could help solve a problem that was essentially a black problem. The editorial made no mention of government policies that created the economic and political conditions for the riots, or governmental action that could be taken to remake the city. This from a newspaper that since its inception in 1942 had consistently advocated government action to spur civil rights in employment, education, and housing for all Americans and, throughout its history, had a single editor, a political liberal named Philip Slomovitz.[8]

In the months after the riots, Jews who considered themselves left of the liberal Jewish center felt more empowered than before to voice their criticism of government policy. The riots proved to them that government programs were token gestures to mitigate social unrest at the expense of true change. An address offered by Jack Carper, the Michigan director of the Jewish Labor Committee, to the Workmen's Circle less than two months after the riots pinned blame on federal legislation for not solving the twin problems of poverty and segregation. In scathing language, he castigated liberals for their blind faith in government programs: "We who know better have allowed ourselves to be misled by an anti-poverty program, by a head start program and by the public proclamations extolling the virtues of integrated housing." The complacent belief that government programs could solve the deep problems of economic inequality and racial injustice enabled liberals to rest easy, Carper explained. With their respite now interrupted by rioting, liberals—and, really, he meant Jewish liberals—were threatening to respond in exasperation, "to throw up our hands and declare—Enough is Enough!" The truth, however, was that these government programs "have not affected the life of the Negro. They have at best affected our lives, they have enabled us to think that we are making our finest effort." For Carper, only once all people had opportunities to secure jobs that paid a living wage and afforded them access to education, housing, and the "good life," would society be redeemed.[9] Yet in his criticism, he offered no indication of how job creation could be achieved and whether the same government that he deemed so incompetent in its civil rights work could take on the task of such a massive social revolution.

Even from Jewish groups firmly entrenched in the liberal center, the theme of government inadequacy resounded. In May 1967, a few months before the riots, the national director of education and urban affairs for the American Jewish Committee suggested to Detroit's local chapter that those groups with "great technical resources in housing, education, [and] employment" must avail their services to the "racial underclass." While the director suggested that the government must also turn its attention to helping cities, he focused on the ways that private "business- and community-backed" programs could offer assistance where the government might fall short.[10]

As President Johnson ordered troops to the city, and Mayor Cavanagh, much like Jewish leaders, offered reassurance that the city was on its way toward normalcy, an undercurrent of skepticism about the government built among residents of the city and its suburbs. Almost immediately, that skepticism manifested itself in the creation of private efforts to heal and rebuild the city that sought to put substantial power to control the future of the city in the hands of private interests.

On July 24, 1967, the day after the riots started, a group of Protestant, Catholic, and Jewish leaders met to establish the Interfaith Emergency Council. Shortly after, in the weeks following the riots, civic leaders, Jews among them, formed New Detroit, a private citizens council. Faith leaders and business leaders responded to the riots with alacrity, charting their own vision for the city and positioning themselves as central to any future order for the city. In both faith and business spheres, Jews participated actively, though with notable anxieties. Jews voiced concerns about joining the work of faith-based urban missions that reflected overwhelmingly Christological goals. In the business community, a few prominent and very affluent Jews made inroads into Detroit's business elite and gradually invited their Jewish friends to act as investors in urban projects. Yet throughout the late 1960s and early 1970s, even as Jews increasingly formed their relationships with Detroit through the private realms of business and faith activism, their footing in both realms remained shaky.

The Interfaith Emergency Council fashioned itself as the central "relief agency" to assist innocent victims of the destruction. Meeting first at a Catholic church, the group, which included black and white Protestants, Quakers, Catholics, and Jews, quickly reassembled at the Cathedral Church of Saint Paul, the seat of the Episcopal Diocese of Michigan located on Woodward Avenue, a few miles south of the riots' epicenter.[11]

Seeking broad-based support, the Interfaith Emergency Council reached out to labor unions, city government, and private agencies to amass funds. When measured against the millions of dollars of destruction, the $100,000 the group raised appears paltry.[12] The group, however, imagined its task as broader than giving money to those in need; rather, it hoped to reframe the discussion of the city by channeling power to citizens to work together in a spirit of cooperation and transcendent purpose. The group's statement of "common purpose" later elaborated: "In this time of domestic crisis a general religion cannot suffice. Nothing less than epochal acts of responsibility are required of us. We sense the need to design new dimensions of action, based on a profound repentance and appreciation for the amount of faith this new action will require of us. The programs we initiate will reflect our contemporary attempt to serve man and thus obey God."[13]

Resonating with early twentieth-century social gospel activism, the leaders of the group shared in a liberal theology and a belief that good works in this world were endowed with divine purpose. Temple Beth El's Rabbi Richard Hertz, along with representatives from the American Jewish Committee, American Jewish Congress, and Jewish Community

Council, attended early meetings, when the group proposed allocating funds for basic provisions for people displaced from their homes, for case workers to monitor families in distress, for back-to-school supplies so that children could start the school year with a sense of normalcy, for short-term loans, and for justice-oriented projects, such as the stationing of clergy at "ghetto police stations" to act as advocates for individuals brought into police custody.[14] The group also disbursed funds to organizations seeking "to focus on the development of economic and political power in the ghetto."[15]

In the same weeks, as interfaith leaders scrambled to gather resources, distribute them to individuals and families in need, and offer "an interpretation of the riot" to their "own constituencies," Detroit's business and civic leaders met together with an equally urgent sense of mission.[16] On July 27, 1967, a group of civic and business people came together at the behest of Governor George Romney and Mayor Cavanagh. Within a week, it unveiled itself as New Detroit and announced a list of thirty-nine black and white leaders who would serve at its helm. Joseph L. Hudson Jr., the president of the J. L. Hudson Company, the largest department store in Detroit, and chair of the Metropolitan Fund of Detroit, stepped into the position of leader. Funds from the Metropolitan Fund of Detroit, described in New Detroit literature as a "privately-supported, regionally-oriented urban affair research and coordination agency" underwrote the immediate costs of the group.[17]

As a citizens' group, New Detroit relied on its members to donate their time, staff from their own offices, and money in return for the power to set the course of action to remake the city. Those asked to join had to prove themselves in control of resources or as representing some other strategic interest of the committee. In its earliest days, the only Jewish person tapped to join the committee was Max Fisher, who had recently acquired a majority share in the landmark downtown Fisher Building (only coincidentally did he share a name with the building, erected in 1928 and named for the Fisher brothers' auto-body company that had become a division within General Motors in 1919). Within the first few months, however, Stanley Winkelman, of Winkelman's department stores; Mel Ravitz, from Detroit's Common Council; and Norman Drachler, superintendent of the Detroit Public Schools, also joined the committee.

If these Jewish men were selected for the mix of the power they wielded and the access to powerful institutions and individuals they had, other members were selected to legitimate New Detroit in the eyes of

Detroiters, especially black Detroiters. Hudson, the chair of New Detroit, boasted that nine of the committee's original members were black and that one-third of these "proudly acknowledged the label of militant."[18] As historian Heather Thompson has explained, New Detroit self-consciously invited black radical leaders to join in its efforts, hoping to co-opt their radicalism and restore black faith in liberal leadership.[19]

New Detroit and the Interfaith Emergency Council met the challenge of the riots, in part, by attempting to leverage public funds from government programs and to lobby for greater federal involvement in urban issues. In a report written nine months after its founding, New Detroit leaders explained, "To meet the complexity and cost of dealing with [urban] problem[s], the New Detroit Committee believes federal involvement in terms of great sums of money and leadership will be needed in order to arrest the continuing growth of inner-city hopelessness and despair."[20] More than anything, however, the faith and business groups saw themselves as operating in the vacuum left by ineffectual government action. They faced the challenge of finding new sources of urban funding, but also stepped into a position of power to dictate urban policy unfettered by the legislative checks that government programs endured and the electoral buy-in they demanded.

Leaders of the Interfaith Emergency Council, strapped for funds almost immediately, realized that their efforts were contingent upon investments from private sources with deep pockets. In a letter to Hudson and New Detroit, sent in the early days of August 1967, interfaith leaders wrote, "We . . . are deeply concerned that the New Detroit Committee should conceive of its function as supporting the efforts of grass roots organizations and groups in the planning and implementation of Detroit's rehabilitation."[21] Admonishing New Detroit against catering only to elite interests, the leaders of the interfaith group hoped to convince the business leaders that their standing in the community and their ability to connect with the needs of real people would be strengthened if New Detroit invested in groups such as the Interfaith Emergency Council. At the same time, however, the Interfaith Emergency Council's internal documents reflected its own concern that faith leaders were not adequately meeting the needs of urban residents, especially black ones. The same Emergency Council leaders who suggested creating a permanent Interfaith Action Council, a body eventually formed in the spring of 1968, also worried about how to balance the interests of constituents who brought large sums of money to the table with those who had fewer resources to give.[22]

The Faith Dilemmas of Metropolitan Urbanism

On the first anniversary of the founding of New Detroit and the Interfaith Emergency Council, a columnist in the *Detroit Free Press* noted, "It was not the politicians who stepped forward after the riot to run the recovery effort. It was the city's business-industry-labor hierarchy."[23] The leaders who had earned Detroit its moniker, the arsenal of democracy, believed they could use their power and money to heal the city, willfully turning a blind eye to the way some of their methods of amassing wealth had created festering wounds of racial and economic inequality already for many decades.

Faith leaders, taking a cue from the private business world and building on a legacy of social gospel ideals that positioned faith as a force of this-worldly reform, hoped to have a place at the drawing board when it came to reconstructing the city. While both groups nodded toward the citizens whose lives were most enmeshed in the city's social welfare complex and whose frustration with the white power structure had long been mounting, neither group took its mandate from broad public consensus. All three of the radical black representatives, including the Reverend Albert Cleage, whom Hudson had so proudly touted as part of the leadership of New Detroit, resigned in January 1968.[24] By the spring of 1968, white clergy members of the Interfaith Emergency Council admitted that many of their efforts might appear as "white [people] planning for black people without consultation with black people," and a splinter group of black clergy formed to present its own recommendations for how to appropriate Interfaith Emergency Council funds.[25]

Interfaith political activism was a centerpiece of Jews' metropolitan urbanism, allowing Jews to make common cause with other liberal leaders who created a spiritualized discourse about urban obligation. Jews were present from the start of the Interfaith Emergency Council and some Jewish leaders offered true support for the group's activities. However, when it came to funding the Interfaith Emergency Council and a similarly conceived interfaith housing program, Jewish leaders were skeptical and tightfisted.[26] At root, they worried that these organizations aimed to act as Christian ministries, bringing the poor and deprived to embrace the religious institutions that uplifted them from their social circumstances.

Additionally, Jewish leaders in the late 1960s were ambivalent about pursuing private channels, whether business or faith, to reform urban ills and social inequality. Since the Great Depression and New Deal, American Jews had defined their liberalism through support for and faith in government action. In the decades after World War II, Jewish agencies emerged as strong supporters of government efforts to fight discrimination through public relations campaigns and to mandate social equality through legislation.[27] That the government could be a source of protection of—not threat toward—Jewish rights provided Jews with a deep sense of security about their Americanness and also a sense of urgency to support government and distinguish themselves as good, or model, citizens.

Thus, it was with a measure of ambivalence that Jews in Detroit, in the years after the riots, supported the privatization of urban policy. Jewish metropolitan urbanism had developed in tandem with faith that government programs could sustain cities, and that citizens, wherever they located themselves in urban geography, could be part of that work by supporting government. Jewish organizations were reluctant to assume that urban problems would be solved primarily through individual or private acts. Throughout the late 1960s, Jews continued to understand the private work they did—raising funds for scholarships, helping with employment training programs—as a complement to long-term legislative solutions to urban problems. Reviewing its activities after the first anniversary of the riots, the Jewish Community Council highlighted the "active role" that Jews "played . . . in obtaining state and national legislation in open housing . . . [and] towards building an open society."[28]

Nonetheless, over the postwar years, Jews had also developed an infrastructure of urban involvement that ran parallel to public sources, but was backed by private Jewish interests and funds. The Jewish Community Council and Jewish Federation relied on private Jewish dollars to support their staff and activities, though they accessed public funds for certain programs. These groups understood the power of the private dollar to set the agenda and saw how top investors used their economic clout to steer programs. From this perspective issued Jewish excitement about private-sourced but public-oriented urban activism and, also, wariness about in whose hands urban power might come to rest.

In the beginning of 1968, the Jewish Community Council sought to establish an urban affairs committee to deal "constructively and effectively" with the "urban crisis." At the same time, leaders expressed reluctance to support fully interfaith urban programs.[29] One memo explained, "Whether Council formally affiliates with a permanently constituted new [Interfaith Action Council] is a decision that has not been made. . . . Since our involvement in the inter-faith approach would be only a fractional one (one of several denominations) we obviously could not have the sole option of selecting programs, and might even be supporting some for which we would have less than complete enthusiasm."[30] Epitomizing Jewish metropolitan urbanism, these Jewish leaders believed in investing in the city but wished to do so on their own terms that would be relevant to the lives that Jews were leading—or should be leading—in the suburbs.

By the mid-1960s, anxiety about "Jewish survival" became a central motif in suburban life. Weaving together demographic concerns about the slowing pace of Jewish population growth, especially after the Holocaust, and normative concerns about the quality of Jewish life and, most specifically, the rising rate of intermarriage between Jews and non-Jews, the discourse of Jewish survival became central to Jewish community life in exactly the same years that the Jewish population center shifted from cities to suburbs. The rhetoric of Jewish survival tended to recommend a greater focus on the internal dynamics of Jewish life and a new guardedness about activities that brought Jews into common cause with other groups.[31]

Jewish concerns about joining Christian-dominated efforts to address the so-called urban crisis limited Jews' investment in certain programs. In 1968, the Interfaith Action Council suggested the creation of Suburban Action Centers with the goal of "interpret[ing] to the predominantly white outlying communities of metropolitan Detroit the seriousness of inner-city ghetto conditions—its poverty and its situations of injustice."[32] A proposal simplistically suggested, "The white community can learn from the black community who want to 'tell it like it is.'"[33] Helping to build confidence in the proposal, a report from the spring of 1968 praised "churches in the Detroit area" as "one of the few organizational entities" committed to contesting the "self-fulfilling prophesies and stories so rampant in the metropolitan community."[34]

Richard Hertz, the rabbi at Temple Beth El, endorsed the proposal to create Suburban Action Centers and an early report noted that congregants at the Birmingham Temple were "eager to become involved."[35] When brought initially before the Jewish Community Council, however, the proposal received little support. Noting that it required "a rather large outlay of funds," the staff recommended the board reject the proposal. Agreeing, the board leaders added that the council's human relations activities already extended into the suburbs and supported similar activities.[36]

In 1969, Shaarey Zedek's Rabbi Irwin Groner tried to muster new Jewish support for Suburban Action Centers. At a meeting of the Jewish Community Council's urban affairs committee, Groner put the issue in straightforward terms: "Since affluent whites control the economy and make the important decisions in American society, and since many of them live and some work in the suburbs, it is therefore necessary to channel our efforts into the suburbs and attempt to organize their residents."[37] The rabbi suggested that the strength of the American economy no longer resided in cities, not only because growing numbers of affluent and middle-class people lived outside of cities but also because industry and jobs were fleeing urban spaces as well. Suburbs, he believed, constituted the new centers of power and, as such, had to be the base for any meaningful political mobilization.[38]

With an annual budget of close to half a million dollars, entirely generated from private sources, Suburban Action Centers were uniquely positioned, according to the rabbi, "to involve suburbs in meeting the urban crisis." He suggested that these centers could function to root out prejudice, whether in housing, hiring, or social practices, in the suburbs and could convince suburban residents that the problems that afflicted cities had consequences for the entire metropolitan region. Groner hoped that with a contribution from the Jewish Community Council, a rabbi could be funded to join the staff of the Suburban Action Centers movement, and that suburban dwellers could learn to appreciate the struggles of urban life as their own struggles. Persuaded, the Jewish Community Council agreed to earmarks funds, though quite modest, for this. Yet its leadership never wholeheartedly committed to the idea for fear that the controlling Interfaith Action Council might enter into projects driven by a Christian missionary impulse that were contrary to Jewish interests.[39]

The organized Jewish community gave far fewer resources to the Interfaith Emergency Council (and its successor Interfaith Action Council) than their Catholic and Protestant counterparts.[40] With clear discomfort about funding activities that channeled social welfare through Christian structures, Jewish leaders proposed that they focus their attention on the particular contributions they could make as Jews to urban problems, which included providing employment training and educational scholarships for city youth.

The magnitude of the problems in Detroit, highlighted by the February 1968 release of the Kerner Commission's report on civil disorders, prompted Jewish leaders to carve out very specific spheres of Jewish urban investment. In 1968, the Jewish Federation established its own urban affairs committee and charged it with fostering "a positive attitude on the part of Jews and Jewish organization with reference to urban affairs,"[41] While communicating its commitment to melding Jewish concerns together with urban concerns, Federation and the Jewish Community Council also highlighted the growing distance between the lives Jews led and circumstances in Detroit. At a February 1968 meeting of the newly constituted Jewish Community Council Urban Affairs Subcommittee, the group agreed that "the entire spectrum of urban problems was beyond the reach of any single group" and that this group must "determine where there was a portion of the responsibility" that it could "constructively and realistically undertake."[42]

From predominantly suburban outposts, Jewish organizations and leaders determined it best to focus on just a few particular areas of urban concern that felt germane to Jews' lives. Lawrence Gubow, a Detroit attorney who was appointed a federal district court judge by President Johnson in 1968 and served as chair of the Jewish Community Council's community relations committee, concurred that Jewish leaders must understand their limitations: "I am only repeating the obvious and the well known when I say that any meaningful attack on these problems is going to have to be made on a scale probably unprecedented in our national history."[43] No one, however, was let off the hook, since, he continued, "In developing this picture of a social problem of vast and overwhelming proportions, I have not been preparing the ground for a cop-out, of a 'what's the use, it's too big a problem for us' approach." Instead, he advised that Jewish groups devote their energy to those urban reform projects to which they were best suited or to which they could most "naturally relate."[44]

Jewish Community Council leaders let their sense of Jewish interests guide their urban activism. For example, they resolved to disburse $25,000 each year to the Higher Education Opportunities Committee, a joint private-public fund to help steward "inner-city college potential youngster[s]" on the path toward college. In the rationale for the fund allocation, Jewish Community Council leaders explained that education "relates directly to . . . a 'traditional Jewish interest'" and that the "association of the Jewish Community with this kind of enterprise is a 'natural' one, as distinguished from attempts to become involved with inner city community organizations, which may be more natural to church groups with membership in the inner city areas."[45]

A report on "The Role of the Jewish Community in the Urban Crisis," given by a staff member of the Jewish Community Council in 1968, proclaimed, "We are basically an urban oriented community."[46] Jewish leaders, however, also understood the value of more specifically labeling certain forms of Jewish urban investments as "natural." Using circular logic, leaders identified Jews by their support of cities. Yet they also directed the scope of Jewish urban activism to those activities that were viable in a suburban context and responded to the challenges of suburban Jewish life. Philanthropic activism, volunteer activism, and state or national legislative activism all enabled Jews to leverage their power in public ways and fueled a positive sense of Jewish identity. The 1968 report suggested, "We are in a position to offer the Negro expertise from within our own power structure" and also to work to "influence . . . the power structure of the total community."[47] Much as Jewish leaders suggested that Jews help foster education programs in cities because education reflected a particular Jewish strength, they also believed that blacks could benefit from learning some of the skills that Jews had historically developed to succeed in urban environments. In essence, Jews could filter a measure of their power to those who were relatively powerless, while, at the same time, confirming their own power and status.

Tempering their involvement in black urban life, however, was Jewish leaders' perception that black leadership had veered onto a radical path that threatened the liberal terms of interracial cooperation. In the weeks and months following the riots, the *Detroit Jewish News* reported on black leaders' anti-Zionist statements and on black efforts to eject Jews from civil rights organizations. Characterizing these activities as stemming from "black power controlling elements," the editors of the paper berated black leaders for "weaken[ing] the force[s] that are striving for unity in the ranks of the freedom loving people."[48] Black radicalism did not spring anew from the 1960s nor was it univocal, yet it issued new threats to Jewish, white, and liberal life in an era when blacks gained more control over urban space than they ever had in the past.[49]

The threat that Jewish leaders felt from black radical politics served as a call, in the eyes of some Jewish leaders, to revivify Jews' connection to black urban life in order to defuse the antisemitism they perceived as operating in tandem with black radicalism. In the wake of the April 1968 assassination of Martin Luther King Jr., Jewish groups found occasion to make public statements about their concern for black urban life and to prescribe liberal interracial politics as the proper course to help black America. The American Jewish Committee, for example, placed a quarter-page advertisement in the *Michigan Chronicle*, a black newspaper, mourning King's death and promising to "intensify our efforts to maximize Jewish participation in the creation of jobs and educational opportunities for Negro youth."[50] A report from 1968 noted, "A group of militant and moderate Afro-American leaders have met with a group convened by the American Jewish Congress for the purpose of formulating a developmental assistance program through the Jewish community."[51] Nationally, Jews across the country pursued similar efforts to thwart what they deemed black radical takeovers by supporting limited means of black community power in cities. The Jewish Federation of Baltimore, for example, designated $35,000 to help "responsible Negro leadership," and Jewish organizations strove to maintain a pocket of middle-class stability in the city, where Jews and blacks with economic means could live together.[52]

In the month after King's assassination, Temple Beth El's Community Affairs Committee also sought to disarm black radicalism and reassert the efficacy of Jewish liberalism. The committee circulated a report entitled "'68 Crisis in Black and White" that included a question-and-answer section with Coleman Young, a black state senator and the future mayor of the city, who also had been a former communist sympathizer. In one leading question, they asked Young, "Are Negros [sic] aware of the number of social welfare programs for [their] benefit in which white people participate?" Young responded, "Yes many are. But they are always aware that in spite of these programs to create better conditions in the inner-city ... conditions have not improved and in some instances have worsened."[53] His answer could be read as a call for revolutionary change or, as the Jewish leaders were wont, as a plea for white liberals to help strengthen existing social welfare programs and supplement them with private forms of urban activism.

Much as leaders of New Detroit sought to control black radicalism by inviting some of its leaders to share in the project of rebuilding the city, Jewish leaders also hoped to establish shared ground with black leaders as a means to deracinate black radical politics. Echoing statements made by private civic groups such as New Detroit, Jews endorsed efforts to hire more black police officers and to empower black citizens to help govern the city.[54] They hoped these sorts of efforts would protect a liberal urban agenda that focused on repairing—not revolutionizing—the city by improving its infrastructure, offering social welfare programs to its poorest inhabitants, and continuing to remediate discriminatory practices. Although some leftist Jews, like famed labor lawyer Ernest Goodman, defended black radical politics and challenges to white capitalism and its systemic racism, most Jewish leaders hoped to find a way to harness separatist, nationalist, and other forms of black radical politics to a liberal vision for the city and its reform.

Jewish Voluntarism and the City

The urban reform efforts pursued by the most powerful Jews in Detroit mirrored and bolstered those of the most powerful white non-Jewish Detroit leaders. In a letter to Joseph L. Hudson, the New Detroit chairman, Rabbi Hertz outlined the activities that Temple Beth El intended to pursue to "cure our city's social problems," including encouraging its members to hire blacks who were unemployed or school dropouts and offer them job training, and providing tutoring programs for inner-city children in the synagogue building. These efforts, the rabbi explained, should be understood as bolstering New Detroit's agenda, since "Temple Beth El stands ready to be of every possible assistance to you and your committee."[55]

Similarly, high-profile Jewish professionals signed on to the agenda of the Jewish Federation's Urban Affairs Committee believing that they could work in partnership with New Detroit. A power struggle between the Jewish Community Council and Federation ensued, as Federation leaders, who tended to be among the wealthier and more powerful Jews in the community, noted that only Federation had the weight to "fix in the community's mind" Jews' true commitment to the urban crisis.[56] Indeed, many of the Jewish men involved in Federation's Urban Affairs Committee—primarily attorneys and real estate developers—hoped to stabilize the city and suggest a path forward for its black residents by invoking a Jewish narrative of productive struggle and opportunity in Detroit. In the spring of 1968, the members of the Urban Affairs Committee agreed, "We should find a way to make our lay sophistication and our professional skills available to the black community. As Jews, we have a long experience in building a sense of community and an identity. The black community needs both of these. In a sense, this would be helping the black community help itself."[57]

On the national level, Jewish leaders likewise instructed urban Jews to carve out specific niches in urban life where they could help direct the course of urban repair away from radical solutions and toward liberal remedies that focused on ways that individuals could work hard and achieve success within the reigning economic and political system. In the summer of 1968, ninety-five Jewish leaders from forty cities met to share ideas about "dealing with America's critical urban problems."⁵⁸ The group emphasized a dual-pronged strategy of, first, actively lobbying for "massive governmental action," especially in terms of congressional appropriations to city programs and, second, creating Jewish-led programs in the city. These programs, the group emphasized, should showcase Jews' natural roles in rebuilding urban life by sharing their skills with black urban citizens and encouraging them to invest in the liberal ideal of cities, as places where hard work would pay off (as many Jews believed it had for them).

The attendees of the 1968 conference came to a consensus that Jewish communities could best contribute to ameliorating urban conditions through investing in educational and employee-training programs. Over the coming years, national Jewish organizations reached out to Jewish urban leaders to encourage them to direct their energies toward those areas. In almost every communication, national Jewish organizations also requested data from local organizations quantifying and describing their level of urban activism. From this data, they generated statistics to prove to themselves and the broader public just how committed Jews were to improving cities for black people.⁵⁹

By the late 1960s, Jewish leaders understood that if Jews and their institutions were going to remain involved in Detroit, they would do so primarily through private voluntary modes, whether in the form of contributing manpower or, as was more often the case, financial power to cities. Although some Jewish agencies attended to the needs of poor and generally elderly Jews who remained in the city longer than other Jewish populations, for the most part Jewish institutions understood their urban engagement as bringing them to interact with non-Jewish populations. Many of their efforts reflected the growth of a private philanthropic complex in Jewish life that tied together entrepreneurial success with charitable acts in a complicated and self-sustaining relationship. The more Jews succeeded, the more charity they gave; the more charity they gave, the more they legitimated the terms of their own success.

Not long after he entered office, Nixon appointed Detroit's own Max Fisher to chair his administration's Voluntary Action Program committee. A longtime supporter of Detroit's Jewish institutions, a member of Shaarey Zedek, a cultural philanthropist, and a vocal Zionist, Fisher was among the most prominent Jews in Detroit. He also was the first Jewish member of New Detroit and an important fixture in Michigan's Republican Party, as a crucial supporter of Governor Romney and then a major funder in Nixon's presidential campaign. Romney, who served under

FIGURE 6.2 Max Fisher with Governor George Romney, 1964. Courtesy of the Max M. and Marjorie S. Fisher Foundation.

Nixon as secretary of housing and urban development, worked closely with Fisher to help him develop the committee on voluntary urban activism.[60]

As a businessperson, with significant real estate holdings in downtown Detroit, Fisher's self-interest in Detroit was obvious. He explained to his biographer that his work as a social activist evolved out of his business consciousness: "In the final analysis, as business helps in meeting social problems it truly helps itself."[61] Fisher used his clout in the Jewish world to draw Jewish representatives into his model of voluntary action, which he hoped would enable government to absolve itself from social welfare responsibilities. Already, many Jewish leaders adhered to the principles of voluntary social activism, generating their own private sources of revenue to fund social welfare programs that increasingly reached into the non-Jewish community. Jewish leaders were in many ways ideally placed for Fisher's brand of voluntarism since they both participated in the faith world—and thus carried legitimacy and authority with them—and tended to occupy economic roles that would align their interests with a pro-business agenda.

In June 1969 in his capacity as chair of Nixon's Voluntary Action Program committee, Fisher convened a meeting with faith leaders to whom he made the case for empowering the private sector over local affairs and charged communities with the responsibility of solving their own problems without governmental interference.[62] He hoped to convince the Protestant, Catholic, and Jewish leaders he gathered that voluntary and private action were far superior to government intervention, especially in urban areas. In the form of New Detroit, he had already worked toward this reality.

A representative from the National Community Relations Advisory Council (NCRAC) attended a second meeting of the Voluntary Action Program committee later that same month in 1969 and reported that attendees posed some "sharp" questions about the surge toward voluntarism. Was voluntarism simply a thin veil for the government's effort to shirk its responsibility? And did the government intend to provide financial incentives for religious groups, already strapped for cash, to become clearinghouses of voluntary activism?[63] Yet NCRAC also understood that, of all faith groups, Jews were particularly well situated to prove how efficacious voluntary action could be, especially in cities.

The next year, in 1970, NCRAC drew up a report on "Jewish Voluntary Action for Community Betterment," noting that "as members of the Jewish community have risen from the poverty of immigrant origin to obtain sufficient security," they participated actively in voluntary projects to benefit the broad community. The report continued, "In the stimulation of voluntary urban projects, [Jewish] agencies . . . have been particularly active." According to NCRAC's calculation, Jewish voluntary activism resulted in the expenditure of over a billion dollars.[64]

In 1970, Detroit's Jewish Federation and Jewish Community Council dissolved their separate urban affairs committees and established a joint one.[65] In name, this move indicated a common purpose to direct Jewish attention to urban activism. Yet it also revealed the narrowing terrain of Jewish urban investment, since now only one committee would exist and would, thus, consolidate Jewish urban concerns. The newly formed urban affairs committee had the support of two Jewish titans of Detroit, Stanley Winkelman and Fisher, both of whom maintained significant private investments in the city and maintained that Jewish urban investment was a linchpin of Jewish identity and security in the United States.

Winkelman, born in 1922, had lived in Detroit since the age of five. After serving in World War II, he returned to Detroit, first, to a block close to the intersection of Dexter and Davison and, then, to an upscale home in Sherwood Forest, a neighborhood adjacent to Palmer Woods. By 1960, he had become president of Winkelman Stores, his family's department store chain that operated from over a dozen locations, including a few in the suburbs. Winkelman's primary business, philanthropic, and volunteer investments remained Detroit centered. He partnered with city cultural institutions, such as the Detroit Institute of Arts, to bring international and cosmopolitan arts programs to the city. Winkelman also served on social action committees for the Jewish Community Council and Temple Beth El, as well as Detroit's Community Relations Commission under Mayor Cavanagh. Reflecting on his role on the city commission, he recalled, "This gave me the opportunity on a citywide level to stimulate positive changes in city policy." Similar to other Jewish liberal leaders of his era, he supported open occupancy and believed in an activist government to orchestrate urban justice.[66]

In 1970, the newly formed joint urban affairs committee of Federation and the Jewish Community Council issued a statement in favor of passing a $100 million state bond to direct funds toward the construction of low-income housing and the removal of urban blight.[67] Winkelman, who served as chair of the committee, wrote, "We see Jewish communal support for this bonding proposal as an appropriate and proper role for our community which has long recognized its responsibility in helping to achieve a society responsive to the needs of all citizens."[68] In remarks he offered to the leaders of Detroit's Federation, Winkelman explained that unless cities were healthy, Jews would be unable to attain their most pressing needs: "We must make a commitment as Jews to a positive role in the urban crisis."

Yet even while lobbying for public dollars to support an urban project, Winkelman and other Jewish leaders asserted that Jews had a very particular stake in the city and one that, by and by, would motivate private forms of urban investment. Men such as Fisher and Winkelman, who did not share a political party affiliation (Fisher was a Republican, Winkelman a Democrat), nonetheless shared the belief that if Jews did not commit themselves to the task of uplifting the city, they would compromise their own priorities. To an audience of the board of the Jewish Federation, Winkelman explained, "The very foundations upon which we build our own institutions and generate support for Israel will be threatened if we as American Jews do not help solve urban problems."

Setting aside partisan politics, Winkelman argued that the task of improving cities was "intimately tied to the health of the Jewish community." Intense urban poverty and unrest threatened to topple Jewish investments, to compromise Jewish success, and to lead to repressive state measures that could limit the rights of all Americans. And although he still maintained faith in the government to help rebuild Detroit, he also explained, "The people in the cities alone cannot get the necessary job done at the state or national levels." Cities and city folk needed the Jews, who lived in the suburbs and had access to power to help "poverty ... be licked and equal opportunity become a reality."[69]

New Views: Looking Inward and Outward

By the late 1960s, Jewish organizations felt more pressed than ever to mount a case to their Jewish constituents for their ongoing urban involvements. Members of the Jewish Community Council suggested organizing a seminar to help Jewish leaders see the relevance of the urban crisis to the Jewish community. Many worried that "negative attitudes" toward Detroit, whether as a result of "white backlash or simple complacency," were growing among Jews and that they needed to be taught to "recognize their wrong feelings."[70] Jewish Community Council leaders were not immune from these same feelings. At a meeting in early 1969, a staff person explained that the council had already devoted serious resources to exploring "the urban crisis and race problems" and "it would be unrealistic to provide money and staff assistance" for a seminar on the urban crisis, especially when other causes, such as the celebration of Israel Independence Day and the memorialization of the Warsaw Ghetto uprising demanded attention.[71] One of the advocates of the urban crisis seminar protested that the Jewish community could remain involved in "solving urban problems" without any detraction "from our primary concern for the welfare of our own community."[72]

The argument that Jewish efforts to help remedy the urban crisis were not mutually exclusive of attention to internal Jewish matters undermined the strongest case in favor of Jewish urban investment. Indeed, by articulating the two spheres as separable, the Jewish Community Council admitted that Jewish internal affairs could progress without attention to the urban environment. In prior decades, when Jews' lives had been enmeshed with urban life, that bifurcation would have been nonsensical. In the shape of metropolitan urbanism, many Jews had continued to feel connected to the urban field, but the nature of the bond was surely changing.

As the immediate impact of the riots faded, Jewish leaders had to remind themselves and their constituents why Jews should continue to care about and invest in a city increasingly remote from their spheres of activity. In 1969, the Jewish Community Council's Urban Affairs Committee compiled a database of all of the urban projects in which Jews were involved and publicized them to the community. They hoped the list would serve as much as a call to action as a record of action, though it also smacked of an apologetic.[73]

Many Jews supported the idea of New Detroit and offered their time or money to support voluntary urban initiatives such as tutoring or employment training programs. Yet most still maintained faith in the government as the best agency to undertake the massive efforts to repair cities. Furthermore, American Jews experienced a shift in how they perceived what constituted Jewish interests in the decade following the riots. Geopolitical and cultural trends, in the form of developing conflicts in the Middle East that seemingly threatened the State of Israel's existence, public memorialization and knowledge of the Holocaust, and burgeoning ethnic pride and identity politics movements, fostered an inward turn among many American Jews. Set alongside Jews' socioeconomic comfort in the suburbs, new sources of anxiety about the terms and possibilities of Jewish survival implanted themselves in the agenda of suburban Jewish institutions.[74]

A NCRAC statement in 1972 offered an empathetic portrait of Jews who felt alienated from cities. This was an "understandable reaction against rising crime rates . . . against pressure on business owners to sell to black buyers at financial loss, against preferences given [to] blacks in admission to college and graduate schools and in employment . . . against school desegregation programs that seem to impair the quality of education available to their children, against public housing that they regard as endangering their neighborhoods and threatening the viability of their institutions."[75] Indeed, according to this litany of grievances, Jews had plenty of reasons to turn their backs on cities and the predominantly black populations now clustered in them.

Yet, in the well-worn voice of prophecy, NCRAC warned Jews that their "understandable" impulse to put the city and its problems out of their minds would make them vulnerable to the very problems they wished to ignore as irrelevant to their lives. Echoing the same logic that had given punch to the "Neighbor, Where Are You Running To?" campaign against neighborhood change in Detroit in the early 1950s, NCRAC told Jews that their suburbs, soon enough, would be gripped by urban woes. Even if suburban Jews might wish to "isolate themselves from the cities," they simply could not. Suburbs were the next frontiers for the problems of the city, including "racial strife . . . crime, drug abuse, [and] infectious disease."[76]

NCRAC took heart in the fact that suburban Jews, as estranged as some of them felt from city life, did not turn their back on a commitment to liberal politics that often oriented them toward city space. Throughout the 1970s, suburban Jews emerged as key proponents of liberal housing policies, civil rights protections, pacifism, feminism, and nascent environmentalism.[77] These movements all demanded a worldview beyond Jews' own predominately white, middle-class suburbs, and many of them tied Jews' political activism to city space. At times, geographic remoteness from the city lowered the personal stakes in supporting urban-directed liberal policies, and some critics noted, though often with only anecdotal or isolated evidence, that those Jews who stayed within the city were less likely to cling to liberal ideals than those who left it.[78]

In an analysis of the 1972 Democratic primary, Detroit's Jewish Community Council reported that Jews' support for liberalism remained strong even as they settled into their lives of material comfort in the suburbs. Tracking voting patterns in the twenty-three precincts with the highest Jewish populations and comparing them to data from earlier elections, the report suggested that suburbanization had done little to change the nature of Jewish electoral politics. Prior to the 1972 primary, when politicians considered proposals to bus city schoolchildren across district and municipal boundaries to help integrate schools, commentators had expected that anti-integrationist candidate George Wallace would capture a substantial share of votes from suburban Jews in Detroit. Yet the primary results did not reflect this shift: half of the votes in the Jewish precincts went to progressive candidate George McGovern and only 12.7 percent to Wallace. (The remaining voters in Jewish precincts supported Hubert Humphrey.) Although Wallace had made modest gains when compared to the Jewish votes he received in the 1968 primary, the majority of Jews still rejected him and his anti-integrationist views in favor of McGovern, a candidate who expressed sympathy for busing policies. In contrast,

Wallace captured roughly one-third of non-Jewish votes in precincts with similar socioeconomic characteristics to the Jewish precincts, and he won the state's primary.[79]

In the decade after 1960, when the Jewish population in the suburbs grew precipitously, no fewer than 80 percent of Jewish voters cast their ballots in favor of Democratic presidential candidates, this despite Nixon's friendly policies toward Israel and the growing fervency of Jews' Zionism. The Jewish Community Council remained satisfied, as of its 1972 report, that Jews in the suburbs remained steadfastly committed to liberal ideals: "The point is that at a time of serious political controversy, voter frustration and anxiety, 87.3% of the Jewish voters once again rejected a simplistic, if not demagogic approach to civic issues."[80]

Even as Jews' commitment to liberal politics endured beyond the city in the 1970s, liberalism did not fare nearly as well in Detroit once Jews and other liberal whites left the city. Mel Ravitz, the Jewish man who had served on the Common Council since 1962 and worked tirelessly to pass fair-housing legislation in Detroit, hoped to capture the mayoral position in 1974. On the face, Ravitz seemed perfectly suited for the job. He had a strong record as a liberal committed to mobilizing interracial support and had the endorsement of the city's liberal unions. In years past, this would have been enough to garner substantial votes in the city. But not so this election, when a conservative white police commissioner and the black state senator, Coleman Young, both outspokenly critical of white liberalism, threw their hats in the ring. New demographic patterns had seriously depleted Ravitz's white liberal support, and many black people who might have voted for him in the past now invested their political capital in the black candidate, whose past association with the Communist Party mattered little to them and whose open support of black radical politics rang true to the times. Ravitz's candidacy did not make it past the primary.

On Election Day in November 1973, Coleman Young narrowly defeated the white police commissioner, revealing the enduring power of white conservatism in the city.[81] Far from a moment of clear triumph of equality over racism, Young's election may have been a "hollow prize," a term that many social scientists used to describe the electoral victories that black politicians won in American cities in the 1970s. Historian Michael Katz wrote, "The irony, of course, is that African Americans inherited city governments at the moment when de-industrialization, cuts in federal aid, and white flight were decimating tax bases and job opportunities while fueling homelessness, street crime, and poverty."[82] To this litany of forces undermining the efficacy of black elected leaders, Katz could have added the rising power of private corporate and foundation entities, whose power seemed to grow in inverse proportion to the strength of elected city leadership.

In 1970, even before Young took office, a small cadre of business executives, including Max Fisher and his friend and Jewish real estate developer A. Alfred Taubman, formed an urban redevelopment organization called Detroit Renaissance. With their sights set on remaking the riverfront area of Detroit, Fisher, Taubman, and Detroit industrialist and power broker Henry Ford II bankrolled a study on waterfront development. Over the next decade, Detroit Renaissance bought up riverfront property at very low costs and, with major funding from the Ford Motor Company, built the Renaissance Center, a complex of massive towers perched on the river. Almost immediately upon construction, the RenCen, as it was called, operated at a massive loss for its investors and the city, all banking on economic growth from the project.

Fisher and Taubman, acting through their own separate partnership, also purchased several other sections of the riverfront property and negotiated for a twelve-year tax abatement (commonly known as the "Max Fisher Bill") to help them develop riverfront luxury housing. Many of Detroit's elected officials, almost all black, protested that these urban redevelopment plans ignored residents' concerns and evaded tax burden in the name of economic development. Ken Cockrel, a black city council member, drew up a petition against granting Fisher and Taubman the tax break, and other protestors wore T-shirts printed in verse: "No Tax Break for Riverfront West; Tax Max [Fisher] and his Pal Al [Taubman]." Despite the clear opposition of elected city officials and citizenry, the project moved forward.[83]

While the vast majority of American Jews throughout the 1970s continued to support the idea of publicly funded social welfare and urban programs, favored by Democratic Party politics, the world of privatized Jewish activism grew ever stronger. Privatized and, often, entrepreneurial, Jewish activism emerged as a central component of Jewish liberalism and molded the ways in which Jews engaged with cities in the coming decades. In the form of private dollars, foundations, and development corporations, which proliferated in the 1970s and 1980s, prominent and wealthy Jews found themselves in positions of power, akin to the elected positions that they had sought and sometimes won in cities in earlier

FIGURE 6.3 The Detroit Renaissance Inc. Board of Directors with a model of downtown Detroit, 1979. *Left to right*: Alan E. Schwartz, Joseph L. Hudson, Robert E. McCabe, Max Fisher, and A. Alfred Taubman. Courtesy of Detroit Renaissance Inc.

decades. Answering now not to the whims of an electorate but rather to their sense of what their power entitled them to, wealthy Jews helped make the case for privatizing spaces, services, and ideas that had once been assumed in the domain of the public. As the government continued to cut funding from public social welfare and urban programs throughout the 1970s and 1980s, focused and wealthy philanthropists, foundations, and development corporations channeled private funds to direct the fate of public life. To be certain, most Jews lived far removed from the kind of wealth and power exercised by these private entities, but many grew sympathetic—and indebted—to them and the complex of Jewish privatized activism.[84]

In the postwar years, Jewish liberalism had hinged upon Jews' support of the kinds of policies that safeguarded putatively public and primarily urban spaces, such as schools, neighborhoods, and workplaces, from overt and categorical acts of discrimination. In these public spaces, according to liberal-subscribing Jews and their leaders, individuals could work hard and gain a greater slice of American opportunity. In the seventies and eighties, the content of Jewish liberalism slowly shifted away from this vision of the public. It is no accident that the shift occurred once most Jews had migrated away from cities, where public spaces had been so essential to Jews' access to power and privilege. Instead, the new Jewish liberalism that emerged in the seventies and eighties tended to be far less concerned with maintaining public spaces and more intent upon providing spaces for economic and entrepreneurial growth that over time would ideally accrue benefit to a broad swath of society. Liberalism, thus, became tied to an agenda of "liberating" spaces and resources from government control and delivering them into the hands of those entities that could best generate profit and social good from them.[85]

For the Jewish children who were born in the suburbs of Detroit in the seventies and eighties, the city of Detroit no longer represented a Jewish space, nor was it a public space for any public they knew. Occasionally, these children might have been driven into the city to watch a sporting event, hear the Detroit Symphony Orchestra, or see an exhibit at the Detroit Institute of Arts, and some children may have engaged in small-scale social justice projects in the city. But the logic of metropolitan urbanism that had stitched their parents' lives to the city frayed as the city itself continued to suffer from the broad consequences of deindustrialization and federal disinvestment.

Still, in the shape of the emerging privatized model of urban development, liberal concern, and Jewish activism, the foundations for a new Jewish urbanism, which emerged in the new millennium, were laid. New Jewish urbanism would reflect the phases of American Jewish urbanism that had come before, yet it also issued forth from the new economic, political, and cultural circumstances of American and Jewish life. In the early decades of the new millennium, some of those same Jewish children who had grown up in the suburbs of the city moved their homes and their business to the city, considering Detroit just the sort of "old new" frontier for Jewish life that could mediate between experimentation in the city and fealty to long-standing beliefs about what the city could do for Jews.

CHAPTER SEVEN

Epilogue

Back-to-the-City Jews and the Legacies of Metropolitan Urbanism

On a sweltering summer day in 2012, I met Eugene and Elaine Driker at their gracious home in Palmer Woods. We set out together in Eugene's late model Buick, heading south on Woodward Avenue toward the parts of Detroit they wanted to show me. Empty streets, with few cars and even fewer pedestrians, rolled by my window. Finally, with Palmer Park, the Bagley neighborhood, Dexter, and the Twelfth Street area behind us, we pulled up in front of Avalon International Breads, a bakery just a few blocks south of Wayne State University's campus in Midtown Detroit. Here, in front of a low mustard-yellow brick building, people mulled about and talked and ate. Inside, a long line and tempting smells met us. The bread list, handwritten on large yellow poster board, told a culinary geography: Hastings Street Challah, Russell Street Rustic Italian, Dexter-Davison Rye, and more.

The bakery, the outdoor tables with red-and-white-striped umbrellas, the line, and the breads were all part of an urban experiment undertaken by Jackie Victor, a Jewish woman raised in the suburbs of Detroit, and her partner to start an organic bakery in a city often referred to as a food desert. The bakery website explained, "A bakery is a living metaphor: a hearth, a place to 'break bread.' But metaphors don't change the world and nor rebuild a city. We wanted to make bread."[1] The metaphor, however, fueled a new era of Jewish urbanism, when the symbolism of places such as organic bakeries in cities was just as important as the bread on their shelves.

Whenever I described my research to Jewish Detroiters, they invariably interrupted me to tell me that my history of postwar Jewish Detroit would not be complete without a chapter examining what was happening with Jews in the city since 2010. They explained that Jews, especially young ones, were "coming back" to Detroit, using this phrase despite the fact that few of the Jews they were talking about had ever lived in the city or left it. Journalistic and photographic reportage on the fall and possible rise of current-day Detroit were easy to come by, and I explained that I did not intend to add my voice to that conversation, which seemed to slip into elegiac prophecy.[2]

What did interest me, however, were the converging and diverging narratives that different segments of the Jewish community told about the Jewish "return" to Detroit. And as I listened to Jews talk about their relationship to Detroit in the new millennium, I was struck by how their narratives were working to reinvent Jewishness through the lens of urbanism, and urbanism through the lens of Jewishness—a theme of Jewish urban reinvention with deep historical resonance.

Members of the Isaac Agree Downtown Synagogue, the president of the Jewish Federation of Metropolitan Detroit, high-ranking employees at Quicken Loans, a Reform rabbi who ministered to Jews in the suburbs and lived in the city, University of Michigan students who spent summers or spring breaks or semesters "abroad" in Detroit, Jewish farmers and bakers, and young people who moved to Detroit after college all agreed that actively investing in Detroit felt like the right thing to do for themselves and the city, against steep odds that only mounted in the new millennium and appeared to culminate in 2013 when the city declared bankruptcy. These different sets of Jewish urban activists persistently told me that Jews had no choice but to be part of the new economic and political work in the city because the metropolitan region and its Jewish community could only be as strong as the city. Their reasoning resembled the logic that had sustained Jewish metropolitan urbanism many decades earlier, when Jewish leaders imagined that Jewish neighborhoods could only be as stable as the rest of the city and, eventually, that even suburban outposts could and should be politically, spiritually, and economically oriented toward the city.

An essential way postwar Jews understood their connection to cities, even as they were moving away from them, was in the belief that cities protected the stability and security of Jews in the United States. This simple belief had rested at the heart of metropolitan urbanism. Yet over time, as cities had become less stable and Jews gained a sense of security in the suburbs, Jews' indebtedness to urban life for stability and security transformed into a deep ambivalence about cities. One could have rightly wondered whether American Jews would continue to understand their communal narrative as so deeply shaped by urban space.

The ideology of metropolitan urbanism had justified a patronage relationship between the wealth and power outside of the city and the distress and poverty within it, but the ideology collapsed on itself as cities experienced new distress at the hands of metropolitan expansion. Starting in the late 1970s in cities such as Detroit, Jews and their children experienced metropolitan regions rich with opportunities, good schools, and efficient infrastructure and witnessed metropolitan centers crippled by economic deprivation and neglect. Jews growing up in the suburbs of Detroit in the 1980s, a time when suburban economies thrived, generally recalled having minimal connections to the city.[3]

When suburbs experienced economic decline in the late 1990s, metropolitan regions, already unmoored from metropolitan centers, floundered. Suburbs increasingly lost industry to global competitors, and racial and class tension erupted in suburban schools with shrinking tax bases and new challenges posed by overcrowding. According to historians and social critics, suburban dwellers now faced the same kinds of dilemmas their urban forebears had. And many made the same choices: to continue to move outward, toward the next ex-urban frontier. Some suburban dwellers, however, perceived the problems in suburbs as an indictment of the suburban idea more generally, and they set their vision, if not their homes and workplaces, on the urban landscape.[4]

So neglected by whites had the city of Detroit become in the beginning of the new millennium that what initially struck many whites, including Jews, when they thought about the city was simply their own absence from it. Although eventually Jewish community leaders would describe the Jews who moved to the city as returning to it—a move to claim the space as still Jewish—initially, the city represented a new frontier appealing only to a few pioneers.

Of course, frontiers are rarely empty spaces, and pioneers are seldom the first settlers. In empirical terms, Detroit in 2010 had about 710,000 people living in it. Whites constituted 10 percent of that population, and blacks comprised about 82 percent of it. Only slightly more than 10 percent of the population had attained a bachelor's degree or a higher degree, and the median value of an owner-occupied home in the city was

$71,000, just about half as much as the median value of a home in the rest of the state. Finally, the average number of people per square mile of the city was 5,144. (To offer some perspective, in Philadelphia, the average was 11,379, in Manhattan it was 69,467, and at its peak, Detroit's population density stood at roughly 13,000 people per square mile.)[5] Millennial Jewish Detroit activists, a broad term I use in this chapter to describe the individuals who invested in various ways in the city since the turn of the millennium, created their own urban reality apart from this empirical portrait.

Most significantly, these activists helped reinvent the geography of Detroit, in effect shrinking a city that earlier Jews had helped to extend. Although some employed more specific geographical designations to talk about the city or considered the rest of the city as germane to their activism, most millennial activists lived and worked in the downtown-midtown corridor, a roughly six- to eight-square-mile section that constituted no more than 6 percent of the city's 139-square-mile terrain. Encompassed in this area was Wayne State University, most of the city's cultural institutions (the Detroit Institute of Arts; the Max M. Fisher Music Center, home to the Detroit Symphony Orchestra; Fox Theater; the Charles H. Wright Museum of African American History; and the main branch of the Detroit Public Library, to name just a few), the large Henry Ford Health System, and the business core of the city. Furthermore, these were among the few square miles of the city that had seen a population increase over the last decade, with high housing occupancy, and contained among the highest percentage of white residents in the city. In an act completely consonant with historical trends, millennial urban activists reshaped the city's topography to meet their needs and ideals.[6]

Furthermore, Jewish millennial activists wed the space of city to their visions of American and Jewish success, as many had before them. For these activists of the new millennium, this involved creating an entrepreneurial hotbed in the city, where new ideas, whatever they might be, could attract the power and capital of investors. The activists all believed that cities fostered creativity and experimentation more than other kinds of places, and that gains, in some form, would best be made from entering at the ground floor of urban revitalization and reinvention in Detroit. Here, they could set the terms of entrepreneurial experimentation and, they hoped, success in the city and also build for a Jewish future in Detroit. To be certain, Jews were not the only white people involved in these enterprises, but Jewish millennial activists tended to couch their work in

Jewish terms and sought to establish places of Jewish community, whether religious or not, to anchor their activism in the city and to reconstruct Jewish life more broadly. Whether moving their businesses, their homes, or some of their community assets to the city, many of them believed they were engaging in a transformative and Jewish act. As individuals, many were, though their activism also tended to confirm political and economic structures that served greater rewards to those who started with greater privilege.

Jewish Millennial Activism in Detroit: Corporate, Grassroots, and Communal

By the summer of 2014, Dan Gilbert, the Detroit-born, Jewish billionaire founder of Quicken Loans, owned sixty downtown buildings, a total of nine million square feet of real estate. With his property holdings, including many of the city's most iconic buildings, he had a tight grip on the economic development of Detroit.[7] Describing Gilbert's Detroit Initiative (or Detroit 2.0), a 2012 press release explained, "We are committed to transforming Detroit—from a shrinking, so-called 'rust belt' city of high unemployment to a thriving commercial hotbed that is the envy of all others."[8] In a *New York Times* interview, Gilbert recalled listening to his grandparents and parents talk about what a vibrant city Detroit used to be. He continued, "It wasn't until my late 20s and early 30s, when I started to travel for business, to places like New York City and Los Angeles, that I realized how much we were missing. As I started visiting these great American cities, it hit me—man, how did we blow this so badly?"[9] With his investments and sheer will, he hoped to stop Detroit from blowing it more.

In the shadows of Gilbert's glass and steel towers, a four-story building—a department store in its past life and, since the 1960s, home of the Isaac Agree Downtown Synagogue—stood decrepitly. The building's multicolored window panels contrasted with the rest of its bleak façade. The Downtown Synagogue, founded in 1921, had lived many lives in different downtown buildings and had more than once been fated for demise. In 2007, a young lawyer named Leor Barak happened upon the building, tucked on a block with a strip club and a bar, and learned that the synagogue was shuttering its doors. Not so, he decided, and he became the president of the only remaining Conservative synagogue in the city. (A

Reconstructionist congregation also met in Detroit and prided itself on its "commitment to a continuing Jewish presence in the city of Detroit.")[10] Young Jews started coming into the city to attend the synagogue and saw it as a hub for the kind of community and social justice activism that mattered to them.[11] In a 2011 interview, Barak, then thirty years old, told the camera, "I almost want to make a T-shirt that says, 'Detroit: Saving the Soul of America.' "[12]

Had the Jewish Federation of Metropolitan Detroit not left the city for Bloomfield Hills in 1992, its building would have perched over the outfield of Comerica Park, the Detroit Tigers ballpark that opened in 2000 only a few blocks north of the Downtown Synagogue. Scott Kaufman, CEO of Federation since 2009, assured an audience convened for a spring 2012 conference titled "What Is Jewish Detroit?" that the organization was not moving back downtown anytime soon. But, he continued, Federation had its sights set on the city to serve as an inspiration and an anchor for the Jewish community. A former real estate developer who was raised in the cooperative housing of Detroit's Lafayette Park, Kaufman created programs to draw young people into the city, contending that without a vital Detroit, the Jewish community of Detroit would not survive. He enthused, "This is the blank canvas opportunity. . . . Change the narrative [about the city]. The energy makes a difference."[13]

Each with its own entrepreneurial energy, Quicken Loans, the Downtown Synagogue, and Detroit's Jewish Federation set the contours for Detroit Jews' engagement with the city in the early decades of the 2000s. I classify these forms of engagement as corporate, grassroots, and communal activism, yet the three categories overlapped, drawing sustenance from one another. Furthermore, they operated within a shared set of political and economic structures that obfuscated the lines between public and private sources of power and sought to dictate the new narrative of the city and Jews' relationship to it.

By the early decades of the twenty-first century, Jewish urban activism in Detroit reflected a privatized and entrepreneurial vision of urban life. For those with access to political and economic privileges, including many Jewish Detroiters, the privatized nature of urban life—security forces, retail districts, or corporate and communally funded programs—provided freedom with few restraints for them. Many of the groups, including Jewish ones, which funded private urban endeavors, explained their work through the language of public-mindedness, thus submerging the distinction between private and public space.

Some millennial urban activists contended that public sources of power—city, state, and federal structures reliant upon the money and consent of a public electorate—were simply incapable of creating strong urban infrastructure, while others argued that funding cuts and economic factors hampered public bodies from operating effectively. These perspectives represented deep ideological divisions about the role of the state, but by the early twenty-first century, they resolved into remarkably similar forms of privatized urban activism, confirmed eventually by the insolvency of the public governance of Detroit. For millennial activists, urban governance had shifted toward the realm of the private investor, corporation, entrepreneur, and foundation seeking control of the city.[14]

How one interacted with the city depended on a structure of private profitability that only grew in importance as the idea of an empowered public receded. A fealty to entrepreneurialism sustained the privatization of the downtown-midtown corridor of Detroit. Increasingly, individuals and institutions understood certain kinds of people, ideas, and places within the city to be scarce and, thus, valuable, and they competed for control over them. Millennial urban activists tended to measure programs, policies, and actions against a standard of profitability; that is, whether their work succeeded in gaining more power over coveted (generally private) resources and whether they could, thus, reproduce their vision of the city on a larger and larger scale.[15]

The privatized-entrepreneurial urbanism that Jews helped shape and legitimate in the new millennium in Detroit had the sum effect of placing more urban power in the hands of fewer urban actors than earlier forms of urbanism had. Promising improved efficiency through competition, privatized-entrepreneurial urbanism also tended to edge out other forms of urban activism that did not meet its standards of efficiency and profitability.

Sidewalk Judaism: Rooting the Grassroots in the Private and Entrepreneurial

To many of its members, the sidewalk illustrated the spirit of the Downtown Synagogue and its intimate connection to urbanism. Praying and singing alongside the city street, Downtown Synagogue goers experienced a mode of Judaism freed from the walls of buildings and institutions, what one scholar has depicted as post-denominational Judaism.[16] They

FIGURE 7.1 The Downtown Synagogue, 2014. Photograph by Karpov the Wrecked Train.

imagined a community that would take its Judaism and Jewish ideals to the streets, literally, and envisioned a city where public or civic spaces, such as sidewalks, could accommodate the kind of diversity that they prided themselves on attracting to their congregation. A growing population of black Jews constituted the congregation's membership and, as of the winter of 2013, three black men and women were in the process of converting to Judaism.

The synagogue's newly hired executive director, a woman named Anna Kohn, explained that unlike other Jewish institutions and places in the city that traded on privacy for security and identity, "We leave our doors open and people wander in."[17] Yet under Gilbert's corporate ventures, which included a private security force stationed to watch live feeds from cameras posted on downtown streets, and in the midst of Jewish communal initiatives to engineer Jewish community life in the city, the sidewalks and putatively public spaces of downtown Detroit increasingly bore the marks of private regulation and entrepreneurial means to gain control over resources and, in this case, the right mix of people.[18]

From 2005 to 2010, the Downtown Synagogue's membership more than doubled from 50 households to 175 (and by 2013, that number grew to 250). Every other Reform and Conservative synagogue, with the exception of one, in the Detroit area experienced a leveling or shrinkage in membership over the same five-year period.[19] The Downtown Synagogue had maintained a small core of older members and had sponsored free High Holiday services in the suburbs since the mid-1990s. But the bulk of its new membership came from twenty- and thirty-something, college-educated Jews, many of whom grew up in the suburbs of Detroit and some of whom had moved into the city. Sixty percent of the synagogue's board members were under the age of forty.[20]

An attorney who grew up in Southfield and thought he would never return to the Detroit area once he had the chance to leave, Harry Reisig was part of the new swell of interest in the Downtown Synagogue. In 2010, in his mid-thirties, Reisig moved to Detroit after years of living outside of Michigan, and he started to work for a program to help incarcerated men readjust to life outside of prison. Reisig hesitated before he decided to attend a Friday night service at the Downtown Synagogue. Having recently stepped away from Orthodox Judaism, he was uncertain about how to connect to his Jewish identity. As he walked toward the building, he saw a small group of people sitting on the sidewalk praying. Almost immediately, one of them, a guy he had known while growing up, asked Reisig if he would chant a section of the Friday night service. Reisig agreed, and within minutes he was, leading the *davening*—the praying—outside the Downtown Synagogue on a sidewalk in downtown Detroit.[21]

Amit Weitzer, a woman who settled in Detroit a year after graduating from the University of Michigan in 2008, started spending time at the Downtown Synagogue even before she moved to Detroit. "I loved that the services spilled outside onto the sidewalk," she remembered about her early experiences. She described a feeling of awakening, after years of being involved in Jewish life, first, in her West Bloomfield congregation and, then, through Hillel, a Jewish student organization, at college. "For the first time, I felt compelled by the possibility of integrating life, work, and being Jewish in one place," she reflected.[22] Another member, Avalon bakery founder Jackie Victor, explained that the cracks—in the sidewalk and in the edifice of the building—were what made the Downtown Synagogue magical: "The magic is that there's all this space for people to step into and become part of it. There are so many cracks, and everyone is needed to fill them."[23]

Cracks and chasms, however, also divided Downtown Synagogue members from other Jews in Detroit, creating a tension that had enabled the Downtown Synagogue to define itself in opposition to other Jewish forces operating in the city and the metropolitan region. For a time, this division had been essential to the identity of the Downtown Synagogue as a grassroots kind of place, far different from the organized Jewish community, including Federation and many of the established suburban synagogues, and the corporate forces located in the downtown-midtown corridor.

When Federation or one of Gilbert's holdings worked to "brand" Detroit, Downtown Synagogue folks often bridled and claimed that they were excluded from the hegemonic visions of corporate or communal interests. But Downtown Synagogue leaders also used the brand to counter-brand themselves. Gilbert's plans to remake Detroit, for example, did not include serious initiatives in the neighborhoods beyond the downtown-midtown corridor. The grassroots folks increasingly defined themselves through the belief that the state of the neighborhoods beyond the city's core would be the ultimate test of whether their work had truly succeeded. And when Federation explained its purpose was to serve the interests of "the community," the grassroots Downtown Synagogue group disputed what one member explained as "the unilateral story of Detroit" and Federation's definition of the Jewish community in favor of a more pluralistic vision.[24]

Branding themselves as concerned with all of Detroit, and as pluralistic and accepting, the Downtown Synagogue group's language slowly wove its way back into the language of the corporate and communal activists, who increasingly sought to explain how all of Detroit would benefit from their visions and how a diversity of Jews was included in their work. By 2013, the leadership of the Downtown Synagogue explained that the fierce tension that had once pitted their supporters against corporate or communal urban activists had receded.[25]

Unsurprisingly, tension remained in the relationship between urban activists, of all varieties, and those Jewish leaders and institutions committed to suburban Jewish life. This tension was critical to how urban and suburban Jews defined themselves, and it often manifested itself through a combination of generational, political, and economic divisions. Many suburban Jewish institutions watched warily as young people gravitated toward Detroit, whether to live or just to socialize. The massive suburban buildings in which suburban synagogues had invested in the 1960s, 1970s, and early 1980s stood on eroding ground.

When I started my research in 2008, I heard rumors that Shaarey Zedek and Temple Beth El were both contemplating moves to suburban locations even more remote from the city, where the congregations expected the Jewish population to settle next. By 2013, some synagogue executive directors worried that the young people who should be filling their congregations' pews and assuming leadership positions were heading downtown instead. Kohn, the executive director of the Downtown Synagogue, acknowledged that when she participated in meetings with synagogue directors from across the metropolitan region, she was consistently the youngest person in the room and sometimes had to deflect criticism that young people were choosing downtown over the suburbs because they wanted to drink and party.[26]

One of the older members of the Downtown Synagogue, a man who had moved to Detroit in 1962 as an assistant professor at Wayne State, recounted to me an incident in which one of the younger members of the congregation, upon telling a suburban Jew that she belonged to the Downtown Synagogue, was chided, "You mean those commies?"[27] From another Downtown Synagogue member, I heard a similar story in which a very wealthy and young suburban businesswoman turned to a dinner companion, also a member of the Downtown Synagogue, and asked whether the congregation was "inclusive." When the member answered, "Yes, it is," the businesswoman replied that she had heard it was "anti-Republican and anti-wealth."[28]

Red-baiting as a response to left-leaning Jewish activism has a long history, of course, and one with which older Jewish Detroiters who lived through the McCarthy hearings in the city would have been familiar. By 2013, the charges that Jewish activists in the city were communists, anti-capitalists, or anti-Republicans communicated the defensiveness that some suburban Jews felt about the back-to-the-city movement and the ways in which they perceived the movement challenging the decisions they had made. Their allegations built upon racist and classist presumptions that to live in the city was to be too urban and cosmopolitan and to undermine true Americanism. Ironically, modern antisemitic discourse had similarly depicted Jews as urban dwellers removed from the land and productive contributions to society.[29]

Young millennial activists involved in the Downtown Synagogue and other Detroit Jewish initiatives often saw the division between urban and suburban communities just as starkly as suburban detractors. Many valued urban cultural life for the kind of experimentation and options it offered. And many sought to live their politics in the neighborhoods they called home, the food they consumed, and the work in which they engaged. In a sense, they craved a return to the local politics that they imagined had marked Jewish urban life in the 1940s and 1950s.

Many Jewish millennial activists described yearning for a spiritual life free from the large, metropolitan-style Jewish institutions that had limned their predominantly suburban childhoods. Yet few could deny that these institutions—synagogues, youth groups, summer camps, and day schools—had given them the tools to believe that Jewish values were hardy enough to serve as the grounding for Jews to encounter the larger non-Jewish community and to help heal the wounds of the non-Jewish city. In material ways as well, their vision depended upon the suburbs, most obviously because sectors of suburban Jews lent financial support to Jewish initiatives in Detroit, essentially bankrolling life in the city that they or their parents had left with deep ambivalence. Even those young Jews who gave to the city the capital of their education and entrepreneurism operated from the base of resources gained in the suburbs.

Financing and Branding the New City

In the summer of 2012, the leadership of the Downtown Synagogue hired Anna Kohn as its executive director, the sole paid staff position at the institution. Kohn fit the profile of many of the young members. She had grown up in the Detroit suburbs in the nineties, where she attended a vibrant and socially engaged synagogue, the Reform Temple Emanu-El in Oak Park, and she developed a strong commitment to social activism, especially prison reform. (Unlike most of the other young members, she did not attend the University of Michigan. Rather she went to Hampshire College where she crafted her own major and dubbed it "Detroitology.") For an institution that prided itself on its lack of institutional trappings, the decision to hire Kohn represented a move toward what Max Weber called routinization, an attempt to re-create order after a period of creativity and innovation. As Kohn described it, she was hired to be the person "at the wheel."[30]

The trail of money that led to Kohn's appointment also routinized—and monetized—the terms of grassroots activism and drew it into close connection with communal and corporate activists. The Mandell (Bill) and Madeleine Berman Foundation offered an initial grant to the Downtown Synagogue as seed money for the position. The careful reader will recall that Bill Berman generated his wealth from real estate development in the suburbs and had encouraged Shaarey Zedek in the late 1950s to move to Southfield. Now, the same Berman decided to fund an urban synagogue, nearly undone by the migration he had supported and from which he had profited decades earlier. With Berman's grant in hand, the Downtown Synagogue approached the Jewish Fund, a philanthropic organization managed by the Jewish Federation, to build upon its seed money and provide three years of funding to cover a director's salary. The Jewish Fund had formed in 1997 shortly after the Detroit Medical Center purchased Sinai Hospital, the city's Jewish hospital founded in 1953 in northwest Detroit. The profits from the sale, roughly $63 million, were placed in a fund dedicated to supporting Jewish and non-Jewish health needs and "furthering positive relations between the Jewish community and the city of Detroit," though the fund did not have the same obligations as a hospital to administer care to the public.[31]

Money from multiple streams flowed toward the Downtown Synagogue. A congregation with nominal annual membership dues ($75 for an individual in 2014), it relied on private donors and foundation grants to stay afloat and pay for necessary renovations to its physical plant. According to Barak, its president, 85 percent of the donations the congregation received came from people living in the suburbs. Presumably, these donors shared the dream of a viable synagogue in the city, even if they did not share the commitment to living in that city. A $2 million capital campaign that commenced in 2013 would depend upon capturing more of these suburban dollars to improve the physical plant of the crumbling building.[32]

Kohn, whose position emerged from the nexus of grassroots, corporate, and communal activists, made it her mission to foster better connections among those three groups. She became friends with the woman who led NextGen, the Jewish Federation's under-forty division, and she worked to repair ruptures between the Downtown Synagogue and Federation that predated her. She also fast developed a relationship with Gilbert's handlers, especially his philanthropic advisor. Gilbert's philanthropic office had yet to make a substantial gift to the Downtown Synagogue as of early 2013, but board members and Kohn indicated that it was likely only a matter of time before their congregation became a beneficiary of Gilbert's largesse.[33]

As more people walked in the door of the synagogue, the core group of young organizers recognized that employees of Quicken and Rock Venture, an umbrella business to manage Gilbert's holdings, were among the crowd. As Kohn explained, the Downtown Synagogue was a "marketable product" that could "offer something that Quicken can never offer."[34]

Indeed, the Downtown Synagogue embodied the very qualities that Gilbert believed were essential to a thriving business environment in Detroit. Not a new congregation, it had nonetheless reinvented itself as a start-up, creative congregation, accepting of a diversity of Jews, and rooted to the city around it.

In a 2011 blog post about his Detroit 2.0 plan, Gilbert envisioned a downtown Detroit "hustling and bustling with young technology-focused people who can find cool lofts to live in, abundant retail and entertainment options close by, safe streets by day and night, and most importantly, numerous start-up and growing entrepreneurial companies where opportunity is endless and creative minds are free to collaborate and do what they do best: CREATE!"[35] In 2012, Gilbert helped launch a campaign called "Opportunity Made in Detroit," airing a minute-long advertisement for the city during World Series Game Four between the Detroit Tigers and the San Francisco Giants (a game the Tigers lost, sealing their defeat in that year's World Series). With narration and a soundtrack by Detroit native Kid Rock, the advertisement explained, "Opportunity. It doesn't stare you in the face. It's not going to yell at you to come'n get it. It doesn't knock." Images of mainly young people—farmers, dancers, artists, architects, scientists, black people, and white people—cascaded in sync with the quickening drumbeat and climaxed with a final question and response: "What does opportunity look like? It looks like Detroit. And opportunity is made in Detroit." A final screen flashed "Quicken Loans: Engineered to Amaze."[36]

Rather circularly, Gilbert maintained that in order for creative people to come to Detroit to create they had to believe the city was, well, a creative city.[37] He and Federation's CEO Scott Kaufman both had a habit of bringing up the case of Groupon, a lucrative company founded by two Detroiters (and a third non-Detroiter) but headquartered in Chicago. Had those two guys, one Jewish, both raised in Detroit's suburbs, thought of Detroit as a viable place to do business, a place that could attract creative people and breed creativity, then Detroit and not Chicago would have benefited from a company that valued itself at $20 billion in 2011.[38]

In an effort to keep young Jews and their talents from leaving the Detroit region, a demographic reality that would deplete the community and force Jewish institutions such as Federation into obsolescence, Kaufman had conducted a survey of Jews who were under forty years old to find out what would make them stay in the area. In the responses he received, he found that young Jews all wanted a deeper connection to the city itself. Kaufman interpreted his findings as a mandate to bring Federation's presence into the city and work to make it attractive enough to keep Jews from fleeing the region. Federation staff admitted freely that Detroit was not the ends of their work; as Miryam Rosenzweig the director of Next-Gen explained, "Federation is interested in seeing a strong city, but we will follow the community's interests. Our role is not to create an activist agenda in Detroit."[39]

Yet in funding ventures in the city that often bore only tenuous connections to the Jewish communal world and in working to rebrand the city, Federation stepped into the fray of activists all intent upon controlling the city's future through branding and funding campaigns. In 2012, Federation used money raised from an annual softball game fund-raiser (Pitch for Detroit) to create the Do It for Detroit Fund. Described by Josh Kanter, a NextGen staff person, as a "social impact program with the goal of engaging young Jewish adults in meaningful service," the fund provided money for five micro-grants in the categories of Education, Environment, Hunger, Arts and Culture, and Health and Nutrition. Kanter explained that none of the applicants was asked to demonstrate a Jewish purpose to their programs, but successful ones would offer volunteer service opportunities in which young Jewish Detroiters, whether in the city or outside, could participate. Although grant winners were ultimately chosen by popular vote at several evening programs, a Federation-based committee chose the three finalists to compete. The grants were modest (about $3,000), but Federation clearly saw itself in the business of brokering and funding private modes of activism in the city that would appeal to young people.[40]

The Downtown Synagogue, likewise, could help showcase the young experimental side of Detroit and become a magnet to anchor the creative economy that urban studies theorist Richard Florida so persuasively instructed American urban leaders was the sine qua non of revitalization. And the Downtown Synagogue could also prove to Jews that Detroit was still a vital place for Jewish life, a goal upon which Federation staked its very existence and a goal enmeshed with Gilbert's real estate investments in Detroit. For these reasons, Kohn was confident that Gilbert would, by and by, financially support the Downtown Synagogue, and for these same reasons, Federation had already channeled funds to the Downtown Synagogue and helped fuel the buzz about it.

For the corporate and communal sectors, making an investment in the grassroots activism of the Downtown Synagogue was tantamount to a self-investment and promised to move forward their visions of the city. Even if the three groups had somewhat divergent visions, they all operated within—and benefited from—a shared model of privatized, entrepreneurial urban reinvention that pivoted upon their access to resources and privilege.

Living in Detroit on Principle and Privilege

Jackie Victor, the cofounder of Avalon Bakery, moved to Detroit in the early 1990s, well before corporate, communal, or grassroots Jewish organizations had become a significant presence in the city. As a child in Bloomfield Hills, she and her family had driven into the city frequently, and she had often wondered about the gulf between her leafy green suburb and the deteriorating city of her family's past. As an undergraduate at the University of Michigan in the late 1980s, she imbibed radical critiques of capitalism and aligned herself with Detroit political activists James and Grace Lee Boggs. After graduation, Victor moved to Detroit to be near the Boggs and to live true to her and their ideology. Still, she described her move to Detroit as a "solitary journey." Before she and her partner opened their bakery, they made very little money and knew very few people like themselves who lived in the city.[41]

Most people, Victor recognized, shared neither her principles nor her privilege to live in the city. Black middle-class residents left the city each day, grateful for the opportunity to move and with no thoughts of returning to the city to join "some counter-insurgency." She explained, "The only people who come back are those who can afford it. The young Jews in Detroit live on air, like I did. They're totally underemployed and doing visionary stuff as if it's their job. They don't have student loans. And they have parents in the suburbs, so they have the privilege of not working 'real' jobs."[42]

Blair Nosan, a twenty-something who moved to Detroit in 2008, after participating in a Jewish farming program in Connecticut, understood that her lifestyle in Detroit corresponded to her socioeconomic privilege. She started a pickling business, called Suddenly Sauer, became an active board member at the Downtown Synagogue, and, through the synagogue, co-created Eden Gardens, a neighborhood farm and education project on the eastside of Detroit. None of her work brought in a true living wage. She reflected, "It is hard to feel as if the work I'm doing is valuable, because it's not being valued with money or the trappings of a 'real' job."[43]

Jewish, college-educated, grassroots activists who moved to Detroit maintained that principles drove their decision. Most, however, acknowledged that without the privileges of their backgrounds, they would have been unable to make such a choice. Communal and corporate sources directly helped sustain that privilege through programs and grants to help young, educated people live in Detroit.

In 2010, the same year Gilbert relocated the headquarters of Quicken Loans to downtown Detroit, he also developed a venture called "Live Downtown" with several other Detroit businesses. Gilbert replicated a program started in 2010 by Hudson-Webber, a Detroit-area foundation, to provide employees of Wayne State University, Detroit Medical Center, and Henry Ford Hospital with a housing subsidy if they rented or bought in the midtown area. By its own reporting a success, the Hudson-Webber program had exhausted its $1.2 million budget after just ten months. Much like that program and, in fact, with ongoing support from the Hudson-Webber Foundation, Live Downtown provided rental subsidies and forgivable loans for employees of several Detroit businesses and industries, including DTE Energy, Compuware, Blue Cross Blue Shield of Michigan, and Quicken Loans, as long as the workers lived in the downtown-midtown corridor of the city. David Egner, the president and CEO of the Hudson-Webber Foundation, described both programs as efforts to "capture" the under-thirty-five-year-old, educated demographic so sorely lacking in the city. While the city provided the perfect environment for creative start-up entrepreneurism, he argued, it would never be able to capitalize on this without building a twenty-four-hour culture to captivate young people's interests and loyalties.[44]

At the same time as Live Downtown emerged as an engine to attract talent to work, live, and, as the saying always goes, play in Detroit, Kaufman hatched a remarkably similar plan with funding from Federation. Called "Live Detroit," Federation's program developed to help stanch the Jewish population loss in the region. Live Detroit provided a rent subsidy of $250 per month to a twenty-five-person cohort of the "next generation's leaders" who chose to make their homes in the city. Recipients of the subsidy agreed to hold frequent Federation-related events in their homes. Still, for Federation the program was unprecedented because it took Federation resources, both in targeted fund-raising dollars and in the form of staffing hours, and distributed them to individuals, not agencies. Kaufman argued that ultimately the program would accrue as much value to the Jewish community as other Federation-funded programs.[45]

Hoping to attract a "diverse group of entrepreneurs, community builders, business professionals and artists dedicated to building community," Live Detroit promised to consider applicants regardless of their "sex, race, color, religion, creed, age, national origin, ancestry, pregnancy, marital status or parental status, sexual orientation, or disability."[46] The program also listed as its priority applicants who demonstrated "commitment to the City of Detroit and the Jewish community."[47] According to Josh Kanter, the staff person who closely administered the program, by the winter of 2013, Federation had received 110 applications from Jews and non-Jews and had chosen twenty-two grant recipients, fourteen of whom were Jewish. He explained that by giving the award to non-Jews and Jews, Federation was fulfilling its mission of building community in Detroit through an appreciation of its diversity.[48]

As of 2013, the director of Federation's NextGen Detroit reported that the Live Detroit fund would fulfill its obligations to the cohort selected for the program, but after another year, the program would likely not seek more funding. She explained, "We have concluded that people want to move to Detroit now, whether or not they're offered a subsidy."[49] Newly renovated lofts and apartments reached full occupancy almost as soon as they were put on the market, and the downtown-midtown area boasted an almost 99 percent occupancy rate. By 2013, other programs, such as the Moishe House and the Repair the World House—Jewish communal living programs in the midtown area—provided communally funded subsidized living for a handful of young Jews in Detroit.[50]

Live Downtown and Live Detroit recipients were restricted, according to the terms of their subsidies, to living in only designated parts of the city. The maps for Live Downtown and Live Detroit were identical: an irregular rectangle of land, running from the Detroit River to the boundary of the midtown area at Interstate 94 and jutting out slightly to the east to encompass Lafayette Park and Eastern Market and to the west toward Corktown. This was the downtown-midtown corridor, the seven-or-so-square-mile area where journalists and commentators set the narrative of Detroit's revival. Private subsidies, ventures, and, even, privately funded security forces differentiated these blocks from the rest of the city, bringing to mind the wall that developers such as Harry Slatkin had hoped would protect the value of their property investments in the 1950s. An even stronger historical parallel, however, could be found in the governmental subsidies that helped whites leave cities for suburbs in the postwar era and had, through a financial system that relied upon racial data as a significant variable for assessing property value and risk, created invisible walls between black cities and white suburbs. In the end, even those people who moved to the downtown-midtown corridor absent specific housing incentives benefited from the powerful private apparatus of urban governance, subsidized often by public dollars, that allowed certain folks in and kept others out.

The Privatized World of Public Urban Space

As Jews had shifted the focus of their attention away from the specific spaces of their neighborhoods and toward the city and metropolitan region in the late 1950s and 1960s, their concern with place-bound activism had diminished. The public spaces of neighborhoods—sidewalks, front lawns, street corners—mattered less to them once they no longer inhabited those spaces, and they increasingly focused their attentions on the policies and laws of urban governance. Many believed that these policies, if ameliorated, would eventually improve public urban space. Still, Jews' lives were much less intertwined with public urban spaces than in earlier decades.

Emerging in the 1970s, prominent Detroit leaders, Jewish and non-Jewish, had approached the city as a setting for private initiatives, arguing that the city would be better managed through private investment and that the investors and the public would both reap benefits. These private efforts in the 1970s and 1980s almost all ended in financial loss, even though similar efforts in other cities, such as Boston and New York City, met with financial success and remade public spaces in these cities.

Business Improvement Districts and Local Development Corporations, according to urban sociologist Sharon Zukin, proliferated in the 1980s as "private organization[s] of commercial property owners that carrie[d] out public functions of financing, maintaining, and governing public space."[51] In their success, these kinds of private entities re-created urban landscapes, often pushing and pricing out undesirable activities and individuals. They also tended to collude with public policy that offered more privileges (such as tax abatements) to those with privilege, and fewer privileges (such as low pay and no benefits for the service industry jobs created by private urban ventures) to those already lacking privilege.[52]

Most Jewish millennial activists in Detroit understood that their work perpetuated a divided city, not only by etching ever more deeply a geographic line between the downtown-midtown corridor and the rest of the city, but also by reproducing and hardening racial and class lines. Leor Barak, president of the Downtown Synagogue, explained simply, "It is the tale of two cities."[53] A Quicken Loans vice president (who was Jewish), charged with organizing Gilbert's Detroit initiatives, similarly noted that despite the growth in the downtown and midtown areas, the steady population loss and "deep-rooted problems" were "not slowing down" in the rest of the city.[54]

Evidenced by the maps designating where individuals could live and be eligible for rent and housing subsidies, Jewish Federation, Quicken Loans, and several other Detroit companies also perpetuated a hierarchical geography of private urban investment. By focusing on one quadrant of the city's map, Detroit millennial activists modeled their activism on the successful private urban initiatives undertaken in several other cities. Privatized efforts held the advantage of not being beholden to the electorate of an entire city and, thus, were free to neglect strategically whole sections of that city.[55]

Some grassroots millennial activists, particularly those involved in urban farming and social-justice-oriented initiatives in the city, protested the way Jewish and non-Jewish activists were redrawing the map of Detroit. Eitan Sussman, a young Jewish man involved in urban agriculture education, posited a direct correspondence between renewal and neglect: "As we're talking about renewal [in the city], we're also talking about displacement. . . . As we're strategically investing in some neighborhoods, that means we're actually strategically pulling out investment in other neighborhoods."[56] Nosan, the young activist working on an urban farming program, believed that agricultural projects outside of the downtown-midtown corridor had the potential to "connect [Jewish activists] to the whole city's needs."[57] And Jackie Victor, in a video produced by Liberty Mutual about responsible entrepreneurship in 2012, reflected, "The big picture is we have a whole city to heal."[58]

Nonetheless, private entities, whether grassroots organizations, communal bodies, or corporations, were subject to few regulations and none of the electoral checks that might have demanded a geographically, racially, and economically broader vision of public urban space than the ones they endorsed. In conversations with Detroit Jewish activists, I heard almost nothing about the city's elected officials or the general electorate. Dave Bing, a black former NBA basketball player who became the city's mayor in a special election in May 2009, offered supportive statements in favor of corporate moves to downtown. Over the next few years, private interests clearly gained traction over the downtown-midtown corridor at the expense of public elected powers, which were constantly hampered by insufficient funds, high-profile scandals, and depleted state and federal resources. When in 2013 the state of Michigan stripped the publicly elected officials of their power and appointed an unelected emergency manager to control the city's finances, the private sector only grew in power. Indeed, when Detroit filed for bankruptcy at the end of the summer of 2013, Eugene Driker predicted that the total evisceration of the public sphere would allow for true "urban reinvention" to occur, freed from the strictures of public governance that, with the deck stacked against them by forces of history and policy, had failed so miserably.[59] Likewise, the white mayor elected in the wake of Detroit's bankruptcy told a *New York Times* reporter "he had no problem with the private sector doing so much to shape his city."[60]

In the middle of the twentieth century, Jews had sought public appointments and elected positions, believing that through these roles they could influence the city's direction. This was much less so the case by the turn of the millennium, when although Jews constituted a substantial set of the private interests in the city, for the most part they did not turn their attention to attaining formal positions of political leadership.

Some of the leaders of groups such as Quicken, Federation, and the Downtown Synagogue subscribed to what historian Thomas Sugrue calls "trickle-down urbanism." They imagined that once the city's core successfully drew moneyed and educated people into it, better services and infrastructure would naturally flow to urban residents outside of the core zone of investment.[61] Barak, the president of the Downtown Synagogue, explained that a long-term economic view justified the focus on downtown and midtown development: "The city must create a larger tax base. When people with wealth come into the city, their dollars will support a larger area and improve social programs."[62] Simply getting people to come spend time and money in the city, according to Federation's CEO, was the first step in stabilizing it, and he believed that Federation could play a crucial role in rebranding the city as "Jewish Detroit," a good place for Jews and a place that Jews, on some level, could possess.[63]

As Gilbert bought up downtown real estate at a breathtaking pace, he and his inner circle of advisors gained unrivaled political, economic, and cultural power in the city. People with whom I spoke frequently bestowed upon him titles of political power: the Downtown Synagogue's president called him, "the unofficial economic mayor" of the city; a staff person of a Jewish organization referred to the "Gilbert Empire," and a Federation newsletter termed an area of the city with a high concentration of Gilbert properties the "Power Block."[64] By controlling the means of economic production and consumption in that area of the city, Gilbert and his holdings engineered a privatized economy that, itself, became a form of governance. The jobs in his companies offered capital to educated people who then had money to spend to satisfy their desires for homes, recreational activities, and cultural opportunities, almost all in spaces that Gilbert owned, maintained, and from which he and his companies profited. Indeed, as Sugrue would agree, "trickle-down urbanism" did not appear to be working to spread wealth or stability to the city's working class or poor, yet it did make it virtually impossible for publicly elected officials to compete with or, even, regulate the private sector when it came to determining the future of the city.[65]

Gilbert's private capital came to determine new public policies. For example, with the purchase of several of his properties, Gilbert received tax incentives, which included exemptions from certain property taxes, and tax subsidies to defray parking costs and other expenses associated with bringing workers into Detroit.[66] A high-level staff member contended that the incentives Gilbert received were not unique: "Every real estate deal done down there [in Detroit] is done with loads of incentives: state, federal, local. We got to get to the point where that's not the case anymore, and there's a long way to go."[67] The same staff person also noted that regardless of incentives, Gilbert also invested a "TON of his own pure cash equity" into his Detroit projects and took significant financial risks in doing so.[68]

As I followed the money, however, I came to realize that some of the big capital Gilbert invested in Detroit had been generated from lending strategies that seriously crippled the city just a few years earlier. This irony had historical precedent in Detroit and among its Jews: in the postwar years, recall, some of the same Jews who worried about "neighborhood change" were also landlords positioned to make a higher profit from house-hungry black tenants than Jews or other whites. Quicken Loans, the most vocal corporate booster of Detroit, thrived during another time when home lending policy was used as an agent of economic exploitation, especially of blacks and lower-middle-class people, and a source of economic gain for already powerful Americans. At the turn of the millennium, bankers generated the idea of subprime lending as a means to extend credit to individuals characterized as high risk in return for their payment of steep interest rates and other unfavorable terms. Eventually, subprime lending spiraled into a default crisis.

Although Quicken emerged from the lending crisis with a far cleaner image than many other loan-making firms, the money funding Gilbert's redevelopment in Detroit was connected to a lending industry that drew profit from exploiting housing inequality and the myriad of inequities connected to it.[69] Avalon Bakery's Victor recalled watching neighborhoods in the city collapse in the face of subprime lending policies. Lower-class families took the opportunity, often dangled in front of them, to refinance their homes and then quickly were unable to meet the high interest costs of their refinancing terms. Homes they had once owned became unaffordable to their occupants.[70] Thus, some of the private capital being invested in Detroit had been generated from the city itself and its citizens who had yet to experience any measurable gains from the downtown-midtown investments.

At the same time, public cultural institutions, established to serve a broad public, also became enmeshed in the growingly privatized economy of the city. The Detroit Institute of Arts (DIA), for example, the city's premier art museum treasured for its Diego Rivera automotive plant murals (*Detroit Industry, or Man and Machine*), had long relied on public tax dollars to keep it afloat. In 1990, 75 percent of its operating budget came from state money; by 2012, the museum received no funding from the state, though it did receive a modest subsidy, raised from a slight and hotly contested increase in property taxes, from the city's surrounding suburbs.[71]

One could imagine the Beaux Arts building closing up shop, dismantling piece by piece the wall frescoes that, even in their own time, stood as ambivalent tribute to the age of industry and the worker. Yet with high occupancy in the downtown-midtown corridor and private dollars continuing to flow in, the DIA stayed its ground and worked to convince private donors that the art museum helped lure creative, young, educated people to the city and was a cultural treasure for the region. The coveted creative class wanted art and culture, and the private sphere that funded their apartments and subsidized their jobs was stepping in to re-create this public space in the city as a reflection of a new private economy.

In the spring of 2013, under the duress of impending bankruptcy, state officials considered selling off some of the DIA's collections in order to grow the city's liquidity and help it dig out of debt. The museum's philanthropic supporters bridled against such a suggestion, and A. Alfred Taubman, the real estate developer who had joined Max Fisher to redevelop downtown in the late 1970s and early 1980s, pronounced the proposal "a crime," suggesting, at least on one level, that the public would be stealing assets that had, in effect, become private property.[72] By the winter of 2014, private foundations and donors, including a notable number of

FIGURE 7.2 Downtown Synagogue member Blair Nosan planting at Eden Gardens, 2013. Photograph by David Guralnick / *The Detroit News*, courtesy of the Detroit News Photo Archive, Detroit, Michigan.

Jews, had raised a significant amount of money, though not yet equal to the appraised value of the museum's collection, in hopes of using private resources to safeguard a public institution. According to a *New York Times* report, the private funds would "essentially relieve the city-owned Detroit Institute of Arts museum of its responsibility to sell some of its collection to help Detroit pay its $18 billion in debts."[73]

The privatized urban economy bestowed rewards upon the people and institutions in Detroit with economic and cultural capital. Victor explained, "It's what's happening in the center city and a few pockets that make it possible—and fun—for me to raise my kids in Detroit. Is it making it better for the other 90 percent [who don't live in these areas]? No. Is it going to? I don't know.... Probably not."[74] When Victor and her partner opened Avalon bakery in 1997, Victor's father, the son of immigrants who had opened a small store in the Hastings neighborhood and a man with deep emotional ties to Detroit, turned to his radical daughter and said, "Aha! You're finally going to become a capitalist." She replied, "No, Dad, I'm going to be an entrepreneurial socialist."[75] She hoped to redistribute the pockets of wealth in the city and the suburbs, starting with one organic loaf of bread at a time. Victor maintained that only by drawing wealth into the city could she attain her vision of bringing real sustenance to the people of Detroit. But she also believed that Detroit's success could not be apprehended entirely in the material realm. "I've always thought Detroit is a very spiritual city," she told a camera crew in 2012, "because if you're completely living life on the surface, you know, and you're only looking at what exists on the physical level, you'll miss it."[76]

Feeding Jewish Futures in Detroit

On a plot of vacant land in an all-black neighborhood on Detroit's east side, twenty-something Blair Nosan tried to produce material and spiritual sustenance for one corner of the city. Working with a fellow member of the Downtown Synagogue, a black Jewish woman who lived in the eastside neighborhood, Nosan helped create and fund Eden Gardens. She offered local and outside groups the chance to learn how to work the soil and grow food from it. She hoped these skills could bring some of the downtown-midtown corridor's energy and creativity to an area of Detroit remote from the so-called revival. The farm might help feed people who lacked access to good food, but Nosan also believed it could construct a new space from which to reinvent the city and heal past wounds. She explained, "Eden Gardens uses growing food as an organizing mechanism, allowing two long segregated communities [Jews and blacks] to come together and slowly build relationships."[77]

When nature writer Rebecca Solnit described Detroit as a post-American city in the pages of *Harper's Magazine* in 2007, the abundant nature in the city—"a pair of wild pheasants, bursting from a lush row of vegetables"—was for her the surest sign that Detroit had moved beyond its urban past. In apocalyptic terms, she imagined an eventual state of grace encasing Detroit, when the city and its old industrial grit would become submerged beneath the topsoil of a new era, a post-urban time. Urban farming, for many poor and minority people living in the city, had become a means of subsistence (Solnit used the word "sharecropping"), not to be romanticized but rather to put food on the table.[78] For Nosan and other Jewish activists invested in urban farming, however, nature's purpose was not to engulf the city. Rather, they hoped that through connecting themselves and their communities with the means of food production, they would emerge better attuned to how cities grow and thrive.

Would Detroit give its bounty to the Jews who chose to invest in it, and at what expense to the city and its diverse inhabitants? Well before the city declared its bankruptcy, the ideal of a fair exchange between the bounty of the city and the well-being of its inhabitants had long been an elusive vision. In the face of structural inequalities written into law and economic policy, the city gave unequally to its different inhabitants, depending on their class and race, and it also, over time, lost support from federal, state, and private sources.

Communal, corporate, and grassroots millennial Jewish urban activists all believed the city could do for them, in material, spiritual, and communal terms, as much as they could do for the city. Yet all three groups extracted costs from the city: for example, a Downtown Synagogue member might pay rent to a landlord who received tax abatements from the city for his real estate holdings; or Gilbert's spokespeople might insist his economic investment was good for the city, but the money he used to buy and refurbish old properties may have come from lending practices that hurt the city and its surrounding areas; or the Jewish Federation might claim that it could rewrite the narrative of Detroit and thus convince young Jews it was a cool place to be, but in order to do so, it recapitulated an old narrative about the city as a dangerous, inept, empty place. As of 2013, the investments that Jews made in the city tended to enact a private entrepreneurial vision of urban life that behooved only a small swath of the public, while, more generally, building its own power from a disempowered urban public.

In the 1980s and 1990s, even as traces of Jews' metropolitan urbanism remained evident, few Jews had made tangible investments, public or private, in the city. One could have concluded that the politics and sensibility of Jewish urbanism, the subject of this book, had ended or been transformed into something entirely different by that time with no clear connection to the city. What changed in the beginning decades of the twenty-first century, then, to spark anew Jewish urbanism in Detroit and to persuade this historian that the theme was far from over in the sweep of American Jewish history?

Historians seeking to understand the new millennium of Jewish urban activism in the future might consider a conversation Eugene Driker had with a fellow Jewish lawyer. On a phone call one day, the man said to Eugene, "For years, you and your wife have been involved in the city when it wasn't very popular. And suddenly, it's become popular for the Jewish community to be involved in the city. And I just want you to know that I'm impressed that you guys were involved in it when it wasn't popular." That evening, Eugene went home to his wife and joked, "I guess we've arrived! Somebody is paying us *koved* [honor, in Yiddish] for these years of laboring in the vineyards."[79]

The imagery of tending the vineyards in the city may tell us something crucial in thinking about this latest chapter in Jewish urbanism. As evidenced by their food activism, social justice work, political organizing, and business, retail, and recreational development efforts, Jewish individuals and organizations imagined the city as providing spaces in need of more careful tending in order to release the fruits of their fecundity.

In earlier decades, urban-dwelling Jews had looked to the suburbs as the new vineyards, away from the hardened soil of urban spaces. Yet Americans in the beginning of the twenty-first century lived with a different suburban reality. By 2014, it would have been foolish to predict large-scale Jewish flight from the suburbs, especially as many suburbs and exurbs, generally wealthy communities more remote from cities than suburbs, thrived, and some tried to reinvent themselves with revitalized main streets, walkable shopping and dining districts, and entrepreneurial opportunities.[80] Still, a greater number of suburbs were playing host to once-imagined urban problems, such as high crime rates and poverty, and many suburbs were also plagued with population loss that resembled urban patterns from earlier decades. Increasingly, those with the means left the crumbling foundations of ranch homes, the empty office parks and shopping centers, and the potholed exit ramps that had marked the postwar era of suburban development. Suburban schools suffered apace the depletion of the tax base, and signs of infrastructural neglect abounded. High oil prices made a mockery of large suburban homes and the long car rides people took to move across low-density landscapes.[81]

For Jews, especially young ones, cities provided an escape from what they had come to regard as the infertile ground of suburban life. Ambivalence about cities—about leaving them and returning to them—ran deep among Jews. Indeed, Jewish urbanism in the United States was fundamentally characterized by uncertainty about what the city should do for Jews and what Jews should do for the city. As such, Jewish urbanism often bred contradictions about matters of politics, economic justice, culture, and spirituality.

Historically, Jewish life in cities had been fraught with contradictions, often born from Jews' encounters with power. Cities in America were the places where Jews gained unprecedented wealth and cultural capital; they were also the places where Jews fought mightiest for their own economic, political, and cultural rights, and for the rights of others. Furthermore, the utopian promises that some Jews found in cities often did not extend to other populations or, even more perniciously, were premised upon the very subjugation of certain groups within America's social, economic, and political structure.

In this most recent chapter of Jewish urbanism in Detroit, the city remained a generator of contradictory impulses—to love, to redeem, to exploit, to disdain, to remake, to be more Jewish, to be less Jewish—for the Jews in its midst. The circuitous pathways of Jews' urban journeys generated the character of modern Jewish life in the United States, as Jews oriented and reoriented themselves to ever-changing city spaces.

Acknowledgments

As a graduate student, I could rely on the fact that a handful of accomplished scholars had a fiduciary responsibility to help me produce good work. After all, they had agreed to let me into their program and university. At some point, in the early stages of researching this book, I had the disturbing realization that this time, I was on my own. Except, I was wrong. The friends, new and old, scholars, students, archivists, and institutions that have helped me write this book are too numerous to name. I was not alone, and for that fact, I am deeply grateful.

I started this project during the 2007–2008 academic year, when I was fortunate to be among the inaugural fellows at University of Michigan's Frankel Center for Advanced Judaic Studies. The theme was "Jews and the City," and to say that I was deeply affected by it would be an understatement. Under the able leadership of Deborah Dash Moore and Anita Norich, our small band of fellows shared work, ideas, lunches, dinners, brunches, play dates, and due dates (just about). My days of intense focus, with frequent trips to the Reuther Library at Wayne State in Detroit, were cut short when one afternoon, while reading in my office, I went into labor two months ahead of schedule. Anita knew to open my office door and went along for the ride to Mott Children's Hospital with me. Our Ann Arbor community, including friends from the Frankel Center and my mother-in-law, Sandra Berman, who came to our house every single evening after our daughter went to bed so that we could return to our son in the NICU, sustained us. This all served as the gestation, if you will, for the book.

We returned to State College, Pennsylvania, with a toddler and baby in tow. Penn State provided a supportive environment to continue research and writing. The Jewish Studies Program, under the leadership of

Brian Hesse (*z"l*), offered material support, and my colleagues in History and Religious Studies, including Jennifer Boittin, Lori Ginzberg, Tijana Krstic, Jennifer Mittelstadt, Adam Rome, and Annie Rose, read early iterations of this work and gave me invaluable feedback. The caregivers at the Bennett Family Center at Penn State and our warm babysitter Jenna Stern all made certain that our children were in good hands while we worked.

In 2009, we moved to Philadelphia and joined the faculty at Temple University. From the first time I met him (when he interviewed me for the job), I knew that working in a department with Bryant Simon would be as good as it gets. His wisdom, energy, creativity, and friendship have propelled the project and made Temple feel like the right place to be. Temple's History department enabled me to make good progress on this project. I owe a debt of gratitude to Patricia Williams for all of her help with administrative matters and processing payments to archives and research assistants. The various chairs of the department—Drew Isenberg, Will Hitchcock, Beth Bailey, and Jon Wells—offered encouragement and helped me plan my sabbatical year. Over one of the most productive lunches of my life, Heather Thompson and I plotted the historical arc of this book. David Farber generously responded to work I presented and pushed me to define the political terrain of this book with greater precision. Richard Immerman and David Watt have been steadfast voices of sane counsel.

Colleagues from other departments, including Rebecca Alpert, Laura Levitt, and Mark Leuchter, also created a warm and collegial environment at Temple. I am grateful to Peter Logan, the director of the Center for the Humanities at Temple, for inviting me to present my research and to Abby Perkiss, then a graduate student, for organizing a symposium on race and integration. From this symposium grew my article "Jewish Urban Politics in the City and Beyond," published in the *Journal of American History* 99, no. 2 (September 2012): 492–519. Thanks to the *JAH* for allowing me to reprint parts of that article in this book, and thanks, as well, to the journal's editor, Ed Linenthal, and the readers, including Beryl Satter, Ken Waltzer, and several anonymous ones, for helping me craft a more forceful and well-supported argument.

At Temple, I serve as the director of the Feinstein Center for American Jewish History. I am appreciative of Nancy Isserman, who has served as the associate director of the center since its founding in 1990; Ed Brown, long-standing chair of the center's advisory board and a deeply thoughtful and wise person; and Arielle Werden-Greenfield, who now serves as the center's graduate fellow. Rather selfishly, I devoted two years of the Feinstein Center's programs to exploring the connection between Jews and American urbanism and then invited folks from near and far to tell me (and the other attendees) their thoughts on that relationship. I am particularly grateful to Lizabeth Cohen, Robert Fishman, Julia Foulkes, Paul Levy, Deborah Dash Moore, Suleiman Osman, Max Page, Inga Saffron, Beryl Satter, Tom Sugrue, Josh Zeitz, and Sharon Zukin for their incredibly engaged participation and ongoing generosity.

As we settled into Philadelphia, my head remained in Detroit. Over the years, I have come to rely on a team of capable archivists there. William Lefevre, Mary Wallace, and the other archivists at the Reuther Library at Wayne State made all of my visits, phone calls, and e-mail exchanges pleasant and productive. Anita Sower also served as an on-site research assistant at the Reuther Library, scanning substantial collections for me. Jan Durecki at Temple Beth El and Judy Cantor at Shaarey Zedek generously shared their wisdom with me, and I benefited many times over from their intimacy with every photograph and paper in their synagogues' collections. Archivists at the American Jewish Historical Society at the Center for Jewish History, the American Jewish Archives in Cincinnati, Columbia University's Avery Architectural and Fine Arts Library, and several other places enabled me easy access to the materials necessary for this book.

My research was literally enlivened by the memories of several Detroit Jews who took me into their homes, their cars, and their confidence to tell me about their experiences in the city. I list these people, many of whom have become friends, in the notes to this book. But I must make special mention of Eugene and Elaine Driker. The Drikers are simply extraordinary, as historical resources and as human beings. I exploited time and again their sharp memories of all things Detroit and came to rely on their willingness to entertain (and almost always answer with astounding accuracy) my questions about street intersections, stores long since closed, real estate firms, and so much more. When it came time to write the book, they emerged as important characters in my story. I shared a draft of the book with them so that they could read over the quotations I attributed to them. What they returned to me was a thoroughly proofread manuscript, with yellow Post-it flags alerting me to infelicities of language and usage and with questions about content. Of course, all remaining errors are mine, but they are markedly fewer thanks to the Drikers!

Among my Detroit people, I also owe special thanks to Patricia Becker. Not only did she, alongside Douglas Towns, create the maps for the book, but she also read the manuscript with her characteristic precision and helped me strengthen its demographic data. Much gratitude, as well to Arthur Horwitz (of the *Detroit Jewish News*) and his wife Gina Horwitz for taking an interest in this project and treating me to a delicious lunch in Rome. Harriet and Al Saperstein, Katie and Dave Elsila, and Martin Herman all were invaluable resources, kindly sharing their experiences and connections with me. Finally, I am thankful to Anna Kohn and Blair Nosan for sharing on multiple occasions their passionate knowledge about the Downtown Synagogue with me.

Through my work at the Feinstein Center, I have developed close collaborations with a number of Philadelphia institutions and individuals and found inspiration for my own work among them. Germantown Jewish Centre, the Gershman Y, the National Museum of American Jewish History, and Congregation Rodeph Shalom all have provided me opportunities to speak to a broad public about my work. A special note of gratitude to the adult learners at Rodeph Shalom: you have a fan in me! From those institutions, Warren Hoffman, Emily August, Ivy Barsky, Josh Perelman, and Rabbis Jill Maderer, Eli Freedman, and Adam Zeff, and our fabulous Germantown Jewish Centre community (including Mindy Brown, who shared her publishing expertise with me as generously as she shared her inimitable chocolate *babka*) have all supported my work in personal and meaningful ways.

Philadelphia's riches extend to a vibrant group of scholars all working on American Jewish studies and, together, we have shared our work. I have benefited immeasurably from discussions in this working group with Rebecca Alpert, Dianne Ashton, Warren Hoffman, Arthur Kiron, Melissa Klapper, Dina Pinsky, Lance Sussman, Deborah Waxman, and Beth Wenger.

I have rather promiscuously shared my work with any person or group of people willing to listen. Audiences at the University of Washington, Yale University, University of Michigan, Michigan State University, Wayne State University, Emory University, University of Illinois–Chicago, Hebrew Union College (Los Angeles), and University of California–Riverside listened and asked important questions. I have also had the opportunity to present my work at various conferences: the Association for Jewish Studies conference (including the Works-in-Progress in Modern Jewish Studies group), the Biennial Scholars' Conference on American Jewish History, the Berkshire Conference of Women Historians, and the Organization of American Historians conference. Colleagues from those worlds and others generously commented on the project and steered me to new sources and better frameworks. I offer particular thanks to Michael Alexander, Sarah Bunin Benor, Jon Butler, Rebecca Davis, Hasia Diner, Susan Glenn, Eric Goldstein, Paula Hyman (*z"l*), Robert Johnston, Ari Kelman, Matt Lassiter, Tony Michels, Noam Pianko, Riv-Ellen Prell, Shari Rabin, Katie Rosenblatt, Jonathan Sarna, Amy Shevitz, Ronit Stahl, Chip Turner, and Beth Wenger. I also am grateful to the Wexner Foundation, its professional staff, and my fellow Wexner Graduate Fellowship alumni for answering e-mail questions, no matter how obscure, creating connections, and teaching me each day about the many faces of Jewish life.

In addition to the Drikers, Patty Becker, and anonymous readers for the University of Chicago Press, several other individuals read substantial pieces (or all) of this manuscript. I profoundly appreciate Rebecca Alpert, Deborah Dash Moore, and Catherine Rottenberg for their insightful and specific feedback and their friendship. To the series editors, Jim Goodman and Becky Nicolaides, I also owe thanks for their suggestions and support. This project entered the University of Chicago Press under the able stewardship of Robert Devens and then, despite my disappointment about Robert's departure from the Press, landed in the extraordinarily capable hands of Tim Mennel, a deeply knowledgeable urbanist in his own right, Nora Devlin, and Erin DeWitt.

I wrote most of this book sitting at my desk overlooking our block in Monteverde Vecchio, a neighborhood up a big hill in Rome. For this, I have my husband to thank. He served as the director of a classics program in Rome over the 2012–2013 academic year, a time when our children learned, first, to endure and, then, to love the Italian language, their classmates and teachers at Sant'Ivo, and the bounty of the city. The staff at the Intercollegiate Center for Classical Studies took care of us in all ways; they fed us, cleaned our apartment, drove us to the doctor, helped our daughter with her homework, and made us feel like family. I offer deep gratitude, especially, to Francesco Sgariglia and Giuseppina Vallefuoco. I am also thankful to the American Academy of Rome for extending library privileges to me. We shared our Roman experience and perplexities with friends, old and new. My weekly (at least) visits with Emma Blake, while our sons practiced Italian, gave wonderful rhythm to the blur of writing days. I am grateful to Temple University for granting me the sabbatical year, to the National Endowment of the Humanities for supporting summer work on the project, and the American Council of Learned Societies for selecting me as a fellow for the year. In ways large and small, this book is a product of our year in Rome.

As for family, my gratitude and love run deep. My parents, Sandy and

Lee Corwin, taught me to follow my passions from when I was a young child and have supported me in all of my journeys. Their wisdom, love, and openness to new ideas and adventures inspire me. My brothers, Alex, Eric, and Ivan, taught me the value of a good argument and are among the people I admire most. I am grateful that they have chosen such charming partners—Lori, Julia, and Allison. My grandmother, Goldie Newman, is the lifeblood of our large family, drawing together its newest members (and singing Yiddish songs to the babies) into a web of love and closeness. My aunts, uncles, and cousins are simply part of who I am, and I thank them all for that. I also deeply appreciate my in-laws and not only because they gave me some street cred in Detroit. Sandra Berman and her partner Joe Ohren, and Marvin and Donna Berman are solid rocks of support, generosity, and love. Marvin and Sandra were both born in Detroit and over the years have shared their own memories and connections with me, come to my talks, and asked me lots of good questions.

Simon, born during my fellowship at the University of Michigan, is six as I write this, and his sister Ella is eight. They are excited that I am writing a book and ask, sometimes, what it is about. Better than this, they are curious about everything around them and approach the world with eagerness and a boundless quest to understand it. Dan, aside from being a hot ticket to Italy, is the person who makes wherever we are feel like home. I am so fortunate to have created this family and this home with him. *Baci, miei cari!*

Archival Collections, Interviews, and Abbreviations

List of Archival Collections

American Jewish Archives, Hebrew Union College, Cincinnati, OH:
- Leon Fram Papers, SC-2885
- Richard C. Hertz Papers, MS-675
- Interview with Leonard Simons, TR-1058

American Jewish Historical Society, New York, NY:
- National Jewish Community Relations Advisory Council Collection, I-172
- Philip Slomovitz Papers, P-84

Archives of American Art, Smithsonian Institute, Washington, DC:
- Oral History Interview with Lawrence A. Fleischman, February 28–March 9, 1970, http://www.aaa.si.edu/collections/interviews/oral-history-interview-lawrence-fleischman-11811.

Bentley Historical Library, University of Michigan, Ann Arbor, MI:
- Sherwin T. Wine Papers
- *Detroit Jewish News*

Columbia University Libraries, New York, NY:
- Percival Goodman Architectural Records and Papers, Avery Architectural and Fine Arts Library
- Percival Goodman Oral History, 1979, Columbia Center for Oral History

Congregation Shaarey Zedek, Archives, Southfield, MI

Stephen S. Clark Library, University of Michigan, Ann Arbor, MI:
- Detroit Map Collection

Walter P. Reuther Library, Archives of Labor and Union Affairs, Wayne State University, Detroit, MI:
- Adat Shalom Records
- Birmingham Temple Records
- Detroit Commission on Community Relations (DCCR)/Human Rights Department Records
- Donald C. Marsh Papers
- Jewish Community Council Records
- Jewish Federation of Metropolitan Detroit Records
- Jewish Labor Committee Records
- Mel Ravitz Papers

Temple Beth El, Rabbi Leo M. Franklin Archives, Bloomfield Hills, MI
Temple Israel, Archives, West Bloomfield, MI

Author's Interviews

- Vadim Avshalumov, February 27, 2013
- Leor Barak, January 27, 2013
- Mandell (Bill) Berman, May 23, 2008
- David Carroll, February 22, 2012
- Bonnie Cousens, September 17, 2009, and July 29, 2010
- Elaine Driker, January 9, 2012, and September 2, 2013
- Eugene Driker, January 4, 2012, and September 2, 2013
- Ben Falik, March 14, 2013
- Marcy Feldman, February 22, 2012
- Stanley Frankel, August 13, 2008
- Josh Kanter, February 27, 2013
- Scott Kaufman, March 22, 2012
- Anna Kohn, February 1, 2013
- Blair Nosan, February 22, 2013
- Oscar Pascal, June 13, 2011
- Miryam Rosenzweig, February 13, 2013
- Alvin Saperstein, June 14, 2011

- Ethel Schwartz, June 22, 2011
- Esther Shapiro, June 14, 2011
- Jackie Victor, February 18 and 20, 2013

List of Abbreviations

AS: Adat Shalom Records, Walter P. Reuther Library, Archives of Labor and Union Affairs, Wayne State University, MI

BT: Birmingham Temple Archives, Walter P. Reuther Library, Archives of Labor and Union Affairs, Wayne State University, MI

FA: Temple Beth El, Rabbi Leo M. Franklin Archives, Bloomfield Hills, MI

IRC: Detroit Commission on Community Relations (DCCR)/Human Rights Department Records, Walter P. Reuther Library, Archives of Labor and Union Affairs, Wayne State University, MI

JCCR: Jewish Community Council Records, Walter P. Reuther Library, Archives of Labor and Union Affairs, Wayne State University, MI

JFR: Jewish Federation of Metropolitan Detroit Records, Walter P. Reuther Library, Archives of Labor and Union Affairs, Wayne State University, MI

JLC: Jewish Labor Committee Records, Walter P. Reuther Library, Archives of Labor and Union Affairs, Wayne State University, MI

MR: Mel Ravitz Papers, Walter P. Reuther Library, Archives of Labor and Union Affairs, Wayne State University, MI

NCRAC: National Jewish Community Relations Advisory Council Collection, American Jewish Historical Society, New York, NY

RH: Richard C. Hertz Papers, American Jewish Archives, Hebrew Union College, Cincinnati, OH

SZA: Congregation Shaarey Zedek, Archives, Southfield, MI

TIA: Temple Israel, Archives, West Bloomfield, MI

Notes

Introduction

1. This, in fact, has been the regnant interpretation of Jewish suburbanization offered by social critics and historians. For a review of some of the most important social criticism on Jews and suburban life, see Lila Corwin Berman, "American Jews and the Ambivalence of Middle-Classness," *American Jewish History* 93, no. 4 (December 2007): 409–434. Also, see Judith Goldstein, *Inventing Great Neck: Jewish Identity and the American Dream* (New Brunswick, NJ: Rutgers University Press, 2006); Hasia Diner, *The Jews of the United States* (Berkeley: University of California Press, 2004), 283–304; Gerald Gamm, *Urban Exodus: Why the Jews Left Boston and the Catholics Stayed* (Cambridge, MA: Harvard University Press, 1999); Albert Gordon, *Jews in Suburbia* (Boston, MA: Beacon Press, 1959); Jonathan Sarna, *American Judaism: A History* (New Haven, CT: Yale University Press, 2004), 282–293; and Edward Shapiro, *A Time for Healing: American Jewry since World War II* (Baltimore: Johns Hopkins University Press, 1992). On Jews' migrations to the Sunbelt, see Deborah Dash Moore, *To the Golden Cities: Pursuing the American Jewish Dream in Miami and L.A.* (New York: Free Press, 1994).

2. My thinking on the connection between Jewish history and place has been influenced by Barbara Mann, *Space and Place in Jewish Studies* (New Brunswick, NJ: Rutgers University Press, 2012); and Julia Brauch, Anna Liphardt, and Alexander Nocke, eds., *Jewish Topographies: Visions of Spaces, Traditions of Place* (Burlington, VT: Ashgate, 2008). Also, see Special Issue: "Jewish Conceptions and Practices of Space," *Jewish Social Studies* 11, no. 3 (Spring 2005). For a theoretical discussion of the "spatial turn," see Santa Arias and Barney Warf, eds., *The Spatial Turn: Interdisciplinary Perspectives* (New York: Routledge, 2009).

3. See Eli Lederhendler, *New York Jews and the Decline of Urban Ethnicity, 1950–1970* (Syracuse, NY: Syracuse University Press, 2001), 1–4; Ezra Mendelsohn, ed., *People of the City: Jews and the Urban Challenge* in *Studies in Contemporary Jewry* XV (New York: Oxford University Press, 1999); Joachim Schlör,

"Jews and the Big City: Explorations on an Urban State of Mind," in Brauch, Liphardt, and Nocke, eds., *Jewish Topographies*; and Yuri Slezkine, *The Jewish Century* (Princeton, NJ: Princeton University Press, 2004). Also, see *Prooftexts* 26, nos. 1/2 (Winter/Spring 2006) for its special issue devoted to Jews and urbanism. I am also grateful for the participants in Temple University's Feinstein Center for American Jewish History's "Jews and the American City" conference in November 2011 who all offered rigorous and impressionistic analysis of Jews' relationship to city space in the United States. See http://www.cla.temple.edu/feinsteincenter/past-events/, accessed July 11, 2014, for a digital recording and transcripts from the conference.

4. See Elizabeth Wilson, *The Sphinx in the City: Urban Life, the Control of Disorder, and Women* (Berkeley: University of California Press, 1992), chapters 1 and 2.

5. Karl Marx's 1844 essay "On the Jewish Question" is the clearest expression of Western anxiety about Jewish urban economic power. Marx drew upon Weber who came to similar conclusions about the contrast between legitimate and illegitimate power, though Weber did not attack Jews with Marx's vitriol. Weber did, however, describe the modern city as a setting for the seemingly illegitimate modes of power to revolutionize life. See http://www.marxists.org/archive/marx/works/1844/jewish-question/index.htm, accessed April 10, 2014; and Max Weber, *Economy and Society,* ed. Guenther Roth and Claus Wittich (Berkeley: University of California Press, 1978). For a useful discussion of Weber, see Michael Alexander, "The Jewish Bookmaker: Gambling, Legitimacy, and the American Political Economy," in *Jews and the Sporting Life,* ed. Ezra Mendelsohn, *Studies in Contemporary Jewry* XXIII (New York: Oxford University Press, 2008). For a sweeping history of how Western society imagined itself through iterations of anti-Judaism, see David Nirenberg, *Anti-Judaism: The Western Tradition* (New York: Norton, 2013), especially chapters 7–13.

6. See Claude Fischer, "The Subcultural Theory of Urbanism: A Twentieth-Year Assessment," *American Journal of Sociology* 101, no. 3 (November 1995): 543–577; Robert Park, "The City: Suggestions for the Investigation of Human Behavior in the Urban Environment," in *The City,* ed. Robert Park, Ernest Burgess, and Roderick McKenzie (Chicago: University of Chicago Press, 1967 [1925]); and Louis Wirth, "Urbanism as a Way of Life," *American Journal of Sociology* 44, no. 1 (July 1938): 1–24.

7. On Louis Wirth's sociological work and its relationship to his own assimilated identity, see Lila Corwin Berman, *Speaking of Jews: Rabbis, Intellectuals, and the Creation of an American Public Identity* (Berkeley: University of California Press), chapter 3; Hasia Diner, "Introduction to the Transaction Edition," in Louis Wirth, *The Ghetto* (New Brunswick, CT: Transaction Publishers, 1998); Elizabeth Wirth Marvick, "Biographical Memorandum on Louis Wirth," in *Louis Wirth on Cities and Social Life*, ed. Albert J. Reiss (Chicago: University of Chicago Press, 1964);

Fred Matthews, "Louis Wirth and American Ethnic Studies: The Worldview of Enlightened Assimilationism, 1925–1950," in *The Jews of North America*, ed. Moses Rischin (Detroit: Wayne State University Press, 1987); and Robert Salerno, *Louis Wirth: A Bio-Bibliography* (New York: Greenwood Press, 1987).

8. For the sociological foundations of theories that correlate mobility and assimilation, see Robert Park, *Race and Culture* (Glencoe, IL: Free Press, 1950); Leo Srole and W. Lloyd Warner, *Social Systems of American Ethnic Groups* (New Haven, CT: Yale University Press, 1945); and Wirth, *The Ghetto*. For the theory as it appears in social history, see Thomas Kessner, *The Golden Door: Italian and Jewish Immigrant Mobility in New York City, 1880–1915* (New York: Oxford University Press, 1977).

9. For an insightful meditation on Jews and power, see David Biale, *Power and Powerlessness in Jewish History* (New York: Schocken Books, 1986).

10. On Jews' investment in a regulatory government, see Marc Dollinger, *Quest for Inclusion: Jews and Liberalism in Modern America* (Princeton, NJ: Princeton University Press, 2000).

11. On rising Jewish socioeconomic power in postwar America, see Rachel Kranson, "Grappling with the Good Life: Jewish Anxieties over Affluence in Postwar America" (Ph.D. diss., New York University, 2012).

12. A number of scholars have concluded that in the postwar years, Jews "became white." See, for example, Karen Brodkin, *How Jews Became White Folks and What That Says about Race in America* (New Brunswick, NJ: Rutgers University Press, 1998); and Matthew Frye Jacobson, *Whiteness of a Different Color: European Immigrants and the Alchemy of Race* (Cambridge, MA: Harvard University Press, 1998). For a study that questions the terms of Jewish racial identity and explores how Jews deployed race as an identity category even as they "became white," see Eric Goldstein, *The Price of Whiteness: Jews, Race, and American Identity* (Princeton, NJ: Princeton University Press, 2006).

13. On the federal disinvestment from cities, see Robert Beauregard, *Voices of Decline: The Postwar Fate of U.S. Cities* (Cambridge, MA: Blackwell, 1993); David Freund, *Colored Property: State Politics and White Racial Politics in Suburban America* (Chicago: University of Chicago Press, 2007); Arnold Hirsch, *Making the Second Ghetto: Race and Housing in Chicago, 1940–1960* (Chicago: University of Chicago Press, 1998); Kenneth Jackson, *Crabgrass Frontier: The Suburbanization of the United States* (New York: Oxford University Press, 1985); Robert Self, *American Babylon: Race and the Struggle for Postwar Oakland* (Princeton, NJ: Princeton University Press, 2003); Amanda Seligman, *Block by Block: Neighborhood and Public Policy on Chicago's West Side* (Chicago: University of Chicago Press, 2005); and Thomas Sugrue, *The Origins of the Urban Crisis: Race and Inequality in Postwar Detroit* (Princeton, NJ: Princeton University Press, 1996). On the splintering of liberalism and the rise, especially, of conservatism, see Darren Dochuk, *From Bible Belt to Sunbelt: Plain-Folk Religion, Grassroots Politics, and the Rise of*

Evangelical Conservatism (New York: Norton, 2010); Kevin Kruse, *White Flight: Atlanta and the Making of Modern Conservatism* (Princeton, NJ: Princeton University Press, 2007); Matthew Lassiter, *The Silent Majority: Suburban Politics in the Sunbelt South* (Princeton, NJ: Princeton University Press, 2006); Lisa McGirr, *Suburban Warriors: The Origins of the New American Right* (Princeton, NJ: Princeton University Press, 2001); Michelle Nickerson, *Mothers of Conservatism: Women and the Postwar Right* (Princeton, NJ: Princeton University Press, 2012). Finally, for a theoretical meditation on liberal democracy and its transformation into neoliberalism, see Wendy Brown, "Neo-Liberalism and the End of Liberal Democracy," *Theory and Event* 7, no. 1 (2003), http://muse.jhu.edu.libproxy.temple.edu/journals/theory_and_event/v007/7.1brown.html.

14. On the privatization of urban space, see Miriam Greenberg, *Branding New York: How a City in Crisis Was Sold to the World* (New York: Routledge, 2008); and Sharon Zukin, *Naked City: The Death and Life of Authentic Urban Places* (New York: Oxford University Press, 2010). For an astute examination of social critics' conversations about the fraying of Jewish liberalism, see Michael Staub, *Torn at the Roots: The Crisis of Jewish Liberalism in Postwar America* (New York: Columbia University Press, 2002).

15. See Richard Harris and Robert Lewis, "The Geography of North American Cities and Suburbs, 1900–1950: A New Synthesis," *Journal of Urban History* 27, no. 3 (March 2001): 262–292. For a historiographical meditation on the urban-suburban binary and its attendant racial and class divisions, see Matthew Lassiter and Christopher Niedt, "Suburban Diversity in Postwar America," *Journal of Urban History* 39, no. 1 (January 2013): 3–14. For an example of an excellent historical study that does not draw a strict division between city and suburb, see Alison Isenberg, *Downtown: A History of the Place and the People Who Made It* (Chicago: University of Chicago Press, 2004). On the emergence of scholarly conversations challenging the binary division between conservatism and liberalism, see "Conservatism: A Roundtable," *Journal of American History* 98, no. 3 (December 2011): 723–773.

16. Cheryl Greenberg, "Liberal NIMBY: American Jews and Civil Rights," *Journal of Urban History* 38, no. 3 (May 2012): 456.

17. Ibid., 463. On Jews' self-interest as a critical factor explaining their involvement in the civil rights movement and antidiscrimination campaigns, see Dollinger, *Quest for Inclusion*; Jonathan Rieder, *Canarsie: The Jews and Italians of Brooklyn against Liberalism* (Cambridge, MA: Harvard University Press, 1985); and Joshua Zeitz, *White Ethnic New York: Jews, Catholics, and the Shaping of Postwar Politics* (Chapel Hill: University of North Carolina Press, 2007).

18. On neoconservatism, see Murray Friedman, *The Neoconservative Revolution: Jewish Intellectuals and the Shaping of Public Policy* (New York: Cambridge University Press, 2005). On the Jewish left in the United States, see Joseph Dorman, *Arguing the World: The New York Intellectuals in Their Own Words* (New

York, Free Press, 2000); Tony Michels, *A Fire in Their Hearts: Yiddish Socialists in New York* (Cambridge, MA: Harvard University Press, 2005); Tony Michels, ed., *Jewish Radicals: A Documentary History* (New York: New York University Press, 2012); Gerald Sorin, *The Prophetic Minority: American Jewish Immigrant Radicals, 1880–1920* (Bloomington: Indiana University Press, 1985). Also Michael Walzer's keynote address at YIVO's "Jews and the Left" conference (May 6, 2012) offers a way of thinking about the rise and decline of the Jewish left. For a video of the address, see http://www.cjh.org/pages.php?pid=45&evID=1965, accessed April 10, 2014.

19. See note 13.

20. Darren Dochuk has also written about white conservative Protestants whose relationship with the city and urban churches led them to far greater urban attachment than most historians have recognized. See Darren Dochuk, "'Praying for a Wicked City': Congregation, Community, and the Suburbanization of Fundamentalism," *Religion and American Culture* 13, no. 2 (Summer 2003): 167–203.

21. Kruse, *White Flight*, 6.

22. Robert Self and Thomas Sugrue, "The Power of Place: Race, Political Economy, and Identity in the Postwar Metropolis," in *A Companion to Post-1945 America*, ed. Jean-Christophe Agnew and Roy Rosenzweig (Malden, MA: Blackwell, 2002), 28.

23. Freund, *Colored Property*, 8. On black suburbanization, see Andrew Wiese, *Places of Their Own: African American Suburbanization in the Twentieth Century* (Chicago: University of Chicago Press, 2004).

24. George Lipsitz, "The Possessive Investment in Whiteness: Racialized Social Democracy and the 'White' Problem in American Studies," *American Quarterly* 47, no. 3 (September 1995): 374. Also, see Brodkin, *How the Jews Became White Folks*; Jacobson, *Whiteness of a Different Color*; David Roediger, *Working Toward Whiteness: How America's Immigrants Became White: The Strange Journey from Ellis Island to the Suburbs* (New York: Basic Books, 2005); and Michael Rogin, *Blackface, White Noise: Jewish Immigrants in the Hollywood Melting Pot* (Berkeley: University of California Press, 1996).

25. Gamm, *Urban Exodus*; and Edward Shapiro, *A Time for Healing: American Jewry since World War II* (Baltimore: Johns Hopkins University Press, 1992). On Jewish nostalgia for urban places, see Hasia Diner, *Lower East Side Memories: A Jewish Place in America* (Princeton, NJ: Princeton University Press, 2000), 131; and Hasia Diner, Jeffrey Shandler, and Beth Wenger, eds., *Remembering the Lower East Side: American Jewish Reflections* (Bloomington: Indiana University Press, 2000).

26. Wendy Cheng, *The Changs Next Door to the Díazes: Remapping Race in Suburban California* (Minneapolis: University of Minnesota Press, 2013); Lily Geismer, "'Don't Blame Us': Grassroots Liberalism in Massachusetts, 1960–1990" (Ph.D. diss., University of Michigan, 2010); Becky Nicolaides, *My Blue Heaven:*

Life and Politics in the Working Class Suburbs of Los Angeles, 1920–1965 (Chicago: University of Chicago Press, 2002); Christopher Niedt, ed., *Social Justice in Diverse Suburbs: History, Politics, and Prospects* (Philadelphia: Temple University Press, 2013); Riv-Ellen Prell, "Community and the Discourse of Elegy: The Post War Suburban Debate," in *Imagining the American Jewish Community*, ed. Jack Wertheimer (Hanover, NH: University Press of New England / Brandeis University Press, 2007), 67–90; and Wiese, *Places of Their Own*.

27. Herbert Gans, *The Levittowners: Ways of Life and Politics in a New Suburban Community* (New York: Pantheon Books, 1967), 37. On the Levittown suburbs, see Barbara Kelly, *Expanding the American Dream: Building and Rebuilding Levittown* (Albany: State University of New York Press, 1993).

28. Marshall Sklare, "Jews, Ethnics, and the American City," *Commentary* 53, no. 4 (April 1972): 70.

29. On liberal political activism in the suburbs, see Geismer, "'Don't Blame Us.'" Also, see Lassiter and Niedt, "Suburban Diversity in Postwar America"; and Sylvie Murray, *The Progressive Housewife: Community Activism in Suburban Queens, 1945–1965* (Philadelphia: University of Pennsylvania Press, 2003).

30. Studies of small-town Jews illuminate a very different landscape that a minority of Jews in the United States experienced. See, for example, Ewa Morawska, *Insecure Prosperity: Small-Town Jews in Industrial America, 1890–1940* (Princeton, NJ: Princeton University Press, 1996); and Lee Shai Weissbach, *Jewish Life in Small-Town America: A History* (New Haven, CT: Yale University Press, 2005).

31. Etan Diamond, *And I Will Dwell in Their Midst: Orthodox Jews in Suburbia* (Chapel Hill: University of North Carolina Press, 2000); and Samuel Heilman, "Orthodox Jews, the City and the Suburb," in *People of the City: Jews and the Urban Challenge*, ed. Peter Medding, *Studies in Contemporary Jewry* XV (New York: Oxford University Press, 1999).

32. Jonathan Sarna, "The Cult of Synthesis in American Jewish Culture," *Jewish Social Studies* 5, nos. 1/2 (Fall 1998–Winter 1999): 52–79.

33. For helping me think through the tropes of unity and diversity in twentieth-century America, I am grateful to Matthew Frye Jacobson's work and a long-ago discussion we had when I was a graduate student. See especially Jacobson, *Whiteness of a Different Color*; and Jacobson, *Roots, Too: White Ethnic Revival in Post-Civil Rights America* (Cambridge, MA: Harvard University Press, 2006). Also, see Gary Gerstle, *American Crucible: Race and Nation in the Twentieth Century* (Princeton, NJ: Princeton University Press, 2002).

34. For studies of these cities, see Lloyd P. Gartner, *History of the Jews of Cleveland* (Cleveland: Western Reserve Historical Society, 1978); Henry Goldschmidt, *Race and Religion among the Chosen Peoples of Crown Heights* (New Brunswick, NJ: Rutgers University Press, 2006); Hirsch, *Making the Second Ghetto*; William Helmreich, *The Enduring Community: The Jews of Newark and MetroWest* (New Brunswick, NJ: Rutgers University Press, 1999); Hillel Levine and Lawrence Harmon, *The Death of an American Jewish Community: A Tragedy of Good Intentions*

(New York: Free Press, 1992); Murray, *The Progressive Housewife*; Antero Pietila, *Not in My Neighborhood: How Bigotry Shaped a Great American City* (Chicago: Ivan R. Dee, 2010); Wendell Pritchett, *Brownsville, Brooklyn: Blacks, Jews, and the Changing Face of the Ghetto* (Chicago: University of Chicago Press, 2002); George Sanchez, "'What's Good for Boyle Heights Is Good for the Jews': Creating Multiculturalism on the Eastside during the 1950s," *American Quarterly* 56 (September 2004): 633–661; Beryl Satter, *Family Properties: Race, Real Estate, and the Exploitation of Black Urban America* (New York: Henry Holt, 2009); and David Varady, "Wynnefield: Story of a Changing Neighborhood," in *Philadelphia Jewish Life, 1940–2000*, ed. Murray Friedman (Philadelphia: Temple University Press, 2003).

35. On Detroit, see Kevin Boyle, *Arc of Justice: A Saga of Race, Civil Rights, and Murder in the Jazz Age* (New York: Henry Holt, 2004); Freund, *Colored Property*; Sugrue, *The Origins of the Urban Crisis*; Jon Teaford, *Cities of the Heartland: The Rise and Fall of the Industrial Midwest* (Bloomington: Indiana University Press, 1993); Heather Ann Thompson, *Whose Detroit? Politics, Labor, and Race in a Modern American City* (Ithaca, NY: Cornell University Press, 2001); and Olivier Zunz, *The Changing Face of Inequality: Urbanization, Industrial Development, and Immigrants in Detroit, 1880–1920* (Chicago: University of Chicago Press, 1982). On Detroit's Jews, see Sidney Bolkosky, *Harmony and Dissonance: Voices of Jewish Identity in Detroit, 1914–1967* (Detroit: Wayne State University Press, 1991); Henry Meyer, "The Structure of the Jewish Community in the City of Detroit" (Ph.D. diss., University of Michigan, 1939); Robert Rockaway, *The Jews of Detroit: From the Beginning, 1762–1914* (Detroit: Wayne State University Press, 1986); and Kenneth Waltzer, "East European Jewish Detroit in the Early Twentieth Century," *Judaism* 49 (Summer 2000): 291–309.

Chapter One

1. See Sylvia Cottler Cohen, "Dexter-Davison Market," October 2006, copy in author's possession. Cohen is the daughter of Norman Cottler, founder and owner of the market.

2. Information about the Drikers' lives from interview with Elaine Driker, January 9, 2012; interview with Eugene Driker, January 4, 2012; and driving tour of Detroit with Elaine and Eugene Driker, June 28, 2012.

3. One can find plenty of theoretical frameworks for thinking about the role of space in shaping human experience. The two texts that have most influenced me are Doreen Massey, *For Space* (London: Sage, 2005); and Yi-fu Tuan, *Space and Place: The Perspective of Experience* (Minneapolis: University of Minnesota Press, 1977).

4. Park, "The City: Suggestions for the Investigation of Human Behavior in the Urban Environment," in *The City,* ed. Robert Park, Ernest Burgess, and Roderick McKenzie (Chicago: University of Chicago Press, 1967 [1925]), 6.

5. For an overview of sociological theory on the neighborhood, see Robert Sampson, *Great American City: Chicago and the Enduring Neighborhood Effect* (Chicago: University of Chicago Press, 2012).

6. On the early Jewish population of the Hastings Street neighborhood, see Phillip Applebaum, "A Tour of Jewish Detroit," published by Southeast Michigan Regional Ethnic Heritage Studies Center (1975); Sidney Bolkosky, *Harmony and Dissonance: Voices of Jewish Identity in Detroit, 1914–1967* (Detroit: Wayne State University Press, 1991), chapter 1; and Robert Rockaway, *The Jews of Detroit: From the Beginning, 1762–1914* (Detroit: Wayne State University Press, 1986). On the class and nationality patterns in the neighborhood, see "The Jewish Population of Detroit in 1904," extracted from Oliver Corwoods, "An Ethnographical Study of Detroit," August 1904 and reprinted in *Michigan Jewish History* 13, no. 2 (June 1973): 15.

7. "The Ghetto!" extracted from the *Detroit News*, September 13, 1896, and reprinted in *Michigan Jewish History* 6, no. 2 (June 1966): 9. Also, see Kenneth Waltzer, "East European Jewish Detroit in the Early Twentieth Century," *Judaism* 49, no. 3 (Summer 2000): 291–309.

8. Bolkosky, *Harmony and Dissonance*, 152–153.

9. Olivier Zunz, *The Changing Face of Inequality: Urbanization, Industrial Development, and Immigrants in Detroit, 1880–1920* (Chicago: University of Chicago Press, 1982), 350–351.

10. Rockaway, *The Jews of Detroit*, 64; and Zunz, *The Changing Face of Inequality*, 153, 392.

11. On Jews' exclusion from the automobile industry, see Zunz, *The Changing Face of Inequality*, 333. On Jews' occupational patterns in the 1920s, see Bolkosky, *Harmony and Dissonance*, 20; and Henry Meyer, "The Structure of the Jewish Community in the City of Detroit" (Ph.D. diss., University of Michigan, 1939), 123–135.

12. On the United Jewish Charities, see Irving Edgar, "Beginnings of the United Jewish Charities," *Michigan Jewish History* 15, no. 2 (July 1975): 5–8.

13. Rockaway, *The Jews of Detroit*, 63.

14. On immigration restriction legislation and its role in reshaping twentieth-century American culture, see Mae Ngai, *Impossible Subjects: Illegal Aliens and the Making of Modern America* (Princeton, NJ: Princeton University Press, 2004).

15. For a copy of the report, see memo from Zeldon Cohen to CRC Neighborhoods Committee, September 24, 1965, with attached copy of "Shifting Jewish Districts," a 1923 Survey of the Detroit Jewish Community, Folder 2, Box 23, JCCR.

16. Jon Teaford, *Cities of the Heartland: The Rise and Fall of the Industrial Midwest* (Bloomington: Indiana University Press, 1993), chapter 4; and Zunz, *The Changing Face of Inequality*, 286.

17. Zunz, *The Changing Face of Inequality*, 286–291.

18. Memo from Zeldon Cohen to CRC Neighborhoods Committee, September 24, 1965, JCCR.

19. On the formation of the Jewish Welfare Federation in 1926, see Bolkosky, *Harmony and Dissonance*, 113. On the progressive era and its fixation on expert data to help rationalize urban and American experience, see Jeffrey Hornstein, *A Nation of Realtors: A Cultural History of the Twentieth-Century American Middle Class* (Durham, NC: Duke University Press, 2005); Sarah Igo, *The Averaged American: Surveys, Citizens, and the Making of a Mass Public* (Cambridge, MA: Harvard University Press, 2007); Alison Isenberg, *Downtown America: A History of the Place and the People Who Made It* (Chicago: University of Chicago Press, 2004); Daniel Rodgers, *Atlantic Crossings: Social Politics in a Progressive Age* (Cambridge, MA: Belknap Press of Harvard University Press, 1998); and Marc Weiss, *Community Builders: The American Real Estate Industry and Urban Land Planning* (New York: Columbia University Press, 1987).

20. For synthetic studies of the relationship between Jewish identity and space, see Barbara Mann, *Space and Place in Jewish Studies* (New Brunswick, NJ: Rutgers University Press, 2012); and Julia Brauch, Anna Liphardt, and Alexander Nocke, eds., *Jewish Topographies: Visions of Spaces, Traditions of Place* (Burlington, VT: Ashgate, 2008). For historical examinations of different modes of Jewish spatial separation, see Charlotte Fonrobert, "The Political Symbolism of the Eruv," *Jewish Social Studies* 11, no. 3 (Spring/Summer 2005): 9–35; Steven Katz, ed., *The Shtetl: New Evaluations* (New York: New York University Press, 2007); and David Ruderman, "The Historical Significance of the Ghetto in Jewish History," in *From Ghetto to Emancipation: Historical and Contemporary Reconsideration of the Jewish Community*, ed. David Myers and William Rowe (Chicago: University of Chicago Press, 1997).

21. The formal and informal residential restrictions that Jews in the United States experienced should help us understand one way in which American exceptionalism has been overstated in the historiography on American Jews. For a broader consideration of this, see Tony Michels, "Is America 'Different'? A Critique of American Jewish Exceptionalism," *American Jewish History* 96, no. 3 (September 2010): 201–224. On the ways in which zoning policies and restrictive covenants were used to inscribe hierarchies in American space, see Robert Fogelson, *Bourgeois Nightmares: Suburbia* (New Haven, CT: Yale University Press, 2005); David Freund, *Colored Property: State Policy and White Racial Politics in Suburban America* (Chicago: University of Chicago Press, 2007); and Seymour Toll, *Zoned American* (New York: Grossman Publishers, 1969).

22. See Deborah Dash Moore, "On the Fringes of the City: Jewish Neighborhoods in Three Boroughs," in *The Landscape of Modernity: Essays on New York City, 1900–1940*, ed. David Ward and Olivier Zunz (New York: Russell Sage Foundation, 1992).

23. Neil Baldwin, *Henry Ford and the Jews: The Mass Production of Hate* (New York: Public Affairs, 2001). On nativism and antisemitism in the United States, see Leonard Dinnerstein, *Antisemitism in America* (New York: Oxford University Press, 1994); Gary Gerstle, *American Crucible: Race and Nation in the Twentieth*

Century (Princeton, NJ: Princeton University Press, 2001); and John Higham, *Strangers in the Land: Patterns of American Nativism, 1860–1925* (New York: Atheneum, 1963).

24. Henry Meyer, "The Economic Structure of the Jewish Community of Detroit," *Jewish Social Studies* 2, no. 2 (April 1940): 127–148. On Jews and the Depression, see Beth Wenger, *New York Jews and the Great Depression: Uncertain Promise* (New Haven, CT: Yale University Press, 1996).

25. Articles of Incorporation of Standard Club and Amendments, 1934, copy obtained from Judge Avern Cohn and in author's possession. See also Shelley Eichenhorn, "Jews, Gentiles: The Social Gap Survives," *Detroit News*, November 14, 1976.

26. Zunz, *The Changing Face of Inequality*, 357.

27. Bolkosky, *Harmony and Dissonance*, 187.

28. Ibid., 17–19, 436. Henry Meyer estimated that the Jewish population in Detroit in the mid-1930s was closer to eighty-two thousand, but demographers since decided that his numbers were inflated. See Meyer, "The Structure of the Jewish Community in the City of Detroit," 9.

29. Henry Meyer, "Some Facts about Jewish Detroit," Jewish Welfare Federation, 1940, Box 548, Folder 3, JFR. On the housing stock in the Twelfth Street area, see Bernard Rosenberg, "Report on the Findings of the 12th Street Survey," n.d. [1947], Box 4, Folder 47:57, Part I, Series 1, IRC, 9.

30. Meyer, "Some Facts about Jewish Detroit," JFR.

31. On the creation of the Federal Housing Administration, see Henry Aaron, *Shelter and Subsidies: Who Benefits from Federal Housing Policies?* (Washington, DC: Brookings Institution, 1972); Kenneth Jackson, *Crabgrass Frontier: The Suburbanization of the United States* (New York: Oxford University Press, 1985), chapter 11; and Adam Rome, *The Bulldozer in the Countryside: Suburban Sprawl and the Rise of American Environmentalism* (New York: Cambridge University Press, 2001), 28–32.

32. According to the 1940 census tract report, 61,553 housing units were in buildings of ten or more units, which represented slightly less than 14 percent of the total housing stock. In 1950, that percentage fell to 11.8 percent. See U.S. Bureau of the Census, *Population and Housing, Statistics for Census Tracts, Detroit, Mich. and Adjacent Area* (Washington, DC: U.S. Government Printing Office, 1942), 193. I thank Patricia Becker for helping me find this information and making these calculations for me, which differ from Thomas Sugrue's calculation that apartment buildings comprised 1.3 percent of the city's housing stock. See Sugrue, *The Origins of the Urban Crisis: Race and Inequality in Postwar Detroit* (Princeton, NJ: Princeton University Press, 1996), 20.

33. David Goldberg and Harry Sharp, "Some Characteristics of Detroit Area Jewish and Non-Jewish Adults," in *The Jews: Social Patterns of an American Group*, ed. Marshall Sklare (Glencoe, IL: Free Press, 1958): 115–116. On

Jewish homeownership in the 1920s, see Zunz, *The Changing Face of Inequality*, 192.

34. To track the changing language of race in American civic discourse, see Gerstle, *American Crucible*; and Matthew Frye Jacobson, *Whiteness of a Different Color: European Immigrants and the Alchemy of Race* (Cambridge, MA: Harvard University Press, 1999). On the rise of interfaith efforts and public relations campaigns against antisemitism and "un-American" behavior, see Stuart Svonkin, *Jews against Prejudice: American Jews and the Fight for Civil Liberties* (New York: Columbia University Press, 1997); and Wendy Wall, *Inventing the "American Way": The Politics of Consensus from the New Deal to the Civil Rights Movement* (New York: Oxford University Press, 2008).

35. Eli Lederhendler, *New York Jews and the Decline of Urban Ethnicity, 1950–1970* (Syracuse, NY: Syracuse University Press, 2001), chapter 1.

36. Jonathan Sarna, "The Cult of Synthesis in American Jewish Culture," *Jewish Social Studies* 5, nos. 1/2 (Fall 1998–Winter 1999): 52–79.

37. For studies that highlight the strength, fleeting as it may have been, of Jewish neighborhood identification in the 1940s and early 1950s, see Lloyd P. Gartner, *History of the Jews of Cleveland* (Cleveland Western Reserve Historical Society, 1978); Arnold Hirsch, *Making the Second Ghetto: Race and Housing in Chicago, 1940–1960* (Chicago: University of Chicago Press, 1998); William Helmreich, *The Enduring Community: The Jews of Newark and MetroWest* (New Brunswick, NJ: Rutgers University Press, 1999); Hillel Levine and Lawrence Harmon, *The Death of an American Jewish Community: A Tragedy of Good Intentions* (New York: Free Press, 1992); Sylvie Murray, *The Progressive Housewife: Community Activism in Suburban Queens, 1945–1965* (Philadelphia: University of Pennsylvania Press, 2003); Wendell Pritchett, *Brownsville, Brooklyn: Blacks, Jews, and the Changing Face of the Ghetto* (Chicago: University of Chicago Press, 2002); George Sanchez, "'What's Good for Boyle Heights Is Good for the Jews': Creating Multiculturalism on the Eastside during the 1950s," *American Quarterly* 56 (September 2004): 633–661; Beryl Satter, *Family Properties: Race, Real Estate, and the Exploitation of Black Urban America* (New York: Henry Holt, 2009); and David Varady, "Wynnefield: Story of a Changing Neighborhood," in *Philadelphia Jewish Life, 1940–2000*, ed. Murray Friedman (Philadelphia: Temple University Press, 2003).

38. On the history of the Catholic Church in Detroit, see Leslie Tentler, *Seasons of Grace: A History of the Catholic Archdiocese of Detroit* (Detroit: Wayne State University Press, 1990).

39. See Annexation History Census Tract Map, 1960, from Patricia Becker's private collection, in author's possession.

40. John Stevens, "Detroit Population Moving Outward," *The Detroiter* (a publication of the Detroit Board of Commerce), November 5, 1951, Box 124, Folder 1, JFR.

41. Map, "Patterns of Restricted Covenants," 1947, Box 584, Folder 5, JCCR.

42. See "Adas Shalom: The Story of a Synagogue," Dedication Volume, March 28–30, 1952, Box 55, Folder 5, AS. On the history of Adas Shalom, also see Dedication Book for "The New Adas Shalom Synagogue," n.d. [1971] Box 55, Folder 3, AS. Note, Adas Shalom changed its name to Adat Shalom shortly after it moved to the suburbs in 1973.

43. Deborah Dash Moore, *At Home in America* (New York: Columbia University Press, 1981), 39.

44. For advertisements, see *Detroit Jewish News*, June 17, 1949, 23.

45. Albert Mayer, "Movement of the Jewish Population in the Detroit Metropolitan Area: 1949–1958," 1958, sponsored by the Jewish Welfare Federation of Detroit, Box 584, Folder 9, JCCR.

46. On the construction of the Lodge, see Charles K. Hyde, "Planning a Transportation System for Metropolitan Detroit in the Age of the Automobile: The Triumph of the Expressway," *Michigan Historical Review* 32, no. 1 (Spring 2006): 88–95. More generally, see Tom Lewis, *Divided Highways: Building the Interstate Highways, Transforming American Life* (New York: Viking, 1997).

47. Albert Mayer, "Jewish Population Study: 1963," sponsored by the Jewish Welfare Federation of Detroit, Box 590, Folder 8, JCCR.

48. Mayer, "Movement of the Jewish Population in the Detroit Metropolitan Area: 1949–1958," JCCR.

49. Freund, *Colored Property*, 233; and "Preliminary Reports: Population Counts for States, 1960," Census of Population, August 1960, Box 37, Folder 10, JFR.

50. See Milton Tambor, "The Historical Development of the Detroit Jewish Community Center," *Michigan Jewish History* 3, no. 3 (June 1963): 15–17.

51. See U.S. Bureau of the Census, *U.S. Census of Population and Housing: 1960, Census Tracts*, Final Report PHC(1)-40 (Washington, DC: U.S. Government Printing Office, 1962), 19.

52. "Cottlers to Open New OP Market," *Detroit Jewish News*, November 13, 1959, 14.

53. James Flink, *The Automobile Age* (Cambridge, MA: MIT Press, 1990).

54. On postwar criticism of the suburbs, see Lila Corwin Berman, "American Jews and the Ambivalence of Middle-Classness," *American Jewish History* 93, no. 4 (December 2007): 409–434. Recent scholarship has offered a more complicated and heterogeneous assessment of the suburbs. See Wendy Cheng, *The Changs Next Door to the Díazes: Remapping Race in Suburban California* (Minneapolis: University of Minnesota Press, 2013); Lily Geismer, "'Don't Blame Us': Grassroots Liberalism in Massachusetts, 1960–1990" (Ph.D. diss., University of Michigan, 2010); Becky Nicolaides, *My Blue Heaven: Life and Politics in the Working Class Suburbs of Los Angeles, 1920–1965* (Chicago: University of Chicago Press, 2002); Christopher Niedt, ed., *Social Justice in Diverse Suburbs: History, Politics, and Prospects* (Philadelphia: Temple University Press, 2013); William Benjamin Piggot, "Globalization from the Bottom Up: Irvine, California,

and the Birth of Suburban Cosmopolitanism," *Pacific Historical Review* 81, no. 1 (February 2012): 60–91; Riv-Ellen Prell, "Community and the Discourse of Elegy: The Post War Suburban Debate," in *Imagining the American Jewish Community*, ed. Jack Wertheimer (Hanover, NH: University Press of New England / Brandeis University Press, 2007): 67–90; and Andrew Wiese, *Places of Their Own: African American Suburbanization in the Twentieth Century* (Chicago: University of Chicago Press, 2004).

55. My thinking on this has been most influenced by the work of Freund, *Colored Property*; Kevin Kruse, *White Flight: Atlanta and the Making of Modern Conservatism* (Princeton, NJ: Princeton University Press, 2007); Matthew Lassiter, *The Silent Majority: Suburban Politics in the Sunbelt South* (Princeton, NJ: Princeton University Press, 2006); Satter, *Family Properties*; and Sugrue, *The Origins of the Urban Crisis*.

56. Interview with Eugene Driker, January 4, 2012.

57. "This Is What We've Been Waiting For . . ." n.d. [1948–1949], Folder "Fram: Building: Correspondence, Building Fund, Architect, 1940s," TIA.

58. Scholars have written about nostalgia for the Jewish urban past in relation to the Lower East Side. See Hasia Diner, *Lower East Side Memories: A Jewish Place in America* (Princeton, NJ: Princeton University Press, 2000), 131; and Hasia Diner, Jeffrey Shandler, and Beth Wenger, eds., *Remembering the Lower East Side: American Jewish Reflections* (Bloomington: Indiana University Press, 2000).

Chapter Two

1. "Incident Report: City of Detroit, Interracial Committee," November 21, 1944, Part I, Series 1, Box 3, Folder "Incidents Housing, 1944," IRC.

2. On the decline of the Jewish left and the rise of Jewish liberalism in the 1940s, see Marc Dollinger, *Quest for Inclusion: Jews and Liberalism in Modern America* (Princeton, NJ: Princeton University Press, 2000); Stuart Svonkin, *Jews against Prejudice: American Jews and the Fight for Civil Liberties* (New York: Columbia University Press, 1997).

3. On redlining policies and their role in creating housing segregation and a discriminatory housing market, see Charles Abrams, *Forbidden Neighbors: A Study of Prejudice in Housing* (New York: Harper, 1955); and Kenneth Jackson, *Crabgrass Frontier* (New York: Oxford University Press, 1985), chapter 11. A recent revisionist history has worked to explain that federal policy was only one factor, among many, fueling an unjust housing market. See Amy Hillier, "Redlining and the Home Owners' Loan Corporation," *Journal of Urban History* 29, no. 4 (May 2003): 394–420.

4. Robert Park, "The City: Suggestions for the Investigation of Human Behavior in the Urban Environment," in *The City*, ed. Robert Park, Ernest Burgess, and Roderick McKenzie (Chicago: University of Chicago Press, 1967 [1925]).

5. On the power of a Jewish liberal establishment, see Stephen Steinberg, *The Ethnic Myth: Race, Ethnicity, and Class in America* (New York: Atheneum, 1981); Svonkin, *Jews against Prejudice*; and Wendy Wall, *Inventing the "American Way": The Politics of Consensus from the New Deal to the Civil Rights Movement* (New York: Oxford University Press, 2008).

6. Marshall Field Stevenson, "Points of Departure, Acts of Resolve: Black-Jewish Relations in Detroit, 1937–1962" (Ph.D. diss., University of Michigan, 1988), 67–68.

7. Kurt Peiser and William Boxerman, "Forward Steps in Jewish Community Organization: Recent Experiences in Detroit," *Jewish Social Service Quarterly* 14, no. 2 (December 1937): 240–250. Also, see Walter Klein, "The Jewish Community Council of Metropolitan Detroit: The Organizing Years," *Michigan Jewish History* 18, no. 1 (January 1978): 20–34; and an unpublished paper by Amy Shevitz on the Detroit Jewish Community Council, in author's possession.

8. "Facts for Your Information," n.d., Folder 9, Box 66, JCCR. The leader of the East Side Merchants Association was also one of the leaders in the Jewish Community Council.

9. Stevenson, "Points of Departure, Acts of Resolve," 68–70.

10. Ibid., 97–98.

11. Donald Marsh, Alvin Loving, and Eleanor Wolfe, "Some Aspect of Negro-Jewish Relationships in Detroit," sponsored by Jewish Community Council, Detroit Branch of the NAACP, and the Graduate School of Wayne State, 1945, draft, Box 9, Folder 5, Donald C. Marsh Collection, Reuther Library, Wayne State University, Detroit, Michigan, 16.

12. Stevenson, "Points of Departure, Acts of Resolve," 99.

13. Sam Lieberman led the East Side Merchants Association starting in 1938, and he worked to provide considerable support for the Sojourner Truth Citizens Committee. See Dominic Capeci, "Black-Jewish Relations in Wartime Detroit: The Marsh, Loving, Wolf Surveys and the Race Riot of 1943," *Jewish Social Studies* 47, nos. 3–4 (Summer/Fall 1985): 225.

14. Thomas Sugrue, *The Origins of the Urban Crisis: Race and Inequality in Postwar Detroit* (Princeton, NJ: Princeton University Press, 1996), 73–75; and Joe T. Darden, Richard Child Hill, June Thomas, and Richard Thomas, *Detroit: Race and Uneven Development* (Philadelphia: Temple University Press, 1987), 114–118.

15. Howard Hill et al., "Survey of Religious and Racial Conflict Forces in Detroit" (September 30, 1943), Box 685, Folder 26, JFR, 17.

16. On Raskin, see Angela Dillard, *Faith in the City: Preaching Radical Social Change in Detroit* (Ann Arbor: University of Michigan Press, 2007), 16; and Stevenson, "Points of Departure, Acts of Resolve," 141. On attorney Ernest Goodman, see Steve Babson, Dave Riddle, and David Elsila, *The Color of Law: Ernie Goodman, Detroit, and the Struggle for Labor and Civil Rights* (Detroit: Wayne State University Press, 2010).

17. Sugrue, *The Origins of the Urban Crisis*, 74. On World War II–era commu-

nism, see Maurice Isserman, *Which Side Were You On? The American Communist Party during the Second World War* (Middletown, CT: Wesleyan University Press, 1982); and Ellen Schrecker, *Many Are the Crimes: McCarthyism in America* (Boston, MA: Little Brown, 1998).

18. On the 1943 riot, see Capeci, "Black-Jewish Relations in Wartime Detroit," 225; and Harvard Sitkoff, "Detroit Race Riot of 1943," *Michigan History* 53 (Fall 1969): 183–206.

19. "Preliminary Returns of Survey on Jewish-Negro Relationship in Detroit" (appended to Howard Hill et al., "Survey of Religious and Racial Conflict Forces in Detroit" [September 30, 1943]), Box 685, Folder 26, JFR, 12.

20. Capeci, "Black-Jewish Relations in Wartime Detroit," 230–231.

21. Hill et al., "Survey of Religious and Racial Conflict Forces in Detroit," 10.

22. Ibid., 10–11.

23. George Schermer, "Report of Meeting," April 18, 1947, Part III, Series 3, Box 19, Folder 12, IRC. On insurance, see letter from George Schermer to Oscar Cohen (of Jewish Community Council), May 5, 1947, Part III, Series 3, Box 19, Folder 12, IRC.

24. Hill et al., "Survey of Religious and Racial Conflict Forces in Detroit," 4.

25. Stevenson, "Points of Departure, Acts of Resolve," 162. On liberal views about the pathology of prejudice, see Stephen Steinberg, *Turning Back: The Retreat from Racial Justice in American Thought and Policy* (Boston, MA: Beacon Press, 1995).

26. "Incident Report," November 21, 1944, IRC.

27. The color-coded system endures in the archives of the Interracial Committee. See, for example, Part I, Series 1, Boxes 4–9, IRC.

28. On the 1945 election, see Stevenson, "Points of Departure, Acts of Resolve"; and Heather Thompson, *Whose Detroit? Politics, Labor, and Race in a Modern American City* (Ithaca, NY: Cornell University Press, 2001), 14.

29. George Schermer, "The Transitional Housing Area," November 10, 1952, Part III, Series 4, Box 27, Folder 27, IRC. On Schermer, see "George Schermer, Rights Expert, Dies at 78," *New York Times*, June 6, 1989. Also author's e-mail correspondence with Judith Schermer (daughter of George Schermer), June 15, 2011.

30. For Schermer's home address, see minutes, September 14, 1950, Box 68, Folder 1, JCCR.

31. Eli Grade and Bette Roth, *Congregation Shaarey Zedek, 1861–1981* (Detroit: Wayne State University Press, 1982), 51.

32. On housing stock, see "Report on the Findings of the 12th Street Survey," n.d. [1947], Part I, Series 1, Box 4, Folder 47:57, IRC.

33. Cited in Sidney Bolkosky, *Harmony and Dissonance: Voices of Jewish Identity in Detroit, 1914–1967* (Detroit: Wayne State University Press), 185.

34. Thomas Kleene, "Anti-Negro Housing Propaganda Circulated in Jewish Community," July 30, 1946, Part III, Series 4, Box 27, Folder 1, IRC.

35. "Manual for Interviewers in the Twelfth Street Area," November 6, 1946, Box 15, Folder 6, JCCR.

36. Memo re: Fraiberg and Weiss conversation about Neighborhood Subcommittee, n.d. [February 1947], Box 15, Folder 6, JCCR. On Fraiberg, see http://jwa.org/encyclopedia/article/fraiberg-selma, accessed April 10, 2014. On the location of Jewish Community Centers in the 1930s and 1940s, see Milton Tambor, "The Historical Development of the Detroit Jewish Community Center," *Michigan Jewish History* 3, no. 3 (June 1963): 15–17.

37. *Detroit Jewish News*, April 11, 1947, copy in Box 15, Folder 6, JCCR; and Neighborhood Subcommittee, January 21, 1947, Box 15, Folder 6, JCCR. On press coverage for cleanup drives, see Louis Fraiberg to Benedict Glazer and Lawrence Crohn, April 16 and 25, 1947, Box 15, Folder 6, JCCR.

38. "Report on the Findings of the 12th Street Survey."

39. Ibid., 16.

40. Ibid., 20.

41. Letter from S. Stahle to Jewish Community Council, June 2, 1947, Box 15, Folder 5, JCCR.

42. On the FHA and mortgages for landlords of black rental properties, see Beryl Satter, *Family Properties: Race, Real Estate, and the Exploitation of Black Urban America* (New York: Henry Holt, 2009). On the FHA and rental properties, see Nathan Connolly, *A World More Concrete: Real Estate and the Remaking of Jim Crow South Florida* (Chicago: University of Chicago Press, 2014), chapter 6.

43. Memo from John Feild to George Schermer, "Community Unrest in Twelfth Street Area," July 17, 1947, Part I, Series 1, Box 4, Folder 47:57, IRC.

44. Letter from B. Edelman to Jewish Community Council, May 7, 1947, Box 15, Folder 6, JCCR.

45. Chicago School sociologists in the early twentieth century originated an "invasion-succession" model to understand changes in neighborhood population. For a review on creation and deployment of this model in sociological scholarship, see Kent Schwirian, "Models of Neighborhood Change," *Annual Review of Sociology* 9 (August 1983): 89–91.

46. "Report of Interviews in the 12th Street and Hamilton Area," July 31, 1947, Part I, Series 1, Box 4, Folder 47:57, IRC. See also "Report of Interviews," August 5, 1947, Part 1, Series 1, Box 4, Folder 47:57, IRC.

47. "Report on the Findings of the 12th Street Survey," IRC, 5.

48. Memo from Feild to Schermer, "Community Unrest in Twelfth Street Area," July 17, 1947, IRC.

49. Louis Fraiberg to Oscar Cohen, October 24, 1947, Folder 6, Box 15, JCCR. For a broader pronouncement on this topic, see "A Guide to Changing Neighborhoods: A Manual of Guidance for Dealing with Intergroup Relations Problems in the Neighborhood Undergoing Change," published by the National Community Relations Advisory Council, 1956, Folder 1, Box 86, JCCR.

50. See Samuel Zipp, *Manhattan Projects: The Rise and Fall of Urban Renewal in Cold War New York* (New York: Oxford University Press, 2010), 125–129.

51. Memo from Louis Fraiberg to Shmarya Kleinman, March 15, 1949, Box 67, Folder 9, JCCR.

52. Publicity flyer reprinted in "A Guide to Changing Neighborhoods," 52–53. See David Freund, *Colored Property: State Policy and White Racial Politics in Suburban America* (Chicago: University of Chicago Press, 2007); Stephen Grant Meyer, *As Long as They Don't Move Next Door: Segregation and Racial Conflict in American Neighborhoods* (Lanham, MD: Rowman and Littlefield, 2001); and Sugrue, *The Origins of the Urban Crisis*.

53. "A Statement about the Twelfth Street Area by the Jewish Community Council of Detroit," n.d. [1947–48], Folder 6, Box 15, JCCR.

54. Letter from Aaron Droock (president of the Jewish Community Council) to rabbis, September 11, 1947, Box 15, Folder 6, JCCR. Also, see "Council Acts to Stem Twelfth Street Rumors," *Detroit Jewish News*, September 19, 1947, 12.

55. "Twelfth St. Property Owners to Act on Housing Problem," *Detroit Jewish News*, October 3, 1947, 6.

56. George Schermer to George Edwards, December 31, 1947, Part I, Series 1, Box 4, Folder 47:57, IRC.

57. Minutes from the Continuing Committee, November 19, 1947, Part I, Series 1, Box 4, Folder 47:57, IRC.

58. David Riesman, "The Suburban Sadness," in *The Suburban Community*, ed. William Dobriner (New York: G. P. Putnam's Sons, 1958), 388.

59. Lila Corwin Berman, "Gendered Journeys: Jewish Migrations and the City in Postwar America," in *Gender and Jewish History*, ed. Marion Kaplan and Deborah Dash Moore (Bloomington: Indiana University Press, 2010); Lisa McGirr, *Suburban Warriors: The Origins of the New American Right* (Princeton, NJ: Princeton University Press, 2001); Sylvie Murray, *The Progressive Housewife: Community Activism in Suburban Queens, 1945–1965* (Philadelphia: University of Pennsylvania Press, 2003); Michelle Nickerson, *Mothers of Conservatism: Women and the Postwar Right* (Princeton, NJ: Princeton University Press, 2012); and Becky Nicolaides, *My Blue Heaven: Life and Politics in the Working Class Suburbs of Los Angeles, 1920–1965* (Chicago: University of Chicago Press, 2002).

60. Nathan Shur to Jewish Community Council, November 19, 1947, Box 15, Folder 6, JCCR.

61. Ibid.

62. Letter from Louis Fraiberg to Mrs. Frances Mueller, April 20, 1948, Box 15, Folder 6, JCCR. See also memo from Oscar Cohen to Frank Trager, S. Andhil Fineberg, Waltor Lurie, Will Maslow, and Irving Saler, June 30, 1948, Box 15, Folder 6, JCCR.

63. Letter from George Schermer to Realtors, January 19, 1948, Part I, Series 1, Box 4, Folder 47:57, IRC.

64. Memo from Joseph Fauman and Eleanor Wolf to Jewish Community Council, re: Midtown area, n.d. [1950], Box 552, Folder 2, JCCR, 2.

65. See letter from Bernard Rosenberg to Joseph Fauman, December 2, 1949, Box 584, Folder 5, JCCR.

66. For a draft of the report, see Bernard Rosenberg, "Afro-Jewish Americans: The Case of Twelfth Street, Detroit," n.d. [Fall 1949], Box 584, Folder 5, JCCR.

67. Letter from Bernard Rosenberg to Joseph Fauman, September 18, 1949, Box 584, Folder 5, JCCR.

68. Letter from Fauman to Rosenberg, n.d. [September 1949], Box 584, Folder 5, JCC.

69. Letter from Rosenberg to Fauman, September 18, 1949, JCCR.

70. Letter from Fauman to Rosenberg, n.d. [September 1949], JCCR.

71. Albert Mayer, "Analysis of Contributions to Allied Jewish Campaign (Women's Division)," n.d. [early 1950s], Box 37, Folder 10, JFR, 21–26.

72. Abe Kasle, "Hebrew School Expansion Program Follows Jewish Population Trends," November 5, 1948, *Detroit Jewish News*.

73. "Jewish Center's Dexter Branch Sets Up Temporary Headquarters," *Detroit Jewish News*, December 24, 1948, 21; and "City Approves Construction of Center Dexter Extension," *Detroit Jewish News*, February 25, 1949, 16. Also, see Milton Tambor, "The Historical Development of the Detroit Jewish Community Center," *Michigan Jewish History* 3, no. 3 (June 1963): 15–17.

74. Letter from Louis Fraiberg to John Feild (of Interracial Committee), February 17, 1949, Box 68, Folder 4, JCCR.

75. "Housing Incident at 2005 W. Philadelphia," February 21, 1949, Part I, Series 1, Box 6, Folder 49:7, IRC.

76. Satter, *Family Properties*, 4–5.

77. "Summary of Meeting on Legal Controls in Housing Incidents," Part I, Series 1, January 31, 1949, Box 6, Folder 49:3, IRC.

78. Letter from Will Maslow (American Jewish Congress) to George Schermer, November 8, 1948, Part III, Series 4, Box 26, Folder 8, IRC; and letter from Sol Rabkin (ADL) to George Schermer, November 19, 1948, Part III, Series 4, Box 26, Folder 8, IRC.

79. "Summary of Meeting on Legal Controls in Housing Incidents," IRC.

80. Letter from George Schermer to Jason McNally (Wayne County prosecutor) and copied to Commissioner Harry Toy, September 16, 1948, Box 5, Folder 48: 125A, IRC.

81. Letter from Harry S. Toy, Police Commissioner, to Rev. John E. Coogan, S. J., Chairman of Mayor's Interracial Committee, September 9, 1948, Part I, Series 1, Box 5, Folder 48: 125A, IRC. For background on Commissioner Toy, see Coleman Young and Lonnie Wheeler, *Hard Stuff: The Autobiography of Coleman Young* (New York: Viking, 1994), 102.

82. Letter from George Schermer to Father E. Coogan, August 30, 1948, 5, Folder 48:125A, IRC.

83. On the lack of violence in the Twelfth Street area, see memo from Fauman and Wolf to Jewish Community Council, n.d. [1950], JCC.

84. Jeffrey Hornstein, *A Nation of Realtors: A Cultural History of the Twentieth-Century American Middle Class* (Durham, NC: Duke University Press, 2005).

85. Letter from George Schermer to real estate agents, May 24, 1949, Part III, Series 4, Box 26, Folder 1, IRC.

86. See "Process Record of a Meeting Called to Explore the Current Social Situation in the Mid-Town Area and to Determine the Most Effective Use of the Community Council Staff Assigned," April 18, 1950, Folder 9, Box 67, JCCR. Also, see Stevenson, "Points of Departure, Acts of Resolve," 165.

87. Joseph Fauman to Ed Swan (of the NAACP), n.d. [1950], Folder 1, Box 68, JCCR.

88. Memo from Fauman and Wolf to Jewish Community Council, JCCR.

Chapter Three

1. "Gross Realty Co. Expands; Acquires Facilities of Hurd Realty Company," *Detroit Jewish News*, July 22, 1955, 16.

2. Henry Meyer, "Some Facts about Jews in Detroit," sponsored by the Jewish Welfare Federation of Detroit, 1940, Box 584, Folder 3, JFR, 10.

3. Albert Mayer, "Occupational Characteristics of the Jewish Population in the Detroit Metropolitan Area," sponsored by the Jewish Welfare Federation of Detroit, 1956, Box 37, Folder 10, JFR, Tables LF-15 and LF-18a.

4. On Jews' economic roles as traders and not land owners, see Jacob Katz, *Tradition and Crisis: Jewish Society at the End of the Middle Ages* (New York: Free Press of Glencoe, 1961), chapter 6; and Derek Penslar, *Shylock's Children: Economics and Jewish Identity in Modern Europe* (Berkeley: University of California Press, 2001). For a set of essays that explores the development of Jews' economic roles in the United States, see Rebecca Kobrin, ed., *Chosen Capital: The Jewish Encounter with American Capitalism* (New Brunswick, NJ: Rutgers University Press, 2012). Finally, for a meditation on the relationship between Jewish history and Jewish power, see David Hollinger, "Rich, Powerful, and Smart: Jewish Overrepresentation Should Be Explained Instead of Avoided or Mystified," *Jewish Quarterly Review* 94, no. 4 (Fall 2004): 595–602.

5. For a history of the profession, see Jeffrey Hornstein, *A Nation of Realtors: A Cultural History of the Twentieth-Century American Middle Class* (Durham, NC: Duke University Press, 2005). Little has been written about Jews' overrepresentation in the real estate profession. For a glimpse into the world of Jewish banking, real estate, and financial ruin in New York City, see Rebecca Kobrin, "Destructive Creators: Sender Jarmulowsky and Financial Failure in the Annals of American Jewish History," *American Jewish History* 97, no. 2 (April 2013): 105–137.

6. "Real Estate Division 'Doing Well,'" *Detroit Jewish News*, June 1, 1951, 3.

7. Letter from Julius Weinberg to Charles Posner, May 15, 1951, Box 68, Folder 1, JCCR.

8. Albert Mayer, "Analysis of the Movement of the Jewish Population of Detroit," sponsored by the Jewish Welfare Federation of Detroit, 1952, Box 37, Folder 11, JFR, 3.

9. Ibid., Table 3.

10. Advertisement printed in *Detroit Jewish News*, January 27, 1950, 15.

11. "More Display Space at A. Pupko," *Detroit Jewish News*, March 3, 1950, 16.

12. For example, see letter from William Knapp (Temple Israel architect) to Louis Schostak, January 26, 1949, Folder "Fram: Building: Correspondence, Building Fund, Architect, 1940s," TIA.

13. Letter from Louis Rosenzweig to Jewish Realtors, June 1, 1950, Box 68, Folder 8, JCCR.

14. Julius Weinberg memo, June 6, 1950, Folder 68, Box 1, JCCR.

15. Ibid.

16. Ibid.

17. Press clipping from *Michigan Chronicle*, July 15, 1950, Box 68, Folder 1, JCCR.

18. Ibid. Also reported in "Negro Paper Applauds JCC Anti-Panic Effort," *Detroit Jewish News*, July 21, 1950, 16.

19. David Naimark, "This Week in Detroit," *Forward*, June 12, 1950, translation in Folder 4, Box 68, JCCR.

20. See two letters from Bernard Edelman to Jewish Community Council, n.d. [1950], Box 68, Folder 8, JCCR.

21. Postcard, May 15, 1951, Box 68, Folder 8, JCCR.

22. Letter from Julius Weinberg to Mrs. M. J. Kritchman, June 28, 1950, Box 68, Folder 8, JCCR. On the Jewish Community Council's commitment to block meetings, see "Meetings Attempt to Crush Propagandizing of Property Owners," *Detroit Jewish News*, October 27, 1950, 21.

23. Richard Marks, "The Impact of Negro Population Movement on Property Values in a Selected Area of Detroit," January 16, 1950, Part III, Series 4, Box 26, Folder 28, IRC.

24. "Race Irrelevant to Values," reprint from *Trends in Housing* (a bimonthly publication of the National Committee Against Discrimination in Housing), May 1960, Box 12, Folder 1, AS.

25. An ever-growing body of literature explores these practices. The sources I have relied upon most include Kevin Kruse, *White Flight: Atlanta and the Making of Modern Conservatism* (Princeton, NJ: Princeton University Press, 2005); Beryl Satter, *Family Properties: Race, Real Estate, and the Exploitation of Black Urban America* (New York: Henry Holt, 2009); Robert Self, *Race and the Struggle for Postwar Oakland* (Princeton, NJ: Princeton University Press, 2003); Amanda Seligman, *Block by Block: Neighborhoods and Public Policy on Chicago's West*

Side (Chicago: University of Chicago Press, 2005); and Thomas Sugrue, *Sweet Land of Liberty: The Forgotten Struggle for Civil Rights in the North* (New York: Random House, 2008).

26. "Process Record of a Meeting Called to Explore the Current Social Situation in the Mid-Town Area and to Determine the Most Effective Use of the Community Council Staff Assigned," April 18, 1950, Folder 9, Box 67, JCCR.

27. "Minutes from Meeting," September 14, 1950, Folder 1, Box 68, JCCR.

28. Letter from Mrs. Munz to Julius Weinberg, January 31, 1950 [*sic*, correct date is 1951], Box 68, Folder 4, JCCR.

29. Letter from "Disgusted" to Rabbi Framm, n.d. [1950], Box 68, Folder 4, JCCR.

30. Letter from Schermer to Executive Board of Michigan Committee on Civil Rights, May 19, 1950, Box 546, Folder 6, JCCR.

31. Letter from Fauman to Isaac Toubin, May 24, 1950, Box 284, Folder 2, JCCR.

32. On the Cobo administration, see Thomas Sugrue, *The Origins of the Urban Crisis: Race and Inequality in Postwar Detroit* (Princeton, NJ: Princeton University Press, 1996), 83–88.

33. For a thorough study of the Schoolcraft Gardens Cooperative project, see Katherine Rosenblatt, "'Collective Bargaining and Collective Buying Go Together like Ham and Eggs': Schoolcraft Gardens, Cooperativism, and the Labor Movement in Postwar Detroit," graduate seminar paper, University of Michigan (copy in author's possession). On the Jewish Community Council's response to the Schoolcraft Gardens Cooperative plans, see letter from Shmarya Kleinman to Jewish leaders, March 8, 1950; letter from Shmarya Kleinman and Boris Joffe to Detroit Common Council, March 9, 1950; and letter from Joseph W. Eaton (president, Schoolcraft Gardens Cooperative) to Walter Klein, March 17, 1950, all in Box 284, Folder 2, JCCR.

34. "JCC, Better Housing Group, Brand City Plan Inadequate—'Slum Spreading,'" *Detroit Jewish News*, March 24, 1950, 20; "Mounting Racial Tension Arousing Civic Leaders," *Detroit Jewish News*, March 31, 1950, 38.

35. Memo from Frances Levenson and Sol Rabkin (joint memo from American Jewish Committee and ADL) to Jewish organizations throughout the United States, July 19, 1951, Box 284, Folder 3, JCCR.

36. Samuel Zipp, *Manhattan Projects: The Rise and Fall of Urban Renewal in Cold War New York* (New York: Oxford University Press, 2010), 125–129.

37. See, for example, *Detroit Jewish News,* March 2, 1951, 8; March 30, 1951, 9, 14; September 21, 1951, 10.

38. "Sale of Property at 3785 Elmhurst to Negro Family," December 17, 1951, Part I, Series 1, Box 8, Folder 51:63, IRC.

39. "Sold to Negroes: Bomb Threatens White Pair," *Pittsburgh Courier*, December 29, 1951; and "Get Bomb Threat for Sale of House to Negro," *Daily Worker*,

January 1, 1952, both in file of "Sale of Property at 3785 Elmhurst to Negro Family," IRC.

40. See copy of leaflet in "Sale of Property at 3785 Elmhurst to Negro Family," IRC.

41. "Can of Naptha Found under Porch but Police Don't Probe Death Notice," *Daily Worker*, January 20, 1952, filed in "Sale of Property at 3785 Elmhurst to Negro Family," IRC.

42. Case file from 20009 Santa Barbara, January 3, 1950, Part I, Series 1, Box 7, Folder 50:13, IRC.

43. George Schermer, "New Neighbors and Property Values," delivered at "Study Conference for Women of the Metropolitan Detroit Area," February 11, 1952, Box 284, Folder 3, JCCR.

44. George Schermer, "Approach to the Racial Factor in the Housing Market," October 23, 1951, delivered at the Greater DT Chapter No. 13, Society of Residential Appraisers, Part III, Series 4, Box 27, Folder 28, IRC.

45. Letter from George Schermer to Charles Potter, February 19, 1952, Part I, Series 1, Box 9, Folder 52:5, IRC.

46. "Report of the Changing Neighborhoods Subcommittee," October 26, 1955, Folder 5, Box 534, JCCR; Marshall Field Stevenson, "Points of Departure, Acts of Resolve: Black-Jewish Relations in Detroit, 1937–1962" (Ph.D. diss., University of Michigan, 1988), 380, 382–383; Sugrue, *The Origins of the Urban Crisis*, 224–225; and "George Schermer, Rights Expert, Dies at 78," *New York Times*, June 6, 1989.

47. "Report of the Changing Neighborhoods Subcommittee," October 26, 1955, JCCR.

48. "Equal Opportunity in Housing: A Handbook of Facts," publication of the National Community Relations Advisory Council, June 1952, copy located in YIVO Library, Center for Jewish History, New York City.

49. Memo from Lewis Weinstein (chair of National Committee on Discrimination, NCRAC) to NCRAC membership, February 27, 1953, Box 84, Folder 4, JCCR.

50. Prior to this, a subcommittee of the Legislative Information Committee had dealt with housing issues. See minutes of NCRAC Committee on Discrimination in Housing, January 19, 1953, Box 58, Folder 4, NCRAC.

51. "Minutes of NCRAC Committee on Discrimination in Housing," January 19, 1953, NCRAC.

52. Ibid.

53. "Draft Statement of Principles on Equality of Opportunity in Housing," NCRAC, April 8, 1953, Box 58, Folder 5, NCRAC.

54. Ibid.

55. "NCRAC Statement of Principle on Equality of Opportunity in Housing," June 30, 1953, Box 58, Folder 7, NCRAC Archive.

56. "Minutes of NCRAC Committee on Discrimination in Housing," January 19, 1953, NCRAC.

57. "A Guide to Changing Neighborhoods: A Manual of Guidance for Dealing with Intergroup Relations Problems in the Neighborhood Undergoing Change," published by the National Community Relations Advisory Council, 1956, Folder 1, Box 86, JCCR, 15; and analysis of returns on "Survey on Community Experiences Re: Changing Neighborhoods," April 1953, Box 58, Folder 5, NCRAC.

58. Will Maslow, "The Uses of Law in the Struggle for Equality," October 25, 1954 (delivered at NCRAC conference, "The Advancement of Community Relations Objectives through Law and Legislation," December 9–11, 1954), Box 10, Folder 5, JLC.

59. Ibid.

60. "Neighborhood Conservation: What Is Neighborhood Conservation," prepared by Detroit City Plan Commission, n.d. [1954–1955], Box 82, Folder 4, JCCR.

61. "Summary of Sub-Committee Meeting Regarding East Side Merchants Association," May 25, 1954, Box 66, Folder 10, JCCR.

62. Selwyn James, "We Refused to Give Up Our Homes," *Redbook*, December 1955 (reprint), Part III, Series 3, Box 22, Folder 2, IRC.

63. "Vital Test Case in Inter-Racial Cooperation," *Detroit Jewish News*, July 22, 1955, 16.

64. Memo from Joseph Fauman to Boris Joffe, re: Changing Neighborhood Problems, September 9, 1955, Box 4, Folder 4, JCCR.

65. Ibid.

66. On Fauman, see "Detroit Sociologist Joins Council Staff as Director of Research," *Detroit Jewish News*, June 13, 1947, 16.

67. "Report of the Changing Neighborhoods Subcommittee," October 26, 1955, Box 534, Folder 5, JCCR.

68. Ibid.

69. Memo from S. Joseph Fauman to Boris Joffe, September 15, 1955, Folder 2, Box 85, JCCR.

70. "Report of the Changing Neighborhoods Subcommittee," October 26, 1955, JCCR.

71. Letter from Charles Abrams to Jules Cohen (NCRAC), June 16, 1953, Box 58, Folder 6, NCRAC. For a critique of Abrams's work, see Stephen Meyer, *As Long as They Don't Move Next Door: Segregation and Racial Conflict in American Neighborhoods* (Lanham, MD: Rowman and Littlefield, 2000).

72. "A Guide to Changing Neighborhoods," 1956, JCCR, 32.

73. Ibid., 36.

74. Ibid., 14.

Chapter Four

1. Advertisement in *Detroit Jewish News*, October 16, 1959, 26.

2. On Slatkin's plan to extend the wall, see letter from Albert Mayer to Jewish

Community Council, February 23, 1953, Box 85, Folder 3, JCCR. On the history of the wall in Detroit, see Thomas Sugrue, *The Origins of the Urban Crisis: Race and Inequality in Postwar Detroit* (Princeton, NJ: Princeton University Press, 1996), 63–65.

3. "Far-Sighted Planning Speeds Local Suburban Integration," *Detroit Jewish News*, February 28, 1958, 10. On the population, see Albert Mayer, "Movement of the Jewish Population in the Detroit Metropolitan Area, 1949–1959," Box 37, Folder 11, JFR, 4.

4. Mayer, "Movement of the Jewish Population in the Detroit Metropolitan Area, 1949–1959," JFR, 6.

5. Eleanor Wolf and Charles Lebeaux, *Change and Renewal in an Urban Community* (New York: Praeger, 1969), 6.

6. Memo from Joseph Fauman to Boris Joffe, May 3, 1957, Box 551, Folder 2, JCCR.

7. Ibid.

8. Changing Neighborhoods Committee minutes, January 16, 1958, Box 551, Folder 3, JCCR.

9. Albert Mayer, "Population Movement as a Factor in Locating a Jewish Community Center," June 25, 1957, Box 37, Folder 10, JFR, 1.

10. "Summary of Delegates Assembly," November 10, 1958, from *Jewish Community Council of Metropolitan Detroit Bulletin*, November 17, 1958, Box 551, Folder 2, JCCR.

11. Changing Neighborhoods Committee minutes, January 18, 1959, Box 6, Folder 3, JCCR.

12. See copy of the Ruritan Park Civic Association Option Agreement, n.d. [1959], Box 551, Folder 2, JCCR.

13. Changing Neighborhoods Committee minutes, January 18, 1959, JCCR.

14. Letter from Ruritan Park Civic Association to neighbors, n.d. [1959], Box 551, Folder 2, JCCR.

15. Memo from Norman Perlstein to files, April 14, 1959, Box 551, Folder 2, JCCR.

16. Flyer for Ruritan Park Civic Association meeting, September 16, 1959, Box 551, Folder 2, JCCR.

17. Letter from Ruritan Park Civic Association to neighbors, n.d. [1959], JCCR.

18. On the Bagley neighborhood, see Wolf and Lebeaux, *Change and Renewal in an Urban Community*; and Damon Stetson, "Community Finds Integration Key," *New York Times*, April 22, 1962, 64.

19. On the composition of the board, see note from Rabbi Segal, October 26, 1962, Box 11, Folder 7, AS; on Jewish funding for the Bagley Community Council, see Wolf and Lebeaux, *Change and Renewal in an Urban Community*, 82.

20. "Hate—or 'Improvement,'" *Detroit News*, October 31, 1961, copy in Box 11, Folder 7, AS.

21. Memo from Abraham Citron to Shmarya Kleinman, June 7, 1961, Box 87, Folder 2, JCCR.

22. Neighborhoods and Housing Committee minutes, November 28, 1961, Box 4, Folder 4, JCCR.

23. Ibid.

24. Mayer, "Movement of the Jewish Population in the Detroit Metropolitan Area: 1949–1958," JFR.

25. Changing Neighborhoods Committee minutes, September 13, 1959, Box 6, Folder 3, JCCR.

26. William Whyte, *The Organization Man* (New York: Simon and Schuster, 1956), 374. For broader consideration of the role that Jewish figures played in postwar social criticism, see Lila Corwin Berman, "American Jews and the Ambivalence of Middle-Classness," *American Jewish History* 93, no. 4 (December 2007): 409–434; Daniel Horowitz, *Vance Packard and American Social Criticism* (Chapel Hill: University of North Carolina Press, 1994); and Rachel Kranson, "Grappling with the Good Life: Jewish Anxieties over Affluence in Postwar America" (Ph.D. diss., New York University, 2012).

27. Memo from Fauman to Changing Neighborhood Subcommittee Chairman, October 14, 1955, Box 4, Folder 4, JCCR. By 1955, the percentage of Jews in the neighborhood had increased to 80 percent. See Albert Mayer, "Russel Woods: Change without Conflict: A Case Study of Neighborhood Transition in Detroit," in *Studies in Housing and Minority Groups*, ed. Nathan Glazer and Davis McEntire (Berkeley: University of California Press, 1960).

28. See Mayer, "Russel Woods," 203. Beryl Satter offers a clear discussion of contract buying and its exploitative possibilities in *Family Properties: Race, Real Estate, and the Exploitation of Black Urban America* (New York: Henry Holt, 2009), 3–7.

29. Column by Edward Pintzuk, incoming president of Russel Woods Association, *Russel Woodsman*, February 1959, Box 551, Folder 2, JCCR.

30. See Pintzuk, *Russel Woodsman*, February 1959, JCCR.

31. Ibid. Much later in his life, Pintzuk earned his doctorate in history from Wayne State University and wrote a very sympathetic portrayal of Michigan's Communist Party and its fellow travelers in the 1950s. See Edward Pintzuk, *Reds, Racial Justice, and Civil Liberties: Michigan Communists during the Cold War* (Minneapolis: MEP Publications, 1997). Also, see Elizabeth Katz, "Lifelong Learner," *Wayne State Magazine*, Spring 2009, 24–26.

32. Mayer, "Russel Woods," 219.

33. Changing Neighborhoods Committee minutes, September 8, 1959, Box 6, Folder 3, JCCR.

34. Eleanor Caplan and Eleanor Wolf, "Factors Affecting Racial Change in Two Middle Income Housing Areas," *Phylon* 21, no. 3 (1960): 230; and Mayer, "Russel Woods," 214.

35. Changing Neighborhoods Committee minutes, September 13, 1959, Box 6, Folder 3, JCCR.

36. For Kleinman's address, see Changing Neighborhoods Committee minutes, June 18, 1958, Box 534, Folder 5, JCCR.

37. On Kleinman, see "Honor Dr. Kleinman for Interracial Work," *Detroit Jewish News*, September 29, 1950, 3; and biographical description for finding aid for Kleinman's papers at Reuther library, http://www.reuther.wayne.edu/node/2687, accessed April 10, 2014.

38. Changing Neighborhoods Committee minutes, March 9, 1960, Folder 4, Box 4, JCCR.

39. Letter from Kleinman to Segal, December 2, 1960, Box 12, Folder 1, AS.

40. See Sidney Fine, "Michigan and Housing Discrimination, 1949–1968," *Michigan Historical Review* 23, no. 2 (Fall 1997): 81–114.

41. "Joint Program Plan for Jewish Community Relations, Discrimination in Housing, 1960–1961," Box 32, Folder 8, JLC.

42. Ibid. According to a statistical study, "outside the South, states with larger union memberships, more Jewish residents, and more NAACP members passed fair housing laws sooner than others" (41). See William Collins, "The Political Economy of State Fair Housing Laws before 1968," *Social Science History* 30, no. 1 (Spring 2006): 15–49.

43. Memo from Samuel Spiegler (Director of Information, NCRAC) to Jewish organizations, December 28, 1959, Box 533, Folder 2, JCCR; and "NCRAC Recommendations for Program in Area of Discrimination in Housing, 1956–1957," Box 10, Folder 4, JLC.

44. Letter from Abe Citron to Arnold Aronson (NCRAC), September 21, 1959, Box 552, Folder 1, JCCR.

45. See memos from Kleinman to Changing Neighborhoods Committee, March 19, 1959, and August 26, 1959; memo from Citron to Changing Neighborhoods Committee, September 4, 1959, Box 584, Folder 6, JCCR; and "Some Consideration in Dealing with Housing Problems" (Cleveland), January 1958, Box 533, Folder 1, JCCR. On the desire to discuss other cities' housing policies, see "Proposed Program for Changing Neighborhoods and Housing Committee," n.d. [1959], Box 552, Folder 2, JCCR.

46. Letter from Abraham Citron to Sol Tax, August 26, 1959, Folder 2, Box 87, JCCR. Sol Tax, "Residential Integration: The Case of Hyde Park in Chicago," *Human Organization* 18, no. 1 (Spring 1959): 22–27. For a study of racial integration in Hyde Park, see Arnold Hirsch, *Making the Second Ghetto: Race and Housing in Chicago, 1940–1960* (New York: Cambridge University Press, 1983), chapter 5.

47. Changing Neighborhoods Committee minutes, November 28, 1961, Folder 4, Box 4, JCCR.

48. Mordecai Kaplan, "A Program for the Reconstruction of Judaism," *Menorah Journal* 6, no. 4 (August 1920): 183–184. More generally, see Mordecai

Kaplan, *Judaism as a Civilization: Toward a Reconstruction of American-Jewish Life* (Philadelphia: Jewish Publication Society, 1994 [1934]).

49. On Mordecai Kaplan and the deep influence he had on American Judaism, see Lila Corwin Berman, *Speaking of Jews: Rabbis, Intellectuals, and the Creation of an American Public Identity* (Berkeley: University of California Press, 2009); Arnold Eisen, *Rethinking Modern Judaism: Ritual, Commandment, Community* (Chicago: University of Chicago Press, 1998), chapter 8; Noam Pianko, *Zionism and the Roads Not Taken: Rawidowicz, Kaplan, Kohn* (Bloomington: Indiana University Press, 2010), chapter 4; Mel Scult, *Judaism Faces the Twentieth Century: A Biography of Mordecai M. Kaplan* (Detroit: Wayne State University Press, 1993); and Special Issue: "Mordecai Kaplan's *Judaism as a Civilization* and the Legacy of an American Idea," *Jewish Social Studies* 12, no. 2 (Winter 2006). On Émile Durkheim, see Émile Durkheim, *The Elementary Forms of Religious Life*, trans. Karen Fields (New York: Free Press, 1995); and Deborah Dash Moore, "David Emile Durkheim and the Jewish Response to Modernity," *Modern Judaism* 6, no. 3 (October 1986): 287–300.

50. Rabbi Morris Adler, "May I Have a Word with You?" *Recorder* (Shaarey Zedek bulletin), May 25, 1956; attached to form letter from Boris Joffe and Samuel Rhodes, May 29, 1956, Box 85, Folder 2, JCCR.

51. Letter from Richard Hertz to Charles Abrams, April 20, 1956, Box 15, Folder 1, RH; also, see flyer for Charles Abrams event, April 18, 1956, Box 15, Folder 1, RH.

52. Changing Neighborhoods Committee minutes, September 12, 1960, Box 331, Folder 1, JCCR.

53. Statement adopted by the United Synagogue of America Board of Directors, November 1963, Box 31, Folder 10, RH.

54. Resolution passed by the National Biennial Convention of the Union of Orthodox Jewish Congregations of America, November 9–13, 1960, Box 31, Folder 10, RH.

55. Open Occupancy Pledge Card, n.d. [1960], Box 569, Folder 6, JCCR.

56. Sample Covenant Card for Open Occupancy in Housing, n.d. [1960], Box 569, Folder 6, JCCR.

57. "Statement on Open Occupancy," February 14, 1961, Box 4, Folder 4, JCCR.

58. "For Fairness and Neighborliness," statement made jointly by Morris Adler (on behalf of the Jewish Community Council), Robert J. Allen (for the Roman Catholic Archdiocese of Detroit), and Richard S. Emrich (for the Detroit Council of Churches), n.d. [1960–1961], Box 82, Folder 5, JCCR.

59. David Goldberg and Harry Sharp, "Some Characteristics of Detroit: Area Jewish and Non-Jewish Adults," in *The Jews: Social Patterns of an American Group*, ed. Marshall Sklare (Glencoe, IL: Free Press,1958),113–115; and Sidney Fine, *Expanding the Frontiers of Civil Rights: Michigan, 1948–1968* (Detroit: Wayne State University Press, 2000), 98.

60. Mel Ravitz, "Some Principles and Problems of Citizen Organization for Neighborhood Conservation," presented at the Conservation Victory Banquet, October 15, 1957, Part I, Series 3, Box 2, Folder 9, IRC. On Ravitz's biography, see finding aid for Ravitz Papers, Reuther Library, http://www.reuther.wayne.edu/node/2818, accessed April 10, 2014.

61. Community Relations Committee minutes, November 18, 1959, Box 534, Folder 5, JCCR.

62. Ibid.

63. Jewish Community Council leaders served on the board of the Fair Housing Practices group. See letter from Citron to Charles Wells (president of Russel Woods—Sullivan Area Association), July 18, 1960, Box 569, Folder 6, JCCR.

64. Community Relations Committee minutes, November 18, 1959, JCCR. Marni Davis has explained that Jews, more generally, were reluctant to endorse laws that constricted the freedom of economic and commercial markets because they "regarded economic liberalism and open markets as inextricably intertwined with social and political tolerance" (52). See Marni Davis, *Jews and Booze: Becoming American in the Age of Prohibition* (New York: New York University Press, 2012).

65. For a fascinating meditation on the ways in which Jews valued privacy as a right, see Jason Schulman, "The Limits of Liberalism: A Constitutional Reconsideration of American Jewish Politics" (Ph.D. diss., Emory University, forthcoming), chapter 5. On the ways in which the government subsidized—and, in fact, socialized—private housing and the American Dream, see Barbara Kelly, *Expanding the American Dream: Building and Rebuilding Levittown* (Albany: State University of New York Press, 1993).

66. Realtor case, April 20, 1960, Part I, Series 1, Box 6, Folder 60:21, IRC.

67. Letter to attendees of November 30, 1960, meeting from Kleinman, November 30, 1960, Box 552, Folder 2, JCCR.

68. Realtor case, April 20, 1960, IRC.

69. Robert L. Wells, "Realty Curb on Scare Tactics Not Needed Here, Council Told," *Detroit News*, April 30, 1961, copy in Part I, Series 1, Box 7, Folder 61:19, IRC.

70. "Burdick, Wise, Baum, Kasle, Kaufman Elected," *Detroit Jewish News*, April 10, 1959, 14.

71. Statement by Tom McNamara, president of Detroit Housing Commission, December 3, 1959, Box 569, Folder 6, JCCR.

72. Letter from Ravitz to Abe Citron, Harry Yudkoff, Joe Fauman et al., July 24, 1960, Box 569, Folder 6, JCCR.

73. Ravitz campaign advertisement, *Detroit Jewish News*, September 8, 1961, 35.

74. "Ravitz Elected to City Council," *Detroit Jewish News*, November 10, 1961, 14.

75. Heather Thompson, *Whose Detroit? Politics, Labor, and Race in a Modern American City* (Ithaca, NY: Cornell University Press, 2001), 30–34.

76. Although law-and-order politics grew to characterize the conservative agenda under President Nixon, liberals were early adapters of the notion that government regulation could engineer social law and order. In 1965, President Johnson told Congress that one of government's "most legitimate functions" was the maintenance of "law and order." See Heather Thompson, "Why Mass Incarceration Matters: Rethinking Crisis, Decline, and Transformation in Postwar American History," *Journal of American History* 97, no. 3 (December 2010): 729.

77. Letter from Ravitz to Mayor Cavanagh, May 1, 1962, Box 3, Folder 8, MR.

78. See Ordinance No. 753-F, Chapter No. 445, Fair Neighborhood Practices Ordinance, effective November 29, 1962, Box 12, Folder 26, MR.

79. "Statement of the Jewish Community Council of Metropolitan Detroit in Support of the Amended Brickley Ordinance," October 31, 1962, Box 11, Folder 7, AS.

80. Ravitz received many letters in support of the Brickley Ordinance. See Box 3, Folder 11, MR.

81. On FHA policies that backed mortgages for landlords of all black buildings, see Nathan Connolly, *A World More Concrete: Real Estate and the Remaking of Jim Crow South Florida* (Chicago: University of Chicago Press, 2014), chapter 6.

82. Letter from Paul Silverstein to tenants, n.d. [November 1962], Part I, Series 1, Box 10, Folder 62:149, IRC.

83. Ibid.

84. Letter from Ravitz and Patrick to members of the Common Council, September 26, 1962, Box 3, Folder 11, MR.

85. Press release from the Cotillion Club, November 9, 1962, Box 3, Folder 11, MR. On NAACP opposition, see Sugrue, *The Origins of the Urban Crisis*, 197.

86. "Scare Peddling Must Stop," *Detroit News*, n.d. [November 1962], copy in Part III, Series 4, Box 32, Folder 1, IRC.

87. "'Panic Sale' Law Violate 8 Times, Enforcers Told," *Detroit News*, December 3, 1962, copy in Part III, Series 4, Box 32, Folder 1, IRC.

88. Jack Walker, "Fair Housing Michigan," in *The Politics of Fair-Housing Legislation: State and Local Case Studies,* ed. Lynn Eley and Thomas Casstevens (San Francisco: Chandler Publishing Company, 1968), 364.

89. "Jewish Community Council of Metropolitan Detroit, Voting Survey," November 8, 1966, election, copy at American Jewish Historical Society, Center for Jewish History, New York City, F574.D2 J29, 6–7.

90. Memo from Kleinman to Father Kern, Reverends Laird, Lenox, Bristah, Symes, Mitcham, and Hopper, Zel Cohen, Louis Rosenzweig, and Harold McKinney, April 23, 1962, Box 331, Folder 1, JCCR.

91. Ibid.

92. On the roots of the interfaith movement and Jews' participation in it, see

Fred Beuttler, "For the World at Large: Intergroup Activities at the Jewish Theological Seminary," in *Tradition Renewed: A History of the Jewish Theological Seminary,* ed. Jack Wertheimer (New York: Jewish Theological Seminary of America, 1997); Benny Kraut, "A Wary Collaboration: Jews, Catholics, and the Protestant Goodwill Movement," in *Between the Times: The Travail of the Protestant Establishment in America, 1900–1960,* ed. William Hutchison (New York: Cambridge University Press, 1989); and Mark Silk, "Notes on the Judeo-Christian Tradition in America," *American Quarterly* 36, no. 1 (Spring 1984): 65–85. For examinations of postwar interfaith activism and collaboration, see Deborah Dash Moore, "Jewish GIs and the Creation of the Judeo-Christian Tradition," *Religion and American Culture* 8, no. 1 (Winter 1998): 31–53; and Kevin Schultz, *Tri-Faith America: How Catholics and Jews Held Postwar America to Its Protestant Promise* (New York: Oxford University Press, 2011).

93. Rabbi Segal, Neighborhood Conference, June 5, 1962, Box 11, Folder 7, AS.

94. "Northwest Detroit Meeting of Religious Leaders on Neighborhood Stability and Open Occupancy," June 5, 1962, Box 331, Folder 1, JCCR.

95. Memo on "Northwest Detroit Meeting on Open Occupancy" (written by the Jewish Community Council Neighborhoods and Housing Committee), May 21, 1962, Box 331, Folder 1, JCCR.

96. "Challenge to Conscience: Conclusions, Recommendations, Major Messages," n.d. [1963], Box 83, Folder 3, JCCR.

97. Richard Hertz, "Open Occupancy—A Moral Imperative," January 2, 1963, Box 40, Folder 3, RH.

98. Robert Bellah, "Civil Religion in America," *Daedalus* (Summer 1988 [Winter 1967]): 97–118.

99. Neighborhoods and Housing Committee minutes, November 21, 1962, Box 11, Folder 7, AS.

100. On black Jews, see Jacob Dorman, *Chosen People: The Rise of American Black Israelite Religions* (New York: Oxford University Press, 2013); Roberta Gold, "The Black Jews of Harlem: Representation, Identity, and Race, 1920–1939," *American Quarterly* 55, no. 2 (June 2003): 179–225; James Landing, *Black Judaism: Story of an American Movement* (Durham, NC: Carolina Academic Press, 2002); and Bernard Wolfson, "African American Jews: Dispelling Myths, Bridging the Divide," in *Black Zion: African American Religious Encounters with Judaism,* ed. Yvonne Patricia Chireau and Nathaniel Deutsch (New York: Oxford University Press, 2000).

101. Letter from Steven Jackson to Mr. Haber, December 5, 1970, Box 12, Folder 1, AS.

102. Letter from Citron to Rev. William Porter (of Warren Ministerial Association), April 5, 1963, Box 585, Folder 1, JCCR.

103. Statement by Mayor Jerome Cavanagh, September 26, 1963, Box 585, Folder 1, JCCR.

104. "Challenge to Conscience," n.d. [1963], JCCR, 12.

105. Hertz, "Open Occupancy—A Moral Imperative," January 2, 1963, RH.

106. "Challenge to Conscience," n.d. [1963], JCCR.

107. Reactivation Meeting of the Executive Committee minutes, Metropolitan Conference on Open Occupancy, June 6, 1963, Box 29, Folder 3, JLC; and memo from Walter Klein to rabbis, September 6, 1963, Box 31, Folder 10, RH.

108. Sidney Fine, *Violence in the Model City: The Cavanagh Administration, Race Relations, and the Detroit Riot of 1967* (Ann Arbor: University of Michigan Press, 1989), 27–28.

109. Stephen Meyer, *As Long as They Don't Move Next Door: Segregation and Racial Conflict in American Neighborhoods* (Lanham, MD: Rowman and Littlefield, 2000), 177–178; Sugrue, *The Origins of the Urban Crisis*, 227; and Thomas Sugrue, *Sweet Land of Liberty: The Forgotten Struggle for Civil Rights in the North* (New York: Random House, 2008), 243.

110. See Angela Dillard, *Faith in the City: Preaching Radical Social Change in Detroit* (Ann Arbor: University of Michigan Press, 2007), chapter 6; and Fine, *Violence in the Model City*, 28–32.

111. Flyer for rally on August 20, 1964, Box 12, Folder 1, AS.

112. "Why Every Detroit Citizen Should Vote 'No' on the Homeowner's Ordinance," n.d. [summer 1964], Box 12, Folder 1, AS. For a list of officers, see letter from John J. Weaver (chairman of Citizens for a United Detroit) to supporters, August 11, 1964, Box 12, Folder 1, AS.

113. Memo from Harold Dubin to Walter Klein, n.d. [1964], Box 87, Folder 2, JCCR; see also "Voting Precincts Located in 'Bagley Area,'" n.d. [September 1964], Box 87, Folder 2, JCCR.

114. Harold Dubin to Walter Klein, n.d. [1964/5?], Box 83, Folder 4, JCCR. See Robert Kirk, "Court Kills Homeowners Law," *Detroit News*, December 30, 1966, copy in Box 83, Folder 6, JCCR.

115. Memo from Dubin to Klein, n.d. [September 1964], JCCR.

116. Discussion of presentation by Dr. Dan Dodson on "Human Values in the Central City—Implications for Jewish Communal Service," May 31, 1963, Box 404, Folder 14, JFR.

117. "Our Complacent Public Officials" (editorial), *Detroit Jewish News*, September 11, 1964, 4.

118. Dubin to Klein, n.d. [1964/5?], JCCR. See Kirk, "Court Kills Homeowners Law," December 30, 1966, JCCR. Complaint for Declaratory Judgment, in *NAACP v. City of Detroit*, December 21, 1964, Part III, Series 4, Box 29, Folder 7, IRC.

119. The text of the act can be found at https://michigan.gov/documents/mhc_mhm_fairhousing_ch2_46844_7.pdf, accessed April 10, 2014.

120. Saul Friedman, "A Neighborhood Fights Fear through Its School," *Detroit Free Press*, December 6, 1965, copy in Box 590, Folder 8, JCCR.

121. Wolf and Lebeaux, *Change and Renewal in an Urban Community*, 20–32. In an earlier article, Wolf specifically used the terminology of the "tipping point," which she adopted from political scientist Morton Grodzin's study *The Metropolitan Area as a Racial Problem* (1958). See Eleanor Wolf, "The Tipping-Point in Racially Changing Neighborhoods," *Journal of the American Institute of Planners* 29, no. 3 (August 1963): 217–222.

122. Saul Friedman, "School Struggles to Retain Racial Balance," *Detroit Free Press*, December 7, 1965, copy in Box 590, Folder 8, JCCR.

123. Ibid.

124. Ibid.

125. "Mumford Action Program (MAP): Statement of Purpose," April 8, 1965, Box 38, Folder 15, JLC.

126. Ibid.

127. Draft press release, May 14, 1965, Box 38, Folder 15, JLC.

128. "MAP: Statement of Purposes," April 8, 1965, JLC.

129. "Ask Power of Arrest at Schools," *Detroit News*, May 4, 1965, copy in Box 38, Folder 16, JLC.

130. Memo from Jack Carper, May 18, 1965, Box 38, Folder 15, JLC.

131. Letter from Bill Goode (of JLC) to Robert Alpern, n.d. [May 1965], Box 38, Folder 16, JLC.

132. On the Jewish Labor Committee, which had been formed in 1934 to support European Jewish unionism, see "Description of Jewish Labor Committee for Workmen's Circle" n.d. [1960], Box 34, Folder 16, JLC. JLC was listed as a supporting organization in "MAP: Statement of Purposes," April 8, 1965, JLC.

133. "'Not Creating Ghetto,' Area Brokers State," *Northwest Record*, August 5, 1965, copy in Part III, Series 4, Box 32, Folder 4, IRC.

134. Wolf and Lebeaux, *Change and Renewal in an Urban Community*, 74.

135. "Minutes of Meeting of MAP Representatives and School Administration Representatives," August 31, 1965 (minutes from September 2, 1965), Box 38, Folder 16, JLC.

136. Saul Friedman, "If the Pasteur Project Fails, Then What?" *Detroit Free Press*, December 8, 1965, copy in Box 590, Folder 8, JCCR.

137. On the changing nature of black-Jewish alliances in the 1960s, see Cheryl Greenberg, *Troubling the Waters: Black-Jewish Relations in the American Century* (Princeton, NJ: Princeton University Press, 2006), especially chapter 6; Jonathan Kaufman, *Broken Alliance: The Turbulent Time between Blacks and Jews in America* (New York: Scribner's, 1988); and Michael Staub, *Torn at the Roots: The Crisis of Jewish Liberalism in Postwar America* (New York: Columbia University Press, 2002), chapter 3. On liberal efforts to placate and engulf black separatists, see Matthew Countryman, *Up South: Civil Rights and Black Power in Philadelphia* (Philadelphia: University of Pennsylvania Press, 2006), 160–162; and Suleiman Osman, *Brownstone Brooklyn: Gentrification and the Search for Authenticity in Postwar New York* (New York: Oxford University Press, 2011), 244.

138. On housing hearings, see Fine, "Michigan and Housing Discrimination, 1949–1968," 81–114.

139. Address by William Gross, president of Independent Real Estate Brokers Association, August 2, 1965, Part III, Series 4, Box 32, Folder 4, IRC.

140. Irving Katcher testimony, February 1966, Part III, Series 4, Box 121, Folder 22, IRC.

141. Allan Grossman testimony, February 1996, Part III, Series 4, Box 121, Folder 22, IRC. On the high rate of case dismissal by the Civil Rights Commission, see memo to Commission on Community Relations from Housing Division to the Commission on Community Relations, July 7, 1967, Part III, Series 4, Box 32, Folder 1, IRC.

142. Albert Letvin testimony, February 1966, Part III, Series 4, Box 121, Folder 22. (Throughout the testimony, his name is misspelled in various ways, but other records indicate Letvin as his proper last name.)

143. Ibid.

144. "Proposed Lafayette Park/Mies van der Rohe Historic District Final Report," 2002, 3, http://www.detroitmi.gov/LinkClick.aspx?fileticket=Y6_kfWpNo8g%3D&tabid=3096&mid=4357, accessed April 10, 2014.

145. Jeffrey Hardwick, *Mall Maker: Victor Gruen, Architect of an American Dream* (Philadelphia: University of Pennsylvania Press, 2004). On the significance of modernism and modernist architecture to the postwar housing movement, see Samuel Zipp, "The Roots and Routes of Urban Renewal," *Journal of Urban History* 39, no. 3 (May 2013): 366–391.

146. Wolf and Lebeaux, *Change and Renewal in an Urban Community*, 145.

147. Ibid., 144.

148. "Proposed Lafayette Park/Mies van der Rohe Historic District Final Report," 2002. Also, see interviews with Alvin Saperstein and Esther Shapiro (resident of Lafayette Park), June 14, 2011.

149. Hardwick, *Mall Maker*, 95.

150. For population figures, see Sidney Bolkosky, *Harmony and Dissonance: Voices of Jewish Identity in Detroit, 1914–1967* (Detroit: Wayne State University Press, 1991), 300.

Chapter Five

1. Letter from Harry Perlis to Rabbi Segal, October 11, 1963, Box 11, Folder 7, AS.

2. Albert Mayer, "Jewish Population Study: 1963," Box 590, Folder 8, JCCR.

3. See Lila Corwin Berman, "American Jews and the Ambivalence of Middle-Classness," *American Jewish History* 93, no. 4 (December 2007): 409–434.

4. Scholars have argued for a more metropolitan perspective on urban, suburban, and rural development that transcends false divides among these zones and

shows their interconnectedness. See Andrew Needham and Allen Dieterich-Ward, "Beyond the Metropolis: Metropolitan Growth and Regional Transformation in Postwar America," *Journal of Urban History* 35, no. 7 (November 2009): 943–969. Two recent edited volumes on suburbs also make clear this shift in perspective toward metropolitanism. See Kevin Kruse and Thomas Sugrue, eds., *New Suburban History* (Chicago: University of Chicago Press, 2006); and Becky Nicolaides and Andrew Weise, *The Suburb Reader* (New York: Routledge, 2006).

5. Joshua Fishman, "Moving to the Suburbs: Its Possible Impact on the Role of the Jewish Minority in American Community Life," *Phylon* 24, no. 2 (1963): 150.

6. Lance Sussman, "The Suburbanization of American Judaism as Reflected in Synagogue Building and Architecture," *American Jewish History* 75, no. 1 (September 1985): 31–47. For studies of synagogue architecture in the United States, see Sam Gruber, *American Synagogues: A Century of Architecture and Jewish Community* (New York: Rizzoli, 2003); Richard Meier, ed., *Recent American Synagogue Architecture* (New York: Jewish Theological Seminary, 1963); and Henry Stolzman and Daniel Stolzman, *Synagogue Architecture in America: Faith, Spirit and Identity* (Mulgrave, Victoria, Australia: Images Publishing Group, 2004). For specific studies of architects who built Jewish spaces, see Joseph Siry, *Beth Shalom Synagogue: Frank Lloyd Wright and Modern Religious Architecture* (Chicago: University of Chicago Press, 2012); and Susan Solomon, *Louis I. Kahn's Jewish Architecture: Mikveh Israel and the Midcentury American Synagogue* (Waltham, MA: Brandeis University Press, 2009). On the role of Jewish architects in postwar architecture, see Gavriel Rosenfeld, *Building after Auschwitz: Jewish Architecture and the Memory of the Holocaust* (New Haven, CT: Yale University Press, 2011). On American religious architecture more broadly, see Peter Williams, *House of God: Region, Religion, and Architecture in the United States* (Urbana: University of Illinois Press, 1997).

7. Ruth Cassel, "Modern Functional Design Characterizes Numerous New Synagogues in Detroit," *Detroit Jewish News*, September 8, 1950, 80.

8. Ibid.

9. Michael Meyer, *Response to Modernity: A History of the Reform Movement in Judaism* (Detroit: Wayne State University Press, 1988), chapter 10.

10. Memo from Richard Hertz to Leonard Simons and Nate Shapero, July 17, 1953, FA.

11. Letter from John D. Rose, secretary of the Townsite Community Church, to Temple Beth El, January 26, 1954, FA.

12. James Hudnut-Beumler, *Looking for God in the Suburbs: The Religion of the American Dream and Its Critics, 1945–1965* (New Brunswick, NJ: Rutgers University Press, 1994), 37.

13. Report on trip to New York City, Rabbi Hertz and Emanuel Harris, February 15–17, 1954, FA.

14. B. Sumner Gruzen, "Selecting a Site for the Synagogue," in *An American*

Synagogue for Today and Tomorrow, ed. Peter Blake (New York: Union of American Hebrew Congregations, 1954), 71.

15. Rachel Wischnitzer-Bernstein, "The Problem of Synagogue Architecture: Creating a Style Expressive of America," *Commentary* 3, no. 6 (March 1947): 240. For biographical information on Wischnitzer-Bernstein, see http://jwa.org/encyclopedia/article/wischnitzer-rachel, accessed November 19, 2009.

16. Wischnitzer-Bernstein, "The Problem of Synagogue Architecture," 241.

17. Eric Mendelsohn, "In the Spirit of Our Age," *Commentary* 3, no. 6 (June 1947): 541. Here I disagree with Rosenfeld's assessment that the Holocaust did not imprint itself on the synagogue designs of postwar Jewish architects. For his argument, see Gavriel Rosenfeld, *Building after Auschwitz: Jewish Architecture and the Memory of the Holocaust* (New Haven, CT: Yale University Press, 2011), 53–77.

18. Maurice Eisendrath, "Introduction," in *An American Synagogue for Today and Tomorrow: A Guide Book to Synagogue Design and Construction,* ed. Peter Blake (New York: Union of American Hebrew Congregations, 1954), xv. On the Union of American Hebrew Congregations, see Meyer, *Response to Modernity.*

19. See William Schack, "Synagogue Art Today: I: Something of a Renaissance," *Commentary* 20 (December 1955): 548–553.

20. Eugene Lipman quoted in ibid., 550.

21. Samuel M. Cohen, "Synagogue Architecture Expert: Irving Lurie," *Synagogue Center* 5, no. 2 (February 1945): 10, 12; and "Architectural Problems," and "Strengthening Synagogue Life," *Synagogue Center* 4, no. 1 (October 1943): 13.

22. "Temple Beth El to Remain at Woodward Avenue Site," *Detroit Jewish News,* December 9, 1955, 17.

23. "Geographic Distribution of Temple Beth El Membership," 1945, 1955, and 1962, Box 16, Folder 23, IRC.

24. The Downtown Synagogue experienced a revival in the new millennium. See discussion in epilogue.

25. For an overview of Reform Judaism, from its European roots to its American expression, see Meyer, *Responses to Modernity.*

26. Jordan Stanger-Ross, "Neither Fight nor Flight: Urban Synagogues in Postwar Philadelphia," *Journal of Urban History* 32, no. 6 (September 2006): 791–812.

27. Board minutes, May 1, 4, 1952, SZA.

28. Board minutes, April 7, 1953, SZA; and board minutes, October 3, 1955, SZA.

29. For a history of the Chicago Boulevard building, see Eli Grade and Bette Roth, *Congregation Shaarey Zedek, 1861–1981* (Detroit: Wayne State University Press, 1982), 51–67.

30. Board minutes, October 3, 1955, and December 12, 1955, SZA. On the timed light, see board minutes, March 11, 1957, SZA.

31. Rabbi Morris Adler, "May I Have a Word with You?" *Recorder* (Shaarey

Zedek bulletin), May 25, 1956, attached to form letter from Boris Joffe and Samuel Rhodes, May 29, 1956, Box 85, Folder 2, JCCR.

32. See introduction to Lily Edelman and Morris Adler, *May I Have a Word with You?* (New York: Crown Publishers, 1967), xiii.

33. "Semi-Annual Congregational Meeting," April 21, 1960, SZA.

34. Conversation with Bill Berman (no relation to author) in Ann Arbor, Michigan, May 23, 2008.

35. On Berman, see "Mandell L. Berman Receives Lifetime Achievement Award," Association for the Social Scientific Study of Jewry, http://www.contemporaryjewry.org/28.html, accessed November 4, 2011.

36. "Transcript of an Oral History of Mandell ('Bill') Berman," conducted by Judy Cantor, October 9, 1990, SZA, 26.

37. On Louis Berry, see "Louis Berry, Hotel Executive, 92," *New York Times*, June 17, 1995.

38. On the decision to retain Goodman, see board minutes, June 11, 1956, SZA. On the list of architects, see board minutes, March 19, 1956, SZA; and on the congregation's interest in Goodman, see board minutes, September 10, 1956, SZA.

39. On purchase price, see board minutes, January 14, 1954, SZA; on sale price, see special meeting of congregation, August 12, 1957, SZA.

40. On the new land, see special board meeting minutes, January 28, 1957, SZA. On the down payment loan, see board minutes, March 11, 1957, SZA.

41. "Berman Oral History," October 9, 1990, SZA, 20.

42. Board minutes, February 10, 1958, SZA.

43. "Berman Oral History," October 9, 1990, SZA, 28–29.

44. Board minutes, September 8, 1958, SZA.

45. On the negotiations, see board minutes, April 9, 1962, SZA; special meeting of board minutes, April 10, 1962, SZA; and special congregational meeting minutes, April 26, 1962, SZA.

46. Letter from Aubrey Ettenheimer to board of trustees, October 28, 1964, FA.

47. Letter from Sidney Karbel to members, September 1, 1964, FA.

48. Ibid.

49. Letter from Ettenheimer to board of trustees, October 28, 1964, FA.

50. "Proposed Building Sites, Temple Beth El," prepared by Byron W. Trerice and Jerome Reiss (real estate agents), n.d. [1964], FA.

51. Letter from Max Sheldon to Norman Allen, June 24, 1965, Box 17, Folder 10, AS.

52. Ibid.

53. On the building committee members, see memo from Max Sheldon to members, August 4, 1965, Box 17, Folder 10, AS; on Hechtman and Goldin, see "Nathan I. Goldin," *Legal Chronicle*, June 18, 1965, Box 17, Folder 9, AS.

54. Letter from Norman Allen to Albert List, July 15, 1966, Box 17, Folder 10, AS.

55. Letter from Allen to List, December 6, 1966, Box 17, Folder 10, AS.

56. See, for example, correspondence between Abe Kasel (building-committee member) and Rudoph Shulman (president of Adas Shalom), July 18 and 20, 1967, Box 17, Folder 10, AS.

57. Letter from Sidney Karbel to Mr. and Mrs. Everet Straus, January 20, 1966, FA.

58. Letter from Aubrey Ettenheimer to Irving Katz, January 18, 1967, FA.

59. "Beth El to Continue in Present Location, Pastoral Letter Asserts," *Detroit Jewish News,* August 11, 1967, 5.

60. Letter from Walter Shapero to Archie Katcher, July 5, 1968, FA. On the decision to retain Yamasaki's firm to design the new synagogue building, see memo from Guthard to Yamasaki and Hertz, February 20, 1968, FA. The memo specifically requested that all parties keep the deal quiet.

61. See letter from Archie Katcher to Oscar Zemon, January 3, 1969, FA; letter from William Frank to Archie Katcher, January 9, 1969; and response from Archie Katcher to Frank, January 17, 1969, FA.

62. Letter from Archie Katcher to Martin Eisenstadt, February 7, 1969, FA. Note to the board is stapled to this letter.

63. See Karla Goldman, "This Is the Gateway to the Lord: The Legacy of Synagogue Buildings for African American Churches on Cincinnati's Reading Road," in *Black Zion: African American Religious Encounters with Judaism,* ed. Yvonne Chireau and Nathaniel Deutsch (New York: Oxford University Press, 2000).

64. "Shaarey Zedek Looks to the Future," n.d. [1957/8?], SZA.

65. Ibid.

66. "Committee Member's Kit," n.d. [late 1950s], SZA, italics in original.

67. Board minutes, March 31, 1959, SZA.

68. Flyer for October 24, 1957, meeting, SZA.

69. On the religious school building, see board minutes, November 11, 1963; on the real estate gift, see board minutes, January 1, 1965; and on the Highway Department, see board minutes, March 25, 1966, all SZA.

70. I know of no study that has compared the cost of synagogue construction to church construction in the postwar suburbs. Certainly, some churches were built at great expense, but synagogue buildings, on the whole, appear to have been more costly. In 1973 Highland Park Baptist Church (a white Protestant Fundamentalist congregation), for example, erected a new building in Southfield, just a mile from Shaarey Zedek that cost roughly $900,000 to build. See Darren Dochuk, "'Praying for a Wicked City': Congregation, Community, and the Suburbanization of Fundamentalism," *Religion and American Culture* 13, no. 2 (Summer 2003): 182.

71. Oral history interview with Percival Goodman, 1979, Columbia Center for Oral History, 435.

72. Ibid. For his defense of moveable partitions, see Myron Schoen and Eugene Lipman, ed., *The American Synagogue: A Progress Report: Proceedings of the Second National Conference and Exhibit on Synagogue Architecture and Art*

(New York: Union of American Hebrew Congregations, 1958), 153. On Goodman, see "The Architect from New York," in *Creators and Disturbers: Reminiscences by Jewish Intellectuals of New York*, ed. Bernard Rosenberg and Ernest Goldstein (New York: Columbia University Press, 1982); Kimberly Elman and Angela Giral, ed., *Percival Goodman: Architect, Planner, Teacher, Painter* (New York: Miriam and Ira D. Wallach Art Gallery, Columbia University, 2000); Paul Goldberger, "Percival Goodman, 85, Synagogue Designer, Dies," *New York Times*, October 12, 1989; and Percival and Paul Goodman, "Modern Artist as Synagogue Builder: Satisfying the Needs of Today's Congregation," *Commentary* 7, no. 1 (January 1949): 51–55.

73. For this description, see Grade and Roth, *Congregation Shaarey Zedek, 1861–1981*, 109.

74. See Congregation Shaarey Zedek brochure, n.d. [2012], copy in author's possession. As early as the 1940s, architects attempted to render a sanctuary design that would expand for the attendance increase at high holidays. See Richard Bennett, "A Synagogue That Can Double Its Capacity," *Interiors* 106 (January 1947): 81.

75. Board meeting, March 19, 1962, SZA.

76. Percival and Paul Goodman, "Tradition from Function," *Commentary* 3, no. 6 (June 1947): 543. Jan Peter Stern sculpted the eternal light, and Robert Pinart created the stained glass panels. On Stern and Pinart, see minutes from annual meeting, October 24, 1962, SZA.

77. For a description of the architecture of Shaarey Zedek, see Stolzman and Stolzman, *Synagogue Architecture in America: Faith, Spirit, and Identity*, 188–191.

78. "Report of Trip to NY," February 15–17, 1954, FA.

79. See *Time*, January 18, 1963, cover.

80. Alvin Toffler, *The Culture Consumers: A Study of Art and Affluence in America* (New York: St. Martin's Press, 1964), 34.

81. Ibid., 66–67; and "Lawrence Fleischman Oral History," February 28, 1970, March 2, 1970, March 7, 1970, March 9, 1970, http://www.aaa.si.edu/collections/interviews/oral-history-interview-lawrence-fleischman-11811, accessed March 28, 2014.

82. See Michigan Historic Site plaque posted outside of Temple Beth El.

83. Progress report of President Robert Canvasser, March 1973, FA.

84. William Grimes, "Tony Rosenthal, 94, Sculptor of Public Art," *New York Times*, August 1, 2009.

85. Rabbi's annual report, May 23, 1972, FA.

86. Letter from George Gladstone to Henry Lenhoff, August 4, 1970, FA.

87. Ibid.

88. For revisionist perspectives on the narrative of postwar American-Jewish declension, see Berman, "American Jews and the Ambivalence of Middle-Classness," 409–434; and Riv-Ellen Prell, "Community and the Discourse of Elegy: The Post War Suburban Debate," in *Imagining the American Jewish Community*,

ed. Jack Wertheimer (Hanover, NH: University Press of New England/Brandeis University Press, 2007), 67–92.

89. Originally printed as Mike Masch, "Who Needs Jewish Liberation?" *Hayom* 2, no. 5 (February 23–March 9, 1972): 2, quoted in Michael Staub, *Torn at the Roots: The Crisis of Jewish Liberalism in Postwar America* (New York: Columbia University Press, 2002), 200.

90. On Wine, see Dan Cohn-Sherbook, Harry Cook, and Marilyn Rowens, *A Life of Courage: Sherwin Wine and Humanistic Judaism* (Farmington Hills, MI: International Institute for Secular Humanistic Judaism, 2003); Lawrence Joffe, "Rabbi Sherwin Wine," *Guardian,* September 18, 2007, http://www.guardian.co.uk/news/2007/sep/18/guardianobituaries.religion, accessed March 5, 2013.

91. B. Z. Sobel and Norman Mirsky, "'Ignosticism' in Detroit: An Experiment in Jewish Religious Radicalism," unpublished, n.d. [late 1960s], Box 3, Folder 17, BT, 2.

92. Letter from Rabbi Fram to Joel Hepner, September 11, 1963, Box 3, Folder 17, BT.

93. Judith Goren, "Evolution of a Temple," in Dedication Book, 1971, Box 1, Folder 20, BT.

94. "History of the Birmingham Temple," 1963–1995, Box 3, Folder 3, BT.

95. Sobel and Mirsky, "'Ignosticism' in Detroit," BT, 3.

96. "Suburban Rabbi: I Am an Atheist," *Detroit Free Press,* December 3, 1964, copy in Box 1, Folder 20, BT; "Masons Bar Congregations Whose Rabbi Rejects God," *New York Times*, February 6, 1965; "The Atheist Rabbi," *Time*, January 29, 1965.

97. "A Word from the Rabbi," *Birmingham Temple Newsletter*, November 20, 1964, Box 41, Folder 19, AS.

98. Harold Schacher, "National Jewish Groups to Get Story on Rabbi Who Is Atheist," *Detroit News*, December 4, 1964, Box 41, Folder 19, AS.

99. "Rabbi Wine: No Proof God Exists as 'Person'; Rabbi Freehof: Jews Should Shun Wine Group," *National Jewish Post and Opinion*, January 1, 1965, Box 41, Folder 19, AS.

100. Sobel and Mirsky, "'Ignosticism' in Detroit," BT, 4.

101. "To Use or Not to Use the Word 'God,'" *Reconstructionist* 30, no. 19 (January 1, 1965): 4; Deborah Waxman, "Faith and Ethnicity in American Judaism: Reconstructionism as Ideology and Institution, 1935–1959" (Ph.D. diss., Temple University, 2010).

102. "Masons Oust Atheist Rabbi, Flock," unknown newspaper, n.d. [1965], Box 3, Folder 16, BT; and Sobel and Mirsky, "'Ignosticism' in Detroit," BT, 4.

103. Bishop Emrich, "The Atheist Rabbi," *Detroit News*, February 7, 1965, Box 41, Folder 19, AS.

104. Sobel and Mirsky, "'Ignosticism' in Detroit," BT, 4.

105. Interview with Bonnie Cousens, executive director of the Society for Humanistic Judaism, September 17, 2009. On congregants' feelings of rejection by their families, see Goren, "Evolution of a Temple," 1971, BT, 3.

106. For a description of Wine as a bachelor, see press clipping, "An 'Ignostic' Rabbi Faces Loss of Title," December 4, 1964, in Box 3, Folder 16, BT; and interview with Cousens, July 29, 2010.

107. Al Tobocman, "About the Building," in *Dedication Book*, 1971, Box 1, Folder 20, BT, 5.

108. Ibid.

109. "A Resolution Presented to the Board of the Birmingham Temple by the Community Relations Committee," January 7, 1964, Box 1, Folder 8, BT.

110. See Box 1, Folder 8, BT. Also, see "Celebration Book Honoring the Birmingham Temple's 40th Anniversary," 2003, Folder 2, Box 1, BT.

111. Goren, "Evolution of a Temple," 1971, BT, 4.

112. Board meeting minutes, June 6, 1967, Box 1, Folder 8, BT.

113. T. V. LoCicero, "The Murder of Rabbi Adler," *Commentary* 41, no. 6 (June 1966): 52.

114. Ibid.

115. Aside from the account in *Commentary*, I am also relying on a number of articles published in the *New York Times*: "Detroit Rabbi Shot before 1,000 in Synagogue," *New York Times*, February 13, 1966, 40; "Wounded Rabbi Gains a Bit; Assailant Dies and Is Buried," *New York Times*, February 17, 1966, 21; "Rabbi Morris Adler, 59, Dies; Shot during Service on February 12," *New York Times*, March 12, 1966, 12; "9,000 at Funeral for Rabbi Shot Fatally in Synagogue," *New York Times*, March 14, 1966, 37.

116. "Detroit Rabbi Shot before 1,000 in Synagogue," 40.

117. Grade and Roth, *Congregation Shaarey Zedek*, 121.

118. "Entire Community Prays for Complete Healing of Rabbi Adler," *Detroit Jewish News*, February 18, 1966, 1.

Chapter Six

1. Peter Golden, *The Quiet Diplomat: A Biography of Max M. Fisher* (New York: Cornwall Books, 1992), 141–142.

2. Thomas Sugrue, *The Origins of the Urban Crisis: Race and Inequality in Postwar Detroit* (Princeton, NJ: Princeton University Press, 1996), 259.

3. Phone interview with Stanley Frankel, August 13, 2008.

4. Matthew Countryman, *Up South: Civil Rights and Black Power in Philadelphia* (Philadelphia: University of Pennsylvania Press, 2006); Robert Self, *American Babylon: Race and the Struggle for Postwar Oakland* (Princeton, NJ: Princeton University Press, 2003); and Sugrue, *The Origins of the Urban Crisis*.

5. Sidney Bolkosky, *Harmony and Dissonance: Voices of Jewish Identity in Detroit, 1914–1917* (Detroit: Wayne State University Press, 1991), 301.

6. "City Restored to Sanity; Firm Action Ends Rioting: Community Aids

Sufferers," *Detroit Jewish News*, July 28, 1967. Eugene Driker and Avern Cohn both recall giving legal aid to individuals who were arrested during the riots. Interview with Eugene Driker, January 4, 2012; and "Oral History of Judge Avern Cohn," conducted by Judy Christie, July 18, 2005, at U.S. Courthouse, 29, copy in author's possession.

7. "Our City's Calamitous Humiliation," *Detroit Jewish News*, July 28, 1967, 1, 8.

8. On Slomovitz and his editorship of the *Detroit Jewish News*, see the guide to his papers at Reuther Library: http://www.reuther.wayne.edu/files/UP001494.pdf, accessed March 15, 2014. Also, see e-mail from Arthur Hurwitz (publisher and executive editor of the *Detroit Jewish News*) to author, September 1, 2013.

9. Partial remarks delivered by Jack Carper, Michigan director of the Jewish Labor Committee to Workmen's Circle District Conference, September 15, 1967, Box 45, Folder 12, JLC.

10. "AJC Urban Affairs Director Urges Partnership to Battle City Woes," *Detroit Jewish News*, May 19, 1967, 25.

11. For a list of participants, see Long-Range Planning Committee: Interfaith Emergency Council minutes, August 15, 1967, Box 29, Folder 6, RH.

12. "Design Plan for an Interfaith Action Council," April 1968, Box 29, Folder 6, RH, 3.

13. Ibid., 2.

14. "Two Proposals from Justice Committee to Interfaith Long-Range Planning Committee," n.d. [August 1967], Box 29, Folder 6, RH; and "Recommendations for Use of Interfaith Relief Funds," August 14, 1967, Box 29, Folder 6, RH.

15. "Committee on Community Organization Report," September 11, 1967, Box 29, Folder 6, RH.

16. Long-Range Planning Committee: Interfaith Emergency Council minutes, August 15, 1967.

17. "A Crisis of People: The New Detroit Committee's Progress Report in Review," n.d. [1968], Box 20, Folder 24, IRC; Heather Thompson, *Whose Detroit?: Politics, Labor, and Race in a Modern American City* (Ithaca, NY: Cornell University Press, 2001), 74–75.

18. Quoted in Thompson, *Whose Detroit?* 74.

19. Thompson, *Whose Detroit?* 75. Also, see Countryman, *Up South*.

20. "A Crisis of People," n.d. [1968], IRC.

21. Press release from Interfaith Emergency Council, August 9, 1967, Box 29, Folder 6, RH.

22. Arlie Porter and James Sheehan, "Proposal for an Interfaith Action Council," October 1967, Box 29, Folder 6, RH.

23. Gary Blonston, "New Detroit: A Race-Relations Lab," *Detroit Free Press*, August 11, 1968, copy in Box 20, Folder 24, IRC.

24. Ibid.

25. Interfaith Emergency Council minutes, March 6, 1968; and Interfaith Action Council meeting with Cavanagh, April 10, 1968, Box 29, Folder 6, RH.

26. By the spring of 1969, Jews were out-funded by all religious groups except for two Lutheran groups. See "Special Report: Status of Denominational Financial Support," May 22, 1969, Box 29, Folder 6, RH.

27. See Stuart Svonkin, *Jews against Prejudice: American Jews and the Fight for Civil Liberties* (New York: Columbia University Press, 1997); and Wendy Wall, *Inventing the "American Way": The Politics of Consensus from the New Deal to the Civil Rights Movement* (New York: Oxford University Press, 2008).

28. Memo from Mrs. Julian Krolik to Urban Affairs Subcommittee, September 10, 1968, Box 5, Folder 6, JCCR.

29. Memo from Mrs. Julian Krolik, January 5, 1968, Box 5, Folder 6, JCCR.

30. "A Proposal for Jewish Community Support of and Involvement in an Inner City Scholarship Project," January 4, 1968, Box 5, Folder 6, JCCR.

31. Lila Corwin Berman, "Sociology, Jews, and Intermarriage in Twentieth-Century America," *Jewish Social Studies* 14, no. 2 (Winter 2008): 32–60.

32. "Suburban Action Centers: A Proposal," n.d. [1968], Box 29, Folder 6, RH.

33. Ibid.

34. Franklin Zweig and Arthur Cryns, "To Change the Climate of Violence in Detroit Proposal: A Crisis-Oriented, Inter-University Training Institute as a Supportive and Consultative Arm to Community Efforts toward Tension Reduction, Racism Reform and Community Development in the Detroit Area," March 20, 1968, Box 29, Folder 6, RH.

35. "Interfaith Action Center's First Week's Highlights," June 7, 1968, Box 29, Folder 6, RH.

36. Urban Affairs Subcommittee minutes, January 26, 1968, Box 5, Folder 5, JCCR.

37. Urban Affairs Subcommittee minutes, January 9, 1969, Box 591, Folder 1, JCCR.

38. On the deindustrialization and decentralization of the postwar economy and its effects on cities, see Barry Bluestone and Bennett Harrison, *The Deindustrialization of America* (New York: Basic Books, 1982); Lizabeth Cohen, *A Consumers' Republic: The Politics of Mass Consumption in America* (New York: Knopf, 2003), chapter 6; Jefferson Cowie and Joseph Heathcott, *Beyond the Ruins: The Meanings of Deindustrialization* (Ithaca, NY: ILR Press of Cornell University Press, 2003); Peter Siskind, "Suburban Growth and Its Discontents," in *The New Suburban History,* ed. Kevin Kruse and Thomas Sugrue (Chicago: University of Chicago Press, 2006); and Sugrue, *The Origins of the Urban Crisis*, 127–130. Although some urban industry moved to suburbs for cheaper and more plentiful land, many urban industries also relocated to different regions of the country, especially the South, where a "Sunbelt economy" emerged from the ravages of northern and midwestern urban economies. See Jefferson Cowie, *Capital Moves:*

RCA's Seventy-Year Quest for Cheap Labor (Ithaca, NY: Cornell University Press, 1999); and Bruce J. Schulman, *From Cotton Belt to Sunbelt: Federal Policy, Economic Development, and the Transformation of the South, 1938–1980* (New York: Oxford University Press, 1991).

39. Urban Affairs Subcommittee minutes, January 9, 1969, Box 591, Folder 1, JCCR.

40. Zweig and Cryns, "To Change the Climate of Violence in Detroit Proposal," March 20, 1968, RH.

41. "Position Statement," June 1968, Box, 116, Folder 6, JFR. On the involvement of national-level Jewish organizations in "urban crisis" politics, see Marc Dollinger, "The Other War: American Jews, Lyndon Johnson, and the Great Society," *American Jewish History* 89, no. 4 (December 2001): 448–450.

42. Urban Affairs Subcommittee minutes, February 9, 1968, Box 5, Folder 5, JCCR.

43. Lawrence Gubow, "Comments on the Role of the Jewish Community in the 'Urban Crisis,'" March 28, 1968, Box 65, Folder 3, JCCR.

44. Ibid.

45. "A Proposal for Jewish Community Support of and Involvement in an Inner City Scholarship Project," January 4, 1968, JCCR. Approval of allocation in Urban Affairs Subcommittee minutes, January 26, 1968, Box 5, Folder 6, JCCR.

46. Urban Affairs Subcommittee minutes, May 22, 1968, Box 5, Folder 6, JCCR.

47. Ibid.

48. "Irresponsible Bigots' 'Power' Pressures," *Detroit Jewish News*, September 15, 1967, 4. Also, see "SNCC Attack on Zionism, Israel Branded 'Anti-Semitic Tragedy,' Affecting Race Relations in U.S.," *Detroit Jewish News*, August 18, 1967, 1.

49. On the roots of postwar black radicalism, see Self, *American Babylon*, 217–220. On rising black urban power, see Michael Katz, *Why Don't American Cities Burn* (Philadelphia: University of Pennsylvania Press, 2011), chapter 3.

50. Letter from Lewis Grossman, president of Detroit Chapter of the American Jewish Committee, April 10, 1968, Box 29, Folder 6, RH.

51. Draft of "To Change the Climate of Violence in Detroit Proposal: A Crisis-Oriented, Inter-University Training Institute as a Supportive and Consultative Arm to Community Efforts toward Tension Reduction, Racism Reform and Community Development in the Detroit Area," March 20, 1968, Folder 6, Box 29, RH; Steve Babson, Dave Riddle, and David Elsila, *The Color of Law: Ernie Goodman, Detroit, and the Struggle for Labor and Civil Rights* (Detroit: Wayne State University Press, 2010).

52. Highlights of presentation by Robert Hiller, "The Northwest Baltimore Corporation," CJWF National Urban Affairs and Public Welfare Committee Meeting, June 7, 1969, Box 26, Folder 10, JFR.

53. "Report from '68 Crisis in Black and White," n.d. [Spring 1968], Box 29, Folder 6, RH.

54. Interfaith Action Council, April 5, 1968, Folder 6, Box 29, RH; "Responses of Jewish Community Agencies and Organizations to the 'Urban Crisis,'" May 7, 1968, Box 591, Folder 1, JCCR. Also, see Babson, Riddle, and Elsila, *The Color of Law*.

55. Letter from Hertz to Hudson, August 11, 1967, Box 29, Folder 6, RH.

56. Letter from Alan E. Schwartz (of Federation) to William Avrunin (of the Jewish Community Council), June 12, 1968, Box 116, Folder 6, JFR.

57. Ad hoc Committee on Urban Affairs minutes, May 27, 1968, Box 116, Folder 6, JFR.

58. *The Jewish Community Newsletter* 1, no. 1 (June–July 1968), Box 88, Folder 5, NCRAC.

59. See, for example, "Jewish Community Activities in the Urban Crisis," May 16, 1968 (published by the Council of Jewish Federations and Welfare Funds), Box 88, Folder 6, NCRAC.

60. Golden, *The Quiet Diplomat*.

61. Ibid., 145.

62. Memo from Michael Klion to Max Fisher, re: Minutes of Meeting—Religious Groups, June 4, 1969, Box 27, Folder 7, NCRAC.

63. Memo from Walter Lurie to Isaiah Minkoff, July 11, 1969, Box 27, Folder 7, NCRAC.

64. "Outline of Patterns of Jewish Voluntary Action for Community Betterment," attached to memo from Walter Lurie to Isaiah Minkoff, March 17, 1970, Box 27, Folder 8, NCRAC.

65. "A Program to Strengthen and Unify Detroit's Jewish Communal Organization," January 29, 1970, Box 31, Folder 11, RH.

66. Stanley Winkelman, *A Life in a Balance: The Memoirs of Stanley J. Winkelman* (Detroit: Wayne State University Press, 2000), 187. See also the guide to Winkelman's papers at the Reuther Library, http://www.reuther.wayne.edu/files/UP001500.pdf, accessed March 15, 2014.

67. "Fact Sheet concerning $100 Million Housing Bond Issue," n.d. [February 1970], Box 116, Folder 6, JFR.

68. Memo from Urban Affairs Committee of Detroit Federation to board of governors of Detroit Federation, February 2, 1970, Box 116, Folder 6, JFR.

69. Stanley Winkelman, "Remarks to Board of Governors," February 2, 1970, Box 116, Folder 6, JFR.

70. Urban Affairs Subcommittee minutes, December 11, 1968, December 18, 1968, and December 30, 1968, Box 22, Folder 1, JCCR.

71. Urban Affairs Subcommittee minutes, January 29, 1969, Box 22, Folder 1, JCCR.

72. Urban Affairs Subcommittee minutes, February 12, 1969, Box 22, Folder 1, JCCR.

73. Urban Affairs Subcommittee minutes, February 19, 1969, Box 22, Folder 1,

JCCR; and memo from Alan E. Schwartz (chair of Urban Affairs Committee), February 14, 1969, Box 116, Folder 6, JFR.

74. On these geopolitical and cultural trends in the 1960s and 1970s, see Hasia Diner, *We Remember with Reverence and Love: American Jews and the Myth of Silence after the Holocaust* (New York: New York University Press, 2009); Matthew Frye Jacobson, *Roots Too* (Cambridge, MA: Harvard University Press, 2006); and Michael Staub, *Torn at the Roots: The Crisis of Jewish Liberalism in Postwar America* (New York: Columbia University Press, 2002).

75. Draft of Equal Opportunity section of Joint Program Plan for 1972–1973, appended to memo from Bennett Yanowitz to Commission on Equal Opportunity, May 12, 1972, Box 28, Folder 6, NCRAC.

76. Ibid.

77. Lily Geismer, "'Don't Blame Us': Grassroots Liberalism in Massachusetts, 1960–1990" (Ph.D. diss., University of Michigan, 2010); and Sylvie Murray, *The Progressive Housewife: Community Activism in Suburban Queens, 1945–1965* (Philadelphia: University of Pennsylvania Press, 2003). Also, see the interviews amassed in the Jewish Women and Feminist Activism in Metro Detroit Collection, http://www2.matrix.msu.edu/~jewish/, accessed January 2012.

78. See, for example, Jonathan Rieder, *Canarsie: The Jews and Italians of Brooklyn against Liberalism* (Cambridge, MA: Harvard University Press, 1985).

79. Harold Dubin, "Report on 1972 Democratic Primary," June 12, 1972, Box 31, Folder 11, RH.

80. Ibid. For further data on postwar Jewish voting patterns that validates the conclusion that Jews remained staunch supporters of the Democratic Party, see Judith Stepan-Norris and Caleb Southworth, "Churches as Organizational Resources: A Case Study in the Geography of Religion and Political Voting in Postwar Detroit," *Social Science History* 31, no. 3 (Fall 2007): 343–380.

81. On the election, see Thompson, *Whose Detroit?* 196–199.

82. Michael Katz, "Why Don't American Cities Burn Very Often?" *Journal of Urban History* 34, no. 2 (January 2008): 191.

83. Golden, *The Quiet Diplomat*, 380–396; and Joe Darden, *Detroit: Race and Uneven Development* (Philadelphia: Temple University Press, 1987), 46–59.

84. I have not found a source that adequately addresses the meteoric rise of Jewish foundations from the 1950s through the beginning of the twenty-first century and how private Jewish dollars, especially those of a few wealthy families, came to set the pace of American Jewish life. A quick review of a list of fifty-six of the top giving Jewish family foundations revealed the dollar power housed in these foundations and the means through which these private funds have set the agenda for Jewish life and American life. For the list, see http://www.jewishresearch.org/quad/01-12/following-money-list.html, accessed November 21, 2013. For excellent journalistic reporting on this, see Josh Nathan-Kazis, "26 Billion Bucks: The Jewish Charity Industry Uncovered," *Forward*, March 24, 2014, http://forward.com

/articles/194978/-billion-bucks-the-jewish-charity-industry-unco/, accessed July 10, 2014. Also see, Shaul Kelner, "In Its Own Image: Independent Philanthropy and the Cultivation of Young Jewish Leadership," in *New Jewish Leaders: Reshaping the American Jewish Landscape,* ed. Jack Wertheimer (Waltham, MA: Brandeis University Press, 2011). For historical overviews of philanthropic foundations, see David Hammack and Helmut Annheier, *A Versatile American Institution: The Changing Ideals and Realities of Philanthropic Foundations* (Washington, DC: Brookings Institution Press, 2013); and Olivier Zunz, *Philanthropy in America* (Princeton, NJ: Princeton University Press, 2012).

85. For a useful discussion of how urban space grounded this shift in liberalism, see David Harvey, *Social Justice in the City* (Baltimore: Johns Hopkins University Press, 1973).

Chapter Seven

1. See Avalon International Breads, http://www.avalonbreads.net/goodies/breads/, accessed March 20, 2013.

2. For recent journalistic accounts of Detroit, see Dan Austin, *Lost Detroit: Stories behind the Motor City's Majestic Ruins* (Charleston, SC: History Press, 2010); Mark Binelli, *Detroit City Is the Place to Be: The Afterlife of an American Metropolis* (New York: Metropolitan Books, 2012); Katja Kullman, *Rasende and Ruinen: Wie Detroit sich neu erfindet* [German, *Rapturous Ruins: How Detroit Reinvents Itself*] (Berlin: Suhrkamp, 2012); and Charles LeDuff, *Detroit: An American Autopsy* (New York: Penguin, 2013). Also, see the Detroit section on the Atlantic Cities website for journalistic portraits of the city at http://www.theatlanticcities.com/hubs/detroit/, accessed March 20, 2013.

3. The growing concentration of wealth and jobs in suburbs reflected postwar trends of urban deindustrialization and decentralization and also the rise of what Joel Garreau called "Edge Cities." See Barry Bluestone and Bennett Harrison, *The Deindustrialization of America* (New York: Basic Books, 1982); Jefferson Cowie, *Capital Moves: RCA's Seventy-Year Quest for Cheap Labor* (Ithaca, NY: Cornell University Press, 1999); and Joel Garreau, *Edge City: Life on the New Frontier* (New York: Doubleday, 1991).

4. For an analysis of a recent trend of suburban neglect and disinvestment, see Becky Nicolaides and Andrew Wiese, "Suburban Disequilibrium," *New York Times,* April 6, 2013, http://opinionator.blogs.nytimes.com/2013/04/06/suburban-disequilibrium/, accessed March 20, 2013; and Eric Klinenberg, "The Suburbs Are Dead," *Playboy,* January 9, 2013, http://www.playboy.com/playground/view/the-suburbs-are-dead, accessed March 20, 2013.

5. All taken from U.S. Census Bureau. See quickfacts.census.gov, accessed March 22, 2013.

6. On the percentage of white residents and the occupancy rates of the downtown-midtown corridor, see Data Driven Detroit's map at http://open.cridata.org/maps/mapas/map.html?mapkey=d3, accessed March 10, 2014.

7. Gilbert's real estate holdings increased rapidly starting from 2010. For 2014 figures, see Ben Austen, "The Post-Post-Apocalyptic Detroit," *New York Times*, July 11, 2014, http://www.nytimes.com/2014/07/13/magazine/the-post-post-apocalyptic-detroit.html?_r=0, accessed July 12, 2014.

8. David Carroll, "Detroit Initiatives," January 23, 2012, report in author's possession. On the extent of Gilbert's holdings, see Kirk Pinho, "There's No Denying Gilbert's Buying," *Crain's Detroit Business*, February 17, 2013, http://www.crainsdetroit.com/article/20130217/NEWS/302179993/reporters-notebook-theres-no-denying-gilberts-buying, accessed March 22, 2013.

9. David Segal, "A Missionary's Quest to Remake Motor City," *New York Times*, April 13, 2013, http://www.nytimes.com/2013/04/14/business/dan-gilberts-quest-to-remake-downtown-detroit.html?pagewanted=all, accessed March 22, 2013.

10. On the Reconstructionist Congregation of Detroit, see http://www.recondetroit.org/. The congregation, originally called T'Chiyah, formed in response to Temple Israel's decision to leave Detroit in the early 1980s. When one segment of the congregation left for the suburbs and took the name T'Chiyah with it, the group that chose to remain in the city formally affiliated with the Reconstructionist movement. See author's correspondence with Toby Citrin, January 31, 2013.

11. On the Downtown Synagogue's history, see "The Isaac Agree Downtown Synagogue: A Brief History & Appreciation," from Martin Herman's collection, in author's possession. On the synagogue's revival, see Louis Aguilar, "Saving Detroit's Last Synagogue," *Detroit News*, December 18, 2008, http://www.detroitnews.com/apps/pbcs.dll/article?AID=/20081218/METRO/812180400/1041/LIFESTYLE04, accessed February 11, 2013; Dennis Archambault, "What Will Be Detroit's Next Hot Spot? Signs Point to Capitol Park," *Model D*, March 16, 2010, http://www.modeldmedia.com/features/capitolpark03152010.aspx, accessed February 13, 2013; Sala Levin, "The Last Synagogue Standing," *Moment*, November–December 2013, http://www.momentmag.com/last-synagogue-standing/, accessed December 2013; and David Sands, "Detroit Synagogue Sparks Resurgence of Downtown Jewish Life," *Huffington Post*, December 12, 2012, http://www.huffingtonpost.com/2012/12/11/detroit-synagogue-downtown-jewish_n_2274095ss.html, accessed February 13, 2013.

12. "Changing the Face of Detroit," on *Detroit 20/20*, ABC, channel 7, February 25, 2011, http://detroit2020.com/2011/02/25/changing-the-face-of-detroit/, accessed February 15, 2013.

13. Scott Kaufman's remarks at "What Is Jewish Detroit?" April 1, 2012, Jewish Communal Leadership Program, University of Michigan. A recording of the conference can be found at http://mediasite.ssw.umich.edu/Mediasite/Play/4053b324671846af861e53ad149ead8b1d, accessed February 6, 2013.

14. For a useful set of essays about the erosion of public space in American cities, see Michael Sorkin, ed., *Variations on a Theme Park: The New American City and the End of Public Space* (New York: Hill and Wang, 1992). Also, see Elijah Anderson, *The Cosmopolitan Canopy: Race and Civility in Everyday Life* (New York: Norton, 2011); and Sharon Zukin, *Naked City: The Death and Life of Authentic Urban Places* (New York: Oxford University Press, 2010).

15. On entrepreneurialism and its connection to city space and so-called neoliberalism, see David Harvey, "From Managerialism to Entrepreneurialism: The Transformation in Urban Governance in Late Capitalism," *Geografiska Annaler* Series B, Human Geography 71, no. 1 (1989): 3–17; and Wendy Brown, "Neo-Liberalism and the End of Liberal Democracy," *Theory and Event* 7, no. 1 (2003), http://muse.jhu.edu.libproxy.temple.edu/journals/theory_and_event/v007/7.1brown.html.

16. See Shaul Magid, *American Post-Judaism: Identity and Renewal in a Post-ethnic Society* (Bloomington: Indiana University Press, 2013).

17. Conversation with Anna Kohn, February 1, 2013; and e-mail correspondence on February 25, 2013, with Martin Herman, former president of the Downtown Synagogue and involved in it since 1989.

18. On Gilbert's private security force, see Matt Helms, "Dan Gilbert Unleashes Internet to Catch 3 Graffiti Vandals," *Detroit Free Press*, July 2, 2014, http://www.freep.com/article/20140702/NEWS01/307020174/Dan-Gilbert, accessed July 10, 2014; and David Segal, "A Missionary's Quest to Remake Motor City," *New York Times*, April 13, 2013, http://www.nytimes.com/2013/04/14/business/dan-gilberts-quest-to-remake-downtown-detroit.html?pagewanted=all, accessed April 15, 2013.

19. See Ira Sheskin, "The 2005 Detroit Jewish Population Study, 2010 Update," Jewish Federation of Metropolitan Detroit, April 2011, http://jewishdetroit.org/pdf/2010-population-study.pdf, accessed March 22, 2013.

20. Data on Downtown Synagogue membership and board composition as of 2013 from conversation with Anna Kohn, February 1, 2013.

21. Harry Reisig's remarks, "What Is Jewish Detroit?" April 1, 2012, Jewish Communal Leadership Program, University of Michigan, http://mediasite.ssw.umich.edu/Mediasite/Play/4053b324671846af861e53ad149ead8b1d, accessed February 6, 2013.

22. Conversation with Amit Weitzer, February 14, 2013.

23. Conversation with Jackie Victor, February 18, 2013. On Victor's involvement in the Downtown Synagogue, see "Jackie Victor on Creating Jewish Community in Detroit," posted at *She Detroit,* December 29, 2011, http://shetroit.com/personal-insights/jackie-victor-on-creating-jewish-community-in-detroit/, accessed February 18, 2013.

24. Conversation with Amit Weitzer, February 14, 2013.

25. Conversation with Anna Kohn, February 1, 2013.

26. Conversation with Anna Kohn, February 1, 2013.

27. E-mail correspondence with Martin Herman, February 25, 2013.

28. Conversation with Blair Nosan, February 22, 2013.

29. Midcentury populist rhetoric tended to combine anti-urbanism and anti-semitism. See Alan Brinkley, *Voices of Protest: Huey Long, Father Coughlin, and the Great Depression* (New York: Knopf, 1982).

30. Conversation with Anna Kohn, February 1, 2013. On his theory of routinization, see Max Weber, *The Theory of Social and Economic Organization*, ed. and trans. A. M. Henderson and Talcott Parsons (New York: Oxford University Press, 1947), section v, "The Routinization of Charisma."

31. For information on the Jewish Fund, see http://thejewishfund.org/. On the history of Sinai Hospital, see "A Sinai Hospital Retrospective," *Michigan Jewish History* 40 (Fall 2000): 16–31.

32. For the sake of full disclosure, I note that my husband and I, who do not live in Detroit, gave a donation to the first phase of the capital campaign in April 2013.

33. Conversation with Anna Kohn, February 1, 2013.

34. Ibid.

35. See Dan Gilbert's posting "Detroit 2.0: It's Real and It's Happening Now," July 17, 2011, posted on his blog *Choose Thinking*, http://choosethinking.com/2011/07/detroit-2-0-its-real-and-its-happening-now/, accessed March 22, 2013.

36. See Quicken Loans, http://www.quickenloans.com/press-room/?s=opportunity&submit.x=0&submit.y=0, accessed April 10, 2014.

37. Corporate and communal activists in Detroit frequently used the term "creative class" to describe the kinds of people they hoped to attract to the city. Many acknowledged Richard Florida's popular and best-selling book *The Rise of the Creative Class* (New York: Basic Books, 2002) as formative in their thinking about what Detroit needed. In his writing about Detroit, economist Edward Glaeser makes a similar argument that, above all else (even federal investment and infrastructure), cities must attract smart and creative people in order to thrive. See Edward Glaeser, *Triumph of the City: How Our Greatest Invention Makes Us Richer, Smarter, Greener, Healthier, and Happier* (New York: Penguin Press, 2011).

38. In my conversation with Scott Kaufman on March 22, 2012, he spoke about Groupon; also, see Gilbert, "Detroit 2.0: It's Real and It's Happening Now."

39. Conversation with Miryam Rosenzweig, February 13, 2013.

40. Conversation with Josh Kanter, February 27, 2013.

41. Conversation with Jackie Victor, February 18, 2013. On James and Grace Lee Boggs, see Grace Lee Boggs, *Living for Change: An Autobiography* (Minneapolis: University of Minnesota Press, 1998); and the documentary film *American Revolutionary: The Evolution of Grace Lee Boggs*, directed and produced by Grace Lee, Caroline Libresco, and Austin Wilkin, 2013.

42. Conversation with Jackie Victor, February 20, 2013.

43. Conversation with Blair Nosan, February 22, 2013.

44. David Egner's remarks at "Motor City Frontiers," panel, part of the Council of American Jewish Museums annual conference, Detroit, Michigan, February 28, 2012 (recording in author's possession and available through the Council of American Jewish Museums); and "Downtown Biz Leaders Launch Detroit Work-Live Incentives," Southeast Michigan Startup Website, July 29, 2011, http://www.semichiganstartup.com/InTheNews/livedowntownprogram072611.aspx, accessed April 10, 2014.

45. Conversation with Scott Kaufman, March 22, 2012; and conversation with Miryam Rosenzweig, February 13, 2013. Also, see program website at www.livedetroitfund.org, accessed February 13, 2013.

46. See Live Detroit Fund, http://www.livedetroitfund.org/faq/.

47. Live Detroit Fund, http://www.livedetroitfund.org.

48. Conversation with Josh Kanter, February 27, 2013.

49. Conversation with Miryam Rosenzweig, February 13, 2013.

50. From 2011 until 2013, the Moishe House, a communal living environment for young Jews, occupied a home on East Ferry Street, near Wayne State University. In the summer of 2013, it relocated to Royal Oak, a suburb of Detroit. A second Moishe House, established through a national organization called Repair the World, stood for a year in the Woodbridge section of Detroit. Although no longer affiliated with the Moishe House movement, Repair the World fellows continued to live communally and work in Detroit in 2013. See "Moishe House Heads from Detroit to Royal Oak," *Detroit News*, October 9, 2013, http://www.thejewishnews.com/on-the-move/, accessed March 19, 2014.

51. Zukin, *Naked City*, 127.

52. Scholars and social critics have written prolifically on the human costs, including job insecurity, low wages, and zero benefits, of service industry jobs and their relationship to forces of globalization. See, for example, Barbara Ehrenreich, *Nickel and Dimed: On (Not) Getting By in America* (New York: Metropolitan Books, 2001); Miriam Greenberg, *Branding New York: How a City in Crisis Was Sold to the World* (New York: Routledge, 2008); Erin Hatton, *The Temp Economy: From Kelly Girls to Permatemps in Postwar America* (Philadelphia: Temple University Press, 2011); and Bethany Moreton, *To Serve God and Wal-Mart: The Making of Christian Free Enterprise* (Cambridge, MA: Harvard University Press, 2009).

53. Conversation with Leor Barak, January 27, 2013.

54. David Carroll's remarks at "What Is Jewish Detroit?" April 1, 2012, Jewish Communal Leadership Program, University of Michigan, http://mediasite.ssw.umich.edu/Mediasite/Play/4053b324671846af861e53ad149ead8b1d, accessed February 6, 2013.

55. For a similar argument about the unaccountability of privatized urban policy, see Mark Binelli, "Detroit, the Billionaire's Playground," *New York Times*,

February 7, 2013, http://www.nytimes.com/2013/02/08/opinion/detroit-sinks-with-belle-isle.html?hpw, accessed February 10, 2013. For a different perspective on how private individuals step into the void of public antipoverty and housing programs, see Ben Austen, "The Death and Life of Chicago," *New York Times*, May 29, 2013, http://www.nytimes.com/2013/06/02/magazine/how-chicagos-housing-crisis-ignited-a-new-form-of-activism.html?pagewanted=all&_r=0, accessed June 1, 2013.

56. Eitan Sussman's remarks, "What Is Jewish Detroit?" April 1, 2012, Jewish Communal Leadership Program, University of Michigan, http://mediasite.ssw.umich.edu/Mediasite/Play/4053b324671846af861e53ad149ead8b1d, accessed February 6, 2013.

57. Conversation with Blair Nosan, February 22, 2013.

58. The film can be found at http://responsibility-project.libertymutual.com/films/the-entrepreneurial-spirit-avalon#fbid=gULypC3a9Sb, accessed February 22, 2013.

59. Conversation with Eugene and Elaine Driker, September 2, 2013.

60. See Austen, "The Post-Post-Apocalyptic Detroit." For a thorough discussion of the historical forces resulting in the bankruptcy, see Nathan Bomey and John Gallager, "How Detroit Went Broke: The Answers May Surprise You—and Don't Blame Coleman Young," *Detroit Free Press*, September 15, 2013, http://www.freep.com/interactive/article/20130915/NEWS01/130801004/Detroit-Bankruptcy-history-1950-debt-pension-revenue, accessed September 18, 2013. Detroit's bankruptcy received national and regional coverage. I followed the stories in the *New York Times*, the *Detroit Free Press*, the *Detroit News*, *Crain's Detroit Business*, and Huffingtonpost.com.

61. See Sugrue's preface to the 2005 edition of *The Origins of the Urban Crisis: Race and Inequality in Postwar Detroit* (Princeton, NJ: Princeton University Press, 2005), xxv.

62. Conversation with Leor Barak, January 27, 2013.

63. On the practice of branding cities, see Greenberg, *Branding New York*.

64. "The Quickening of Detroit," posted at *My Jewish Detroit*, http://myjewishdetroit.org/2012/10/the-quickening-of-detroit_a-stroll-along-webward-avenue/, accessed March 22, 2013.

65. See John Gallagher interview with Sugrue, *Detroit Free Press*, February 23, 2014, http://www.freep.com/article/20140223/OPINION05/302230041/Thomas-Sugrue-Gallagher-Detroit-bankruptcy-future-city, accessed February 24, 2014.

66. Carroll, "Detroit Initiatives," January 23, 2012.

67. David Carroll's remarks, "What Is Jewish Detroit?" April 1, 2012, Jewish Communal Leadership Program, University of Michigan, http://mediasite.ssw.umich.edu/Mediasite/Play/4053b324671846af861e53ad149ead8b1d, accessed February 6, 2013.

68. E-mail correspondence with David Carroll, September 2, 2012.

69. On Quicken and the subprime crisis, see Michael Hudson, "Claims of High-Pressure Sales, Fraud at Odds with Quicken Loans' Straight-Shooting Image," *Public Integrity*, February 4, 2011, http://www.publicintegrity.org/2011/02/04/2156/claims-high-pressure-sales-fraud-odds-quicken-loans-straight-shooting-image?fb_action_ids=757467300970270&fb_action_types=og.comments&fb_source=aggregation&fb_aggregation_id=288381481237582, accessed January 8, 2014; and Alain Sherter, "Mortgage Mess: Why Quicken Loans May Not Be as Squeaky Clean as It Claims," CBS News *Moneywatch*, February 8, 2011, http://www.cbsnews.com/8301-505123_162-43550469/mortgage-mess-why-quicken-loans-may-not-be-as-squeaky-clean-as-it-claims/, accessed January 8, 2014.

70. For an urban perspective on the subprime lending crisis, see Manuel Aalbers, ed., *Subprime Cities: The Political Economy of Mortgage Markets* (Malden, MA: Wiley-Blackwell, 2012).

71. See "DIA Millage Passes: Detroit Institute of Arts Expects $23 Million Annually after Tight Race in Macomb," *Huffington Post,* August 8, 2012, http://www.huffingtonpost.com/2012/08/08/dia-millage-detroit-institute-of-arts-_n_1753989.html, accessed January 8, 2014.

72. Mark Stryker and John Gallager, "DIA's Art Collection Could Face Sell-Off to Satisfy Detroit's Creditors," *Detroit Free Press*, May 23, 2013, http://www.freep.com/article/20130523/NEWS01/305230154/DIA-Kevyn-Orr-Detroit-bankruptcy-art, accessed January 8, 2014.

73. Randy Kennedy, Monica Davey, and Steven Yaccino, "Foundations Aim to Save Pensions in Detroit Crisis," *New York Times,* January 13, 2014, http://www.nytimes.com/2014/01/14/us/300-million-pledged-to-save-detroits-art-collection.html?_r=0, accessed January 14, 2014. Also, see the remarks of Graham Beal (director, president, and CEO of the Detroit Institute of Arts) at "Motor City Frontiers" panel, February 28, 2012.

74. Conversation with Jackie Victor, February 20, 2013.

75. Conversation with Jackie Victor, February 18, 2013.

76. The film can be found at http://responsibility-project.libertymutual.com/films/the-entrepreneurial-spirit-avalon#fbid=gULypC3a9Sb.

77. E-mail correspondence with Blair Nosan, January 29, 2013. On Eden Gardens, see Blair Nosan, "Growing in Eden Gardens," *The Jew and the Carrot* blog, *Forward*, November 13, 2012, http://blogs.forward.com/the-jew-and-the-carrot/165799/growing-in-eden-gardens/, accessed January 29, 2013; and Niraj Warikoo, "Jewish Centers Promote Food Justice in Detroit," *Detroit Free Press*, December 8, 2012, http://www.freep.com/article/20121208/NEWS05/312080065, accessed January 29, 2013. In 2013, Nosan moved to New York City to pursue a master's degree at the Jewish Theological Seminary, but the Downtown Synagogue continued to run Eden Gardens.

78. Rebecca Solnit, "Detroit Arcadia: Exploring the Post-American Landscape," *Harper's Magazine,* July 2007, 73.

79. Interview with Eugene Driker, January 4, 2012.

80. See, for example, Ryan Call, D. Jamie Rusin, and Sean Slater, "New Suburbanism: Reinventing Inner-Ring Suburbs," *UrbanLand: The Magazine of the Urban Land Institute*, July 8, 2013, http://urbanland.uli.org/industry-sectors/public-spaces/new-suburbanism-reinventing-inner-ring-suburbs/, accessed April 10, 2014; and Prema Katari Gupta, *Creating Great Town Centers and Urban Villages* (Washington, DC: Urban Land Institute, 2008).

81. See Sam Roberts, "Suburbs' Share of Poor Has Grown Since 2000," *New York Times*, May 20, 2013, http://www.nytimes.com/2013/05/20/nyregion/suburbs-are-home-to-growing-share-of-regions-poor.html?hp, accessed May 22, 2013. On the urban-style problems in Detroit's suburbs, see David Muller, "While Companies Move into Downtown Detroit, Suburbs Continue to Suffer," *MLive.com*, March 8, 2013, http://www.mlive.com/business/detroit/index.ssf/2013/03/while_companies_move_into_down.html, accessed March 20, 2013.

Index

Page numbers in italics refer to illustrations.

AAA. *See* Archives of American Art (AAA)
Abrams, Charles, 104, 120–21
activism: civic, 142; and housing, 123, 130, 136; interfaith, 131, 134, 198; left-leaning, 227; legislative, 203; millennial, 220–23, 227–28, 235–36, 242; philanthropic, 203; political, 17, 46, 119–22, 150, 198, 212, 232, 260n29; private urban after riots, 192–97; privatized Jewish, 214–15; social gospel, 195; spiritual politics of, 119–22; voluntary, 203, 206–8. *See also* grassroots; philanthropy; urban activism; voluntarism
Adas/Adat Shalom, 37–39, 112–13, 117–18, 132, 134, 150, 158, 167–68, 252, 253
ADL. *See* Anti-Defamation League (ADL)
Adler, Morris (rabbi), 120–21, 159–61, *161*, 165, 186–88
African Americans. *See* black people; Negroes
AJA. *See* American Jewish Archives (AJA)
AJC. *See* American Jewish Committee (AJC)
AJHS. *See* American Jewish Historical Society (AJHS)
Alamo sculpture (Rosenthal), 178–79
Allied Jewish Campaign, 78
Alpern, Robert, 142–43
altruism, 52
ambivalence: of Jews toward cities, 8–9, 11, 78, 108, 151, 176, 192, 198–99, 218–19, 228, 243; of Jews toward suburbs, 149, 168–69, 186

American exceptionalism, and residential restrictions, 263n21
Americanization, 52, 227. *See also* assimilation
American Jewish Archives (AJA), 247, 251, 253
American Jewish Committee (AJC), 34–35, 50, 120–21, 142, 194–96, 203–4
American Jewish Congress, 50, 72–75, 97, 99, 103, 195–96, 204
American Jewish Historical Society (AJHS), 247, 251, 253
American-Jewish synthesis, cult of, 35
Americanness, 104, 199. *See also* whiteness
animosity: of blacks toward Jewish landlords, 55; of Jews toward cities, 11
Ann Arbor, MI, 121–22, 178–79, 190, 245
anti-capitalism, 54, 94, 227
Anti-Defamation League (ADL), 50, 72–75, 82–83
antidiscrimination, 128–29, 137, 145, 187, 258n17. *See also* discrimination
anti-poverty, 194, 304–5n55
antisemitism: and anti-urbanism, 303n29; black/Negro, 53, 55; and black radicalism, 203; Ford's, 29; and housing, 75; interfaith efforts and public relations campaigns against, 265n34; as less acceptable, 34–35; modern discourse, 227; and nativism, 29, 263–64n23; in neighborhoods, 23; pre-Enlightenment, 3; and racism, 57–58. *See also* racism
anti-urbanism: and antisemitism, 303n29; and white conservatism, 11–12

apartment buildings, 21, 24, 34, 40–41, 71, 89, 118, 129, 234, 239, 264n32. *See also* housing
A. Pupko's (store), 80–81
architects, *81*, 154–56, *160*, 162–63, 165, 172, *177*, 184–85, 230, 290n38, 291n60, 292n74; Jewish, 155, 288n6, 289n17; modernist, 148, 153, 174
Architect Selection Committee, 163, 165
architecture: modernist, 154–56, 162–63, 165, 169, 172, 174–76, 287n145; religious, 288n6; sanctuary design, 291–92n72, 292n74; synagogues, 152–57, 165, 168–70, 172, 174, 176, 180–82, 288n6, 289nn15–17, 289n21, 292n77
Archives of American Art (AAA), 251
Archives of Labor and Union Affairs. *See* Walter P. Reuther Library, Archives of Labor and Union Affairs
assimilation, 4–5, 12–13, 49; and identity, 256–57n7; and mobility, 257n8. *See also* Americanization
Astor Place (New York, NY), 178–79
automobile industry: in Detroit, role of, 15; Jews' exclusion from, 25, 56, 262n11
Avalon International Breads (Avalon Bakery), 217, 225, 232, 239–41
Avery Architectural and Fine Arts Library. *See* Columbia University, Avery Architectural and Fine Arts Library
Avrunin, William, 139
Avshalumov, Vadim, 252

back-to-the-city Jews: and integrated housing, 148; and legacies of metropolitan urbanism, 217–44
Bagley Community Council, 112–14, 130, 132, 138, 141, 146, 150
Bagley Elementary School, 36–37, 112–13
Bagley neighborhood, 18–19, 34–44, 59, 70, 77, 80, 92, 109–14, 117–18, 130, 132, 138–47, 150, 154, 158, 217
Baltimore, MD, 15, 42, 204
Barak, Leor, 221–22, 229, 235–36, 237, 252
Baum, Victor (judge), 140–41
Bentley Historical Library, 251
Berman, Mandell (Bill), 162–65, *163*, 165, 171, 228–29, 246, 252
Berman Foundation. *See* Mandell (Bill) and Madeleine Berman Foundation

Berry, Louis, 162–63
BIDs. *See* Business Improvement Districts (BIDs)
Bing, Dave, 236
Birmingham Masonic Temple, 181–86, *185*, 200, 252, 253
Birmingham (suburb), 190–91
black Jews, 134, 224, 241, 284n100
black people, 26–28, 75–76, 83, 91, 99, 111, 121, 124, 128, 192, 211, 213–14, 220, 238; and antisemitism, 53, 55, 203; and churches, 52, 170; in Detroit, 36, 109, 133, 196–97, 219; and housing, 53, 72–76, 283n81; and Jews, 55–56, 286n137; and liberalism, 127, 130, 138, 286n137; in neighborhoods, 47–51, 56, 59–62, 65–68, 72, 87, 89–90, 101–5, 116–17, 241; population, 219; and radicalism, 11, 138, 144–45, 197, 203–5, 213, 297n49; and riots, 51–56; and separatism, 7, 53, 107–8, 137, 145, 204–5, 286n137; and suburbanization, 259n23; and urbanism, 12, 203, 206; and urban power, 297n49; as urban underclass, 12; women, 52, 144, 224. *See also* Negroes
Blenheim Forest District Improvement Association, 109
Bloomfield Hills, *31*, 42, 45, 167, *178*, 222, 225, 232
B'nai B'rith, 103
boardinghouses, 28, 63. *See also* housing
Boggs, James, and Grace Lee, 232, 303n41
Bonstelle Theatre, 160
Booker T. Washington Business Association, 135
Boston, MA, 15, 235
Boston-Edison, 30, 58, 88, 116, 156–57
bourgeois excess, 42
Boyle Heights (Los Angeles, CA), 15
B. Pupko's (store), 80–81
branding, cities, 226, 228–32, 237, 258n14, 304n52, 305n63
Brickley, James, 128
Brickley Ordinance, 128–31, 137–38
Bronx (New York, NY), 35
Brooklyn (New York, NY), 15
Brownsville (Brooklyn, NY), 15
Business Improvement Districts (BIDs), 235
Butzel, Fred, 52

capital, cultural, 240, 243–44
capitalism, 7–8, 51, 56, 64, 105–6, 136, 148, 204–5, 232–33, 240; anti-, 54, 94, 227; and democracy, 79–80, 105; and privilege or power, 10–11
Carper, Jack, 194
Carroll, David, 252
Cathedral Church of Saint Paul, 195
Catholic Church, 28, 35–36, 44, 47, 49, 74, 121–22, 134, 183, 195, 201, 208; in Detroit, history of, 265n38
Cavanagh, Jerome (mayor), 127, 131, 135, 137, 192, 194, 196, 209
"Changing Neighborhoods" (lecture), 120
Changing Neighborhoods Committee, 101–3, 109–12, 114, 117, 119
Charles H. Wright Museum of African American History, 220
Chicago, IL, 15, 21–22, 26, 57–58, 62, 118–19, 148, 176, 230, 248
Chicago Boulevard, 32, 159, *159*, 160, 165, *166*, 172, 175–76
Chicago School sociologists, 270n45
churches: abandoning, 131; black, 52, 170; construction of, 291n70; and integration, 134; and metropolitan community, 200; urban, 259n20. *See also* faith; religion; synagogues; *and specific churches*
Cincinnati, OH, 42, 78, 180–81, 247
cities: branding, 226, 228–32, 237, 258n14, 304n52, 305n63; as changing spaces, 244; definition of, 43; disinvestment from, 7, 11–12, 152, 169, 216, 257–58n13; financing, 228–32; geography and meaning of reinvented, 1–2; interstitial spaces of, 4; land annexation, and growth, 26, 36; leaving, price of, 168–72; and new Jewish urbanism, 210–16; as real and imagined places, 1; as stability and security, 218; success in, 29; and unity, 14. *See also* inner city; urbanism
Citizens for a United Detroit, 138
citizenship, 3–4, 28, 136, 151, 199
Citron, Abraham, 118–19
civil rights, 6, 16, 54, 76, 83, 90, 93–95, 121, 145–46, 153, 185, 192–94, 203, 212; Jewish involvement in movement, 10–11, 258n17; legislation, 112; liberal agenda, 78–79; and race, 94
Civil Rights Congress (CRC), 93–94

Civil Rights Federation, 54
Clairmount Street, 32
Clark (Stephen S.) Library, 252
class: and liberalism, 56; and nationality, 4–5, 262n6; and poverty, 56; and race, 6, 88, 116, 133, 219, 227, 235–36, 242, 258n15; reform, 56; and suburbs, 13; and urban spaces, 30. *See also* middle class
Cleage, Albert, Reverend, 137, 198
Cleveland, OH, 15, 118, 121–22, 165
Cleveland Heights, 35
Cobo, Albert (mayor), 90–91, 94–95, 125–26, 275n32
Cockrel, Ken, 214
Cohen, Sylvia Cottler, 261n1
Cohen, William, 97, 99
Cohn, Avern, 294–95n6
Columbia University, Avery Architectural and Fine Arts Library, 247, 251
Columbia University, Columbia Center for Oral History, 251
Comerica Park, 222
Commentary, 13, 155, 294n115
Commission on Community Relations, 95–96, 101, 125–26, 128–30, 132, 135, 145, 252, 253
Commission on Human Resources, 120–21
Commission on Law and Social Action, 74–75
Common Council, 23, 66, 90–91, 123, 126, *126*, 128–30, 135, 137–38, 196, 213
communal living, 234, 236, 242, 304n50. *See also* housing
communism, 31, 48–49, 53–55, *55*, 60, 64, 70, 73–74, 79, 103, 105, 204, 227; and liberal housing politics, 89–96
Communist Party, 54, 93–94, 213, 279n31
Congregational Church, 36–37, 58, 112, 132, 156
Congress on Racial Equality, 144
conservatism, 95, 125, 127; and anti-urbanism, 11–12; and liberalism, 9, 13, 213, 258n15, 283n76; and neighborhoods, 50, 100; and suburbanism, 11–13; white, 11–13, 90–91, 107–9, 137–39, 213, 259n20. *See also* neoconservatism
Conservative Jewish Theological Seminary, 119
Conservative Judaism, 31, 37, 58, 112, 120–21, 129, 150–51, 156–58, 165, 221–22, 224–25

conversion to Judaism, 224
Corktown, 234
Corporation and Securities Commission, 125
cosmopolitanism, 14, 35, 115, 209, 227; of cities, 147; and identity, 180; and liberalism, 88–89; and parochialism, 4; suburban, 147, 172–80. *See also* metropolitanism; urbanism
Cotillion Club, 130, 135
Cottler Cohen, Sylvia. *See* Cohen, Sylvia Cottler
Cottler, Norman, *19*, 261n1
Coughlin, Father, 34–35
Council of American Jewish Museums, 304n44
counter-insurgency, 232
Cousens, Bonnie, 252, 293n105, 294n106
Covenant Card Campaign, 121–22
CRC. *See* Civil Rights Congress (CRC)
creative class, 239, 303n37
Crown Heights (Brooklyn, NY), 15
cultural capital, 240, 243–44
Culture Consumers, The (Toffler), 176

DAC. *See* Detroit Athletic Club (DAC)
Daily Worker, 92–93
davening (praying), 225
Davidson, Morris, 92–94
Davis, Richard, Mrs., 55
Davison Street, 18
Dearborn Independent, 29
decentralization: and deindustrialization, 296n38, 300n3; geographical, 157; urban, 149, 154
declension, postwar American-Jewish, 292–93n88
deindustrialization: and decentralization, 296n38, 300n3; of Detroit, 15; and disinvestment, 216; and segregation, 15
democracy, 7–8, 34–35, 48–49, 83–84, 96, 101, 118, 120, 122–23, 138, 198, 212–13; and capitalism, 79–80, 105; and community, 155
Democratic Party, 127, 209, 212–14; Jewish support of, 214, 299n80. *See also* Republican Party
demographics, 9, 11, 13, 14–15, 35, 41, 49, 65–66, 80, 82, 99, 105, 110, 113, 139, 141–42, 150–51, 191, 200, 213, 230, 233,
247–48; Jewish survey, 27–28, 59. *See also* Jewish population
demography, 32, 110
denominationalism, 121, 134, 153–54, 161–62, 199–200, 223–24
Department of Synagogue Architecture, 156
desegregation: and housing, 90; and schools, 211. *See also* integration; segregation
Detroit Athletic Club (DAC), 29–30
Detroit Board of Education, 141–42
Detroit City Plan Commission, 100, 123
Detroit Council for Better Housing, 90–91
Detroit Free Press, 140–41, 182, 198
Detroit Golf Club, 44
Detroit Institute of Arts (DIA), 176–77, 209, 216, 220, 239–40
Detroit Jewish News, 38, 41, 66, 78, 80–81, 92, 101, 106, 127, 139, 152–53, 156, 187, 192–93, 203, 248, 251, 295n8
Detroit-Leland Hotel, 29–30
Detroit Medical Center (DMC), 229, 233
Detroit News, 112–13, 130, 143, 183
Detroitology, 228
Detroit Public Library, 220
Detroit Renaissance, 214, *215*
Detroit River, 23, 181, 234
Detroit Symphony Orchestra, 176, 216, 220
Detroit Tigers, 222, 230
Detroit 2.0 plan, 221, 230
Dexter Avenue, 18, 33
Dexter-Davison area, 18–19, *19*, 22, 29, 41, 45–47, 60, 209, 217
Dexter-Davison Market, 18, *19*, 41, 45
Dexter neighborhood, 32–36, 40–41, 44, 58–59, 70–71, 77, 80, 82, 85–86, 92–93, 107, 115–16, 120, 126, 129, 156–58, *159*, 217
DIA. *See* Detroit Institute of Arts (DIA)
diaspora, 35
discrimination, 23, 29, 57–58, 74–75, 79, 85, 87, 90, 94, 113–14, 118–19, 121–40, 143, 145–46, 149, 185–87, 192, 199, 204, 216; in housing, 75, 96–105, 136, 267n3; in neighborhoods, 96–101. *See also* antidiscrimination; prejudice; racism; segregation
disinvestment, 7, 11–12, 152, 169, 257–58n13; and deindustrialization, 216; suburban, 300n4
displaced persons, 62, 69, 91, 195–96

INDEX

diversity, 13–14, 23–24, 29–33, 42, 148, 183, 224, 226, 230, 234; and unity, 3, 260n33
DMC. *See* Detroit Medical Center (DMC)
Dochuk, Darren, 259n20
Do It For Detroit Fund, 231
Dorchester (Boston, MA), 15
downtown-midtown corridor, 220, 223, 225–26, 233–37, 239, 241, 301n6
Downtown Synagogue, 157, 218, 221–32, *224*, 235–37, 240, 241–42, 248, 289n24, 301n11, 306n77
Drachler, Norman, 196
Driker, Elaine and Eugene, 18–20, 30, 32–33, 39–40, 43–45, *45*, 217, 237, 242–43, 247, 249, 252, 294–95n6
Durkheim, Emile, 120, 281n49

Eastern European Jews, 23, 51–52. *See also* European Jews
Eastern Market, 234
East Side Merchants Association, 52–53, 56, 100, 268n8, 268n13
economics: and inequality, 194, 198; and Jews, role of, 4, 256n5, 273n4; and liberalism, 282n64; and race, 132; suburban, 219; urban, 35, 219, 240, 256n5, 296–97n38. *See also* socioeconomics
Edelman, Bernard, 85–86
Eden Gardens, 232, *240*, 241, 306n77
edge cities, 300n3
Egner, David, 233, 304n44
Eight Mile Road, 36, 109
Eliot Street, 160
Emrich, Richard, Bishop, 183
Enlightenment, 3, 28
entrepreneurialism, 192, 206, 214, 216, 220, 222–23, 230–34, 236, 240–43; and grassroots, 223–28; and neoliberalism, 302n15
environmentalism, 212
"Equal Opportunity in Housing: A Handbook of Facts" (NCRAC study), 96
ethnicity: as artificial barrier in housing, 136; and neighborhoods, 4, 24, 105; and urban spaces, 4–5, 30
ethnography, 47, 69
Ettenheimer, Aubrey, 166–67
European Jews, 23, 26; and unionism, 56, 286n132. *See also* Eastern European Jews
exceptionalism, American: and residential restrictions, 263n21

313

exploitation, 3, 50–56, 62, 70, 74, 79, 83, 88, 94, 128–29, 138, 147, 238–39, 244, 279n28

Fair Election Practices Committee, 160
fair housing. *See* housing
Fair Housing Act (Michigan), 140
Fairmount Temple, 165
Fair Neighborhoods Practices Ordinance (FNPO), 127–31, 134, 137, 145–47
faith: and business, 8, 195, 197; interfaith social gospel movement, 195, 198; and metropolitan urbanism, 198–205; and spirituality, 108. *See also* churches; religion; spirituality; synagogues
Falik, Ben, 252
Farmington Hills, 42, 168, 184, *185*
fascism, 60, 64, 70, 155
Fauman, Joseph, 69–70, 102–3, 109–10
Federal Housing Act (1949 and 1954), 99–100, 123. *See also* National Housing Act (1934)
Federal Housing Administration (FHA), 34, 62, 72, 104, 106–7, 129, 264n31, 283n81
Feinstein (Meyer and Rosaline) Center for American Jewish History, 246–48, 256n3
Feldman, Marcy, 252
feminism, 212
FHA. *See* Federal Housing Administration (FHA)
Fisher, Max, 189–91, *190*, 196, 206–10, *207*, 214, *215*, 239
Fisher Building, 162–63, 189, 190, 196
Fisher (Max) Bill, 214
Fisher (Max M.) Music Center, 220
Fleischman, Lawrence A., 176–77, 251
Florida, Richard, 231, 303n37
FNPO. *See* Fair Neighborhoods Practices Ordinance (FNPO)
Ford, Henry, 29
Ford, Henry, II, 214
Ford Motor Company, 214
foundations, 214–15, 239–40, 299–300n84. *See also* philanthropy
Fox Theater, 220
Fraiberg, Louis, 61
Fram, Leon (rabbi), *81*, 181–83, 251
Frankel, Sam, 167–68
Frankel, Stanley, 252

Frankel (Jean and Samuel) Center for Advanced Judaic Studies, 245
Freehof, Solomon, 182–83
Freund, David, 12
Fullerton Street, 47, 49, 57
fundamentalism, 291n70

Gans, Herbert, 13
Garreau, Joel, 300n3
General Motors, 183, 196
geographic spaces, 11–14, 22–23, 29
geography: and decentralization, 157; and mobility, 5, 114; narratives of, 46; and race, 104
geopolitics, 211, 299n74
German Jews, 23
Gesu Parish, 44
ghettos, 23, 28, 73, 96, 135, 145–46, 196, 200, 210
Gilbert, Dan, 221, 224, 226, 229–30, 229–31, 233, 236–39, 242, 301n7
Gladstone Street, 30, *31*, 160, 181
Glaeser, Edward, 303n37
Glazer, B. Benedict (rabbi), 91
globalization, and service industry jobs, 235, 304n52
Goldin, Nathan, 167–68
Goodman, Ernest, 54, 204–5
Goodman, Percival, 163–65, *164*, 172–76, 173, 178–79, 251
goodwill, 53, 65, 70, 83, 89, 119, 122, 193, 284n92; legislating, 127–31
gradualism, neighborhood association for, 65–70
Graham family, 92–93
grassroots, 96, 192, 197, 229, 231–33, 236, 242; and activism, 221–23; private-entrepreneurial, 223–28. *See also* activism
Great Depression, 29, 115, 158–59, 198–99
Greater Detroit Committee for Fair Housing Practices, 124
Greeks, 35
Green Acres, 19, 43–44
Greenberg, Cheryl, 10
Greenfield Road, 36
Grodzin, Morton, 286n121
Groner, Irwin (rabbi), 201
Gross, Harry, 77
Gross, William, 77, 145–46

Grosse Pointe, 118
Grossman, Allan, 145–46
Gruen, Victor, 148–49
Gubow, Lawrence, 202
"Guide to Changing Neighborhoods" (NCRAC manual), 103–5

Harper's Magazine, 241
Hastings Street, 22–27, 30, 32–33, 44, 51–54, 56, 70, 100, 147–48, 158, 217, 240; class and nationality patterns in neighborhood, 262n6; delicatessen, *24*
Hebrew schools, 28, 35, 70–71, 92, 193
Hebrew Union College, 181, 248, 251, 253
Hebrew verses: in architecture, 170
Hechtman, Samuel, 167–68
Henry Ford Health System, 220
Henry Ford Hospital, 233
Herman, Martin, 302n17
Hersh, David, 71–72
Hertz, Richard C. (rabbi), 120–21, 133–36, 153–54, 159–60, 175–76, *177*, 179, 181, 195–96, 200, 205, 251, 253
Higher Education Opportunities Committee, 202
High Holidays, 36, 66, 225, 292n74
Highland Park Baptist Church, 291n70
Hillel (Jewish student organization), 225
historical frameworks, 8–14
Hitler, Adolf, 155
Holocaust, 200, 211, 289n17
homelessness, 193, 213–14
home loans, 107. *See also* housing; mortgages
homeownership, 6, 24–25, 33–34, 36, 40, 47–51, 60, 62, 65, 67–68, 74, 86–88, 90–92, 100–101, 103, 107, 109, 112–16, 125, 137–46, 264–65n33
Homeowner's Rights Ordinance (HRO), 137–40, 145
hospitals, 229, 233, 245, 303n31
House Un-American Activities Committee (HUAC), 94–95
housewives, 46, 67. *See also* women
housing: activism, 123, 130; black, 53, 74, 283n81; and desegregation, 90; discrimination, 75, 96–105, 136; 267n3; fair, 64, 112, 123, 130, 140, 280n42; federal policies, 113; home loans, 107; integration, 64, 84–86, 89–96, 113, 119, 130, 132–33, 136, 143, 148; interfaith politics,

131–37; Jewish, 105; laws, 112, 280n42; liberal politics and communism, 89–96; middle-class urban market decline, 145–49; modernist, 154–56, 162–63, 165, 169, 172, 287n145; politics of, 89–96, 109–14, 131–37; private and American dream, 282n65; and privatization, 304–5n55; and property values, 86–89; and race, 50, 55, 60, 66–67, 86, 138; ready-made market, 110; reform, 90, 92, 104, 123–25, 140–45; segregation, 118, 267n3; statement, 68; unjust, 267n3; and urbanism, 118; white, 62. *See also* apartment buildings; boardinghouses; communal living; mortgages; open housing/occupancy; private housing; public housing; real estate profession
Housing Commission (Detroit), 53, 127
HRO. *See* Homeowner's Rights Ordinance (HRO)
HUAC. *See* House Un-American Activities Committee (HUAC)
Hudson, Joseph L., Jr., 196–98, 205, *215*
Hudson-Webber Foundation, 233
humanism, 180–81
Humanistic Judaism, 180
Humphrey, Hubert, 212
Huntington Woods, 40–42
Hurd Realty, 77
Hyde Park (Chicago), 15, 118–19
hypocrisy, 10, 76, 89, 149, 153, 186

iconoclasm, 180–83
identity: assimilated, 256–57n7; cultural, 2; geographic, 32; group, 3–4, 6; Jewish, 2, 9–10, 16, 40, 114, 180, 182, 203, 209, 225, 263n20, 265n37; political, 2, 9–10; and spaces, 263n20; spiritual, 8, 14; urban, 6–7, 14, 21, 123
immigration, restrictive legislation, 25, 262n14
Independent Real Estate Brokers Association, 145–46, 170
inequality, 48, 124, 191, 239, 242; economic, 194, 198; social, 123–24, 198–99
inner city, 23, 158, 169–70, 179, 185, 197, 200, 202, 204–5
integration, 11, 23, 53, 68, 71, 115, 117, 129–30, 142–43, 147–49, 169, 194, 212; and housing, 64, 84–86, 89–96, 113, 119, 130, 132–33, 136, 143, 148; populist attack against, 86; pro-integrationism, 94; racial, 50, 73, 105, 113–14, 125, 140, 148, 246; religious, 134; and schools, 143; urban, 136. *See also* desegregation; segregation
intellectualism, intellectuals, 13, 42, 115, 155
interfaith, 16, 34, 91, 121–22, 183, 191, 195–201; activism, 131, 134, 198; efforts against antisemitism, 265n34; housing politics, 131–37; as movement, 136, 283–84n92. *See also* faith
Interfaith Action Council, 197, 199–201
Interfaith Emergency Council, 195, 197–98, 201
intermarriage, 200
International Workers' Order, 31
Interracial Committee (Detroit), 47, 57–75, 87, 91–96, 101, 125; color-coded system, 57, 269n27
Interstate 94, 234
invasion-succession model, for changes in neighborhood population, 270n45
Isaac Agree Downtown Synagogue. *See* Downtown Synagogue
Israel, Israelites, 120, 173, 177, 210–11, 213
"It's Good to Live in the City" (pamphlet), 100

JCC. *See* Jewish Community Center (JCC)
Jeffries, Edward (mayor), 57
Jewish Community Center (JCC), 41, 45–46, 60, 71, 110, 132, 193, 270n36
Jewish Community Council, 51–103, 108–13, 116–34, 138–42, 150, 191–92, 199–202, 208–13, 252, 253; Changing Neighborhoods Committee, 101–3, 109–12, 114, 117, 119; Community Relations Committee, 124, 202; and Federation, 205, 208–9; formation, 32; Internal Relations Committee, 81–82; Interracial Committee, 47, 57–75, 87, 91–96, 101, 125; name change, 108; Neighborhoods and Housing Committee, 117, 119, 126, 132, 134; Urban Affairs Committee, 199, 201–2, 205, 208–9, 211
Jewish Daily Forward, 84–85
Jewish Family and Children's Services, 193
Jewish Federation, 59, 80, 110, 139, *163*, 199, 202, 204–5, 208–10, 218, 222, 225–26, 229–31, 233–34, 236, 237–38, 242, 252, 253

Jewish identity, 2, 9–10, 16, 40, 114, 182, 203, 209, 225; and spaces, 263n20; and suburbanization, 180; urban and cosmopolitan, 180
Jewish Labor Committee (JLC), 50, 97, 117, 143, 194, 252, 253, 286n132, 295n9
Jewish Labor Council, 142
Jewish metropolitan urbanism, 17, 107–8, 145, 198–200, 242; changing, 211, 216; epitomized in suburbs, 200; formation of, 5–8, 106–49; historical frameworks, 8–14; as historical phenomenon, 46; and interfaith political activism, 198; legacies of, 217–44; narratives of, 187–88; sacred suburban sites of, 150–88; as term, 107. *See also* Jewish urbanism; metropolitan urbanism; urbanism
Jewish Museum (Berlin), 154
Jewish neighborhoods, 6–7, 48–50, 58, 62–63, 68–69, 74, 87, 110, 113, 125, 139, 142, 144–45, 149, 158; changing, 32, 36, 77–105; first in Detroit, 21–27; historical in Detroit (map), 20; and identity, 265n37; landmarks (map), 20; locating and relocating in Detroit, 18–46; maps, 20, 37, 39; planning for, 27–32; reimagined, 114–19; in suburbs, 36–43; synagogues (map), 20; as targets of black settlement, 101–5. *See also* neighborhoods
Jewishness, 3, 5, 32, 63, 104, 108, 112, 118, 121, 136, 154, 183, 218
Jewish population, 2–3, 15, 23, 27, 32–34, 38–40, 49, 58, 80, 99, 108, 110, 142, 150–53, 158, 200, 206, 212–13, 226–27, 233; predominance, 1950 (map), 37; predominance, 1960 (map), 39; in suburbs, 150. *See also* demographics
Jewish Theological Seminary, 119, 306n77
Jewish urbanism, 2, 6–9, 13, 15–17, 118, 242–44; and activism, 119–22; changing nature of, 15; entrepreneurial, 223; new perspectives, 210–18; and nostalgia, 43–46, 267n58; urban crises and privatization of, 189–216. *See also* Jewish metropolitan urbanism; urbanism
"Jewish Urban Politics in the City and Beyond" (Berman), 246
"Jewish Voluntary Action for Community Betterment" (report), 208
Jewish Welfare Federation, 28, 32–33, 263n19

Jews: and American cities, 1–17, 256n3; automobile industry exclusion of, 25, 56, 262n11; black, 134, 224, 241, 284n100; and blacks, 55–56, 286n137; economic roles, 4, 256n5, 273n4; marginalization of, 34–35, 48–49, 56–57, 75; as metonym for urban, 3; and millennial activism, 220–23, 227–28, 235–36, 242; as neighbors, 48, 63; and power, 257n9; in real estate profession, 273n5; self-definition, 6, 151, 158; and survival, 200, 211; values of, 108, 120–21, 124, 151, 228; as wanderers, 1, 3, 12–13; whiteness in postwar years, 6, 257n12. *See also* Jewish identity; Jewish neighborhoods; Jewish population
"Jews and the American City" (conference), 256n3
JLC. *See* Jewish Labor Committee (JLC)
Joffe, Boris, 97, 99
Johnson, Arthur, 43
Johnson, Lyndon B., 127, 192–93, 194, 202, 283n76
Journal of American History, 246
Judaism, 1, 180–87, 223–28; anti-, 256n5; Conservative, 31, 37, 58, 112, 120–21, 129, 150–51, 156–58, 165, 221–22, 224–25; conversion to, 224; Humanistic, 180; Orthodox, 14, 31, 49, 66–67, 121, 157, 225; post-denominational, 223; Reform, 30–31, 44, 51, 54, 81, 120–21, 151, 153–58, 163, 165, 172, 181–82, 184, 218, 224, 228; social definition of, 119–20; suburban, 172
Judaism as a Civilization (Kaplan), 119–20
Judenrein (Jew-free), 118
Judeo-Christian, 108, 135

kaddish (mourner's prayer), 157, 186
Kahn, Albert, 31, 153, 158–59, *160*, 165
Kanter, Josh, 231, 234, 252
Kaplan, Mordecai, 119–21, 281n49
Katcher, Archie, 169–70
Katcher, Irving, 145–46, 170
Katz, Michael, 213–14
Katzin, Samuel, 148
Kaufman, Scott, 222, 230–31, 233, 252
Kennedy, John F., 127
Kerner Commission, 201–2
Kid Rock, 230

INDEX

King, Martin Luther, Jr., 137, 203–4
King, Sol, 165
KKK. *See* Ku Klux Klan (KKK)
Kleinman, Shmarya, 117–19
Knapp, William, *81*
Kohn, Anna, 224, 227–29, 231, 248, 252
Kopman Building Company, 38
Kruse, Kevin, 12
Ku Klux Klan (KKK), 29, 34–35

Lafayette Park, 148–49, 222, 234
land annexation, and city limits growth, 26, 36
Lawndale (Chicago, IL), 15
Lederhendler, Eli, 35
legacies: of metropolitan urbanism, 217–44; of social gospel ideals, 198; of wandering, 1, 3, 12–13
"Let's Think Clearly" (housing statement), 68
Letvin, Albert, 146–47, 287n142
Levin, Carl, 19
LeVine, Harry, *81*
liberal electorate, suburbanization of, 137–39
liberalism, 12; black, 127, 130, 138, 286n137; and civil rights, 78–79; and class reform, 56; and conservatism, 9, 13, 94, 213, 258n15, 283n76; and cosmopolitanism, 88–89; economic, 282n64; and fate of Jewish neighborhoods, 50–51; and housing politics, 89–96, 105, 212; Jewish, 8, 10, 50–55, 74–76, 80–82, 85, 89–96, 105, 112–13, 117–19, 123, 139, 143, 149, 151, 193–94, 204, 209, 214, 216, 258n14, 267n2, 268n5; and progressive urban politics, 137–39; and public equality, 10; suburban, 10; urban, 8, 12–13, 59, 300n85; white, 49, 130–31, 136, 204, 213. *See also* neoliberalism
Lieberman, Sam, 268n13
literature, 2, 111, 118, 196
Live Detroit, 233–34
Live Downtown, 233–34
Livernois Avenue, 36, 80
Local Development Corporations, 235
Lodge (John C.) Freeway (M-10), 38, 106, 156, 266n46
Lonely Crowd, The (Riesman), 67
Los Angeles, CA, 15, 221, 248

Lower East Side (New York, NY): as densely inhabited, 23; and nostalgia, 267n58
Lutherans, 132

M-10. *See* Lodge (John C.) Freeway (M-10)
Mandell (Bill) and Madeleine Berman Foundation, 228–29
Manhattan (New York, NY), 36, 220
MAP. *See* Mumford Action Program (MAP)
maps: historical Jewish neighborhoods of Detroit, *20*; Jewish population predominance (1950), *37*; Jewish population predominance (1960), *39*
Marks, Richard, 135
Marsh, Donald C., 53–56, 252
Marx, Karl, 256n5
Maslow, Will, 99–100
Mattapan (Boston, MA), 15
Max Fisher Bill, 214
Max M. Fisher Music Center, 220
Max Sheldon Realty Company, 167
Mayer, Albert, 80, 110, 114, 132, 150–51
Mayflower Congregational Church, 36–37
McCabe, Robert E., *215*
McCarthy hearings, 227
McGovern, George, 212–13
McNichols Road (Six Mile Road), 36
Mendelsohn, Eric, 155
Metropolitan Conference on Open Occupancy, 133, 135–36
Metropolitan Detroit Conference on Religion and Race, 136–37
Metropolitan Fund of Detroit, 196
metropolitanism, 287–88n4; beyond neighborhoods, 122–27. *See also* cosmopolitanism; urbanism
metropolitan Jews: as term, 8–9
metropolitan urbanism, 5–8, 16–17, 145, 198–205; changing, 211, 216; characteristics of, 149; and cities as stability and security, 218–19; development of, 122; faith dilemmas of, 198–205; formation of, 149; framework of, 152; ideals of, 147; ideology of, 218–19; landscapes of, 189; legacies of, 217–44; narratives of, 151, 187–88; and synagogues, 180; as term, 5, 9, 191. *See also* Jewish metropolitan urbanism; urbanism
Meyer, Henry, 264n28
Michigan Association of Reform Rabbis, 182

Michigan Chronicle, 83, 203–4
Michigan Civil Rights Committee, 93
Michigan State Highway Department, 113, 171
midcentury populist rhetoric, 303n29
middle class: 114–16, 133, 135, 140–41, 151, 160–61, 180, 187, 201, 204, 212, 232, 238; and progressive era reform, 52; urban housing market decline, 145–49. *See also* white collar
midtown, 217, 233–34, 236–37, 239. *See also* downtown-midtown corridor
Midtown Neighborhood Council, 65–70, 74, 87–88, 93, 113–14
Minneapolis, MN, 121–22
minority groups, 95, 98, 105
Miriani, Louis (mayor), 125–27
mobility, 24, 26–29, 31, 38, 50, 80, 110, 187; and assimilation, 257n8; geographic, 5, 114; as Jewish skill, 1, 3, 12–13; and socioeconomics, 114
model citizens, 199
modernism, 3, 179–80, 183, 184, 187; architecture and housing, 148, 153, 154–56, 162–63, 165, 169, 172, 174–76, 287n145
Moishe House, 234, 304n50
mortgages, 34, 41, 43, 49, 62, 72, 98, 124, 129–30; home loans, 107. *See also* housing
Mott (C.S.) Children's Hospital, 245
Mount Sinai, 172
Mumford Action Program (MAP), 142–44
Mumford High School, 142, 144
My Jewish Detroit, 305n64

National Association for the Advancement of Colored People (NAACP), 43–44, 53, 55, 65, 76, 130, 135, 138, 144, 280n42
National Committee Against Discrimination in Housing (NCDH), 87
National Community Relations Advisory Council (NCRAC), 96–99, 103–5, 118, 208, 211–12, 251, 253
National Housing Act (1934), 88. *See also* Federal Housing Act (1949 and 1954)
nationalism, nationality, 3, 4–5, 83, 107–8, 145, 204–5
National Jewish Post and Opinion, 183
Nation of Islam, 137
nativism, 3, 29, 34; and antisemitism, 29, 263–64n23

Nazism, 44, 93, 103, 118, 155
NCDH. *See* National Committee Against Discrimination in Housing (NCDH)
NCRAC. *See* National Community Relations Advisory Council (NCRAC)
Negroes, 26–27, 52–53, 56, 58, 60–61, 63–64, 68, 73–74, 82–85, 87, 95–97, 99–103, 110–11, 117–18, 121, 124, 134, 139, 141–42, 144, 169, 193–94, 203–4. *See also* black people
"Neighbor, Where Are You Running To?" (campaign), 80–86, *84*, 89, 212
neighborhoods: black, 47–51, 56, 59–62, 65–68, 72, 87, 89–90, 101–5, 116–17, 241; changing, 32–36, 57–64, 77–105, 109–14, 117, 119–20, 270n45; conservation, 50, 100, 116, 123; and conservatism, 50, 100; discrimination in, 23, 96–101; ethnic, 4, 24, 105; and gradualism, 65–70; idea of, 21–27; sociological theory on, 262n5; as term, 42; and urbanism, 42; white, 58, 62, 65, 73, 87, 99, 106, 109, 111, 115, 133. *See also* Jewish neighborhoods; suburbs; *and specific neighborhoods*
Neighborhoods and Housing Committee, 117, 119, 126, 132, 134
"Neighborhoods in Transition" (panel), 110
neoconservatism, 10, 258–59n18. *See also* conservatism
neoliberalism, 257–58n13; and entrepreneurialism, 302n15. *See also* liberalism
Newark, NJ, 15, 35
New Deal, 6, 198–99
New Detroit, 195–98, 204–6, 208, 211
New Frontier, 127, 216, 219
New Jersey, 35, 100–101
New York, NY, 15, 23, 26, 34–35, 38, 41, 69, 73, 97, 118, 123, 134, 139, 148, 154, 165, 176, 178–79, 221, 235, 267n58
New York Times, 101, 182, 186–87, 221, 237, 240, 294n115, 305n60
NEXTGen, 229, 231, 234
Nixon, Richard M., 8, 206–8, 213, 283n76
Northwest Hebrew Congregation, 36–37
Northwest Memorial Park cemetery, 37
Nosan, Blair, 232, 236, *240*, 241, 248, 252, 306n77
nostalgia, 13, 35, 259n25; and Jewish urbanism, 43–46, 267n58; and Lower East Side (New York, NY), 267n58

INDEX

Oakland County, 40–41
Oak Park, 38–42, 45, 182, 228
"On the Jewish Question" (Marx), 256n5
open housing/occupancy, 95, 104–5, 113–14, 117–19, 122, 131–37, 140, 143, 145–46, 148, 150, 199, 209
Organization Man, The (Whyte), 114–15
Orthodox Judaism, 14, 31, 49, 66–67, 121, 157, 225

pacifism, 212
Paige, Mary, 55
Palmer Park, 44–45, 59, 81, *81*, 117, 217
Palmer Woods, 18–19, 44, 45, 181, 209, 217
Park, Robert, 22
Park Heights (Baltimore, MD), 15
Parkside (Philadelphia, PA), 15
parochialism, and cosmopolitanism, 4
particularism, and universalism, 35
Pascal, Oscar, 252
Pasteur Elementary School, 19, 44, 140–42, 144
Patrick, William, 128, 130, 135, 137
Patrick-Ravitz Ordinance, 137–38
Philadelphia, PA, 15, 26, 35, 42, 71, 74, 118, 148, 157–58, 220, 246–48
philanthropy, 15–16, 25, 176, 203, 206, 209, 215, 229, 239, 299–300n84. *See also* activism; foundations
Pikesville (Baltimore, MD), 15
Pinart, Robert, 292n76
Pintzuk, Edward, 115, 279n31
Pitch for Detroit (fund-raiser), 231
Pittsburgh, PA, 42
Pittsburgh Courier, 92–93
Poles, 23, 35
politics: and activism, 17, 46, 119–22, 150, 198, 212, 232, 260n29; geo-, 211, 299n74; of home in northwest, 109–14; and housing, 89–96, 131–37; and identity, 2, 9–10; Jewish urban, 6, 15, 119–22; law-and-order, 283n76; and leadership, 143, 237; progressive, 7–8, 52, 137–39, 263n19; and socioeconomics, 212–13; spiritual, 119–22; suburban, 12, 201; urban crisis, 297n41; of urban spaces, 47–76
population, Jewish. *See* Jewish population
populism: attack against integration, 86; midcentury rhetoric, 29, 303n29
poverty: anti-, 194, 304–5n55; and class, 56; and segregation, 194; urban, 210

power: black urban, 297n49; and capitalism, 10–11; civic, 192; and history, 273n4; Jewish urban economic, 256n5; and Jews, 257n9; and places, 1, 15–17; public urban, 8; and social divisions, 4–5; socioeconomic, 51, 257n11; and spaces, 132–33; and status, 203; and suburbs, 201
Power Block, 237–38
Practical Home Builders, 167–68
prejudice, 56–57, 60, 66, 83, 90, 96, 117, 120, 125, 130, 139, 201. *See also* discrimination; racism
privacy, 4, 14, 42, 224; as right, 282n65
private housing, 91–92, 97–100, 104, 124–25, 282n65; property rights, 79, 88, 91–92, 138
privatization, 199, 258n14; and activism, 192–97, 214–15; and antipoverty, 194, 304–5n55; and housing, 304–5n55; of grassroots, 223–28; of Jewish urbanism, 189–216; of public urban spaces, 235–41; and urban crises, 189–216; and urban policy, 304–5n55; of urban spaces, 235–41, 258n14
privatized-entrepreneurial urbanism, 223–28, 231–32
progressive era, 263n19; middle-class reformers, 52; social agenda, 7–8; urban politics, 137–39
property, valuing, 86–89. *See also* housing
Protestants, 121–23, 129, 134, 195, 201, 208, 259n20, 291n70
public housing, 54, 91, 95, 124, 148, 211
public spaces: erosion of, 302n14; urban, privatization of, 235–41
Pupko, Abe, 80–81
Pupko, Ben, 80–81

Quakers, 195
Queens (New York, NY), 15, 118
Quicken Loans, 218, 221–22, 229–30, 233, 236–39, 306n69

race: as artificial barrier in housing, 136; changing language in civic discourse, 265n34; and civil rights, 94; and class, 6, 88, 116, 133, 219, 227, 235–36, 242, 258n15; and economics, 132; and geography, 104; hierarchies of, 76, 79, 95; and housing, 50, 58, 60, 66–67, 86, 138;

race (*cont.*)
    and injustices, 194; and integration, 50, 73, 105, 113–14, 125, 140, 148, 246; and intimidation, 72–73; and intolerance, 50–51; and racism, 103; and religion, 56, 136–37; and riots, 51, 56; and succession, 66; tipping point in changing neighborhoods, 141, 286n121; and underclass, 194; and urban crises, 210. *See also* racism
racism, 56–57, 64, 66–67, 71, 74, 87–88, 90–91, 93–95, 103–4, 109–12, 204–5, 213, 227; and fears, 129; and race, 103; white, 137. *See also* antisemitism; discrimination; prejudice; race; segregation
radicalism, 42, 54, 56–57, 64, 74, 104, 181; black, 11, 138, 144–45, 197, 203–5, 213, 297n49
Raskin, Jack, 54, *55*
Ravitz, Eleanore, *126*
Ravitz, Mel, 123–24, *126*, 126–31, 135, 137, 143, 196, 213, 252, 253, 282n60
real estate profession, 80–86, 129, 145–46, 147, 162; Jews' overrepresentation in, 273n5; and property valuations, 86–89; regulation of, 70–76. *See also* housing
Reconstructionism, 183, 221–22, 301n10
Redbook, 100–101
Reform Judaism, 30–31, 44, 51, 54, 81, 120–21, 151, 153–58, 163, 165, 172, 181–82, 184, 218, 224, 228
reinvention, 7–9, 184, 186, 220, 230, 241, 243; of cities, 1–2; through suburban synagogues, 152–56; urban, 9, 13–17, 191–92, 218, 231–32, 237
Reisig, Harry, 225
religion: and architecture, 288n6; as artificial barrier in housing, 136; and integration, 134; Jewish practices, 60, 98, 121; and race, 56, 136–37; social gospel movement, 195, 198; and spaces, 116. *See also* churches; faith; spirituality; synagogues; theology; *and specific religions*
Renaissance Center, 214
Repair the World House, 234, 304n50
Republican Party, 90, 128, 206–7, 209, 227. *See also* Democratic Party
Reuther, Walter, 147–48, *161*
Reuther Library. *See* Walter P. Reuther Library
Rich, Benjamin, 82, 86, 125
Riesman, David, 67

riots: 12, 150, 169, 189–99, 203, 211; legal aid for arrested, 294–95n6; private urban activism after, 192–97; and responsibility, 51–57
Rivera, Diego, 239
Rock Venture, 229
Rodeph Shalom, 157, 248
Rohe, Mies van der, 147–48
"Role of the Jewish Community in the Urban Crisis" (report), 202–3
Romney, George (governor), 196, 206–7, *207*
Roosevelt, Franklin D., 6
Rosenberg, Bernard, 69–70
Rosenfeld, Gavriel, 289n17
Rosenthal, Bernard, 178–79
Rosenzweig, Louis, 81–82
Rosenzweig, Miryam, 231, 252
Roth, Philip, 35
routinization, 228, 303n30
Roxbury (Boston, MA), 15
Rubin, Irving, 113–14, 130, 138
rural development, 287–88n4
rural living, 13–14
Ruritan Park, 111–12
Ruritan Park Civic Association, 111–12
Russell Street, 217
Russel Woods, 33, 115–17, *116*, 126
Russian Jews, 24

sacred places/spaces, 1, 17, 170, 174, 176
sacred suburban sites, of Jewish metropolitan urbanism, 150–88
SAI. *See* Sholem Aleichem Institute (SAI)
Saperstein, Alvin, 248, 252
Schatten, Bernard, 86
Schermer, George, 57–60, 63–64, 66–68, 71–75, 87–88, 90–91, 93–96, 101, 125
Schoolcraft Gardens cooperative, 90, 275n33
schools: and desegregation, 211; districting, 40; Hebrew, 28, 35, 70–71, 92, 193; and integration, 143; parochial, 35–36; and reform, 140, 144–45; suburban, 219, 243; urban, 139–45. *See also specific schools*
Schostak, Louis, 81, *81*
Schostak Brothers and Company, 80–81
Schwartz, Alan E., 176, *215*
Schwartz, Ethel, 253
secularism, 16, 23, 31, 49
Segal, Jacob (rabbi), 112–13, 117–18, 132, 150, 167

INDEX   321

segregation, 29, 46, 73, 90, 96, 130, 134, 143–44, 146, 211, 241; and deindustrialization, 15; of Detroit, 15; and housing, 118, 267n3; and poverty, 194. *See also* desegregation; discrimination; integration; racism
self-interest, 10, 48, 85, 98, 207, 258n17
Self, Robert, 12
service industry jobs: and globalization, 235, 304n52
Seven Mile Road, 36
Shaarey Zedek, 58, 120–21, 129, 158–59, *159*, *160*, 162–63, 165–66, *166*, 170–72, *173*, *174*, *175*, 174–76, 179–80, 184, 186–87, 201, 206, 226–29, 247, 252, 253, 291n70, 292n74, 292n77
Shaker Heights (Cleveland, OH), 15
Shapiro, Esther, 253
sharecropping, 241
Sheldon, Max, 167
Sheldon (Max) Realty Company, 167
Sherwood Forest, 209
Sholem Aleichem Institute (SAI), 31
Shulman, Rudolph, 291n56
Shur, Nathan, 67–68
Silverstein, Paul, 129
Simons, Leonard N., 251
Sinai Hospital, 229, 303n31
Six Mile Road (McNichols Road), 36
Sklare, Marshall, 13
Slatkin, Harry, 106–7, 234
Slomovitz, Philip, 193, 251, 295n8
small towns, 2, 260n30
Smokler, Bert L., 162
social class. *See* class
social criticism, 13, 42, 114–15, 151–52, 187, 219, 255n1, 258n14, 279n26, 304n52
social divisions, and power, 4–5
social gospel movement: ideals and faith dilemmas of metropolitan urbanism, 198; and private urban activism, 195
socialism, 23, 31, 117, 137, 240–41
Socialist Workers Party, 137
social justice, 136, 153, 157–58, 160–61, 180, 216, 221–22, 236, 243
social welfare, 7, 10–11, 27–28, 56, 71–72, 94–95, 192, 198, 201, 204, 207–8, 210, 214–15
socioeconomics: and ambitions, 103; and depravity, 151; and diversity, 33; and elections/politics, 212–13; homage to, 152; and Jewish spaces, 42; and lifestyle, 232; and mobility, 114; and neighborhoods, 63; and power, 51, 257n11; and privilege, 151–52, 232; profiles, 22, 30–31; and status, 21–22; and suburbs, 211; and success in cities, 29. *See also* economics
sociology, 3, 5, 13, 21–22, 43, 49, 53, 67, 80, 102, 116–20, 123, 126, 235, 262n5, 270n45
Sojourner Truth Citizens Committee, 53–54, 268n13
Solnit, Rebecca, 241
Southfield, 38–42, 45, 154, 156, 159–60, 162–64, *166*, 166–68, 172, *174*, *175*, 184, 186, 225, 228–29, 291n70
spaces: civic, 223–24; geographic, 11–14, 22–23, 29; and identity, 263n20; imagined, 1, 21; interstitial, 4; and Jewish architecture, 288n6; liberating, 216; and power, 132–33; religious, 116; sacred, 1, 17, 170, 174, 176; shaping human experience, 261n3; and socioeconomics, 42; suburban, 172, 176, 180. *See also* urban spaces
Spanish Loyalist Army, 55
spatial divisions, 4, 43
spatial turn, and understanding human experience, 2, 255n2
spirituality, 17, 108, 120, 198, 243; and identity, 8, 14; and justice, 176; in suburbs, 180–86; and urbanism, 180–86. *See also* faith; religion
spiritual politics, of Jewish urban activism, 119–22
Standard Club, 29–30, 32
Stearns, Betty, 111
Stephen S. Clark Library, 252
Stern, Jan Peter, 292n76
Strauss, Nathan, 53–54
Strawberry Mansion (Philadelphia, PA), 15, 35
subprime lending crisis, 238–39, 306n69–70
suburban, as term, 40
Suburban Action Centers, 200–201
suburbanization, 2, 11–12, 15, 151, 191, 212, 255n1; black, 259n23; Jewish identity, 180; of liberal electorate, 137–39; and progressive urban politics, 137–39; schismatic, 181; and synagogues, 153, 161–68. *See also* suburbs
suburbs, 1, 5–9, 11–17, 19, 38, 81, 106, 108, 110, 118, 120–21, 127, 136, 142, 147–54, 191–92, 194, 200–201, 209–13, 216–19,

suburbs (cont.)
225, 227–30, 232, 234–35, 239–41, 243; ambivalence toward, 149, 168–69, 186; assessment and criticism of, 266–67n54; as centers of power, 201; and city limits, 36–40; and conservatism, 11–13; and cosmopolitanism, 172–80; definition of, 43; development of, 147–48, 243; disinvestment in, 300n4; economics/economies of, 219; Jewish metropolitan urbanism, epitomized in, 200; Jewish neighborhoods in, 36–45; Jewish population in (1963), 150; and Judaism, 172; and liberalism, 10; neglect, 300n4; politics of, 12, 201; as sacred sites of Jewish metropolitan urbanism, 150–88; schools in, 219, 243; sense of security in, 218–19; and socioeconomics, 211; as spaces, 172, 176, 180; spiritual urbanism in, 180–86; and synagogues, 148, 152–56, 161–68, 176, 182, 186–88, 226; and urbanism, 13, 42, 180–86; urban-style problems in, 307n81; and white conservatism, 11–13. *See also* neighborhoods; suburbanization; *and specific suburbs*

succession: invasion-, 270n45; neighborhood, natural forms of, 61; process of, 49; racial, 66

Sugrue, Thomas, 12, 237–38, 247, 264n32

Sunbelt economy, in South, 296–97n38

surveys, 14–15, 24–28, 32, 38, 54–56, 61, 99, 122–23, 140, 153, 156–57, 189, 230; Jewish, 27–28, 59

Sussman, Eitan, 236

Sussman, Lance, 248

Synagogue Architects Panel (UAHC), 155–56, 163, 165

synagogues, 23, 27–28, 31, 42, 65, 85, 92, 98, 108, 120–22, 150, 225–26, 228: architecture, 152–57, 165, 168–70, 172, 174, 176, 180–82; construction of, 291n70; historical (map), 20; metropolitan, 156–61, 182; and suburbs, 148, 152–56, 161–68, 176, 182, 186–88, 226; urban, 223. *See also* churches; faith; religion; *and specific synagogues*

Taubman, A. Alfred, 214, *215*, 239
T'Chiyah congregation, 301n10
Teaneck, NJ, 100–101

Temple Beth El, 30, *31*, 44, 51–52, 60, 81, 91, 120–21, 133–34, 135, 138, 148, 153–54, 156–60, *160*, 166–72, 175–81, *177*, *178*, 184, 193, 195–96, 200, 204–5, 209, 226–27, 247, 252, 253; historic site plaque, 292n82

Temple Emanu-El, 228
Temple Israel, 44–45, 81, *81*, *82*, 181–82, 252, 253, 301n10

theology, 120, 133–34, 195. *See also* religion
Time magazine, 176, 182
tipping point, 141, 286n121
Tobocman, Al, 184, 185
Toffler, Alvin, 176
topography, 21–23, 38, 42, 180, 220
Torah scrolls, *166*, 185
totalitarianism, 34
Toy, Harry, 73–74
trickle-down urbanism, 237–38
Truth, Sojourner, 53
Twelfth Street neighborhood, 22, 25, 29–40, 44, 47, 58–77, 80, 82, 85–89, 92, 95, 99, 107, 113, 156–58, 217

UAHC. *See* Union of American Hebrew Congregations (UAHC)
UAW. *See* United Automobile Workers (UAW)

underclass: black urban, 12; racial, 194
undesirables, in neighborhoods, 28, 111, 115, 235

unionism, 56, 286n132
Union of American Hebrew Congregations (UAHC), 154–56, 161–65, *164*
Union of Orthodox Jewish Congregations, 121
United Automobile Workers (UAW), 147–48, 160, *161*
United Hebrew Schools, 70–71, 193
United Jewish Charities, 25–28, 262n12
United Synagogue of America, 121

unity: and black radicalism, 203; and cities, 14; and diversity, 3, 260n33; and groups, 14; and national strength, 34

universalism: and neighborhood change, 97; and particularism, 35

urban activism, 5, 131–32, 191, 199, 202–4, 206–8, 220, 222–23, 226; Jewish, 117, 203, 218, 242; and open occupancy, 136; private after riots, 192–97; spiritual politics of, 119–22. *See also* activism

INDEX

urban affairs, 7, 194, 196, 199, 201–2, 208–9
Urban Affairs Committee, 199, 201–2, 205, 208–9, 211
urban crises, 11–12, 297n41; in 1960s, 11–12; politics, 297n41; and privatization of Jewish urbanism, 189–216; and race problems, 210; report, 202–3
urban development, 30, 206–7, 216
urban identity, 6–7, 14, 21, 123, 180
urbanism, 7–8; anti-urbanism, 12, 303n29; and blacks, 12, 203, 206; changing, 6, 15; citywide, 5; economics/economies of, 35, 219, 240, 256n5, 296–97n38; and housing, 118; and industry, 15, 296–97n38; and liberalism, 8, 12–13, 59, 300n85; narratives of, 12, 17; neighborhood-based, 5; and neighborhoods, 42; and nostalgia, 43–46, 267n58; politics of, 5–6, 12, 15, 47–76, 137–39, 246; and poverty, 210; privatized-entrepreneurial, 223–28, 231–32; and reform, 153, 192, 202, 205; and reinvention, 9, 13–17, 191–92, 218, 231–32, 237; spiritual, 180–86; and suburbs, 13, 42, 180–86; and synagogues, 223; trickle-down, 237–38. *See also* cities; cosmopolitanism; Jewish metropolitan urbanism; Jewish urbanism; metropolitanism; metropolitan urbanism
"Urbanism as a Way of Life" (Wirth), 3
Urban League, 52, 135, 138
urban policy, 4–6, 21, 88, 131–32, 197, 199; and privatization, 304–5n55
urban spaces, 2, 4–5, 9–10, 105, 115, 135–36, 152, 201, 216, 219, 243; and class, 30; and ethnicity, 4–5, 30; and liberalism, 300n85; local politics of, 47–76; privatization of public, 235–41, 258n14; and social class, 30. *See also* spaces
urban zones, 4, 108

Victor, Jackie, 217, 225, 232, 236, 239–41, 253
voluntarism, 25, 69, 193, 203, 205–10, 231. *See also* activism
Voluntary Action Program, 206, 208

Wallace, George, 212–13
Wallace, Mary, 247
Walter P. Reuther Library, 245, 247
Walter P. Reuther Library, Archives of Labor and Union Affairs, 252, 253

wandering/wanderers, Jewish legacy of, 1, 3, 12–13. *See also* mobility
War on Poverty, 127
Washington (Booker T.) Business Association, 135
Wayne State University, 18, 53, 69, 80, 110, 123, 148, 160, 217, 220, 227, 233, 245, 247, 248, 252, 253
Weber, Max, 228, 256n5, 303n30
Weequahic (Newark, NJ), 15
Weitzer, Amit, 225
welfare, social. *See* social welfare
West Bloomfield, 42, 45, 167, 225
West Philadelphia Street, 71, 74
white backlash, 139, 210
white collar, 23, 29, 122. *See also* middle class
white conservatism, 90–91, 107–9, 137–39, 213; and anti-urbanism, 11–12; and suburbs, 13; and urban attachment, 259n20
white flight, 2, 11–13, 213–14, 243
white neighborhoods, 58, 62, 65, 73, 87, 99, 106, 109, 111, 115, 133
whiteness, of Jews in postwar years, 6, 257n12. *See also* Americanness
white population, in Detroit, 219
Whyte, William, 114–15
Wine, Sherwin T. (rabbi), 180–85, 251, 294n106
Winkelman, Stanley, 138, 196, 208–10
Winkelman's department stores, 138, 196, 209
Wirth, Louis, 3–4, 256–57n7
Wischnitzer-Bernstein, Rachel, 154
Wishnetsky, Richard, 186–87
Wohlgelernter, Max, 66–67
women, 3, 94, 181, 248; black, 52, 144, 224; Jewish, 67–68, 127; white, 144. *See also* housewives
Woodward Avenue, 23, *31*, 36, 71, 109, 137, 156–58, 160, 167, 170, 176, 179, 195, 217
Workmen's Circle, 31, 117, 194
World War I, 26
Wright (Charles H.) Museum of African American History, 220
Wynnefield (Philadelphia, PA), 15

Yamasaki, Minoru, 148, 169, 176–77, *177*, 179, 291n60

Yiddish, 23, 35, 51, 59, 84, 152, 243, 250
Young, Coleman (senator), 204, 213–14

Zeidman, Elaine. *See* Driker, Elaine and Eugene

Zionism, 1, 30–31, 44, 203, 206, 213
zoning, 4, 28–29, 40–41, 90–91, 108, 115–16, 167, 263n21
Zukin, Sharon, 235, 247
Zunz, Olivier, 30

Historical Studies of Urban America

EDITED BY TIMOTHY J. GILFOYLE, JAMES R. GROSSMAN, AND BECKY M. NICOLAIDES

Series titles, continued from front matter

PUERTO RICAN CITIZEN: HISTORY AND POLITICAL IDENTITY IN TWENTIETH-CENTURY NEW YORK CITY *by* Lorrin Thomas

STAYING ITALIAN: URBAN CHANGE AND ETHNIC LIFE IN POSTWAR TORONTO AND PHILADELPHIA *by* Jordan Stanger-Ross

NEW YORK UNDERCOVER: PRIVATE SURVEILLANCE IN THE PROGRESSIVE ERA *by* Jennifer Fronc

AFRICAN AMERICAN URBAN HISTORY SINCE WORLD WAR II *edited by* Kenneth L. Kusmer and Joe W. Trotter

BLUEPRINT FOR DISASTER: THE UNRAVELING OF CHICAGO PUBLIC HOUSING *by* D. Bradford Hunt

ALIEN NEIGHBORS, FOREIGN FRIENDS: ASIAN AMERICANS, HOUSING, AND THE TRANSFORMATION OF URBAN CALIFORNIA *by* Charlotte Brooks

THE PROBLEM OF JOBS: LIBERALISM, RACE, AND DEINDUSTRIALIZATION IN PHILADELPHIA *by* Guian A. McKee

CHICAGO MADE: FACTORY NETWORKS IN THE INDUSTRIAL METROPOLIS *by* Robert Lewis

THE FLASH PRESS: SPORTING MALE WEEKLIES IN 1840S NEW YORK *by* Patricia Cline Cohen, Timothy J. Gilfoyle, and Helen Lefkowitz Horowitz, in association with the American Antiquarian Society

SLUMMING: SEXUAL AND RACIAL ENCOUNTERS IN AMERICAN NIGHTLIFE, 1885–1940 *by* Chad Heap

COLORED PROPERTY: STATE POLICY AND WHITE RACIAL POLITICS IN SUBURBAN AMERICA *by* David M. P. Freund

SELLING THE RACE: CULTURE, COMMUNITY, AND BLACK CHICAGO, 1940–1955 *by* Adam Green

THE NEW SUBURBAN HISTORY *edited by* Kevin M. Kruse and Thomas J. Sugrue

MILLENNIUM PARK: CREATING A CHICAGO LANDMARK *by* Timothy J. Gilfoyle

CITY OF AMERICAN DREAMS: A HISTORY OF HOME OWNERSHIP AND HOUSING REFORM IN CHICAGO, 1871–1919 *by* Margaret Garb

CHICAGOLAND: CITY AND SUBURBS IN THE RAILROAD AGE *by* Ann Durkin Keating

THE ELUSIVE IDEAL: EQUAL EDUCATIONAL OPPORTUNITY AND THE FEDERAL ROLE IN BOSTON'S PUBLIC SCHOOLS, 1950–1985 *by* Adam R. Nelson

BLOCK BY BLOCK: NEIGHBORHOODS AND PUBLIC POLICY ON CHICAGO'S WEST SIDE *by* Amanda I. Seligman

DOWNTOWN AMERICA: A HISTORY OF THE PLACE AND THE PEOPLE WHO MADE IT *by* Alison Isenberg

PLACES OF THEIR OWN: AFRICAN AMERICAN SUBURBANIZATION IN THE TWENTIETH CENTURY *by* Andrew Wiese

BUILDING THE SOUTH SIDE: URBAN SPACE AND CIVIC CULTURE IN CHICAGO, 1890–1919 *by* Robin F. Bachin

IN THE SHADOW OF SLAVERY: AFRICAN AMERICANS IN NEW YORK CITY, 1626–1863 *by Leslie M. Harris*

MY BLUE HEAVEN: LIFE AND POLITICS IN THE WORKING-CLASS SUBURBS OF LOS ANGELES, 1920–1965 *by Becky M. Nicolaides*

BROWNSVILLE, BROOKLYN: BLACKS, JEWS, AND THE CHANGING FACE OF THE GHETTO *by Wendell Pritchett*

THE CREATIVE DESTRUCTION OF MANHATTAN, 1900–1940 *by Max Page*

STREETS, RAILROADS, AND THE GREAT STRIKE OF 1877 *by David O. Stowell*

FACES ALONG THE BAR: LORE AND ORDER IN THE WORKINGMAN'S SALOON, 1870–1920 *by Madelon Powers*

MAKING THE SECOND GHETTO: RACE AND HOUSING IN CHICAGO, 1940–1960 *by Arnold R. Hirsch*

SMOLDERING CITY: CHICAGOANS AND THE GREAT FIRE, 1871–1874 *by Karen Sawislak*

MODERN HOUSING FOR AMERICA: POLICY STRUGGLES IN THE NEW DEAL ERA *by Gail Radford*

PARISH BOUNDARIES: THE CATHOLIC ENCOUNTER WITH RACE IN THE TWENTIETH-CENTURY URBAN NORTH *by John T. McGreevy*